Knowledge-Based Systems for General Reference Work: Applications, Problems, and Progress

Library and Information Science

Consulting Editor: *Harold Borko*
Graduate School of Education and Information Studies
University of California, Los Angeles

The list of books continues at the end of the volume.

Knowledge-Based Systems for General Reference Work: Applications, Problems, and Progress

John V. Richardson Jr.
Graduate School of Education and Information Studies
University of California, Los Angeles
Los Angeles, California

Academic Press
San Diego   New York   Boston   London   Sydney   Tokyo   Toronto

Copyright © 1995 by ACADEMIC PRESS, INC.

Academic Press, Inc.
A Division of Harcourt Brace & Company
525 B Street, Suite 1900, San Diego, California 92101-4495

United Kingdom Edition published by
Academic Press Limited
24-28 Oval Road, London NW1 7DX

Library of Congress Cataloging-in-Publication Data

Richardson, John V., 1949-
    Knowledge-based systems for general reference work: applications, problems, and progress / by John V. Richardson.
        p.   cm. -- (Library and information science series)
    Includes index.
    ISBN 0-12-588460-5
    1. Reference services (Libraries)--Automation.   2. Expert systems (Computer science)   I. Title.   II. Series: Library and information science series (New York, N.Y.)
    Z711.R554   1995
    025.5'2'0285--dc20   94-31851
                                                        CIP

PRINTED IN THE UNITED STATES OF AMERICA
95   96   97   98   99   00   BB   9   8   7   6   5   4   3   2   1

To Mudge, Hutchins, and Cheney for passing the torch

And for all reference librarians who will to become expert

I am . . . convinced that we have reached a point where no substantive gain in the quality of library service will be possible without the initiation of a systematic, aggressive, and long-term research effort. We simply will not see any major advances in theory or practice if we continue to rely on the intuitive infallibility of the professional in the field as we have in the past.

—Michael H. Harris, *College & Research Libraries*

Contents

One
Applications

Two —————————————————————————————
Problems

4 ————————————————————————————————

Modeling the Reference Transaction   89

5 ————————————————————————————————

The Development of a Knowledge Base for Expert
System in Reference Work   150

6 ————————————————————————————————

Evaluative Criteria for Shells   180

Deborah Henderson, Lauren Mayer, and Pamela Monaster Karpf

7

User Interface Issues in General Reference Work   203

Karen Howell

Three

Progress

8

A Review of KBS Applications in General
Reference Work   253

Preface

The primary purpose and goal of this book is to improve the quality of reference service rendered in libraries. I hope to do so by providing the results of original research that advances our understanding of the reference professional's knowledge and by creating a text that can be adopted by library and information science (LIS) instructors who wish to incorporate technologically based solutions into their curriculum. My audience consists of reference librarians with a professional concern to improve service as well as public service managers who allocate resources. Within reference service, this book focuses on question answering, which is a complex and difficult task. Reference work involves three major variables: the user, the librarian, and resources. We may be able to achieve only a Pareto optimization of reference service, making an improvement in one variable without making anything else worse. Nevertheless, knowledge-based systems (KBS) offer an opportunity to improve the quality of service rendered.

My specific objectives for the readers of this book are fairly extensive and include the ability:

1. To comprehend concepts central to artificial intelligence.
2. To understand the principal component parts of KBS.
3. To appreciate the nature of expertise and KBS limitations.
4. To grasp the major techniques in knowledge acquisition.
5. To understand the major ways of representing knowledge.
6. To recognize the major KBS development efforts under way in libraries in North America, the United Kingdom, and elsewhere.
7. To visualize the architectural logic of an expert's knowledge about reference work.
8. To comprehend the social, technological, economic, political, and ecological implications of adopting KBS in general reference work.

Applications, Problems, and Progress

The subtitle of the book is applications, problems, and progress in regard to expert systems. In order to accomplish the objectives set out above, the book follows this tripartite structure. Applications are covered most clearly in Chapter 8, which exhaustively reviews the more than 50 extant prototypes. Chapter 3 covers what is feasible, Chapter 4 models the reference transaction, and Chapter 7 covers interface issues so that future applications may be more successful.

Problems are covered throughout the book, starting with Chapter 1, which discusses the discipline's traditional emphasis on reference sources. We need to shift toward the procedural knowledge of reference work, not just the declarative knowledge related to working in reference departments. Chapter 5 presents my original research into the general rules about doing reference work. A forthcoming work will present 1500 detailed rules and I also hope to build a second-generation expert system using these rules. The chapter on feasibility reveals that there are alternative ways of conceptualizing the intellectual work of an expert, and Chapter 9 directly points out limitations in extant systems.

Encouraging words about the shift to a balanced or complete paradigm for doing reference work occur in Chapter 1. Similarly, the chapter on modeling is quite positive, in that reference work can be based on research and can be modeled, and systems that act like human experts can be implemented. Chapter 9 tries to avoid the technological optimism inherent in many books on expert systems by identifying the short-term factors that will influence the development of KBS.

The scope of artificial intelligence (AI), and more specifically expert systems, is fuzzy. So, perhaps, an explicit statement about what this book is not is appropriate here. This book does not cover computer vision, robotics, word processing, spreadsheets, or database management. Nonetheless, this book does touch on related AI topics such as natural language processing, learning theory, logic programming, game theory, artistic creativity, and problem solving and planning as it applies to general reference work.

Theory and Practice

Some readers may want to know about the balance between theory and practice in this book. Those interested in the theoretical aspects will have to look no further than the first chapter, which presents the findings of my original research into the history of teaching reference work. There are also three other theoretical research chapters: modeling the reference transaction (Chapter 4), the logic of ready reference work (Chapter 5), and the appropriate criteria to apply in selecting a KBS shell (Chapter 6).

In addition, there are several highly practical chapters focusing on what

KBS work has already been done in the field, and an extensive evaluation of 40 KBS shells to help readers select the most appropriate shell for their domain.

Other readers, notably LIS instructors looking for a recommended teaching order, might consider Chapters 1, 9, 3, 4, 5, and 8. It would be useful for students to read Chapter 2 first if they have absolutely no background in expert systems. I hope that this work will be a necessary supplement to the existing reference textbooks such as Katz's *Introduction to Reference Work* (McGraw, 1987 and 1992) or Cheney and Williams's *Fundamental Reference Sources* (ALA, 1980).

Attitudes and Skills

Other readers may wonder what new skills and attitudes they may acquire by reflecting on matters covered in this book. Reading this book may result in two new attitudes: (1) the attitude that KBS has a place in the field of LIS, especially in reference work and the LIS curriculum; and (2) a critical attitude toward quality service. Successful KBS work demands a logical and systematic approach. Such an attitude toward the field cannot help but improve the quality of reference service.

Likewise, readers should come away with some new skills: (1) they should be able to communicate critically about KBS and its role in reference work; and (2) they should be able to write a modest prototype KBS after thoughtful consideration of Chapter 1 on teaching and learning reference work, Chapter 4 on modeling the reference transaction, and Chapter 5 on the knowledge base or logic of general reference work.

Acknowledgments

I wish to thank many individuals for their contributions to my thinking on this subject and several institutions for support while writing this book. Foremost, I thank the graduate students in my introductory, required two-quarter reference sequence at UCLA: GSLIS 420 "Information Resources and Services I" in the fall of 1986 (notably Bob Tennant for his term paper on the automation of the reference function), 1987 (particularly Ed Pai for suggesting a menu approach to the ESIE assignment), 1989 (especially Raleigh Muns for demonstrating the use of ALA Booklist criteria as components of weighted confidence factors), and 1990, as well as GSLIS 421 "Information Resources and Services II" in the winter of 1989 and 1991. My two new courses, GSLIS 220 "Information Access" (Winter 1993) and

GSLIS 226 "General Reference Work" (Spring 1993 and 1994), must also be mentioned here. As they developed their own KBS prototypes, these students helped me to consider and clarify many points raised in the text.

Robert M. Hayes, Principal Investigator of the Council on Library Resources (CLR)-funded "Long Range Strategic Planning" grant, provided the initial funding for my KBS work in the summer of 1986. Boyd Sutherland, my CLR Research Assistant, developed the initial literature review during that summer. Several subsequent research assistants carried on that task or helped interview expert librarians: notably Kuang-pei Tu and Shirley Meridith, my GSLIS doctoral student advisees; Adelaide Hulbert (MLS, 1991); Jan Strance (MLS, 1991); Chris Werner (MLS, 1991); and Myra Jimenez, my undergraduate student research project advisee in cognitive psychology. Joo Yun Cho (MLS, 1994) helped make revisions and connected the text and graphic files into an acceptable format for the publisher; I greatly appreciate her superb editing and close reading of the text. I thank Beverly P. Lynch, former Dean of GSLIS, for her interest in and support of this topic, and Marcia Bates, GSLIS chair, who provided much-appreciated last-minute RA funds. Gordon Brooks of the State of California Answering Network (LAPL) provided a brief but useful bibliography of books on computer chess and access to his personal collection. Kenny Crews, one of my former doctoral students, generously shared his extensive collection of photocopies on reference quality with me.

I am especially proud of my coauthors' contributions and their professional development since they worked with me during their graduate programs at UCLA's GSLIS. Karen Howell (MLS, 1987) wrote the chapter on interface issues. Upon graduation, she joined the Library of Congress as part of its Special Recruit Program and worked in its Automated Systems Office for several years. She returned to Southern California and works as Systems Development Librarian for the University of Southern California's Center for Scholarly Technology. The chapter on evaluation criteria for KBS shells was written, under my direction, by an impressive group of three graduate students for their MLS specialization paper. At present, Deborah Henderson works for the Wadsworth (WLA) Veterans Administration as Medical Reference Librarian, while Lauren Mayer is a Senior Children's Librarian at the Aquilar Branch of the New York Public Library in Manhattan, and Pamela Monaster Karpf is a Reference Librarian at the Beverly Hills Public Library. Another former student, Songqiao Liu, an analyst for Getty, coauthored the appendix describing about 40 KBS shells. He wrote his Ph.D. qualifying examinations on KBS under my direction and is likely to make a significant technological contribution to the intersection of cataloging and KBS. Joo Cho is editorial assistant for the *Library Quarterly*.

I have also presented my ideas at a number of conferences and thus I thank those attendees who helped clarify my thinking at those stages: the

1988 ASIS Mid-Year meeting in Ann Arbor, Michigan; the 1988 Special Libraries Association meeting; the 1989 New Mexico Library Association; the American Library Association meeting of June 1990, where I presented an early version of Chapter 1, which won the 1990 Justin Winsor Award for Excellence in Library History Research; the conference on Libraries and Expert Systems at Charles Sturt University, New South Wales, Australia, in July 1990; the Association for Library and Information Science 1991 conference, where I presented an earlier version of Chapter 5, which won the 1991 ALISE Research Paper Competition; the American Library Association's LITA 1991 Pre-Conference on expert systems in Atlanta, Georgia; ALA's RASD 1992 Pre-Conference in San Francisco, where I presented a prize-winning paper based on Chapter 4; and my 1991–1992 protegees in ACRL's Pilot Project in Electronic Mentoring, Library and Information Science Research List on Expert Systems (LISRES-L).

I am especially indebted to my mates at Charles Sturt University's School of Information Studies, where I was a Visiting Fellow during the summer of 1990: Brian Cornish, then Dean of the School and my host; Sydney Davis, for conversations about computers and chess; Craig Mc-Donald, for discussions on flowcharting and other (perhaps more) useful modeling techniques; and John Weckert, for conversations about philosophical issues related to knowledge and KBS. I wish them the best of success with their new Centre for Intelligent Systems in Information Management.

I thank all of my colleagues at the University of Illinois Advanced Research Institute during the summer of 1991 for the intellectual camaraderie, and especially Bernie Frohmann for raising philosophical issues related to knowledge, KBS, T2, and cyberpunk, as well as Lynne Howarth for introducing me to Ishikawa diagrams.

Finally, several people have read drafts of various portions of this book, notably my cataloging and reference colleagues at UCLA: Ling Hwey Jeng, Assistant Professor (now at the University of Kentucky); Joanne Passet (now of Indiana University); and Linda Smith of the University of Illinois; and a select group of UCLA's GSLIS students and graduates: Steve Coffman, Los Angeles County Public Library's FYI; Laura Friesen-Lynn, MLS student; and Peter Hadley, former GSLIS Laboratory Librarian. My good friend, the late Bruce Goeller, Senior Staff Member in the System Sciences Department of the Rand Corporation, critiqued the flowchart in Chapter 4, offered several helpful suggestions for its improvement, and served as a sounding board for many of my inchoate ideas.

The institutional support I have received includes UCLA Academic Senate's Committee on Research funding, which supported a research assistant in the early stages of my work; the Council on Library Resources, which funded my study of the logic behind doing reference work, reported in Chapter 5, as Grant 8027; and finally, UCLA for the 1990 two-quarter sabbatical from my teaching and administrative responsibilities, which was much appreciated. At Academic Press, I acknowledge Hal Borko, the series editor of "Library and Information Science," Marvin Yelles, Senior Vice-President and Editorial Director, and Holly Garrett, Production Editor.

John V. Richardson Jr.

Introduction

By way of introduction, the following paragraphs provide summaries of each chapter. Throughout this book, the theme is that KBS would be ideally based on a mode of reference work that relies on a format-based search strategy. Such an approach gives us a basis for evaluating extant systems or developing better ones.

In Chapter 1, I argue that if we are to have truly KBS, then they must be based on what we have discovered about teaching and learning to do reference work during the past 100 years. Hence, this chapter provides the context for a historically valid approach to developing KBS in reference work. The fact that this chapter won the 1990 Justin Winsor Prize given by the American Library Association for outstanding historical writing would tend to validate this view. In terms of scope, this chapter examines the interwoven relationships between nine reference textbook authors. Collectively, these authors have written the six leading textbooks, totaling 15 editions between 1930 and 1992.

Based on my analysis of these textbooks, the essential paradigm includes: (1) the material format or type of reference work; (2) the method of classifying a reference question, the so-called Mudge method or Hutchins heuristic; and (3) the mental traits of the librarian as well as of the person on the other side of the reference desk. Second, this chapter identifies several intellectual schools of thought among the textbook authors: structuralist, proceduralist, and psychologicalist.

The intent of Chapter 2, "Expert Systems Defined," is to orient the interested reference librarian to what constitutes a KBS, specifically, its component parts, the individuals involved in expert systems development work, and who should care about KBS in reference work and why.

Computers, especially microcomputers, are prevalent in library settings and hence available for supporting a more analytical decision-making process. Librarians are increasingly familiar with the widespread utility of the first three kinds of microcomputer applications for the library environment: (1) spreadsheet and database programs, (2) statistical packages, and (3) the now ubiquitous word-processing software. The fourth and newest kind of microcomputer application is a KBS. The phrase "expert systems" (ES) can be rather broad as well as vague (definitions do appear in Chapter 2) and is sometimes referred to as decision support in general, so this chapter includes general problem solving as well as expert systems more narrowly defined.

Chapter 3, "The Feasibility of Expert Systems," describes early work in reference service using KBS, identifies other areas of potential, and then discusses ES's utility in reference service. This chapter points out how the domain must be narrow and then raises serious questions about the ownership of the knowledge contained in such systems and who is responsible for its accuracy.

In Chapter 4, the author explicitly assumes that the best approach to developing a KBS is to model the human expert. In fact, we know quite a bit about the expert's decision-making process because a considerable amount of the professional literature is devoted to the reference transaction. The purpose of this chapter is to review and synthesize the research literature. Much of this literature adopts, either implicitly or explicitly, a systems analysis approach or input–process–output–feedback (IPOF) model. This chapter critiques that approach.

The second purpose of Chapter 4 is to develop an original model or paradigm of the process. Such a model is necessary to create a sophisticated or even viable KBS for general reference work. While the literature is quite rich in descriptive articles, only a handful of analytical models exist. The extant models are usually represented by line drawings and less often, but more recently, as a flowchart or flowsheet, a technique or method whereby detailed charting of the steps in the process takes place. Despite the fact that the flowcharting technique itself was developed between 1915 and 1920 to study manufacturing processes, it has found a more general applicability in reference work.

Nevertheless, flowcharting does involve some distortions of reality by treating the reference interview as a discrete process rather than the continuous process that it is. These models also assume that the process is linearly progressive and composed of simple rather than complex interdependent steps. Therefore, we do not know all its component parts nor which is the optimal model. Until the appearance of this chapter, no one yet had synthesized all of what we know about the process by thoroughly and evaluatively reviewing the previous research literature. In that respect, this chapter extends the teaching and learning paradigm by examining the research literature as well as the textbook presentations.

As Chapter 5 points out, the major bottleneck in developing any KBS is knowledge acquisition. Yet, in reference work, and more specifically in the narrow domain of question answering, inductive techniques exist for compiling and decompiling the private knowledge of experts. This chapter reports on the formalized reasoning process that takes place in the reference librarian's mind after a clear understanding of the inquirer's question has been reached. It covers general strategies, that is, the basic or intermediate-level rules for selecting any one of the common reference formats, which are sometimes referred to as types of sources or classes of information.

In alphabetical order, the set of 12 formats includes abstracts/digests, atlases/gazeteers, bibliographies/catalogs, biographical sources, dictionaries, directories, encyclopedias, handbooks, indexes, quotations, statistical sources, and yearbooks. In addition, this chapter reveals the surface-level rules for selecting specific sources within these sets, which are often referred to as the "tools of choice." This chapter is based on my original research funded by the Council on Library Resources (CLR), and a more modest version won the 1991 ALISE Research Paper Competition. This CLR-funded research has identified more than 1500 specific rules, more than can be presented here. As mentioned earlier, I hope to present these in a forthcoming work as well as to build a second-generation KBS based on these specific rules.

Assuming that most reference librarians will not want to do computer programming, the criteria for selecting a KBS shell are ably presented in Chapter 6 by Deborah Henderson, Lauren Mayer, and Pamela Monaster Karpf. The authors argue that PC-based shells are the most appropriate development tool for novice KBS developers. While many commercially available shells exist, the best or most appropriate for developing KBS in the library reference domain have not been identified. Furthermore, neither have the selection criteria for this domain been fully articulated. The purpose of this chapter is to develop an original and discrete set of criteria based on a literature review and experimentation with several shells. A comprehensive, if not exhaustive, list of 48 criteria has been compiled that will aid librarians, who may be developing their first KBS, in making informed choices/decisions in selecting the shell that will best meet the needs of their library, and ultimately their user community (see Appendix A).

In her typically thorough fashion, Karen Howell wrote Chapter 7 to synthesize the research literature about user interface design so that librarians can evaluate the user interfaces of KBS applications they plan to purchase, determine whether a KBS shell provides facilities to create interfaces that will meet their end user's needs, and most importantly, design usable systems that bring about the productivity and training benefits promised by KBS. The chapter first examines the importance of the user interface in a KBS and deals with some misconceptions about designing user interfaces. Next the chapter discusses general user interface principles and special considerations about the design of the user interface for KBS, makes suggestions for designing the user interface for a KBS in the general reference domain, presents an interface development and evaluation process, and concludes with resources for help in designing a user interface. The overarching objective of this chapter is to improve the interface design of KBS.

The purpose of Chapter 8 is to identify all the existing prototype expert systems and descriptively review them based on evaluative criteria. Arranged in chronological order, this chapter presents more than 50 known prototype KBS for reference work. Each system is described, analyzed, and evaluated, many for the first time. This assessment is also the first independent evaluation of most of these systems. There are a few exceptions; this chapter omits Bruce Bennion's chemistry ES work at his request but includes systems such as the Information Machine (1987) and PRONTO (1989), which are not strictly speaking KBS, but are useful prototyping efforts, nevertheless. The reader will note that my students' supervised work is rather immodestly, listed (see UCLA 420/421 "Information Resources & Services") as is my own development work (see Information Transfer Associates' Question Master). The chapter concludes with a prototypic KBS, which could serve as the start of a set of design specifications. The goal of the chapter is to provide the reader with a clear understanding of the state of the art regarding expert systems in reference work.

The final chapter speculates on the short- to long-term future, especially the development constraints, for KBS in general reference work. In order to do so, the STEPE model is adopted. STEPE stands for social, technological, economic, political, and ecological. The overarching goal of this chapter is to answer the question: What is the most important consequence of further KBS development? The future is unpredictable, but KBS promises the distinct possibility of improved access to information on the part of those whom the library seeks to serve.

John V. Richardson Jr.

One

Applications

1

Learning Reference Work:
The Paradigm★

Library schools throughout the United States have treated reference work as one of the core courses in their curricula ever since 1890, when the New York State Library School (NYSLS) at Albany offered an advanced, senior course entitled "Reference Work." Newly appointed NYS Reference Librarian Dunkin Van Rensselaer Johnston systematized the pioneering efforts of librarians such as Samuel Swett Green of the Worcester Free Public Library, Justin Winsor of the Boston Public Library, and Melvil Dewey at Columbia College who established general or ready reference work as a basic information service for library users. Reference work rapidly became a legitimate topic for advanced study; for instance, Helen Sperry, a student at the NYSLS, completed her thesis on "Reference Work in Popular Libraries" in 1894. In the 1890s, other pioneering schools including Drexel, Pratt, and Armour incorporated reference work into their one-year programs as a basic course.

Oddly, however, no systematic examination of the history of reference teaching nor any evaluation of the teaching paradigm in this field has been offered. Indeed, only the first few chapters in the history of reference teaching have been written.[1] This chapter is the first comprehensive description and analysis of this topic. An examination of how instructors teach this subject could substantially improve service in all types of libraries, as the next generation of reference librarians enters the field. Furthermore, such an examination is especially necessary if truly expert systems in general reference work are going to emerge.

As a conceptual framework, this paper adopts Thomas Kuhn's position that textbooks posit a paradigm—the "normal science" or given way of doing things in certain fields. As Kuhn noted, "Textbooks expound the

★ This chapter originally appeared in *Library Quarterly* 62 (January 1992): 55–89 as "Teaching General Reference Work: The Complete Paradigm and Competing Schools of Thought, 1890–1990." © 1992 by the University of Chicago Press.

body of accepted theory, illustrate many or all of its successful applications, and compare these applications with exemplary observations with experiments."[2] As such, textbooks can reasonably be used to explore the understanding of a field by its authors, readers, and by the practitioners of that specialty.

In an earlier article, I demonstrated the utility of this approach in my examination of the teaching of government publications.[3] I also suggested that this model could be applied equally well to other areas in library and information science, thereby providing additional insight into the profession's teaching paradigm. Because the field has completed one hundred years of teaching this subject, it especially behooves reference faculty to reflect on this topic. Such introspection will aid the primary audience: our students, and through them, most significantly, the users of the library's collection.

This chapter is not a history of reference work per se.[4] Nor does this piece provide a needed international perspective. For instance, turn-of-the-century scholar–librarians such as E. C. Richardson routinely relied on the British Museum's *List of the Books of Reference in the Reading Room*[5] and recommended it to would-be or novice reference librarians; instructors in pioneer library schools cited it as well. Similarly, one might ask what has been the United Kingdom's experience with the now multivolume *Guide to Reference Materials* by A. J. Walford[6] or our contemporary Indian colleagues' experience with Krishan Kumar's textbook.[7] Such a comparative approach, however worthwhile, is out of scope here.

To state my purpose positively, this article describes what textbook authors have been trying to do in teaching of reference work to novice librarians, and more distinctively, states the way they think it could be. By identifying the common assumptions presented in these textbooks, I will reveal the operative paradigm in this field.

Three questions have guided the exploration of this topic: (1) What have we done? (2) In what direction should instructors be moving in teaching general reference work to would-be librarians? and (3) How might this knowledge be applied to expert systems development work?

1.1

Precursors and Supplements to the Modern Textbooks

The pioneer library schools depended primarily on the lecture method to impart knowledge of reference books. Initially, no one thought to save the student's time in note taking during these lectures; professors simply spelled out the author's name and the more difficult reference titles as necessary. By the turn of the century, however, instructors had adopted hecto-graphed lists, and, in conjunction with lists of books compiled by local libraries to increase the usefulness of their collections, a core list or basic bibliography of reference books emerged.

1.1.1 Dunkin Van Rensselaer Johnston

As mentioned earlier, Johnston taught the first course in reference work ever offered. He was appointed assistant reference librarian at the New York State Library in 1883 and promoted to the head reference librarian's post in 1888; he started teaching in the NYSLS in 1890. Reflecting on Johnston's teaching methods at Albany, Josephine A. Rathbone, herself a reference instructor at Pratt Institute for nearly fifty years, wrote that he taught reference via "a series of epigrammatic comments on the books."[8] These potentially sterile lectures were supplemented by practical problems based on actual reference questions encountered at the state library rather than questions designed to illustrate various points of the particular reference books. His problem-oriented method encouraged the students to examine the tools first hand. According to Rathbone, though, "his personality made the value of the course rather than any methods . . . he made every subject interesting because he was interesting."[9] For her, Johnston's reference course succeeded because of his "brilliant mind, a keen sense of humor and a broad culture."[10]

Johnston encouraged each of his students to "handle a great variety of general reference books, e.g., indexes, dictionaries, encyclopedias, general and special, handbooks, statistical almanacs, registers, atlases, etc."[11] Indexes might appear at the head of this list of reference formats because Johnston was particularly conscious of his department's recent acquisition of many periodicals indexed by Poole's cooperative effort.

In any event, to help students in his reference course, Johnston immediately began compiling his own lists of the best reference books. He organized the list by format: dictionaries, general and miscellaneous handbooks, literary reference books, registers and statistical works, reference books in history, general and specialized periodicals, and periodical indexes. By 1899 this list had expanded to more than 500 unannotated titles. Enough to justify widespread dissemination, it appeared as a sixty-page pamphlet entitled *Selected Reference Books* in the Library School Bulletin series.[12] Reprinted in 1903 as *Material for Course in Reference Study,*[13] it was the earliest textbook for reference work. Following this same structural approach (namely by format), other similar efforts began to appear across the country.

1.1.2 Alice B. Kroeger

Kroeger created what became the most authoritative list of reference titles during her service as Librarian and Director of the Library School of the Drexel Institute in Philadelphia.[14] Like Johnston, she had frequently lectured on reference books in several of her library school's classes subsequent to 1894. Later, she taught a distinct course "Reference Work and Bibliography," hoping that

> by instruction in the use of reference-books and bibliographies, which is intended to give to the students such familiarity with these tools of the librarian as will enable them more quickly to meet the needs of the reading public.[15]

She, too, valued problem assignments drawn from inquiries made by readers along with occasional quizzes spanning the entire enterprise as well as the narrowest technical details.[16]

Based on her course outline, her *Guide to the Study and Use of Reference Books,* published by ALA in 1902, received an enthusiastic reception; shortly thereafter, a reprint edition was needed. (See Table 1.1 for a bibliographical analysis of each edition in terms of edition, date, editor, number of titles covered, total pages, and cost.) According to the preface, the

> selection of the [800] books in this volume has been made from a study of the reference departments of the principal libraries of Philadelphia, Boston, New York, St. Louis [her family's hometown], and Washington, and practically covers the course of study in reference books as pursued in the Drexel Institute Library School.[17]

To assist students, she included an oft-reprinted "How to Study Reference

Table 1.1
Bibliographic Characteristics of the Eleven Editions of the *Guide to Reference Books,* 1902–1995

Edition	Date	Editor	Titles	Total pages	Cost
1st	1902	Kroeger	800	104	$1.25
2nd	1908	Kroeger	1200	147	$1.25
3rd	1917	Mudge	1790	235	$2.50
4th	1923	Mudge	2225	278	$3.00
5th	1929	Mudge	2900	370	$4.50
6th	1936	Mudge	3873	504	$4.25
7th	1951	Winchell	5500	645	$10.00
8th	1967	Winchell	7500	741	$15.00
9th	1976	Sheehy	10,540	1015	$30.00
10th	1986	Sheehy	14,000	1560	$60.00
Projected:					
11th	1995	Balay	18,000	2000	$120.00

Books." As a result, Kroeger shifted the discipline's discussion from definition (namely what to teach) to process (namely how to study reference).

An astute observer of other practitioners, Kroeger also realized that many reference librarians simply used the titles with which they were already familiar. In response, she appended a subjective "List of 100 [*Best*] Reference Books"[18] based on her own experience answering readers' questions in the library.

The question of whether there was an irreducible minimum number of reference titles any novice librarian must know and use occurred to Kroeger. In her mind there were only four types of sources: "no library, however small and whatever its character, can be complete without a dictionary, an encyclopedia, an atlas, and a biographical dictionary."[19]

If that order was important, she broke from it in her published *Guide* by reordering encyclopedias and dictionaries first, followed by special subjects including biography, geography, and periodicals. In justifying this new format order, Kroeger wrote that her work was arranged "to a certain extent in the order of usefulness of the books."[20] In this respect, she split with such scholar–librarians as E. C. Richardson who, in 1893, argued that "the following classes are reference books under all definitions: general bibliographies, general encyclopedias, general dictionaries of words, persons, places, or things, atlases, and general indexes."[21]

Her readers demanded a second edition. The 1908 volume contained more foreign works among the now 1200 titles. She also acknowledged James I. Wyer's contribution (see below). Because of her untimely death, however, another editor would issue the third edition.

1.1.3 Isadore G. Mudge

Mudge served the longest period as editor of the *Guide to Reference Books*. A student of Johnston's at Albany, she gained extensive experience in reference work: head of reference and instructor of "Elementary Reference"[22] at the University of Illinois (1900–1903); head librarian, Bryn Mawr (1903–1908); part-time instructor of "Reference I, II, and III" as well as of documents at Simmons College Library School (1910–1912). Ironically, after Kroeger's sudden death in the fall of 1909, the American Library Association Publishing Board approached Mudge, then a reference librarian at Columbia University, to take over the task of issuing supplements to Kroeger's *Guide*. Several years earlier, Mudge had had the same idea as Kroeger—to publish a list of reference books—but Kroeger already had a proof copy of the list compiled by the time the two of them met to discuss this topic of mutual interest at an American Library Association meeting.[23]

Mudge's new edition of the *Guide* followed the same organization, by format, as did earlier volumes.[24] In 1923, she concurred with Kroeger that "certain basic works, a dictionary, an encyclopedia, an atlas, a biographical dictionary," are essential, but she went further, stating that a "book of quotations, handbook of statistics, a state or government manual, are needed everywhere."[25]

Interestingly, Mudge's third edition published in 1917 acknowledged that students in library schools were one of her primary user groups. A fourth edition followed in 1923. Anticipating Wyer's nearly completed textbook, Mudge asserted that her new fifth edition would provide "a textbook for the student, who either independently, or in library school, library training class or college class in bibliography, is beginning a systematic study of reference books."[26] Mudge used her own work as a text in classes that she taught at the New York Public Library (NYPL) from 1915 to 1925 and then at Columbia, where she was a lecturer and then associate professor in the School of Library Service from 1927 to 1938.

> As her own experience grew, so did her ability, and in her teaching, she eventually developed a succinct phrase that she believed encapsulated the components of effective reference: material, mind, and method. The 'method' was of special import and suggests the precursor to today's concern for effective search strategies. The reference librarian's approach to the question, the analysis of the question and its background and, of course, the identification of alternative approaches were basic to success in the encounter.[27]

She never published this approach, so Mudge's methodological ideas would await fullest articulation by one of her students, Margaret Hutchins (see below). Nevertheless, when Mudge died in 1957, she had established a reputation as "the best known and most influential reference librarian in the history of American librarianship."[28]

1.1.4 Constance M. Winchell

After Mudge retired in 1941, the Editorial Committee of the American Library Association approached Winchell to carry on the work for the forthcoming seventh edition of *Guide to Reference Books*.[29] She was well prepared.

After taking her A.B. in humanities from the University of Michigan, Winchell received her certificate in librarianship from the NYPL Library School in 1920 and then her M.S.L.S. from Columbia's Library School in 1930. She had already joined the reference library staff at Columbia University. Winchell advanced through their ranks: reference assistant, 1925–1933; assistant reference librarian, 1933–1941; and finally, chief reference librarian, 1941–1962.[30] Without explaining what she meant by the term "principles" (perhaps she would use "paradigm" today), Winchell wrote that the "fundamental principles of reference work remain more or less constant through the years."[31] Despite this fact, she broke with the traditional order of formats, claiming a radical departure from all earlier editions with the new eighth edition of 1967. No longer following the Dewey Decimal Classification, she divided the work into five major sections. In Part A, "General Reference Works," she shifts the order of formats to include bibliographies first, followed by encyclopedias, dictionaries, periodicals, newspapers, government publications, dissertations, biography, and. genealogy. Unlike general reference work, her four subject fields demanded a different order: "(1) Guides and manuals; (2) Bibliographies; (3) Indexes and abstract journals; (4) Encyclopedias; (5) Dictionaries of special terms; (6) Handbooks; (7) Annuals and directories; (8) Histories; (9) Biographical Works; (10) Atlases; (11) Serial Publications."[32] Her only explicit justification for this change is that it was consonant with "the content of courses in library schools."[33] Like earlier editors, she also intended her work to serve as a "textbook for the student who . . . is pursuing a systematic study of reference books."[34] In the October 1955 issue of *Wilson Library Bulletin,* David Kaser summarized the sentiment of an entire generation of would-be reference librarians fresh out of library school: "Have Winchell; Will Travel."[35]

1.1.5 Eugene P. Sheehy

In 1961, as preparation for assuming the *Guide*'s full editorship,[36] Eugene Sheehy took on the task of preparing "Selected Reference Books,"[37] the semiannual supplements that appeared in *College and Research Libraries.* When the ninth edition appeared in 1976, Sheehy was listed as the fourth editor. As long as the *Guide to Reference Books* was small in size and modest in cost,[38] teachers of reference work could rely on it as a "text." Over the course of six decades that dependence lessened until the current editor had to make an explicit confession.

> Although there has been less and less emphasis in recent years on the *Guide*'s early function as a study aid for library school students and greater stress on its use by the practicing librarian and research worker, the criterion of *usefulness* which governed Miss Kroeger's first edition remains salient.[39]

Sheehy continued to accept Winchell's rearrangement of Part A, "General Reference Works," desiring only to delete one small subsection because it was repeated elsewhere in the *Guide.* Otherwise, the overall arrangement, as evidenced by its letter codes, seems now to follow the main-class notation of the Library of Congress classification scheme, which was itself informed by the letter symbols used by Cutter in his expansive classification. Wrongly, the *Guide* recently came under attack for following conventional thought regarding its arrangement by formats. Dickinson[40] naively accused it of being a historical rather than a dynamic guide to reference works without realizing the importance of certain traditional assumptions—what I shall call the essential paradigm—to which it has been steadfast and true.

1.2
The Textbooks

Harshly critical of library schools' dependence on the lecture method of imparting knowledge, the 1923 report by C. C. Williamson to the Carnegie Corporation served as a major impetus for authors to write the necessary textbooks.[41] The subsequent accrediting agencies, notably the Board of Education for Librarianship suggested by Williamson, was another factor calling for an improvement in the quality of instruction. Funded by a small subvention from Carnegie, the American Library Association enlisted the services of W. W. Charters, a professor of education at Carnegie Institute of Technology, to develop a series of textbooks, one of which was James I. Wyer's *Reference Work*.[42]

In the interim, however, little wonder a bibliography of reference materials such as the *Guide to Reference Books* could find a niche in the teaching of reference work. Its paradigmatic influence on the textbooks for reference work is addressed next. In the following subsections, the date(s) in parentheses represents the appearance date of the author's textbook.

1.2.1 James I. Wyer (1930)

Astutely intending his own work to complement Mudge's *Guide,* Wyer nostalgically dedicated his textbook to the New York State Library School, which had recently merged with the New York Public Library school to create Columbia's program.[43] His book appeared as the second in the W. W. Charters series of Library Curriculum Studies funded by the Carnegie Corporation. Intending his textbook for students and prospective librarians, Wyer adopts a tripartite organizational scheme: Materials, methods, and administration. As for reference materials, he does not list specific titles, but prefers to deal with classes or groups of materials, which by their "character and content are of most value to the scholarly service which libraries seek to render."[44] He concurred with the *Guide*'s editors that dictionaries are most important, followed by encyclopedias, atlases including the related formats of maps and gazetteers, and bibliographies. Interestingly, Wyer omitted biographical dictionaries but innovatively (compared to the

Table 1.2
Relative Presentation Order of Formats in Reference Textbooks, 1930–1987

Reference formats	Wyer	Shores1	Shores2	Hutchins	Shores3	Katz1	Cheney1	Katz2	Katz3	C & W2	Katz4	Katz5
Dictionaries	1	1	1		1	10	6	12	11	6	10	10
Encyclopedias	2	2	2		2	5	7	4	4	7	4	4
Atlases	3	5[a]	6	4	5	13	9	13	12	9	11	11
Bibliographies	4	11	10	1	11	1	1	1	1	1	1	1
Yearbooks	5	3[a]	3		3	6		6	6		6	6
Directories	6	4[a]	5		6	12		7	9		8	8
Indexes/Abstracts	7	10	8		10	4	4	3	3	4	3	3
Catalogs	8						2	2	2	2	2	2
Handbooks			4	7	7	8		8	7		7	7
Serials			7	6	9	[b]						
Magazines//Periodicals		6				2[c]		[d]	[d]			
Newspapers		7						[d]				
Society/Institution Pubs.		8										
Government Pubs.		9	9	2	12	14	5	14	13	5	12	12
Biographical Sources				3	4	11	8	11	10	8	9	9
Statistical Sources				5				10				
Manuals					8	9		9	8			
Audiovisuals				9	14		3[c]		[c]	[c]	[c]	[c]
Pamphlets										[c]	[c]	[c]
Almanacs						7		5	5		5	5
Total formats covered	8	11	10	9	14	14	9	14	13	9	12	12

[a] Treated collectively as continuations.
[b] Treated collectively as serials.
[c] Treated as bibliography.
[d] Treated as index.

formats covered in the *Guide*) added yearbooks, directories, indexes, and catalogs to his list of what he considers conventional reference book formats (see Table 1.2). Pressed to select "the cornerstones of a reference collection," Wyer chose dictionaries, encyclopedias, and atlases.[45]

Wyer never presented a straightforward rule of thumb for how one answers a reference question in the methods section of his text, perhaps encouraging the student to discover the heuristic for herself. Instead, the second portion, the methods section, is largely a description of the reference process or what he prefers to call "the use of print" in the specific subject fields of chemistry and fine arts and in four different types of libraries. Nevertheless, Wyer argued that for any "reference question [to be] completely and satisfactorily answered involves three factors: inquirer, reference librarian, sources of materials."[46] To paraphrase Wyer, the reader must connect with the material via the reference librarian; otherwise there is an incomplete circuit.

In his discussion of the psychological interaction, Wyer's diction in referring to the person on the other side of the desk is significant. In the first portion of his text, he passingly refers to "library users" and only once to "patrons." Otherwise, he consistently refers to the public as readers or inquirers. In his section on management, he also reports on the psychological preparation, or mental traits, necessary to succeed as a reference librarian.[47]

Wyer had identified several dimensions of the essential teaching paradigm: the *material formats,* the *reference method,* and the *mind* of the librarian as well as the reader or inquirer. While subsequent textbook authors may accept this prescription as the scope of reference work, most emphasize only one of the essential elements without further debate.

1.2.2 Louis Shores (1937, 1939, 1954)

After turning "his back on the humanistic culture"[48] represented by a B.A. in English from the University of Toledo, Shores earned his B.S. in library service from Columbia University. In 1929, he studied reference under Mudge, "a great teacher who was herself the personification of everything desirable in a reference librarian."[49] After that he undertook advanced study of social science techniques in the University of Chicago's Graduate Library School, and then earned his Ph.D. from Peabody College in 1934. His earliest reference textbooks reflect the social science "methodological" concerns picked up in his advanced course of study. The so-called "preliminary edition" of *Basic Reference Books* appeared in a paperback edition in March 1937[50] and was based "on nine years of reference experience in school, public and college libraries, and seven years of reference teaching in four institutions" (as professor and director of the Peabody Library School, 1933–1946; and professor at McGill, Summer 1930, at Dayton University,

Summer 1931, and at one other unidentified school).[51] Most of his text is organized by six types of reference materials: dictionaries; encyclopedias; continuations: yearbooks, directories, atlases; serials; indexes; and bibliographies. He instituted some innovations within formats; for instance, dictionaries are arranged by their vocabulary size.

Shores's interest in quantitative issues appears several times through the text. First, Shores responded to the question of the minimum number of reference titles that a beginning reference librarian needs to know. Stating that "the assumption of the core collection is certainly debatable,"[52] he admitted that day-to-day "reference is done with a comparatively small collection of titles."[53] Consequently, he listed the top ten titles that should be in any library's ready reference collection. Shores quoted an unnamed source saying that 80 percent of all reference questions could be answered using an unabridged dictionary and the *World Almanac;* by adding an encyclopedia he concluded that "the estimate can be raised to 98 percent."[54]

His first[55] and second[56] editions included the statistical summary of his Spring 1935 reference book survey, entitled "core collections." The first edition grouped 117 titles into six reference formats, where each title is distinctively labeled "essential" or "desirable" according to responses by school, public, and college reference librarians as well as reference instructors at Columbia, Emory, the University of North Carolina, and Peabody.

Two years later, readers of his second edition found modest changes, though it continued to follow the same outline based on format or type of reference material. The former chapter on continuations became yearbooks, handbooks, and directories. Rather awkwardly, he referred to atlases as "representations." He grouped serials, indexes, and government publications in a chapter by themselves, as were bibliographies. More logically, Shores moved the core collection to an appendix but organized it alphabetically by author, ignoring the role of format. Despite the passage of nearly twenty years, his last edition of 1954, retitled *Basic Reference Sources,* reflects relatively few changes in Shores's "structuralist" thinking.[57] Shores, like other structuralists, held that the primary principle of organization is still the format of reference material, although he recognizes that special subjects belong in a separate section, which he labeled part 2.

He conceded a paradigmatic shift in emphasis by subtitling the third edition "an introduction to materials and methods." Nevertheless, his own emphasis remained on the former. Shores came down on the side of reference materials, characterizing the debate as teaching the books "per se" as opposed to teaching the titles only "incidentally."[58] Furthermore, Shores discussed functional concerns briefly, mainly the meaning of reference work. The two separate chapters (the introduction to reference and reference organization) found in the first and second editions have been combined into a single introductory chapter, now called "the practice of reference."

Basing this chapter on ALA's functional analysis work of the early 1940s, Shores defined for the novice what reference is, but not *how* to do reference work. He rejected case studies of reference situations or scenarios involving problems such as difficult inquiries, inarticulately expressed inquiries, and potential ethical conflicts. For Shores, *method* really meant only three things: (1) the art of abstracting, (2) citing through comparative bibliographic form, and (3) the art of annotation.[59] This approach is more accurately called reference literary criticism. Confident for the most part that John Dewey was correct, Shores's students learned by doing rather than just being told how to do it.[60]

In the first edition of *Basic Reference Books* (March 1937), however, Shores does list three different and detailed heuristics of how novice reference librarians should solve reference question problems. He also provided a list of thirty-seven (expanded to forty-one in the second edition) "representative question types and the probable kinds of reference tools which hold the answer."[61] This approach strongly echoed Hutchins's heuristic, which she published in the January 1937 issue of *Library Quarterly*. By the third edition of 1954, Shores explicitly encouraged the Hutchins heuristic of answering reference questions by analyzing and classifying the question according to the "proper answer source."[62] Nevertheless, Shores still emphasized format and only secondarily management issues in his brief, introductory first chapter. Hence, Shores is primarily a structuralist (namely one who emphasizes an approach by format) in his orientation to reference work.

The third edition of Shores's text continued to be reprinted into the next decade; the ninth printing occurred in August of 1965.

1.2.3 Margaret Hutchins (1944)

Hutchins graduated Phi Beta Kappa from Smith College and in June 1908 she earned a B.L.S. with honors at the University of Illinois where she studied reference under Frances Simpson, to whom she dedicated her textbook. Entering reference immediately after graduation, she stayed at Illinois through 1927 except for two summers, 1926 and 1927, when she taught at the Chautauqua Library School.[63] Her work as a reference specialist at the Queens Borough Public Library resulted in a 1930 "Trial List of Books Recommended for Reference Use."[64] "In writing to Phineas Windsor to request a release from her Illinois commitment she said, "'It offers the opportunity to teach reference to the training class.'"[65] Apparently she felt called to teach.

During this same period Hutchins also taught one summer at Columbia's School of Library Service. Desirous of more advanced training, she returned to school, studying under Isadore G. Mudge in 1929/1930 as did

Louis Shores and Constance Winchell. Hutchins was awarded an M.L.S. from Columbia University in 1931 and joined the School of Library Service as an instructor that July. She rose to assistant professor in 1935 and retired in 1953, having served as an associate professor since 1946.

Her 1944 textbook, *Introduction to Reference Work,* represents the culmination of a long career in reference and its administration, "thirty-five years devotion to the subject, two thirds of which were spent in actual practice of reference work in university and public libraries."[66] Rather than revise Wyer's now dated work or make a detailed survey of reference materials as Shores had, Hutchins's text "deals with the principles and methods of reference work in general."[67]

Adopting Mudge's method, which had been taught to her at Columbia, Hutchins explicitly states the heuristic process of answering questions for the first time:

> The study of reference books [is] . . . not, however merely a multiplication of books, but types of books, with a training of the power to analyze a question or problem and connect it, first, with the proper type of book and, second, with the right individual book.[68]

In chapter 4, she similarly stated that reference work is a reasoning process involving the classification of the question followed by the formation of hypotheses. Not unlike Shores's statement of Mudge's method, the rule of thumb was to interview the inquirer to clarify the question and then classify the question in relation to type of reference material (i.e., format).

Hutchins posited four categories of questions: (1) bibliographical, including use of the card catalog, government publications, and quotations; (2) biographical; (3) historical and geographical; and (4) current information and statistical sources. These categories become separate chapters in the second part of her textbook wherein she points out problems and pitfalls of such questions to the novice reference librarian. Therefore, specific reference titles receive scant attention except as exemplars in the process. In classroom lectures and discussion of reference titles, Hutchins argued, by quoting W. C. Bagley and A. J. H. Keith,[69] that "the emphasis should be upon *rational* mastery rather than upon mechanical mastery, upon *understanding* or *comprehension* rather than upon *memorization.*"[70] Her students learned the necessity of clarification and then the role of classification in successfully answering reference questions.

Of all the textbook authors, Hutchins most clearly elaborates the methodological dimension of teaching paradigm. While Hutchins recognized the necessity of teaching formats, she was the consummate proceduralist, emphasizing method in reference work. As such, she aligned herself most closely with Wyer and Mudge rather than with Shores. Her textbook enjoyed considerable longevity; a sixth printing appeared in 1959.

1.2.4 William A. Katz (1969, 1974, 1978, 1982, 1987, 1992)

Katz shares little in common with the preceding *Guide* editors and authors of textbooks. For that matter, he was not a student of Mudge or Hutchins; although he likes to claim that "I learned everything I know from Cheney, and a bit from Shores."[71] With a newspaper background and a dissertation on a historical topic completed in the Graduate Library School at the University of Chicago, Katz nevertheless developed a strong interest in education for librarianship, especially reference work.[72] Part of his interest in this topic came from his practical experience. Katz worked as a reference librarian for the King County (Washington) Library in the late 1950s "and for a time at the University of Washington Library as a [undergraduate] student."[73] He also gained valuable editorial experience in ALA's Editorial Department; in fact, his first textbook acknowledged Pauline J. Love "for doing her best to teach me the rudiments of publishing."[74]

Starting in 1964, he taught reference as an associate professor at the University of Kentucky's Department of Library Science until he accepted the call to the State University of New York at Albany as a professor in 1966 shortly after earning his doctorate.[75] In the late 1960s, while serving as editor of *RQ* Katz was approached by Frances Cheney to write a reference textbook: "she had contacts at McGraw-Hill."[76] Jean Key Gates, editor of the newly established McGraw-Hill Series in Library Education, read his manuscript on reference work. However, the *two*-volume idea belonged to another editor at McGraw-Hill who "decided two was better than one. Who was I to argue . . . and it all worked out well enough."[77] Indeed, it was excellent timing. Katz could capitalize on burgeoning library school enrollments in the 1960s and the increased demand for current textbooks. Of course, the delay in issuing a new edition of Shores's textbook helped Katz capture a major share of the market with his 1969 *Introduction to Reference Work*.[78]

Consciously reflecting two dimensions of the reference work, the first volume treated "basic information sources," while the second covered "reference services." "Processes" was added to the subtitle of the second volume in 1974; however, Katz still focused on formats and types of questions. He believed that "the neat categorization of reference types by direction [i.e., bibliographies and indexes], and by source [i.e., encyclopedias and dictionaries] is not always as distinctive in an actual situation."[79] Hence, Hutchins's heuristic appeared after a fashion, but his source for this approach was actually Charles Bunge's 1967 doctoral work.[80] In the 1974[81] and even the 1978[82] edition, Katz explains reference work from the functional analysis perspective strongly reminiscent of W. W. Charters and James I. Wyer. He admits to strong admiration of Wyer, but includes Hutchins, "particularly as they are clear thinkers and wrote with style. Style, after all, is everything."[83]

While he believes that one should adopt an analytical approach to the reference process, the analytical process of Mudge and Hutchins was not at all clear in his various editions.[84] Katz can be considered both a structuralist (one who emphasizes format) and a functionalist (one who emphasizes activities). Apparently Hutchins's heuristic—classifying the reader's question by type of reference source—had started to slip from the profession's memory as recently as the early 1970s when instructors began to emphasize the clarification process (i.e., the reference interview).

1.2.5 Frances N. Cheney and Wiley J. Williams (1971, 1980)

A sociology undergraduate of Vanderbilt University in 1928, Cheney worked in their library and became head of the reference department in 1930. She studied part time in the Peabody Library School between 1930 and 1934, earning a B.S. in library science. Cheney also studied with Hutchins at Columbia and was awarded her M.S. in June 1940. She continued to serve as head of reference until 1943, when she joined the Library of Congress. After serving there as a Bibliographer in the General Reference and Bibliography Division, she returned to Nashville to head the Joint University Library's Reference Department from 1945 to 1946. Peabody appointed her an assistant professor that year. Promoted to associate professor in 1949, she became the school's associate director in 1960 and was promoted to professor in 1967. She retired an emerita professor in 1975.[85]

Not unlike Sheehy, Cheney also served an apprenticeship editing *Wilson Library Bulletin*'s "Current Reference Books" beginning in November 1942 when Shores went into military service. Reflecting upon her 5800 reviews, it may well be said that she was "the Profession's Number-One Reference Reviewer."[86] Echoing Shores's title and orientation, Cheney published *Fundamental Reference Sources* in 1971, a much-awaited basic text on reference work.[87] Along with Winchell, it served as the required text when she taught Peabody's Library Science 220, "Introduction to Bibliography," which she described as the "study of basic types of reference sources with emphasis on bibliography; some attention to reference methods, organization, policies, devices, measurement, citation, and bibliographic form."[88]

In her textbook, "sources of bibliographic information are discussed first because they are used in selecting, acquiring, organizing, and retrieving the body of recorded knowledge."[89] In this respect the textbook follows the tradition established by editors of the *Guide to Reference Books*. When queried why she omitted other elements of the paradigm, notably the method, she responded: "because the title is *Fundamental* reference sources."[90]

Despite its traditional emphasis on a single dimension of the reference work—the materials—readers demanded a new edition, and her colleague at Peabody, Wiley J. Williams, joined her as coauthor for the 1980 edition, which followed the same organizational pattern. A new edition is under way, which will include a chapter on the history of reference work and an additional chapter covering handbooks.

1.2.6 Thomas, Hinckley, and Eisenbach (1981)

These authors reflect a west coast, uniquely California, experience. Diana Thomas holds an M.L.S and Ph.D. in librarianship from the University of California, Berkeley. She briefly served as acting reference librarian at Mills College (1971–1972) and then joined the faculty of the Graduate School of Library and Information Science at the University of California, Los Angeles (UCLA). Ann Hinckley earned her M.L.S. from UCLA in 1964 and joined the library staff in interlibrary loan (1964–1967), then reference librarian (1967–1970), and assistant head of reference (1970–1973), and she served as head of reference (1973–1990). Elizabeth Eisenbach earned her M.L.S. from UCLA in 1962 and worked as a librarian from 1962 to 1966 until she joined the faculty of UCLA's Graduate School of Library and Information Science as a lecturer. Appointed a senior lecturer in 1980, she retired in 1987.[91] Together these three authors possess six decades of teaching and reference experience. Not surprisingly, then, G. Edward Evans, another UCLA faculty member at the time and consulting editor of Academic Press's Library and Information Science series, suggested that they write a textbook for his series in 1976.[92]

Unlike most earlier textbook authors, they chose not to discuss specific titles at length. In their introduction, the authors stated that "the student must start with a good working knowledge of the reference sources. This must be taught in the classroom and generally forms the core of most reference courses."[93] Although "matching the question to the sources" is discussed in chapter 5, their textbook does not explicitly recommend Hutchins's heuristic—classify the question by type of source and the rules for selecting specific sources.

Thomas gave two reasons for omitting the materials element of the traditional paradigm: (1) UCLA used extensive format-by-format syllabi in the two-quarter required course; and (2) an emphasis on the tools takes a lifetime.[94] In response to other authors' coverage of titles, she disdained the "scissors and paste book" approach. As for the alternative, she admitted that "it is harder to give students a sense of broader issues" encountered in reference work: "how do you get the soul into reference . . . [if one covers just the titles]?" However, if one wants a list, she offered Enoch Pratt Free Library's *Reference Books,* "my favorite and *vade mecum.*"[95]

More than ever (or at least since Wyer's text), *The Effective Reference Librarian (ERL)* shifted students' attention to the interaction between the reference librarian and the person on the other side of the reference desk. Much of the emphasis in *ERL* is on the latter. Previous authors have almost never used the term, but the *ERL* authors use the term "patron" eight times in the introduction.[96] More frequently, however, they use the "user" (twelve times); "clientele" is used six times. In latter chapters "inquirer" appears occasionally. When asked if they considered what to call the person on the other side of the reference desk, the third author replied, "Oh yes. Patron is offensive; it suggests patronizing while client seems pretentious."[97]

1.3
The Essential Paradigm

Based on an analysis of the preceding six textbooks, a tripartite paradigm for teaching reference work can be seen: (1) the *material* format or type of reference work; (2) the *method* or procedural rules for reference question answering; and, (3) the *mental traits* of the reference librarian as well as the person on the other side of the reference desk. The complete paradigm can be viewed graphically in Figure 1.1. Paradigm, following Kuhnian thought, is a world view that dictates "model problems and solutions to a community of practitioners."[98] Questions raised as a result are determined to be "interesting" based on the operating paradigm. A complete paradigm for reference work might be said to include each and every dimension mentioned by any of the preceding textbook authors. However, most of the reference textbook authors tend to focus on one or two of the three dimensions identified in Figure 1.1, overemphasizing it. Table 1.3 identifies the reference textbook authors by school of thought (or paradigmatic emphasis).

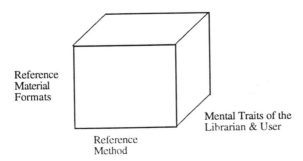

Reference Material Formats

Reference Method

Mental Traits of the Librarian & User

Figure 1.1
The Complete Paradigm for Teaching Reference Work

Because of the relative emphasis on a specific dimension, three different schools of thought emerge. These are: (1) structuralist, (2) proceduralist, and (3) "psychologicalist," if I may be permitted to coin a term. Briefly, a structuralist is one whose work is based primarily on the achievements realized by focusing on the material format. Members of the procedural school stress method—*how* one answers reference questions. The third school concerns itself with the psychological dimension of reference work. Each of these schools will be considered in more detail, by looking at the dimension and the kinds of questions they find interesting, based on the paradigm.

1.3.1 Material Format: Types of Reference Sources

One essential dimension of the teaching paradigm is the format of reference material (see Figure 1.3). In the earliest years of teaching, say from 1890 to 1930, this element had already been intuitively obvious to a generation or more of reference librarians. Several textbook authors have adopted this structural approach to teaching—notably the *Guide* editors, Shores, and Cheney and Williams—almost to the exclusion of the other dimensions.

As a structuralist, one might ask such questions as, What is the best order to present formats to novice librarians? and Are there some indispensable reference formats? An examination of the six textbooks makes it quite clear that some formats receive much more emphasis than others.

Indeed, among structuralist reference librarians and instructors the intellectual debate rages over the classification and priority of the various formats. For instance, in 1902, Kroeger recognized two categories: "the reference books and bibliographies."[99] Her classification reflects an earlier view that among all the materials at hand "the more copious and extensive bibliographies stand foremost."[100] Even so, she listed dictionaries first in her *Guide,* in part, because these were the most useful to the new class of library reader entering libraries at the turn of the century. The earlier type

Table 1.3
Textbook Authors by Paradigmatic Emphasis

Paradigmatic emphasis	Textbook authors
Structural (material format)	*Guide* editors; Wyer; Shores; Katz (vol. 1), Cheney, and Cheney & Williams
Procedural (method)	Wyer (in passing), Hutchins
Psychological (mental traits)	Wyer; Thomas, Hinckley, Eisenbach

of reader—a scholar—did not often need a dictionary, but did value bibliographies, especially lists of the best works in a field.

The range of and relative attention to formats merit some further examination. By 1954, half a century after Kroeger, Shores could identify nearly 150 different reference types. Whether this large number is really helpful heuristically for the proceduralists is addressed below in the section on the reference method. In any event, these other formats attract little attention among structuralists, proceduralists, or functionalists; Hutchins covers pamphlets, society and institutional publications are discussed by Shores, and Katz discusses almanacs.

Yet, other obvious formats such as microforms, and more recent technologies including online and CD-ROM sources, receive almost no attention. This latter situation may be due to the structuralists' ambivalence about their reference utility, their slowness to recognize the reference potential of these sources, or more stubbornly, their unwillingness to treat seriously a source that does not stand up on the shelf by itself. Instead, two formats, discussed below, have claimed most of our teaching time since the beginning.

1.3.1.1 Dictionaries and Encyclopedias

For decades, many reference librarians and instructors agreed with New York State School Library Inspector Leon O. Wiswell's 1916 declaration, "By far the most important single general reference work is the English Dictionary."[101] Dictionaries, along with encyclopedias, were two "indispensable reference books," which gave "direct aid" in answering reference questions.[102]

Dictionaries can also claim primacy because of a logical dependency. One must know how to use a dictionary before anything else. In other words, the new kind of readers entering the library needed to understand the meaning of words before they could use other works in the library's collection. On the other hand, the fact that reference authors introduce their students to dictionaries first also appears pedagogically sound in that this format is already familiar; almost every student owns at least one dictionary.

Sheehy and Mudge agree on the close relationship between the dictionary and encyclopedia. Sheehy distinguishes between the two by noting that "theoretically, the dictionary is concerned only with the word, not with the thing represented by the word, differing in this respect from the encyclopedia which gives information primarily about the thing."[103]

For the structuralist reference textbook author, the encyclopedia seems to have reigned as the supreme format for a long time. Mudge went so far as to refer to encyclopedias as "the backbone of a reference collection."[104] As late as 1969, Katz still argued that "encyclopedias are the most used single source."[105]

1.3.1.2 Bibliographies/Catalogs and
Indexes/Abstracting Services

Despite the common practice of treating dictionaries first and then encyclopedias, an extraordinary shift away from dictionaries occurred in the mid-1940s with the appearance of Hutchins's textbook. Hutchins, a proceduralist, already leading a revolution in one dimension of the paradigm (discussed below), shifted the relative order of formats as well (see Table 1.2). She had become aware that a complex structure for bibliographical control had emerged in the second quarter of the twentieth century; hence, specific reference tools for the control of and access to information had become more significant for reference librarians and their service population. Bibliographies, as noted, have always been important guides for scholars. Now, however, they could access the universal library collection with the appearance of such tools as, for example, the *National Union Catalog*. In 1969, Katz observed that such bibliographies are vital "bridges to information."[106]

Increasingly sophisticated reference titles began to appear in these two categories. With more comprehensive but complex bibliographies and indexes, it became easier for the reference librarian to answer such questions as, Does this title or article exist: who published it or where did it first appear? Cheney, another structuralist, covered bibliography first because, as she says, "I happen to believe they are the bedrock of reference sources. They are usually less well known to the average l.s. student than dictionaries and they put the fear of God in the beginner."[107]

After the Second World War, the growth of knowledge and its dissemination through serial literature rather than monographs created another shift; Katz began to emphasize indexes. The H. W. Wilson Company, which brought serials under increasing bibliographical control, led some reference librarians to refer to this period as the "Golden Age of Indexing." Later, citation indexes from the Institute for Scientific Information also found a more prominent place in reference textbooks.

The increasing primacy of bibliographies, catalogs, and indexes over dictionaries and encyclopedias suggests the debate about order may continue among structuralists. As for the best order, at least two reference textbook authors have explicitly responded to the concern. Shores thought that "there is no reason why a different order should not be adopted"[108] for presenting such material to novice reference librarians; Cheney has said "about *order*. Any one is O.K. if you can defend it."[109]

Reference textbook authors have observed that certain formats contain the direct answer to the question, while others, such as bibliographies, can require two steps to get to the ultimate source for the answer. Unfortunately, the field has not provided any strong research basis for the proper ordering except on the basis of use (see further discussion below). Even this definition of "best" has its difficulties. For instance, the reference librarian may not be using the best source, just the source they happen to own in that particular library.

Finally, many teachers of traditional reference classes will claim in defense of their sole focus on the formats and subsidiary titles: "But we have time only to teach reference books."[110] From a proceduralist viewpoint, however, the structural approach is an incomplete analysis of how one actually answers reference questions. Sources are ordered by format because it simplifies the decision-making process. One needs to know the different formats and their functions, but that is not enough for a proceduralist.

1.3.2 Method

Process or method is the second essential dimension of the paradigm. Simply stated, the proceduralist believes that the reference librarian should classify the question by type of source (i.e., format), and then select a specific source within that format to answer the question. Mudge taught this technique to her classes and her disciple, Hutchins, published it in the literature in 1937 and again in 1944. Interestingly, Hutchins is the sole textbook author to emphasize this process, though Wyer does cover it.

The proceduralist's response to the structuralist's approach is that there are too many titles for instructors to teach or for students to examine firsthand. Furthermore, as recently as 1979, there was still no consensus about the core reference titles to cover in class.[111]

The proceduralist believes that an analytical approach must be taken to the formats. Because reference questions can be answered by using a variety of different formats, more time must be spent on the procedural rules for when to select a particular format. Of course, by identifying 147 types of reference materials, Shores did not really help here; and besides, textbook authors have only discussed, at length, as many as fourteen and as few as eight formats. Total agreement on the absolutely essential formats exists for only two: bibliographies and, oddly enough, atlases. In addition, all but one textbook author would include dictionaries, encyclopedias, and indexes as essential. A structuralist would not spend much time talking about the importance of formats, their distinctions, or similarities; the *titles* are important to them.

From the proceduralist viewpoint, the novice reference librarian is still faced with a variety of choices concerning which format to use. And the novice must next choose from among many specific sources to arrive at the correct "tool of choice." Parenthetically, if the librarian already knows the correct title, then there is no decision necessary; so, learning the specific titles has validity from either perspective. Without a doubt, however, the proceduralist school views the reference decision as a complex multiple-choice classification task.

Historically, Samuel Swett Green may be credited with originally stating the reference professional's "trick of the trade" (also known as a rule of thumb or heuristic), if he meant that the novice librarian should practice analyzing the reference question by form and then find a specific source from memory when he referred to the "habit of mental classification."[112] Nevertheless, only one textbook author, Margaret Hutchins, explicitly states this fundamental theory of how to answer reference questions. Because Hutchins learned it from Mudge who taught her students this element as part of her tripartite approach to reference work at Columbia,[113] it may most properly be referred to as Mudge's method or Hutchins's heuristic. In any event, the earlier as well as later textbook authors do not *explicitly* discuss this essential element in the paradigm.

Larsen's 1979 examination of classroom instruction would suggest a similar neglect.[114] It is as though somehow the reason for emphasizing format rather than specific titles has slipped from the professional memory. Writers such as Wallace J. Bonk have argued that the procedural approach is more important than specific titles.[115] Similarly, Leontine Carroll called for "emphasizing types rather than titles [because it] would be less time consuming and thereby permit more time for a greater emphasis on problems and solutions."[116] Mudge and Hutchins stress format because it is the underlying basis for how one does reference: answer questions, even questions the librarian has never heard before. As mentioned earlier, the general strategy is analysis by format, followed by the specific strategy of selecting a tool of choice from within that format. For a proceduralist, classroom instruction emphasizes the "rules of reference"—the various formats, their similarities, differences, and when one should use one format over another—and only then the rules that lead to specific tools. Granted, however, this approach requires reference instructors to become more analytical in their approach and that is more work.

1.3.3 Mental Traits: The Librarian and the Person on the Other Side

There is a third component of the complete paradigm, one that also can be viewed as a separate school of thought: a focus on the mental traits of the reference librarian and of the person on the other side of the reference desk. In his psychological approach to reference work, Wyer presented the twenty-seven necessary mental traits or "personal qualifications deemed [to be] of first importance in reference work."[117] Table 1.4 lists the important mental traits of reference librarians as identified by the textbook authors.

Table 1.4
Important Mental Traits of Reference Librarians

Mental traits	Wyer	Hutchins	THE '81	Katz '82
Intelligence	1st		2nd	
Accuracy	2nd	5th		
Judgment	3rd	4th		2nd
Professional knowledge	4th		16th	1st
Dependability	5th			
Courteousness	6th			
Resourcefulness	7th			
Tact	8th		1st	
Alertness	9th			
Interest in Work	10th			
Memory	11th	1st	13th	
Mental curiosity	12th		7th	
Interest in people	13th			
Imagination	14th	2nd	3rd	4th
Adaptability	15th			
Perseverance	16th	3rd	8th	5th
Pleasantness	17th		11th	
Cooperativeness	18th			
System	19th			
Health	20th			
Initiative	21st			
Industriousness	22nd			
Speed	23rd		14th	3rd
Poise	24th		12th	
Patience	25th			
Forcefulness	26th			
Neatness	27th			
Suitability to reader	28th	6th		
Ingeniousness			4th	
Helpfulness			5th	
Empathy			6th	
Energy			9th	
Sensitivity			10th	
Humor			15th	

The traits were developed for the Library Curriculum Study of the American Library Association.[118]

 With few exceptions, subsequent textbook authors ignore the list as well as the concept. Teaching solely the tools was satisfactory for them, until the growth of reference sources made the structuralist approach inefficient. When the *Guide to Reference Books* contained less than two thousand titles, librarians could usually remember the right source. However, by the time Hutchins's textbook appeared, the *Guide* had grown to nearly four thousand sources. Not surprisingly, Hutchins then mentioned Wyer's list in her section on reference staff member selection[119] and delineated her six most important characteristics in the section on qualities needed for success.[120] Katz, who seems to have flirted with the psychologicalist approach in his 1982 edition, chose to mention five of the Wyer characteristics in his introduction subsection entitled "The Reference Librarian."[121] And, as might be expected, *The Effective Reference Librarian* discussed fifteen traits[122] possessed by good reference librarians, many of which are from Wyer's list. The six most important traits are: (1) imagination, (2) judgment, (3) professional knowledge, (4) memory, (5) perseverance, and (6) speed.

The psychological school of thought also recognizes and describes the traits held by the person on the other side of the desk. In other words, the textbooks use a psychological approach that is based on the user's questions and then teach those titles that contain the answer. Thus, the psychologicalists hope to find a more efficient way to teach reference work by focusing on that person on the other side of the desk.

Every textbook author seems to have spent some time thinking about what to call that person. The word or term used to describe this person shows a subtle, but significant, semantic shift over time. Indeed, the aesthetics of language can reveal one's philosophical orientation to reference service. Four terms have been used to identify or describe the person: (1) patron, (2) reader or inquirer, (3) user, and (4) customer or client.

1.3.3.1 Patron

Despite colloquial references to "patrons" in library school hallways and even in lectures, reference textbook authors have consistently avoided this term with few exceptions. Their disdain for referring to the person as a patron is manifold. First, the authors do not wish to be patronizing. Second, the term seems to be offensive to some authors.[123] More important, though, the term suggests an undesirable psychological situation, a vertical relationship between the reference librarian and the person. Such a philosophical orientation even manifests itself architecturally in libraries, by having the person stand while the reference librarian sits.

1.3.3.2 Reader/Inquirer

Reference textbook authors, from Wyer to the present, have consistently used the word, "reader," meaning "one engaged in research or study" to describe the person on the other side of the reference desk. Of those terms available, this word best describes the activity or purpose for being in the library and making use of reference service. Among the various authors, though, Thomas, Hinckley, and Eisenbach demonstrate the most ambivalence in using this term. The reason becomes clear upon examination of the next term.

1.3.3.3 User

A strong paradigmatic shift or revolution occurs in this element of the teaching paradigm in 1971. Although Kroeger uses the phrase "users of libraries"[124] and similarly Wyer refers in passing to the "library user,"[125] the term is not used in a textbook until Cheney's *Fundamental Reference Sources* (1971). The word is hopelessly vague and inaccurate; yet, it suggests the using of books versus the ability to take time to read books. It also suggests the risk of substituting knowledge for wisdom and mere information for knowledge.

The growth of knowledge and the subsequent shift from dictionaries and encyclopedias to bibliographies and indexes may account for this shift from reader to user. In the 1960s and earlier, the person on the other side of the desk probably did have time to read, but the so-called information explosion has some basis in reality. Sometimes there is too much data, but never enough relevant information. Starting in the 1970s, reference textbook authors reflected this new reality by adopting the term "users."

1.3.3.4 Customer/Client

One's terminology can be revealing. As noted earlier, "patron" may suggest an unwise vertical relationship, just as some will object that customer or client implies some sort of business connotation. Thomas, Hinckley, and Eisenbach used this term. Although there is today no consensus, such terms as customer or client may not be unrealistic, especially with the appearance of profit centers in public libraries and the growing demand for high-quality reference service. One could add a plethora of possible alternatives, all of which will have negative and positive connotations depending on context and intent. What is clear is that the term shifted from reader to user in Cheney's 1971 textbook, and perhaps there is another shift under way, led by the psychologicalists, to client or customer.

1.4

Conclusions

As stated above, the essential paradigm for teaching and learning general reference work consists of: (1) the reference material's format; (2) the reference method of clarification and classification; and (3) the mental traits of the librarian as well as the person on the other side of the desk. Each of these dimensions also represents a school of thought.

A couple of revolutions have occurred over time. First, the paradigm has undergone a shift from formats to method and back again. Within the dimension of format, the emphasis has shifted from dictionaries and encyclopedias to bibliographies, catalogs, and indexes. The methodological dimension has been overshadowed by an emphasis on the other two dimensions, while the third and final element, mental traits, has experienced a semantic shift from reader to user, and soon it may shift to customer or client.

1.4.1 Material Format

Structuralists concern themselves with lists of specific reference titles, whether it is the number of vital reference titles in the next *Guide to Reference Books* or each school's individual sampling of recommended reference tools. Instead, structuralist reference textbook authors and instructors might consider articulating the principles or "rules of reference" within a particular format. Rereading Hutchins would be useful. In the meantime, research needs to be undertaken to elucidate the conditions under which certain types of reference material formats are useful. Some of the prototype expert systems work that has been done in general reference promises to identify the essential or core titles.

1.4.2 Method

The Mudge method or Hutchins heuristic of classifying the inquirer's question by format and then specific source is another component to successful reference work. Perhaps researchers should treat this principle as a hypothesis and test it. Otherwise, it is an untested assumption that a question can best (i.e., most efficiently) be answered by connecting it to the format first, and then to the specific title. Proceduralists could extend Hutchins's heuristic by elucidating the procedural rules for when to select a specific type of source (i.e., What are the characteristics of the basic formats? How are they unique or how do they overlap?) and the declarative rules for when to select a specific title (i.e., Why are certain sources the "tools of choice"?).

1.4.3 Mental Traits

Despite evidence[126] that interest has shifted to one dimension of the complete paradigm (namely increased interest about the person on the other side of the desk), most of the reference textbooks ignore the substantial research into the psychological dimension of reference. Such work could be incorporated into future editions of the reference textbooks. What we have learned from studies of online public access catalogs may also be relevant to users of printed catalogs and bibliographies.

In conclusion, despite the *Guide*'s being edited at Columbia, the School of Library Service there has lost its teaching influence in this field. That influence has shifted to State University of New York, Albany, where Katz continues to offer a traditional, structural approach to reference work. Strongly influenced by the Columbia connection, the next edition of Cheney and Williams is also likely to offer the same kind of approach. If a new edition of the *ERL* were to appear, it would probably continue to offer the necessary psychological perspective.

The point is that a complete, balanced perspective is possible: (1) a presentation of the structure of reference works; (2) the process of answering reference questions by clarification and classification; and (3) a psychological understanding of the interaction between librarian and user. Perhaps only then will the field have reference librarians trained, educated, and capable of rendering high-quality reference service.

Endnotes

1. Mildred E. Singleton's 195-page "Reference Teaching in the Pioneer Library Schools, 1883–1903" (M.S. Thesis, Columbia University, June 1942) provides a superb start. Fran Miksa's transcriptions of student shorthand notes of Walter Biscoe's lectures in the School of Library Economy at the Columbia College should soon be considered as well because he is seeking a publisher for his work.

2. Thomas S. Kuhn, *The Structure of Scientific Revolutions, Foundations of the Unity of Science*, vol II, No. 2 (Chicago: University of Chicago Press, 1962), 10.

3. John V. Richardson, "Paradigmatic Shifts in the Teaching of Government Publications, 1895–1985," in *Journal of Education for Library and Information Science* 26 (Spring 1986): 249–266; reprint ed., *Encyclopedia of Library and Information Science*, vol. 44: 242–258.

4. For research universities and colleges, this history is best traced by Samuel Rothstein, "The Development of Reference Services in American Research Libraries," Ph.D. dissertation, University of Illinois, 1954; reprint ed., *The Development of Reference Services through Academic Traditions, Public Library Practice, and Special Librarianship*, ACRL Monograph No. 14 (Chicago: American Library Association, 1955), and Richard E. Miller, Jr., "The Development of Reference Services in the American Liberal Arts College, 1876–1976," Ph.D. dissertation, University of Minnesota, June 1984.

5. British Museum, *List of Books Forming the Reference Library in the Reading Room of the British Museum*, 4th ed. 2 vols. (London: Trustees of the British Museum, 1910).

6. Albert J. Walford, ed. *Guide to Reference Materials*, 3d ed. 3 vols. (London: Library Association, 1973).

7. Krishan Kumar, *Reference Service*, 2d ed. (Sahibabad, Dist. Ghaziabad, U.P.: Vikas Publishing House, 1980). His first edition appeared in 1978. A good start on the international perspective is provided in Frank Gibbon's "From Librarianship to Library Science: The Professional Education of Librarians in the United Kingdom, the United States, and Australia," in *Reference Services and Library Education: Essays in Honor of Frances Neel Cheney*, ed. Edwin S. Gleaves and John M. Tucker (Lexington, MA: Lexington Books, 1983), 247–263. Any analysis should include Denis J. Grogan's *Practical Reference Work*, Outline of Modern Librarianship series (London: C. Bingley, 1979) and Donald E. Davinson's *Reference Service* (London: C. Bingley, 1980; reprint ed., New York: K. G. Saur, 1980). Readers interested in examining

material other than textbooks should consult: Marjorie E. Murfin and L. R. Wynar's *Reference Service: An Annotated Bibliographic Guide* (Littleton, CO: Libraries Unlimited, 1977) and the 1984 supplement, which covers 1976 to 1982.

8. Mildred E. Singleton, "Reference Teaching in the Pioneer Library Schools, 1883–1903," 73.

9. Ibid.

10. Ibid.

11. New York State Library, Albany, *Handbook* (Albany: NYSL, 1891), 40.

12. New York State Library, Albany, "Selected Reference Books," *New York State Library Bulletin* 4 (1899): 149–218.

13. New York State Library, Albany, *Material for Course in Reference Study,* NYSL Bulletin No. 83 (Albany: NYSL, 1903).

14. Alice B. Kroeger, *Guide to the Study and Use of Reference Books; A Manual for Librarians, Teachers and Students,* ALA Annotated Lists (Boston: American Library Association Publishing Board, 1902; reprint ed., Boston: American Library Association Publishing Board, 1904; id., *Guide to the Study and Use of Reference Books,* 2d rev. and enl. ed. (Chicago: American Library Association Publishing Board, 1908).

15. Alice B. Kroeger, "Drexel Institute Library School," *Library Journal* 23 (5–9 July 1898): C62–C63.

16. Kroeger best expresses her methods and principles of teaching reference in two other documents: "Library School Pedagogics" n.d. and "Evolution of the Curriculum of the Drexel Institute Library School," *ALA Bulletin* 2 (22–27 June 1908): 210–213.

17. Kroeger, *Guide,* 1st ed., vii–viii.

18. Ibid., 80–82.

19. Ibid., 80.

20. Ibid., vii.

21. E. C. Richardson, "Reference-Books," *Library Journal* 18 July 1893): 254. A functionalist, Richardson also authored a book, *The Reference Department* (Chicago: American Library Association Publishing Board, 1911).

22. A two-page typed outline for the two-semester course, "Elementary Reference," providing the "Program of Course" and "Order of Topics and Lectures," survives in the University of Illinois's Library School Archives, "Miscellaneous Papers." Although she claims originality only for the five-minute in-class oral review of a reference book, Mudge expresses her early methods and principles of teaching reference in the following brief article: "Instruction in Reference Work," *Library Journal* 27 (June 1902): 334–335.

23. Mildred E. Singleton, "Reference Teaching," 166.

24. Isadore G. Mudge, *Guide to the Study and Use of Reference Books by Alice Bertha Kroeger,* 3d ed. (Chicago: American Library Association Publishing Board, 1917).

25. Isadore G. Mudge, *New Guide to Reference Books; Based on the Third Edition of Guide to the Study and Use of Reference Books by Alice B. Kroeger as Revised by I. G. Mudge,* 4th ed. (Chicago: American Library Association, 1923, 231).

26. Isadore G. Mudge, *Guide to Reference Books,* 5th ed. (Chicago: American Library Association, 1929), v.

27. John N. Waddell, "The Career of Isadore G. Mudge: A Chapter in the History of Reference Librarianship," (D.L.S. dissertation, Columbia University, 1973), p. 265, quoting Hutchins's class notes from Mudge's Library Service 301–302 "Bibliography and Bibliographical Methods."

28. Mudge, Isadore Gilbert (1875–1957)" by John N. Waddell and Laurel A. Grotzinger, *Dictionary of American Library Biography* (Littleton, CO: Libraries Unlimited, 1978), 377, and "Mudge, Isadore Gilbert" by David H. Kraus, *Encyclopedia of Library and Information Science,* vol. 18, 287–291.

29. Constance M. Winchell, *Guide to Reference Books,* 7th ed. (Chicago: American Library Association, 1951).

30. "Winchell, Constance Mabel (1896–1983)," by Pamela S. Richards, *Supplement to the Dictionary of American Library Biography* (Englewood, CO: Libraries Unlimited, 1990), 163–165. "Winchell, Constance (Mabel)," *A Biographical Directory of Librarians in the United States and Canada,* ed. Lee Ash and B. A. Uhlendorf (Chicago: American Library Association, 1970), 1195. See, also, Waddell, "The Career of Isadore G. Mudge," 178–179.

31. Winchell, *Guide to Reference Books,* 8th ed., vi. (Chicago: American Library Association, 1967).

32. Ibid.

33. Ibid.

34. Ibid.

35. David Kaser, "Have Winchell; Will Travel." *Wilson Library Bulletin* 30 (November 1955): 263–264.

36. The eleventh edition is projected to appear around June of 1995, according to Robert Balay, the new editor (Balay to Richardson, 16 July 1990).

37. Eugene P. Sheehy, "Selected Reference Books of 1961–1962." *College and Research Libraries* 24 (January 1963):31–38.

38. Quoted in the preface to the ninth edition, Constance Winchell advised Sheehy, "try not to let it get as big as the Manhattan telephone directory" (p. ix).

39. Sheehy, *Guide to Reference Books,* 10th ed., ix. (Chicago: American Library Association, 1986).

40. Donald C. Dickinson, "The Way It Was, the Way It Is: 85 Years of the Guide to Reference Books," *RQ* 27 (Winter 1987): 220–225.

41. C. C. Williamson, *Training for Library Service* (New York: Carnegie Corporation, 1923). See, also, Sarah K. Vann's *The Williamson Reports: A Study* (Metchuen, NJ: Scarecrow Press, 1961).

42. John V. Richardson, "Theory into Practice: W. W. Charters and the Development of American Library Education," in *Reference Services and Library Education: Essays in Honor of Frances Neel Cheney,* ed. Edward S. Gleaves and Mark Tucker (Lexington, MA: Lexington Books, 1983), 209–223.

43. James I. Wyer, *Reference Work: A Textbook for Students of Library Work and Librarians.* Introduction by W. W. Charters. Library Curriculum, no. 2. (Chicago: American Library Association, 1930), v.

44. Ibid., xi.

45. Ibid., 22.

46. Ibid., 96.

47. Ibid., 235–238.

48. Louis Shores, "Basic Reference," *Reference as the Promotion of Free Inquiry* (Littleton, CO: Libraries Unlimited, 1976), 4.

49. Louis Shores, *Basic Reference Books* (1937), 369.

50. Louis Shores, *Basic Reference Books: An Introduction to the Evaluation, Study, and Use of Reference Materials with Special Emphasis on Some 200 Titles.* (Chicago: American Library Association, March 1937).

51. Ibid., v. See, also, "Shores, Louis," Who's Who in Library Service, 3d ed., 446–447 and id., 4th ed., 632. "Shores, Louis (1904–1981)," by Lee Shiflett, Supplement to the Dictionary of American Library Biography (Englewood, CO: Libraries Unlimited, 1990), 123–129. Shores's ideas and career offer interesting possibilities for biographers, but at this point only brief biographical entries and unpublished sources of background information about Shores exist. Nevertheless, the author has benefitted from discussions with Lee Shiflett, who is writing a book-length biography, and second, from Dean Rowan's "Louis Shores and His Feelings

About Reference," GSLIS 420 "Information Resources and Services" Term Paper, UCLA, 1 December 1986.

52. Louis Shores, "We Who Teach Reference," *Journal of Education for Librarianship* 5 (Spring 1965): 241.

53. Ibid.

54. Shores, *Basic Reference Sources* (1937), 375.

55. Ibid.

56. Louis Shores, *Basic Reference Books: An Introduction to the Evaluation, Study and Use of Reference Materials with Special Emphasis on Some 300 Titles.* 2d ed. (Chicago: American Library Association, 1939).

57. Louis Shores, *Basic Reference Sources: An Introduction to Materials and Methods,* with Helen Focke. 3d ed. (Chicago: American Library Association, 1954).

58. Shores, "Basic Reference," 5.

59. Shores, "We Who Teach," 244.

60. Ibid.

61. Shores, *Basic Reference Books* (1937), 384–385 and (1939), 405–408.

62. Shores, *Basic Reference Sources,* 9.

63. "Hutchins, Margaret," by Charles D. Patterson, *Encyclopedia of Library and Information Science,* vol. 11, 123–127. Note his useful appendix entitled "Selected Bibliography" and "Hutchins, Margaret (1884–1961)," by Frances Neel Cheney, *Dictionary of American Library Biography* (Littleton, CO: Libraries Unlimited, 1978), 259–260. Hutchins deserves a fuller biographical study; the School of Library Service archives contain the "Hutchins Papers." Fortunately, some of Hutchins's own teaching material has survived, for example, "Syllabus for the Study of Bibliography and Reference for Use in Connection with Library Service 262," 4th ed. (1947).

64. Margaret Hutchins, *Trial List of Books Recommended for Reference Use.* (Queens Borough, NY: Queens Borough Public Library, 1930).

65. Hutchins to Phineas L. Windsor, 21 August 1927, quoted by Patterson, "Hutchins," p. 124.

66. Margaret Hutchins, *Introduction to Reference Work.* (Chicago: American Library Association, 1944), v.

67. Ibid.

68. Hutchins, "The Artist-Teacher in the Field of Bibliography; An Application of Modern Educational Theories and Techniques to the Teaching of the First-Year Library School," *Library Quarterly* 7 (January 1937): 103.

69. Ibid., 106, quoting W. C. Bagley and J. A. H. Keith, *An Introduction to Teaching* (New York: Macmillan, 1924), 224–225.

70. Hutchins, "The Artist-Teacher," 106.

71. William Katz to John Richardson. Letter, 8 August 1988.

72. Katz earned his doctorate at the University of Chicago as "Willis Armstrong Katz."

73. Katz to Richardson, 8 August 1988.

74. William A. Katz, *Introduction to Reference Work,* vol. 1, *Basic Information Sources,* vol 2, *Reference Services.* McGraw-Hill Series in Library Education. (New York: McGraw-Hill, 1969), vol. 1, viii.

75. Ibid. Additional biographical information on Katz includes *Who's Who in Library Service,* 1966, 357; *A Biographical Directory of Librarians,* 1970, 572; *Who's Who in Library and Information Service,* 1982, 255; and the CD-ROM version of the *Directory of Library and Information Professionals* (1988).

76. Katz to Richardson, 8 August 1988.

77. Ibid.

78. Katz, *Introduction to Reference Work,* 1969.

79. Katz, *Introduction to Reference Work,* 1969, vol. 1, 15.

80. Charles A. Bunge, "Professional Education and Reference Efficiency," Ph.D. dissertation, University of Illinois, 1967.

81. William A. Katz, *Introduction to Reference Work,* vol. 1, *Basic Information Sources,* vol. 2, *Reference Services and Reference Processes,* 2d ed. McGraw-Hill Series in Library Education. (New York: McGraw-Hill, 1974).

82. William A. Katz, *Introduction to Reference Work,* vol. 1, *Basic Information Sources,* vol. 2, *Reference Services and Reference Processes,* 3d ed. McGraw-Hill Series in Library Education. (New York: McGraw-Hill, 1978).

83. Katz to Richardson, 8 August 1988.

84. See, for example, his 1974 edition, vol. 1, 3.

85. Based on standard biographical sources including *Who's Who in Library Service,* 3d through 5th editions, *Who's Who in Library and Information Service,* and the CD-ROM version of the *Directory of Library and Information Professionals.* Cheney also deserves a biographical study, perhaps in a collective biography along with Hutchins; Cheney's papers are held by Vanderbilt University Library's Special Collections Department.

86. "Friends Salute the Profession's Number-One Reference Reviewer," *Wilson Library Bulletin* 47 (September 1972): 86–88.

87. M. Sangster Parrott, Review of Francis N. Cheney, *Fundamental Reference Sources,* in *School Libraries* 21 (Winter 1972): 64.

88. Library Science 220, "Introduction to Bibliography," School of Library Science, George Peabody College, Fall 1971. 40 Pp. plus additional handouts (in Richardson's possession).

89. Frances N. Cheney, *Fundamental Reference Sources.* (Chicago: American Library Association, 1971), 12.

90. Frances N. Cheney to John Richardson. Letter, 23 October 1986.

91. Based on interviews and standard biographical sources including Lee Ash, ed., *A Biographical Directory of Librarians in the United States and Canada,* 5th ed. (Chicago: American Library Association, 1970), 310; *Who's Who in Library and Information Services* (Chicago: American Library Association, 1982), 495, 217, 137; and the CD-ROM version of the *Directory of Library and Information Professionals.* Eisenbach has expressed her rather reactionary philosophy in an article entitled, "No Case Histories, No Papers, No Texts—Only the Reference Desk, or Learning by Doing," *RQ* 11 (Summer 1972): 331–335.

92. Actually the authors had signed a contract with another professional publisher, but the president dictated content and wanted a separate chapter about online reference (interview with Ann T. Hinckley, Los Angeles, 5 October 1988). Referring to it as "T.H.E. book" among themselves, they divided topics up (two chapters apiece) by what they each knew best; it took five years to finish, writing every Tuesday and Wednesday evening (interview with Diana M. Thomas, Los Angeles, 2 May 1987 and 22 July 1988).

93. Diana M. Thomas, Ann T. Hinckley, and Elizabeth R. Eisenbach, *The Effective Reference Librarian,* Library and Information Science series. (New York: Academic Press, 1981), 3.

94. Interview with Diana Thomas, 22 July 1988.

95. Ibid.

96. Once on page ix of the preface and perhaps for alliterative purposes in chapter 5, "Desk Technique and the Library User," they refer to the "problem patron" (p. 128ff).

97. Interview with Elizabeth R. Eisenbach, Los Angeles, 10 October 1985.

98. Thomas S. Kuhn, *The Structure of Scientific Revolutions,* viii.

99. Kroeger, *Guide to Reference Books* (1902), vii.

100. A. R. Spofford, "Works of Reference," in *Public Libraries in the United States of America* (Washington, D.C.: U.S. Bureau of Education, 1876), 687.

101. Leon O. Wiswell, *How to Use Reference Books* (New York: American Book Company, 1916), 25.

102. Kroeger, *Guide* (1902), vii.

103. Sheehy, *Guide* (1986), 146.

104. Shores, *Basic Reference Books* (1937), 376.

105. Katz, *Introduction to Reference Work* (1969), vol. 1, 13.

106. Ibid., 33.

107. Cheney to Richardson, 23 October 1986.

108. Shores, *Basic Reference Books* (1937), v–vi.

109. Cheney to Richardson, 23 October 1986.

110. Hutchins, *Introduction,* 101. Edward Shils has written thoughtfully about the "grip of the past . . . [and] the endurance of past practices" in *Tradition* (Chicago: The University of Chicago Press, 1981).

111. John C. Larsen, "Information Sources Currently Studied in General Reference Courses" *RQ* 18 (Summer 1979):341–348.

112. Samuel S. Green, "Personal Relations Between Librarians and Readers," *American Library Journal* 1 (November 1876): 77. The context is: "But having acquired a definite notion of the object concerning which information is desired, the habit of mental classification, comes to his aid. He sees at once in what department of knowledge the description sought for may be found, and brings to the inquirer an authoritative treatise in this department." For a different view of his "mental classification," see Constance Miller and James Rettig, "Reference Obsolescence," *RQ* 25 (Fall 1985): 52–58.

113. "Mudge," *DALB,* 378 and "Mudge," *ELIS,* vol. 18, 289, which labels Mudge's three M's "a glib prescription."

114. Larsen, "Information Sources," 341–348.

115. Wallace J. Bonk, "Core Curriculum and the Reference and Bibliography Courses," *Journal of Education for Librarianship* 2 (Summer 1961): 28–33 and "Core Reference Course," *Journal of Education for Librarianship* 4 (Spring 1964): 196–208.

116. Leotine D. Carroll, "Down with the Lists: This is the Way We Teach," *RQ* 6 (Fall 1966), 30.

117. Wyer, *Reference Work,* 233.

118. Ibid., 234. For an analysis, see Note 42 above.

119. Hutchins, *Introduction to Reference Work,* 161.

120. Ibid., 32–34.

121. Katz, *Introduction to Reference Work* (1982), vol. 2, 28.

122. Thomas et al., *The Effective Reference Librarian,* 1–3. While several of their traits sound like societal expectations of "the woman next door," one of their traits, helpful, is in fact straight out of the Scouting Movement's Law; see "Boy Scouts" and "Girls Scouts and Girl Guides," *Encyclopedia Americana,* vol. 4 and 12 (1990), 383 and 763, respectively.

123. Interview with Elizabeth R. Eisenbach, 10 October 1985.

124. Kroeger, *Guide* (1902), vii.

125. Wyer, *Reference Work,* 5.

126. Charles A. Bunge, "Interpersonal Dimensions of the Reference Interview: A Historical Review of the Literature," *Drexel Library Quarterly* 20 (Spring 1984): 4–23.

2

Expert Systems Defined*

An expert is a person who has made all the mistakes which can be made
in a very narrow field.

—Niels Bohr

Computers, especially microcomputers, are prevalent in library settings and hence available to support a more analytical decision-making
process.[1] Librarians are increasingly familiar with the widespread utility of
the first three kinds of microcomputer applications for the library environment: (1) spreadsheet and database programs; (2) statistical packages; and
(3) the now ubiquitous word processing software. The fourth and newest
kind of microcomputer application is an expert system. This category is
broad as well as vague (definitions do appear below) and is sometimes
referred to as "decision support" in general but it includes general problem
solving as well.

2.1

Historical Development

Expert systems grew out of artificial intelligence (AI), an interdisciplinary research program drawing upon the disciplines of anthropology, cognitive science, decision sciences, linguistics, mathematics, neuroscience, philosophy (especially epistemology and logic), and psychology, but based
originally within the computer science community.[2] Much of the early work

*Portions of this chapter originally appeared in "Toward an Expert System for Reference
Service: A Research Agenda for the 1990s." *College and Research Libraries* 50 (March 1989):
231–248; reprinted, "Toward an Expert System for Reference Service: A Research Agenda
for the 1990s," in *Expert Systems and Library Applications; An SLA Information Kit* (Washington,
DC: Special Libraries Association, 1991), pp. 95–112. © 1989 by the American Library Association.

and subsequent advances in (AI), or "machine intelligence" as it was then called, focused on chess playing.

For a variety of reasons, chess playing is a particularly interesting problem domain that has some relevant parallels with reference work. In chess, both players have the same goal, to win; in reference work, both the inquirer and librarian seek to find the answer. Next, chess is a complex problem domain with about 38 legal moves each turn, 10^{43} possible positions, and 10^{120} possible branches or games.[3] Like reference work, it is a closed system. Unlike reference, however, chess rules are explicitly spelled out and agreed on internationally. In chess, one piece, the King, is of inestimable value, although it is sometimes represented as equal to 255 or some other large number to prevent the computer program from trying to win by capturing all the opponent's pieces and promoting its pawns to queens and then thinking that it has won. By contrast to the King, the Queen is worth nine; the rook, five; the bishop and the knight, three; and the pawn, one point. Arguably, service to the inquirer is of estimable value in libraries, or at least it should be, but numerical values have yet to be assigned. Finding the correct answer should have the largest value, otherwise a system might solve all the smaller pieces, such as a good interview, and think it had successfully accomplished its task.

Chess has implicit tactics and strategies as does reference work. However, chess has had an internationally recognized hierarchy, at least since the 1890s, which sorts players out according to their relative expertise; reference has nothing similar.[4] These rankings make it easier to measure both an individual's and a computer's status and/or progress.[5] Furthermore, chess players have written down their moves in notable games for the past two to three centuries, though in greater detail since the last century. In addition, players have published expert commentary and analysis on completed as well as adjourned games. Reference has nothing comparable; perhaps a new journal column could do so. In the meantime, a useful study or classroom assignment would be to collect real reference questions and expert answers, asking novices or more advanced practitioners: (1) to identify the theory behind the answer, (2) to analyze the alternative answers, and (3) to explain why the expert's solution is satisfactory.

Computer chess was an avocational interest among the Enigma Cypher Group in Bletchley, England, led by Alan Turing who published a seminal paper entitled "On Computable Numbers" in 1937.[6] This article laid the groundwork for computing chess, and clearly, Turing's programming ideas were influenced by other chess players including I. Jack Good, Donald Michie, Harry Golombek, a chess master, and Hugh O'D. A. Alexander, the British chess champion. By 1951 at the University of Manchester, Turing had written *Turochamp* on their Ferranti Mark I computer. It played legal chess, but lost to a beginner, Alick Glennie.[7]

Intrigued by the difference between experts and beginners, Adrian de Groot studied the differences between chess grand masters and novices. First, he showed these two groups a position on a chessboard for five seconds and then he withdrew it. He found that the grand masters could reconstruct a board position with 20–24 pieces, but that the novices could barely remember the positions for even a handful of pieces.[8] A similar study of reference librarians' ability to recall a question and the steps taken to reaching a satisfactory resolution might be insightful.

In 1950, Claude E. Shannon offered a major advance toward real machine intelligence in "Programming a Computer for Playing Chess." He observed that for chess (1) there are a finite number of possible positions, (2) there are a finite number of possible moves at each position, and (3) the rules result in a win, loss, or draw. Next, he argued that chess playing can be viewed as a tree where the top equals the positions and the possible moves, the branches. The following four principles articulated by Shannon influenced chess programming for the next couple of decades and suggests an analogously productive approach for studying reference work:

1. Examine all moves to a fixed depth.
2. Give numerical value to moves.
3. Weigh points based on pieces and position.
4. Choose move with maximum evaluation.[9]

Similar rules exist for reference work (see Chapters 1 and 5).

Chess programming continued to improve until on 21 January 1967, a computer program called MacHack Six, written by Richard Greenblatt and Donald Eastlake among others, beat a human in a regular chess tournament, making checkmate in 21 moves. During the same year, a University of Chicago master's student, studying reference work, wrote a program that could answer some basic biographical questions that the librarian could not. Not surprisingly, people began to wonder whether it would be possible to beat a master or even a grand master; in response, Donald Michie said: "if one were to succeed in creating such a program, it would be possible to program anything one liked."[10]

Unfortunately, programming reference work did not continue to progress as it did in the chess world. For instance, in 1970 Mikhail Botvinnik, an ex–World Champion, wrote his *Computers, Chess and Long-Range Planning,* which has many interesting parallels for reference work. Shortly thereafter, the first world championship for computers was held in August 1974; those in attendance witnessed the Soviet program, Kaissa, beat Ostrich, an American program. At the Association for Computing Machinery's Tournament in 1981, a Cray Blitz beat a United States Chess Federation (USCF) Master for the first time. To do so, the program used full-width searching (i.e., brute force), a killer heuristic, and an alpha-beta[11] backward pruning algorithm. The program had the capability of six-ply look ahead. On the basis of that win, the program earned a provisional rating of 2258. In October 1983, Belle by Ken Thompson and Joe Condon earned the USCF rating of 2203, a score equivalent to a United States Master. That's well ahead of 99 percent of all chess players.

Machine intelligence has even changed the rules of chess. For more than a century, the endgame chess rule declares a draw if there have been 50 moves without a pawn move or capture. However, computer analysis of certain endgame positions has shown that previously theoretical draws were actually winnable and hence, the endgame rules of chess had to be changed.[12]

So what is the state of computer chess and what might reference librarianship expect? Computer chess already plays significantly better than 85% of all tournament players. For quick decisions or longer thought-out decisions the computer may be stronger, but the human still holds the middle ground (see Figure 2.1). Despite the fact that the computer is strong on chess tactics but not on strategy, it is a powerful player and has increased its playing strength dramatically. Computers, just as humans do, play a stereotypical, but strong "book opening" (the frequently named but standard moves that players often play to get a game started). In reference work, librarians engage in stereotypical behavior regarding categorization of inquirers (see Chapter 4), which speeds initial decision making.

Computers may become unbeatable (see Table 2.1) if they are programmed to look for the *best* next move and always find it;[13] at least theory suggests that the computer playing White would always win in this case.

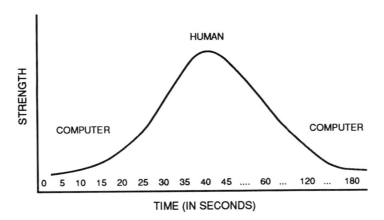

Figure 2.1

Human versus Computer Chess-Playing Strength. Based on narrative in T.D. Harding, *New Computer Chess,* 2d ed. (Oxford: Pergamon Press, 1985), 149.

Table 2.1

Increasing Strength of Computer Chess Programs

Year	Strength	Program, programmer(s)	Source
1967	1243	MacHack Six, R. Greenblatt and D. Eastlake	7
1967	1493	MacHack Six, R. Greenblatt and D. Eastlake	4, 5
1967[a]	1640	MacHack Six, R. Greenblatt and D. Eastlake	7
1968	1529	MacHack Six	5
1969			
1970	1200?	Chess 2.0, D. Slate, Larry Atkin, and Keith Gorlen at Northwestern	3, 5
1971			
1972			
1973			
1974[a]	1734, 1736	Chess 4.0, Northwestern University	3, 4, 7
1974	1400?	Kaissa, Institute of Control Science, USSR	3, 5
1975	1243	TECH, James Gillogly, Carnegie-Mellon University	7
1977[a]	ca. 2000	Chess 4.5, Northwestern University	5
1977	1200?	Ostrich, M. Newborn, G. Arnold, I. Vardi	3, 5
1977	2000?	Chess 4.6, Northwestern University	1, 3
1977	1600?	Duchess, ?	3
1977	1600?	Kaissa, ICS, USSR	3
1978[a]	2244	Belle, AT&T Bell Laboratories	5
1980	2168	Chess 4.9, Northwestern University	3, 5
1980[a]	2294	Belle, AT&T Bell Laboratories	5
1980		Ostrich, M. Newborn, University of Montreal	2
1981	2258	Cray Blitz, R. Hyatt and A. Gower at University of Southern Mississippi	2, 5
1981[a]	2306	Belle, AT&T Bell Laboratories	5
1983	2203?	Belle, Ken Thompson and Joe Condon	1
1983	2153	Cray Blitz	8
1983	2066	NuChess, D. Slate and W. Blanchard	8
1983	2178	Belle, K. Thompson and Joe Condon (Bell)	8
1985[a]	2352	Hitech, MIT	6
1986	2500?	Cray Blitz, University of Southern Mississippi	
1987	2600?	ChipTest, ?	
1988[a]	2558	DeepThought, ?	
1990	2552	DeepThought, Hsu et al.	1

Source: (1) *Scientific American,* October 1990, 44; (2) *Discover,* December 1982, 112; (3) David Levy, *The Joy of Computer Chess* (1984), 77; (4) Peter W. Frey, *Chess Skill in Man and Machine* (1983), 171; (5) David E. Welsh, *Computer Chess* (1984), 10, 11, 16, 18, 20, 21, 23; (6) Carl Ebeling, *All the Right Moves* (1987), [i], 105; (7) David Levy, *Chess and Computers* (1967), 84, 101; (8) David E. Welsh and Boris Baczynskyi, *Computer Chess II* (1985), 260.
[a] Highest score/strength to that date

Indeed, one of the great human players, Capablanca, reportedly used this tactic: "I see just one move ahead—the best move."[14] Despite this obviously promising approach, recent computer chess programming work shows a shift taking place from the *best* node to an approach in finding the node that is most likely to contribute the most information toward terminating the search for the next move. If computer modeling of reference work requires too much computer processing, then this latter approach may be adopted.

Machine intelligence versus human players has shown that even chess experts can be beaten in situations when they: (1) lack concentration or do not take the game seriously, (2) are overly confident and not consistent in their playing. Even so, chess masters normally make a low percentage of unforced errors; when they do, their errors are primarily due to time pressures. Most writers agree that the chess computer programs lack initiative and do not yet possess pattern recognition abilities like human players. What would research about the quality of reference service say? A parallel study of reference work might be informative here.

2.2
Definitions

Readers looking for a formal definition of an expert system may appreciate the following quotations. Donald Waterman of the Rand Corporation defined an expert system in 1985 as "a computer program using expert knowledge to attain high levels of performance in a narrow problem domain."[15] That same year, Goodall in Oxford wrote that "an expert system is a computer system that uses a representation of human expertise in a specialist domain in order to perform functions similar to those normally performed by a human expert in that domain."[16] Yet, another definition of an expert system is:

> a program that relies on a body of knowledge to perform a somewhat difficult task usually performed only by a human expert. The principal power of an expert system is derived from the knowledge the system embodies rather than from search algorithms and specific reasoning methods. An expert system successfully deals with problems for which clear algorithmic solutions do not exist.[17]

Perhaps the most formal definition, however, comes from the British Computer Society (BCS):

> An expert system is regarded as the embodiment within a computer of a knowledge-based component from an expert skill in such a form that the system can offer intelligent advice or make an intelligent decision about a processing function. A desirable additional characteristic, which many would consider fundamental, is the capability of the system, on demand, to justify its own line of reasoning in a manner directly intelligible to the inquirer. The style adopted to attain these characteristics is rule-based programming.[18]

As an operational definition, the BCS comes close; it might also include an explanation facility regarding system prompts, the ability to handle uncertainty, and actual learning from experience while the system is operating.

Readers may increasingly encounter related terms such as knowledge systems, knowledge-based systems (KBS) or reference advisory systems (RAS).[19] While some library and information science authors imply a level of complexity with such terms, what is clear, however, is that the phrase "knowledge-based system" is broader than just expert systems. For example, a knowledge-based system might be a natural language or vision system, or an expert system.

The point of these definitions is that such systems provide heuristic rather than algorithmic solutions to problems. In reference work most of our decisions are qualitative; rarely do we have hard numbers involved except for budgetary matters, reference book circulation, and number of questions asked. Thus far, solutions seem to be based on rules of thumb or tricks of the trade. We could benefit from a more quantitative approach to our decision-making process.

The basic assumption underlying expert systems is that "Knowledge is Power."[20] In general, the more we know, the better the resulting decision. Perhaps, now, the reader understands why so many individuals are fascinated with the possibilities of an expert system. Its proper role in the decision support of reference librarians and their problem solving will be discussed in the next chapter.

2.3
Expert System Building Blocks

As illustrated in Figure 2.2, an expert system is composed of three parts: (1) the knowledge base (of facts and rules); (2) an inference engine; and (3) the interfaces (for the system's developer and the end user). The objective of expert systems work has been to separate domain-specific knowledge (i.e., the knowledge base) from general problem solving (i.e., the inference engine) in order to promote flexibility and transparency of the knowledge required to do a particular task. The synergistic combination of these two elements can result in a potentially powerful system.

2.3.1 Knowledge Base

The first building block is the knowledge base within a domain. In our field, this knowledge base consists of several kinds of knowledge, including the explicit declarative facts and implicit procedural rules for doing general reference work.[21] Roughly speaking, 20 percent of reference knowledge is declarative, while the other 80 percent is procedural. It is worth

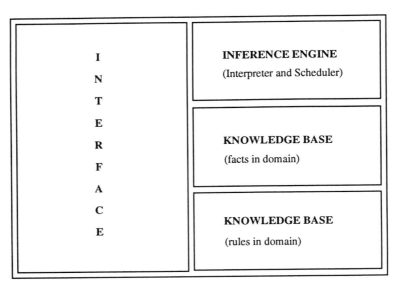

Figure 2.2
Components of an Expert System. Adapted from work by N. Shahla Yaghmai.

noting that the reference knowledge base is more than a database that contains only isolated or even related facts. However, there are significant advantages to defining knowledge as consisting merely of facts and rules (see Chapter 3).

2.3.1.1 Declarative Knowledge (Factual, Static, or Crystallized)

According to James Parrott at the University of Waterloo, a fact is an atomic sentence (predicate) that has at least one constant among its arguments. This means that the sentence makes a specific (or partially specific) statement about what holds *true* in the world *now*. Facts are indispensable in an artificial intelligence application, since they represent the specific data that are required if specific conclusions are to be drawn.[22]

In answering reference questions, the fact base may be said to contain all the requisite reference materials, specifically the reference formats, types or classes, and then the specific tools of choice, as discussed in Chapter 1. Operationally defined, the fact base could be the 14,000 titles listed in the current edition of *Guide to Reference Books*.[23] On the other hand, librarians may well define their fact base as all the reference books in their departmental collection; in that case, this figure ranges from 35,000 to 82,000 works for most academic libraries.[24] Another way to define it would be the total number of titles a reference expert actually uses in the course of her work. In this case, the number might be substantially smaller, perhaps on the order of 1000 titles (see Chapter 5). In reference work, the tools are public knowledge (see Figure 2.3).[25] These tools are listed in readily available sources, such as *Guide to Reference Books,* readily accessible to anyone who is interested. In that sense, the declarative knowledge can be said to be codified, diffuse, and objective.[26] Nevertheless, there is more to learning reference work than just the tools—the packages of information, the objective facts related to publication.

2.3.1.2 Procedural Knowledge (Strategic or Dynamic)

The other important component of the knowledge base is the rule base. Buchanan and Duda have defined a rule as:

> a conditional sentence relating several fact statements in a logical relation. The nature of the relation varies from rule to rule. Often rules record mere empirical associations, rules of thumb based on past experience with little empirical justification. Other rules are statements of theoretical associations, definitions, or causal laws.[27]

Generally speaking, though, rules constitute information about courses of action. As discussed in Chapter 1, this knowledge for reference work is

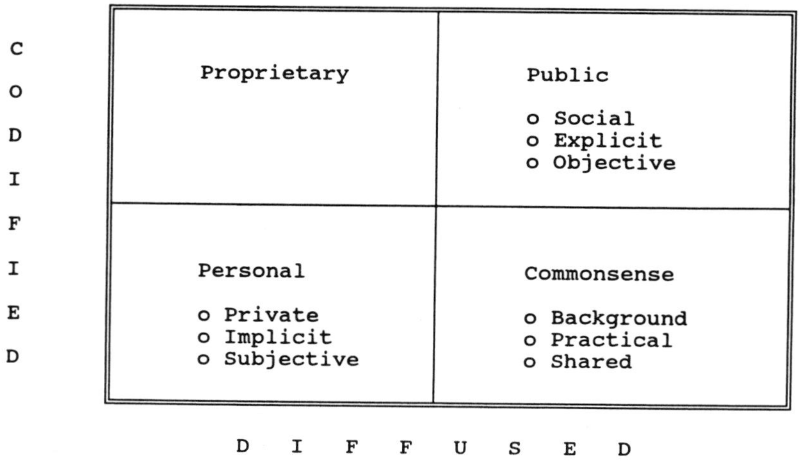

Figure 2.3
Modified C/D Theory of Knowledge. Adapted from Max Boisot, *Information Management* (1987), Figure 3.9.

largely procedural, making decisions about which tools to use. As an example, a simple reference rule might be stated as:

IF the user wants to know the meaning of a word,

THEN consult a dictionary type source.

More complicated situations will require compound rules. For instance:

IF the user wants the proper pronunciation of a word

AND the user wants a prescriptive pronunciation

THEN consult *Webster's 2nd Unabridged Dictionary*.

The entire collection of such simple and compound rules is commonly called the heuristics of the domain.

Another way of distinguishing rules is the difference between characteristic and discriminant rules. For example, as a rule it may be true that most dictionaries will assist with the correct spelling of words (a characteristic rule of the format). However, there is another kind of rule, one that identifies differences. Compare two etymology dictionaries, say, the *Oxford English Dictionary* and Klein's *Comprehensive Etymologies;* one discriminant rule is that the former is a group effort, while the latter is the work of one individual, but even so it covers more words. In other words, discriminant rules focus on some individuating criterion.

Experts possess four different kinds of knowledge: personal (which, as we have seen, can be private, implicit, and subjective); commonsense (including background), practical, which is shared; proprietary, and public knowledge (which is social, explicit, and objective but may be shallow or deep as well). Thus, substantial research or knowledge engineering may have to be undertaken before even core knowledge can be made public (see the following discussion and Chapter 5).

2.3.1.3 Commonsense Knowledge

Following Figure 2.3, this quadrant is knowledge that is diffuse (i.e., general) but not codified (i.e., not written down). It is also called background, practical, shared (e.g. perceptual skills), or world knowledge. An example of such background knowledge might be the function of various reference formats. For instance, most inquirers are at least vaguely aware that dictionaries help with spelling problems or that indexes contain a list of articles. Another reference example would be a biographical search for a Mr. Smith; the human immediately knows that "Mr." implies that the person is male, but the computer has to be programmed to know that.

Parenthetically, most "theories" of reference work also fall into this commonsense quadrant primarily because researchers have not advanced the procedural approach of Mudge (who clearly did not codify what she knew) and Hutchins (who codified it for librarians, but they seem to have forgotten, so it is no longer especially diffuse). Hence, the field has only naive theories—ones not informed by rigorous public scrutiny. Thus, much needs to be done to formalize (i.e., codify) what we now know as common-sense and make it public.[28]

2.3.1.4 Proprietary Knowledge

This kind of knowledge is codified, but not diffuse (see Figure 2.3). Usually, it is not available free of charge to the public. Several ES programs are commercially viable, such as, Educational Testing Service's BookWhiz, Information Transfer Associates' dictionary module, and Oryx Press's BookBrain (see Chapter 8).

Some have questioned the ownership of the knowledge base in expert systems.[29] If the knowledge acquisition research is undertaken in a university, then that institution may claim ownership. On the other hand, work supported by United States government contracts may not be copyrightable at all. The creator of Answerman, Samuel T. Waters, who works for the United States federal government and thus cannot make a copyright claim, advocates making the software "freely available to others so that the knowledge bases are readily accessible to all."[30]

2.3.1.5 Shallow, Intermediate, and Deep Knowledge

Finally, the hierarchical view is yet another way of looking at knowledge. Knowledge can be said to be shallow or deep along a continuum. For example, shallow or surface-level knowledge relates to the selection of specific sources, but such surface knowledge is relatively unstable. New reference books appear; existing works are revised. Hence, maintenance of such expert systems is a significant concern.

Intermediate rules (a kind of metalevel set of rules), in the middle, are those related to the classification of the user's question to match a particular format or type of source. Regrettably, most reference textbook authors do not explicitly articulate these surface or intermediate-level rules.

Deep knowledge consists of axioms, first principles, and theories about information transfer in reference work. Ideally, the urge to discover more rules will cause expert system developers to go deeper into the domain's theory in their search. Indeed, the mere conceptual framework or architecture of knowing any domain implies a deeper underlying theoretical structure. Indeed, there may be a *ceteris paribus* condition[31] beyond which we cannot go, but deeper knowledge of the metarules will be necessary for truly expert systems in reference work.

Perhaps a helpful way of looking at such deep knowledge is the following formula:

Domain Theory + Problem-Solving Knowledge = Heuristic Rules[32]

Such knowledge is stable because it is quite general and rather abstract. Interestingly, expert system developers in reference work have taken the top–down (i.e., surface level first) versus bottom–up (i.e., deep) approach. Adopting the latter would mean a more stable theory or system of rules, which, of course, might be of less practical interest to practitioners but which might lead to a true information science (i.e., definitions, axioms, first principles, and laws).

2.3.1.6 Explicit and Implicit or Tacit Knowledge

Finally, some researchers make the distinction between explicit and implicit knowledge.[33] If the domain expert can articulate knowledge, then it is explicit knowledge. Textbooks and other professional literature contain explicit knowledge or "theory-like representations of what we believe we know."[34]

On the other hand, much of our knowledge may be acquired during apprenticeships or face-to-face relationships. The difficulty is that some, perhaps many experts but especially apprenticed experts, may do a task a particular way rather automatically and quite successfully without knowing why they do it that way. In this case, "one cannot elicit that which no-one knows that they know."[35] While we may not know everything about something, we may still be able to articulate a theory. Here, the difficulty may be that we may have used the rules so often that they simply become "compiled," and we cannot express them explicitly.

In summary, different kinds of knowledge may mean we need different knowledge elicitation techniques.

2.3.2 Inference Engine

The inference engine (see Figure 2.2) contains general problem-solving knowledge and consists of an interpreter and a scheduler.[36] The interpreter determines which rules to invoke while the scheduler decides when these rules fire and in what order. The engine must be programmed as part of the system's programming language or, in the case of a shell,[37] the engine will be already built in. The inference engine is the computer equivalent of thinking or, more specifically, reasoning. Specific inference strategies or inference mechanisms vary, but such methods of reasoning include: (1) production rule-based methods that are either backward chaining or forward chaining; (2) induction systems; and (3) frame based using inheritance.

Furthermore, the most powerful engines allow for uncertainty[38] or probability factors because many domains contain information that is imprecise, incomplete, vague, and even unreliable. It might be useful to classify information as (1) foreseeable; (2) conceivable; (3) realizable; (4) assumable; (5) arguable; (6) doubtless; (7) uncontroversial; (8) undeniable; (9) provable; and (10) safe.[39] In dealing with these situations, some writers have also cautioned developers to distinguish between uncertainty and ignorance.[40] Other desirable expert system features include explanation capabilities such as why the system needs certain information and how this information is used.

2.3.2.1 Production Rules

Following is an illustration of a production rule situation that could employ either forward or backward reasoning. Suppose the reference librarian is trying to answer a question. She knows she has a set number of ready-reference books in which to look. At the same time, she knows what the question is about. Should she:

Strategy A: look through all the books working back to the question, or

Strategy B: work forward from the question eliminating possible reference formats.

Which strategy will work better? Is "mixed-mode" chaining possible?

Strategy A, an example of backward chaining, is "an inference method where the system starts with what it wants to prove."[41] It moves from right to left, from the conclusion back to the condition. The librarian may have to look at numerous reference books before she finds the answer. Strategy B, an example of forward chaining, is "an inference method where rules are matched against facts to establish new facts."[42] Here, the system works from left to right, from condition forward to conclusion. The reference librarian has to know the rules related to formats and then select a specific book that she owns in order to check it and see if it contains the user's answer. Which strategy is best depends on the nature of the domain (see discussion in Chapter 3). In this instance, a combination of both approaches makes sense. The reference librarian may work forward on format because there is a relatively large number of possible formats and then work backward from titles owned within the identified format because there is a limited number of titles within any format.

2.3.2.2 Induction Systems

Some experts find it easier to give examples from their past experience in the domain rather than to express their knowledge directly in the form of abstract IF–THEN rules. Parenthetically, these IF–THEN phrases are technically called Horn Clauses, while "the process of discovering knowledge from examples is called induction."[43] If experts can identify enough sample cases along with the relevant attributes related to their decision-making process as well as the ultimate decision, then machine induction can take the place of prolonged labor-intensive interviewing. The resultant generalized form for statements of fact could be:

The ⟨attribute⟩ of ⟨object⟩ is ⟨value⟩ with certainty ⟨CF⟩.[44]

An obvious advantage of this approach is the lessened burden on the knowledge engineer.

Some expert systems shells, notably RuleMaster, use the strategy of inducing general rules from example problems and solutions. Shells can use a variety of specific induction techniques including: (1) the concept learning system;[45] (2) the genetic algorithm;[46] (3) CART;[47] (4) Interactive Dichotomiser 3 (ID3);[48] (5) AQ11;[49] and (6) BACON.[50]

For instance, the expert could evaluate titles according to ALA's *Booklist* guidelines (i.e., the training set) and then provide the relevant factors or attributes for each title. Having given this data to the shell, the system could create or induce the rules automatically. An alternate approach might have reference librarians collect enough typical reference questions, the relevant attributes, and the sources used to satisfy the query and use these as the basis for the training set. Groups of rules are likely to result, clustering around the various reference formats. In the future, this kind of powerful automated knowledge acquisition holds great promise.[51]

2.3.2.3 Frame-Based Systems

Yet another approach is a network of nodes connected by relations and organized in a hierarchy. Hence, one might envision a framework of concepts with attributes (often called "slots"). For example, each frame might contain a specific reference tool and the slots would be filled with all its identified attributes. When a particular reference query matches this pattern, the resultant action would be the recommendation of that title. Similar reference tools such as the *Dictionary of National Biography* (*DNB*) and the *Dictionary of American Biography* (*DAB*) share certain characteristics; mainly they list deceased white males, but they differ on geographical coverage. In this instance, the daughter *DAB* could inherit the common characteristics from the father and save programming time.

2.3.3 Interfaces

The interface is the common bridge or boundary between the user and the computer system (see Chapter 7). It provides a way for the user to give the computer information that it can use internally, and at the same time, it provides users with the system's advice or recommendations in terms that they can understand. For obvious reasons, the interface is usually a technical subset of English or some other language (see Chapter 7). Less obviously, the content of the interface may be determined by predetermined tree structures (see Chapter 5).

The end–user interface can be structured in a variety of ways including socratic dialogues that ask for the user's response to a set of questions; text-based menus that the user must read and then select the proper alternative; windows or touch screens; a command line or prompt; and natural language. At present, the latter structure is least common in expert systems. Mark Stefik estimates that 42 percent of development time is spent on developing the interface.[52] Finally, some expert system interfaces have graphic capabilities as well.

During system development there may be a developer interface that is different from the one the end user will eventually see. The interface may differ if the user is the (1) reference librarian; (2) paraprofessional staff; (3) library and information science students; or (4) the library's clientele. Depending on which group is selected, significant interface design issues arise related to the appropriate transaction style and the degree of technical language in the interface.

Finally, the life cycle of expert system development is graphically represented in Figure 2.4. The life cycle revolves around (1) the design phase and (2) the development, testing, and validation phases. Many elements are involved with a project's success. Besides the familiar involvement of a principal investigator, project leader, and director, several other individuals will be involved during an expert system's development cycle, including: (1) computer programmers; (2) domain experts; (3) knowledge engineers; (4) software developers; and (5) end users.

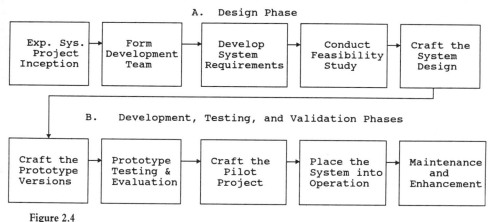

Figure 2.4

A Typical Expert System Life Cycle. From John Walters and Norman R. Nielsen. "A typical expert system life cycle" in *Crafting Knowledge-Based Systems,* Copyright © (New York: John Wiley, 1988). Reprinted by permission of John Wiley & Sons, Inc.

The project director is responsible for assembling the development team, articulating the design philosophy (end user or librarian's assistant, colleague, or expert), and system role (i.e., consultation, checklist, programmed system, communication, training, or knowledge refinement), and reminding the team of those issues. Library management must be interested in the solution of reference service problems and support the development work; otherwise, the project is not likely to be successful. Restated, the most successful expert systems seem to have had a champion fairly high up in the library's administration (see Chapter 8).[53]

2.3.4 Computer Programmers

Expert systems can be custom built from scratch. In this case, programmers will play a major role in the development process. In the early history of expert systems, the major players did not include nonprogrammers. Fortunately, the development of expert system shells or, more generally, expert system development tools (ESDT) has made it easier for nonprogrammers to play a larger role. Indeed, most librarians do not have programming skills nor do they want to acquire them. Nevertheless, they will have to interact with programmers if the decision is made to develop a system from the ground up.

Programmers have a range of computer languages that may be appropriate for developing an expert system.[54] The major AI language options are either LISP or Prolog.

2.3.4.1 LISP (LISt Processing)

John McCarthy invented the AI language of choice in the United States.[55] This third-generation language (3GL), in which the computer is told what to do and it does it, is the second-oldest high-level computer language after FORTRAN. It processes symbolic data (knowledge bases are symbolic data structures) represented as linked list structures, and LISP can handle nested subroutines. The de facto standard is CommonLISP.[56] Such an approach could characterize each and every reference book by topic, frequency of appearance, types of indexes, and so on, much like ALA's *Booklist* guidelines. LISP programmers might rely heavily on the *Guide to Reference Books,* which contains much of the declarative knowledge about reference books. LISP programming has been tried for POINTER, a government documents expert system (see Chapter 8). A variety of PC implementations exist, but novices may wish to peruse the literature and experiment first with XLISP, a public-domain version.[57]

2.3.4.2 Programming in Logic (Prolog)

Invented in France in the 1960s, Prolog has been selected by the Japanese government for their Fifth Generation Computer Project.[58] In contrast to LISP, Prolog can be described as a procedural language (that is, you tell the computer *how* to do it and it does it), although its statements can be either declarative or procedural. The rules in Prolog can be viewed as defining logical relationships, rather than saying how something should be done.[59] "In its declarative form, it proves something is true by searching through a database of facts and rules."[60] As a symbolic language, it is most useful for solving problems that involve relationships between objects. Prolog is based on predicate calculus, especially Horn Clause axioms, which are used to structure the program and guide its execution. A variety of PC implementations of Prolog exist, including Marseille and Edinburgh (or Mellish), which are two different syntaxes; novices may wish to peruse the literature[61] and experiment first with PD Prolog, a public-domain version.[62]

Finally, as a rule of thumb, librarians should not assume that programmers are knowledgeable about particular domains.[63] A programmer's culture is different from librarianship; in some settings, programming virtuosity may be prized above the domain's analytical skills and system (i.e., technical) requirements. In that case, user requirements or usability testing may be ignored.

2.3.5 Domain Experts

Expertise is achieved through training and experience. And experience develops intuition.[64] To state Richardson's rule, however: 85 percent of our reference librarians are MLS competent; another ten percent are truly good; but only five percent are really expert. In other words, an expert is one who aspires to be more than merely proficient.

A critical question, then, is: Who among us is expert and how are they different? A partial answer would be someone who is talented, capable, interested, motivated more by the intrinsic than extrinsic rewards, and who has the time to master the domain knowledge. A more complete answer is provided by Figure 2.5.

A suitable expert to work on the development of an expert system must be more than "mildly dedicated,"[65] he must have already solved the problem, be articulate about it, and available for at least one year. "Eager and bright" does not equal knowledgeable.[66]

Johnson defines an expert as

a person who, because of training and experience, is able to do things the rest of us cannot; experts are not only proficient but also smooth and efficient in the

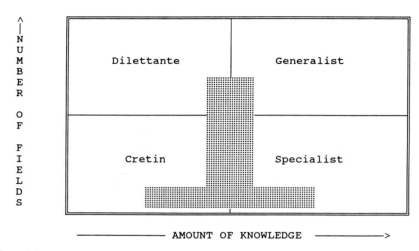

Figure 2.5
Characteristics of Individuals in Relation to Their Amount of Knowledge and Mastery of Fields. T-person in shaded area. Courtesy of Bruce Goeller, Rand Corporation with the GE Think Tank.

actions they take. Experts know a great many things and have tricks and caveats for applying what they know to problems and tasks; they are also good at plowing through irrelevant information in order to get at basic issues, and they are good at recognizing problems they face as instances of types with which they are familiar. Underlying the behavior of experts is a body of operative knowledge we have termed expertise.[67]

Reviewing research on expertise, Robert Glaser and Michelene T.H. Chi have identified seven characteristics of experts. As such, experts:

1. excel mainly in their own domain;
2. perceive large meaningful patterns in their domain;
3. are fast;
4. have superior short-term and long-term memory;
5. see and represent a problem in their domain at a deeper (more principled) level than do novices;
6. spend a great deal of time analyzing a problem qualitatively; and
7. have strong self-monitoring skills.[68]

In attempting to distinguish experts from novices, Marianne LeFrance points out that

experts not only know more *quantitatively* than those with less expertise but that they know what they know in *qualitatively* different ways from those possessing less knowledge.[69]

She goes on to summarize the recent work in cognitive psychology about experts.

- Experts are schema driven rather than data driven.
- Experts focus on goals rather than effects.
- Experts' knowledge is more functional than that of novices.
- Expert knowledge is chunked differently from that of novices.
- Experts' knowledge is more complex than novices' knowledge.
- Experts sometimes behave like robots.
- Experts have greater episodic memory than do novices.[70]

To achieve this status, individuals progress through a series of stages from novice, advanced beginner, competent practitioner, proficient professional to expert (see Figure 2.6).[71] Rosbottom distinguishes a novice from an expert based on know what (i.e., propositional knowledge, sometimes called semantic) rather than the expert's know how (i.e., procedural knowledge, sometimes called syntactic).[72]

Johnson, summarizing twenty years of work on the stages of learning, identifies three phases:

- Phase I, Stage of Cognition or Thought;
- Phase II, Associative Phase of Learning; and
- Phase III, Stage of Automaticity.

Furthermore, Johnson argues that

in Phase I . . . an individual must learn from instruction or from observation of performance what actions are appropriate in which circumstances. In Phase

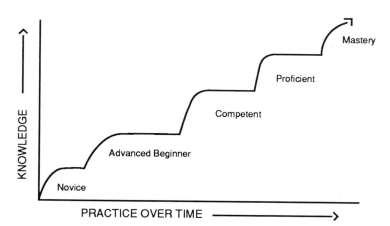

Figure 2.6
Growth of Knowledge over Time

II, . . . the relationships discovered or taught in Phase I are practiced (with feedback) until they become smooth (fluent and efficient) and accurate (proficient). In Phase III, . . . relationships are "compiled" through overpractice to the point where they can be done "without" thinking.[73]

Summarizing this section, Weckert concludes that "a common thread here is that experts tend to group things together differently from novices. They notice patterns when novices do not, and find meaningful relationships where novices only find individuals."[74] In fact, it may take ten years of experience to achieve expertise in a particular domain.[75]

The primary responsibility of the domain expert in the development process is to ensure that the knowledge base is accurate and complete. Perhaps someone should test the hypotheses that novice reference librarians know or learn the characteristic rules first; and that the difference between them and expert librarians is that the latter know more of the discriminant rules. Certainly, more work could be undertaken on the identification of experts in the reference field.[76]

2.3.6 Knowledge Engineers, Elicitors, or Crafters

The knowledge engineer (KE) is another crucial member of the development team because he is responsible for crafting the knowledge base, getting it to fit into a usable form for the computer program. Not unlike a systems analyst, this individual must be logical, analytical, detail oriented, and have strong interviewing skills. The KE must be able to generate questions about the domain and accurately collect this information. Specifically, such engineers are responsible for identifying assumptions behind the problem, clarifying findings, stating generalizations, and proposing hypotheses.

The different kinds of knowledge may require that knowledge elicitation draw upon a variety of different techniques including (1) introspection, (2) direct observation, (3) structured interviews, (4) case histories of reference work, (5) verbal protocol analysis, (6) discourse analysis, (7) multidimensional scaling, and (8) concept sorting/classification. The following section is a discussion of the advantages and disadvantages of each technique.

Incidentally, the International Association of Knowledge Engineers (IAKE) administers an examination for practitioner certification. Interested individuals can write Milton White, Ph.D., Chairman of International Association of Knowledge Engineers, 11820 Parklawn Drive, Suite 302, Rockville, MD 20852 or email him at iake@780.bitnet and CompuServe 71531,104.

2.3.6.1 Introspection

Many of the expert systems in reference work were developed with the domain expert serving as the knowledge engineer. In these cases, the participant is using a form of Aristotelian induction by simple enumeration. In other words, the expert interviews himself and writes down the process, often in the form of rules and facts. Some researchers have questioned the validity of the process, though it is a convenient and economical approach.

2.3.6.2 Direct Observation

As a form of anthropological participant–observer, direct observation demands that the knowledge engineer observe the expert in the day-to-day work environment. This technique has been labeled an "authentic method."[77] Of course, the KE need not use current problems but could pose a typical set of reference questions such as those developed during the thirty years of quality of reference studies. The advantage of this approach is that the knowledge base is "developed by those who practice" and it is validated by evidence. The major disadvantage is its expense because it is labor intensive, and it may not get at tacit knowledge.[78]

2.3.6.3 Structured or Unstructured Interviews

A closely related approach is to conduct an informal or structured interview with the expert.[79] Perhaps the most familiar technique discussed thus far, "it quickly generates a lot of knowledge that indicates the terminology and main components of the domain."[80] It too has disadvantages. A review of psychological research suggests that

> when people attempt to report on their cognitive processes, that is, on the processes mediating the effects of a stimulus on a response, they do not do so on the basis of any true introspection. Instead, their reports are based on a priori, implicit causal theories, or judgments about the extent to which a particular stimulus is a plausible cause of a given response. This suggests that though people may not be able to observe directly their cognitive processes, they will sometimes be able to report accurately about them. Accurate reports will occur when influential stimuli are salient and are plausible causes of the responses they produce, and will not occur when stimuli are not salient or are not plausible causes.[81]

2.3.6.4 Case Histories or Studies

This method is probably the most familiar technique to readers. Hence, only the most relevant literature is cited here.[82]

2.3.6.5 Verbal Protocol Analysis

Similar to observing and interviewing, protocol analysis clearly requires at least two individuals; usually, the knowledge engineer asks the expert to give a verbal report or "think out loud" while performing the task.[83] Parenthetically, some writers refer to the technique as "process tracing."[84]

This approach is best suited for exploratory situations, and if audio or videotaped, it is convenient to review.[85] In fact, videotaping is impersonal after the subject becomes accustomed to its presence. Gammack and Young favor this method because

> it goes beyond what experts can explicitly *tell* you in a problem solving situation to permit inference of what knowledge they must be using but either cannot verbalize or are unaware of.[86]

Unfortunately, there are major disadvantages: experts may need prompting at points where they touch lightly on some aspect of the problem; these prompts may interrupt the flow; the experts may not be highly articulate; the knowledge engineer may not know enough to ask the right questions; the coding is labor intensive; there is an absence of necessary correlation between the verbal report and the actual behavior; questions about validity may arise; analyzing data may be difficult, especially if it is only audiotaped, because the nonverbal cues may be absent; the protocols may still be incomplete; the participants may become uncomfortable because it is an obtrusive technique; and finally the technique may not be appropriate in confidential situations.[87] Hence, some individuals advocate applying task analysis first and then protocol analysis.

2.3.6.6 Discourse Analysis

Discourse analysis may also be more appropriate when there is little explicit or "compiled" knowledge of the domain. This technique is relatively unobtrusive and may be especially good for developing categories.[88] In some instances, it is possible to develop the expert's analytical model by reading the professional literature (e.g., textbooks, monographs, and journal articles). Johnson refers to this technique as a "reconstructed method."[89]

This approach works well when the domain is well understood and the task steps are accepted. Once again, however, the codified explanation may not be how they actually do it; rather how they are *supposed* to do it or what sounds plausible. And, of course, it may not even work as articulated.[90]

2.3.6.7 Multidimensional Scaling

The concepts identified as part of protocol analysis can be sorted using a number of multidimensional scaling techniques including factor analysis.

> These techniques identify similarities among objects and group them conceptually. One such [technique] is the repertory grid method arising from Personal Construct Theory. . . . For expert knowledge elicitation this technique seems appropriate when there are a number of closely related concepts, typically not well differentiated by novices, and expertise consists in being able to make discriminations. . . . The method yields a set of dimensions defining the space containing the domain objects. Clustering on these dimensions gives the structure that differentiates these domain objects from one another.[91]

Readers looking for a quantitative data reduction technique should consider factor analysis.

2.3.6.8 Concept Sorting/Classification

The technique of concept sorting gets at the global as well as meta-knowledge of the domain that experts carry in their heads.[92] Concept sorting involves a five-step process. First, build an initial set of concepts related to the domain by (1) conducting personal interviews, (2) scanning glossaries such as the *ALA Glossary* (1983), (3) checking back-of-the-textbook indexes, and (4) sitting in on introductory or tutorial lectures. Second, write down one concept per card. Third, ask a reference expert to sort these concepts into any number of groups. Cutter asserted that there are different kinds of concepts: individual, concrete general, and abstract.[93] Fourth, ask the expert to identify and describe the common theme within each group. Fifth, ask the expert to relate these groups by organizing them into a hierarchy.

For the question and answer dialog domain, one might find 40 to 50 basic concepts (see Chapter 4). These could be sorted into as few as three groups: inquirer, reference librarian, and reference sources.

In summary, knowledge engineers must consider these nonmutually exclusive techniques to explore and refine the knowledge base so that the programmer can transfer this information into code understandable by the machine. Feigenbaum has worried about the knowledge acquisition bottleneck,[94] pointing out that there are few individuals who have met the necessary criteria as listed above. Furthermore, Brul and Blount suggest "knowledge elicitor,"[95] while Walters and Nielsen rightly prefer the phrase "knowledge crafter," pointing out that the process is not an exact science like engineering aspires to be, but is still an art.[96] In any event, the primary responsibility of this individual is to ensure overall quality during the knowledge elicitation phase.

2.3.7 Software Developers

If librarians adopt a custom or semicustom application (i.e., the shell approach), they may want to consult with the original software developers. What is the company's history; are they likely to be in business next year? What documentation is provided? What kind of warranty do they offer on their product? What kind of service do they offer; is the quality of the support staff high? Are they readily available: through a post office box, a toll-free telephone number, 24 hours or just 9 to 5 eastern standard time? Are new versions released regularly? What about bugs or special fixes for the library environment? These are serious questions that may have to be faced, especially when much of the system development time is spent debugging. In discussing more than 40 shells, Appendix B covers many of these points.

2.3.8 End (Ultimate) User

Although many people may use the system during its development, the end user is the person for whom the system is designed. End users could include: (1) reference librarians, (2) the paraprofessional staff, (3) library and information science students, or (4) the library's clientele. Depending on which group is selected, significant interface design issues arise related to the appropriate transaction style and the degree of technical language in the interface (see Chapter 7).

2.4
Vested Interests in Expert Systems Development

Based on the preceding discussion, it ought to be obvious that several groups should be challenged by the development of expert systems in general reference work. "The analysis of problems for the purpose of automating them always causes reflection upon the subject matter itself."[97] The discussion below is organized around the perceived advantages and disadvantages for each group.

2.4.1 End Users

The major advantage for end users is consistent, high-quality answers to their questions. Second, reference librarians are not always available when the library is open; however, an expert system could be present in the reference department all the time.[98] Furthermore, there is no reason why technologically oriented users with the ability to access the library's existing online services remotely could not have access at any time. Third, it presents an independent, self-help situation for those users who would rather not ask the reference librarian.[99] Finally, if the user does not receive an answer, an expert system could be designed so that those users could leave messages for the reference librarian.[100]

On the other hand, "people may prefer people;" expert systems may lack the warmth and touch of human reference librarians. Unless there are several microcomputers, an expert system can be monopolized by a single user. Furthermore, the extant prototype expert systems (see Chapter 8) seem uninspired; familiar users can predict its responses.

2.4.2 Reference Librarians

Librarians should know, however, that several advantages of developing expert systems for general reference work exist. The primary professional motivation for librarians should be improving decisions about which reference titles to consult in answering a user's question. In addition, such a system should free one from routine questions[101] so they can deal with the tasks less easily automated, provide relief during high-demand periods,[102] result in lower risk of job burnout,[103] and offer some respite from work overload, boredom, and frustration.[104]

While change may be threatening, it does not have to be so. The introduction of an expert system could threaten job security, lead to less pay for professional services, and cause librarians to forget *basic* reference work. Nevertheless, it should be obvious that "there are not enough reference librarians who have perfect recall of their collections even as far as knowing which exclusive categories all the books fit into, and no librarian could have complete recall as to the specifics contained in each . . . reference book in the collection."[105]

2.4.3 Reference Department Paraprofessionals

An expert system could play a significant part in the paraprofessionals' education as support staff. However, this group may be the one most likely to be replaced by second-generation expert systems.

2.4.4 Reference Department Heads

Middle managers have a vested interest in the development of these systems; in particular, managers should benefit from the presence of high-quality, consistent expert "librarians." Managers could cover staff shortages,[106] conserve their scarce resources,[107] reap the potential cost savings, if reference staff was actually replaced, and stem the "brain drain" due to staff turnover.[108] Finally, such expert systems are likely to be relatively affordable and will always provide at least a minimal level of reference service.

2.4.5 Library Directors

Directors and other senior library managers should welcome this new technology for a couple of reasons. First, the potential of their existing investment in expensive microcomputer hardware has not begun to be fully tapped. Second, continuing education of the support staff must be provided; expert systems could play a large role in training paraprofessionals. Armed with the necessary skills to accomplish the job at hand, the library staff should be more satisfied in their work environment. In the final analysis, top management must support the introduction of this new technology or it will not be successful.

2.4.6 LIS Faculty

The existence of expert systems technology calls for a consideration of the curricular implications as well as teaching and learning methodologies.[109] Adoption of an expert systems approach would allow faculty to spend valuable class time on the important material, making explicit tacit knowledge about relationships within the domain.[110] Reid-Smith argues that

> if a shell is used, then the library science student's main task will be the acquisition, analysis, and arrangement of information. These are the tasks which are already professional to the librarian, but in the course of gaining skills the student will also gain the knowledge.[111]

This knowledge may be gained substantially faster according to a recent summary of research on computer-based learning.[112] Without a doubt, this approach has the potential to change the paradigmatic emphasis of traditional reference courses away from sources to process.

However, there may be some significant disadvantages. Faculty will have to spend time on the curricular implications of expert systems and revise their teaching methods and materials. Along the way, faculty will have to learn new information. Nevertheless, LIS admission committees for masters and doctoral programs might do well to recruit students with strong analytical skills who can make the most of this approach. The ETS's Graduate Record Examination (GRE) now reports this type of information.

2.4.7 LIS Students

Students in library and information science are an important audience for an expert systems teaching approach. First, an operational system could serve as a tireless, personal tutor teaching the novice. If the student wants or needs endless repetition, the computer can provide it. More importantly, an expert systems approach, which requires students to construct their own system, makes students think about the implicit as well as explicit knowledge related to the reference process.

In one of the first systematic studies of this approach, students reported that the value of this method lay in the organization of their knowledge, and not so much the content, that was most affected, although various forms of conceptual and procedural differentiation occurred for each student. Evidence also emerged that students had acquired knowledge of conditions of applicability for domain-specific concepts and procedures, and knowledge consequences of actions (so-called conditional knowledge.) Overall the study reveals that the prior class instruction had not established an understanding of the domain's vital relation-ships, and that they were totally unaccustomed to synthesis. Students reported afterwards that a major result of this experience was a shift in their problem-solving approaches—away from rote manipulation with understanding. A further byproduct was an improved understanding of their own thought processes and the development of cognitive strategies.[113]

Another study reports that novices improved their decision-making quality using expert systems and were more confident of their decisions than those who did not use expert systems.[114]

2.4.8 Reference Book Authors and Publishers

Expert systems have advanced beyond the AI laboratory and offer potential investment opportunities. Publishers are already interested in the commercial possibilities presented by these systems. In particular, Oryx Press and the Educational Testing Service have elementary and secondary reading advisory systems for sale (see Chapter 8). Potential reference book authors could use expert systems to identify new tools that do not exist but which are predicted by the rules.

In summary, it should not be necessary to try to quantify (by adding or weighting) the assertions in the final section of this chapter. Objectively and rationally, the advantages clearly appear to outweigh the limitations, at least enough to justify an examination of the feasibility of expert systems in general reference work.

Endnotes

1. See, for example, Peter Hernon and John V. Richardson, *Microcomputer Software for Performing Statistical Analysis: A Handbook Supporting Library Decision Making* (Norwood, NJ: Ablex Publishing Corporation, 1988).

2. Readers interested in the contributions from these other disciplines should read Howard Gardner's *The Mind's New Science: A History of the Cognitive Revolution* (New York: Basic Books, 1985).

3. Dawn Stover, "The World's Next Chess Champion?," *Popular Science* 238 (March 1991): 70 and Herbert A. Simon, "On How to Decide What to Do," *Bell Journal of Economics* 9 (1978): 496.

4. See chapter 14 entitled "Ratings" and several of the chapter references in B.M. Kazic, D. Djaja, M.E. Morrison, and A. Elo, *The Chess Competitors' Handbook* (London: B.T. Batsford Limited, 1980).

5. The "Progress of the Prodigies" is charted in David Short, *Nigel Short: Chess Prodigy; His Career and Best Games* (London: Faber, 1981).

6. Alan M. Turing, "On Computable Numbers, with an Application to the Entscheidungsproblem," *Proceedings of the London Mathematical Society* 42 (1937): 230–265; reprinted in Martin Davis, ed. *The Undecidable* (New York: Raven Press, 1965); reprinted in Darrel C. Ince, ed. *Mechanical Intelligence* (New York: North Holland, 1992).

7. Alex G. Bell, *The Machine Plays Chess?* (Oxford: Pergamon Press, 1978), 17–21.

8. G.W. Baylor, ed., *Thought and Choice in Chess* (The Hague: Moutnon Publishers, 1965). Work since then is neatly summarized in Colin Davis, "Attention, Memory, and Thought," an unpublished September 1990 12-page paper written in the School of Psychology, University of New South Wales, Australia.

9. Claude E. Shannon, "Programming a Computer for Playing Chess," *Philosophical Magazine* 41, 7th series (1950): 256–275.

10. D. Bronstein and G. Smolyan, *Chess in the Eighties,* translated by Kenneth P. Neat. Pergamon Russian Chess Series (Oxford: Pergamon Press, 1982).

11. For more information on alpha-beta searches, see N. Nilsson, *Problem-Solving Methods in Artificial Intelligence* (New York: McGraw Hill, 1971), especially pp. 140–149; D.E. Knuth and R.W. Moore, "An Analysis of Alpha-Beta Pruning," *Artificial Intelligence* 6 (Winter 1975): 293–326; and M.M. Newborn, "The Efficiency of the Alpha-Beta Search on Trees with Branch-Dependent Terminal Node Scores," *Artificial Intelligence* 8 (April 1977): 137–154.

12. A. John Roycroft, "A Prophecy Fulfilled," *E.G.* 5 (November 1983): 218–219 and id., "The '50-Move Rule'" *E.G.* 6 (May 1986): 16.

13. This approach depends on brute force processing power of the computer to look ahead so many "ply"—meaning a move and the other player's response. For instance, if there are "20 possible moves each time; on average, that means 160,000 positions at four-ply; 64 million if you continue until 6-ply." See T.D. Harding, *The New Chess Computer Book,* 2nd rev. ed. (Oxford: Pergamon Press, 1985), p. 212.

14. Alternatively, Feng-hsiung Hsu, Thomas Anantharaman, Murray Campbell, and Andreas Nowatzyk, "A Grandmaster Chess Machine," *Scientific American* 263 (October 1990): 44–50 credit Richard Réti with this quotation.

15. Donald A. Waterman, *A Guide to Expert Systems* (Reading, MA: Addison-Wesley Publishing Company, 1985), 11.

16. Alex Goodall, *The Guide to Expert Systems* (Oxford: Learned Information, 1985), 11.

17. Kamran Parsaye and Mark Chignell, *Expert Systems for Experts* (New York: John Wiley & Sons, 1988), 1.

18. Chris Naylor, *Build Your Own Expert System for the IBM-PC and Compatibles* (Wilmslow, England: Sigma Press, 1987), 1.

19. Within librarianship, some authors such as Kenneth Quinn, Lloyd Davidson, and Robert Carande have backed away from the term expert systems and promise less with the phrase "reference advisory system" (RAS). Often, this phrase means a less complex system, a kind of automated library guide or pathfinder. Yet, there is no reason to expect less than an *expert* system, if the reader follows the development of ideas presented in this book.

20. See Eliot Freidson, *Professional Powers; A Study of the Institutionalization of Formal Knowledge* (Chicago: University of Chicago Press, 1986) and Dennis H. Wrong, *Power; Its Forms, Bases, and Uses* (New York: Harper and Row, 1979).

21. See John Anderson, *Language Memory and Thought* (Hillsdale, NJ: Lawrence Erlbaum Associates, 1976). More recently, in *Computational Intelligence I,* ed. A. Martelli and G. Valle (Amsterdam: North-Holland, 1989), J. Rosbottom's "The Expertise of Expert Systems," pp.

261–267 warns against confusing "knowledge how" with "knowledge that." He argues the former is what experts know, but expert systems are programmed with the latter.

22. James R. Parrott, *Using Expert Systems in Reference Service: Course Notes* (Waterloo: University of Waterloo Press, 1989), 28.

23. Eugene P. Sheehy, *Guide to Reference Books,* 10th ed. (Chicago: American Library Association, 1986).

24. Mary Biggs and Victor Biggs, "Reference Collection Development in Academic Libraries: Report of a Survey," *RQ* 27 (Fall 1987): 67–69.

25. Thanks to Terry Crowley who pointed out that this figure is strongly reminiscent of the conceptual framework—hidden, know others, others know, and unknown—presented in John D. Ingalls and Joseph M. Arceri, *A Trainers Guide to Andragogy, Its Concepts, Experience and Application* (Washington, DC: GPO, 1972).

26. Max Boisot, *Information and Organizations; The Manager as Anthropologist* (London: Fontana, 1987), 54ff.

27. Bruce G. Buchanan and Richard O. Duda, "Principles of Rule-Based Expert Systems," *Advances in Computers,* vol. 22, ed. Marshall C. Yovits (New York: Academic Press, 1983), 178.

28. Consider Jerry R. Hobbs and Robert C. Moore, eds. *Formal Theories of the Commonsense World,* Ablex Series in Artificial Intelligence (Norwood, NJ: Ablex Publishing Corporation, 1985).

29. Diana Woodward, "Proprietary Expert Systems: A Threat to Intellectual Freedom," American Society for Information Science Mid-Year Meeting, 18 May 1988.

30. Waters to Richardson, 15 April 1988.

31. Meaning "other things being equal."

32. Luc Steels, "The Deepening of Expert Systems," *AI Communications* 1 (August 1987): 11.

33. See Michael Polanyi, *The Tacit Dimension* (London: Routledge and Kegan Paul, 1967); Dianne C. Berry, "The Problem of Implicit Knowledge," *Expert Systems* 4 (August 1987): 144–151; and A. Janik, "Tacit Knowledge, Working Life, and Scientific Method," In *Knowledge, Skill and Artificial Intelligence* (Berlin: Springer-Verlag, 1988), 53–63. In his Libraries and Expert Systems conference paper entitled "How Expert Can Expert Systems Really Be?" given at Charles Sturt University on 24 July 1990, John Weckert provides an excellent discussion and distinction between implicit or tacit knowledge and explicit knowledge. These ideas have been further developed in a paper with Craig McDonald, entitled "The Nature of Expertise."

34. John G. Gammack and Richard M. Young, "Psychological Techniques for Eliciting Expert Knowledge," In *Research and Development in Expert Systems: Proceedings of the Fourth Technical Conference of the British Computer Society Specialist Group on Expert Systems,* ed. Max A. Bramer (Cambridge: Cambridge University Press, 1985), 333.

35. Ibid., 328.

36. See Raymond L. Kirchener, Jr., "Building a General Purpose Inference Engine for Expert Systems," M.S. thesis, University of Louisville, 1985.

37. According to Parsaye and Chignell (1988, 344), "an expert system shell can be considered a reasoning system out of which all the knowledge has been emptied. When knowledge about a new domain is entered into the shell appropriately, an expert system is created."

38. Perry L. McCarty, Jr., "The Management of Uncertainty in Expert Systems," Ph.D. dissertation, University of California, Berkeley, 1987.

39. Drew McDermott and Jon Doyle, "Non-monotonic Logic I," *Artificial Intelligence* 13 (1980): 41–72.

40. Glenn Shafer, *A Mathematical Theory of Evidence* (Princeton, NJ: Princeton University Press, 1976) and J.A. Barnett, "Computation Methods for a Mathematical Theory of Evidence," *Proceedings of the IJCAI-79* (1981): 868–875.

41. Donald A. Waterman, *A Guide to Expert Systems* (Reading, MA: Addison-Wesley Publishing Company, 1985), 77.

42. Waterman, 78.

43. Waterman, 361.

44. Bruce G. Buchanana and Richard O. Duda, "Principles of Rule-Based Expert Systems," In *Advances in Computers,* vol. 22, ed. Marshall C. Yovits (New York: Academic Press, 1983), 178.

45. Earl B. Hunt, Janet Mavin, and Phillip J. Stone, *Experiments in Induction* (New York: Academic Press, 1966).

46. John H. Holland, *Adaptation in Natural and Artificial Systems: An Introductory Analysis with Applications to Biology, Control, and Artificial Intelligence* (Ann Arbor: University of Michigan Press, 1975) and David E. Goldberg, *Genetic Algorithms in Search, Optimization, and Machine Learning* (Boston: Addison-Wesley, 1989).

47. Leo Breiman, J. Frieman, R. Olshen, and C. Stone, *Classification and Regression Trees* (Belmont, CA: Wadsworth Inc., 1983).

48. John R. Quinlan, "Discovering Rules by Induction from Large Collections of Examples," in *Expert Systems in the Micro-electronic Age,* ed. Donald Michie (Edinburgh: Edinburgh University Press, 1979), 169–201, and id., "Learning Efficient Classification Procedures and Their Application to Chess-End Games," in *Machine Learning: An Artificial Intelligence Approach,* ed. Ryzsard Michalski, Jaime Carbonell, and Tom Michell (Palo Alto, CA: Morgan Kaufmann Publishers, 1983).

49. R. Michalski and R. Chilauski, "Knowledge Acquisition by Encoding Expert Rules versus Computer Induction from Examples: A Case Study Involving Soybean Pathology," *International Journal of Man–Machine Studies* 12 (January 1980): 63–87.

50. P. Langley, "Data-Driven Discovery of Physical Laws," *Cognitive Science* 5 (1981): 31–54.

51. John H. Holland, Keith J. Holyoak, Richard E. Nisbett, and Paul R. Thagard, *Induction; Processes of Inference, Learning, and Discovery,* Computational Models of Cognition and Perception Series (Cambridge, MA: The MIT Press, 1986).

52. Mark Stefik, "Expert Systems: Perils and Promise," Videotaped Lecture, University of California, Berkeley, 25 April 1985.

53. A similar finding appears in L. Fried, *Commercial Use of Expert Systems: A Survey of U.S. Corporations,* Report No. BIP 86-1068 (Menlo Park, CA: SRI International, 1986).

54. For a discussion of the pros and cons of several languages, see Richard Wexelblat, *History of Programming Languages* (New York: Academic Press, 1981) or William J. Birnes, *McGraw-Hill Personal Computer Programming Encyclopedia; Languages and Operating Systems,* 2d ed. (New York: McGraw-Hill, 1988). Mac users should read Allen Munro, "Choosing a Programming Language," *MacWorld* 4 (October 1987): 142–149, which covers forty-eight implementations including LISP and Prolog.

55. For a brief history of LISP, advantages, and structure, see Steven Cherry, "The World According to LISP," *Micro: The 6502/6809 Journal* 57 (February 1983): 65–69. The first part of Patrick H. Winston, *Artificial Intelligence* (Reading, MA: Addison-Wesley, 1984) contains a nonmathematical introduction to AI followed by a competent discussion of LISP. Steven L. Tanimoto, *The Elements of Artificial Intelligence: An Introduction Using LISP* (Rockville, MD: Computer Science Press, 1987) contains exercises. Other readers may prefer Robert Wilensky's *Common LISPcraft* (New York: Norton, 1986).

56. Mark Bridger and John Frampton, "Creating a Standard LISP," *PC Tech Journal* 3 (December 1985): 98–117. IBM's CommonLISP retails for $10,000, Golden CommonLISP for $495, and Mac implementations from $399 to $600 for Allegro to $995 for Expert CommonLISP or ExperLISP. PC Scheme (Texas Instruments) retails for $95, WaltzLISP for $169, muLISP for $250, IQLISP for $270, and Star Sapphire LISP for $495.

57. See David Betz, "An XLISP Tutorial: This Public-Domain Language Lets You Experiment with Artificial Intelligence," *BYTE* 10 (March 1985): 221–236.

58. IBM implementations include Arity/Prolog for $95–$795, Turbo Prolog for $99.95, M Prolog for $195–$495, ALS Prolog for $199–$499, and Prolog-2 for $895.

59. Both John Malpas, *Prolog; A Relational Language and Its Applications* (Englewood Cliffs, NJ: Prentice-Hall, 1987) and Nigel Ford, *Prolog Programming* (New York: John Wiley and Sons, 1989) are quite good on this aspect.

60. Boyd Sutherland, *Selection of A Reference Service Expert System Shell,* supervised by John Richardson as a Council on Library Resources Supporting Study under the Long Range Strategic Planning for Libraries and Information Resources in the Research University grant; Robert M. Hayes, Principal Investigator (Los Angeles: UCLA Graduate School of Library and Information Science, Summer 1986), 8. A good discussion of the difference between procedural versus declarative knowledge can be found in Ralph Alberico, "More on Knowledge Representation," *Small Computers in Libraries* 7 (December 1987): 10–16.

61. For a brief article, see William F. Clocksin, "A Prolog Primer: An Introduction and Tutorial to the Popular Artificial Intelligence Language," *BYTE* 12 (August 1987): 147–158. Coauthored with C.S. Mellish, the third edition of Clocksin's book-length treatment, *Programming in Prolog,* was published by Springer-Verlag in 1987. Beginners interested in the Edinburgh syntax may consult Ivan Bratko, *Prolog Programming for Artificial Intelligence* (Reading, MA: Addison-Wesley, 1986). Feliks Kluzniak and Stanislaw Scapakowicz, *Prolog for Programmers* (London: Academic Press, 1985) comes highly recommended for its practical information for intermediate programmers. Serious programmers may want Leon Stirling and Ehud Shapiro, *The Art of Prolog: Advanced Programming Techniques* (Cambridge, MA: MIT Press, 1986). Doctoral research includes Peter L. Davies's "Prolog and Expert Systems," Ph.D. dissertation, University of Durham, 1987.

62. Robert Morein, "PD PROLOG: A Public-Domain Version of the Fifth-Generation Language," *BYTE* 11 (October 1986): 155–165.

63. Ibid.

64. Edward Gufeld, "How to Develop Intuition?," *En Passant* No. 99, December 1989, 19–23. Intuition might be defined as an unproven rule.

65. Ibid.

66. Ibid.

67. Paul E. Johnson, "What Kind of Expert Should A System Be?" *The Journal of Medicine and Philosophy* 8 (1983): 78–79.

68. Robert Glaser and Michelene T.H. Chi, "Overview" in *The Nature of Expertise,* ed. Michelene T.H. Chi, Robert Glaser, and M.J. Farr (Hillsdale, NJ: Lawrence Erlbaum Associates, 1988), xvii–xx.

69. Marianne LeFrance, "The Quality of Expertise: Implications for Expert–Novice Differences for Knowledge Acquisition," *SIGART Newsletter,* No. 108 (April 1989): 6–14.

70. Ibid., 7–14.

71. Hubert L. Dreyfus and Stuart E. Dreyfus, *Mind Over Machine; The Power of Human Intuition and Expertise in the Era of the Computer* (New York: Free Press, 1986), Chapter 5. This continuum is neatly summarized in Robert J. Trotter, "The Mystery of Mastery," *Psychology Today* (July 1986): 32–38.

72. J. Rosbottom, "The Expertise of Expert Systems," in Alberto Martelli and Giorgio Valle, eds. *Computational Intelligence, I; Proceedings of 'Computational Intelligence 88'.* (Amsterdam: North Holland, 1989), 261–267. Actually, Rosbottom is drawing upon distinctions first raised by Gilbert Ryle, *The Concept of Mind* (London: Hutchinson's University Library, 1949), see Chapter 2.

73. Johnson, "What Kind of Expert," 79.

74. John Weckert and Craig McDonald, "The Nature of Expertise," draft manuscript.

75. Ten years is generally taken as the standard based on the length of time chess players move from novice to highly proficient.

76. Future work might be patterned on the methodology presented in John Pekkanen, *The Best Doctors in the United States,* rev. ed. (New York: Seaview Press, 1981).

77. Johnson, "What Kind of Expert," 81ff.

78. Ibid.

79. Kathryn J.A. Tournat, "Issues in Knowledge Acquisition for Expert Systems Development: Comparing Structured Interview Techniques for Initial Expertise Elicitation," M.S. thesis, California State University, Long Beach, 1988.

80. Gammack and Young, "Psychological Techniques," 107.

81. Richard E. Nisbett and Timothy D. Wilson, "Telling More Than We Know: Verbal Reports on Mental Processes," *Psychological Review* 84 (May 1977): 231–259.

82. See Raya Fidel, "The Case Study Method: A Case Study," *Library and Information Science Research* 6 (1984): 273–288; Lawrence B. Mohr, "The Reliability of the Case Study as a Source of Information," 65–93, in *Advances in Information Processing in Organizations,* vol. 2, ed. Lee S. Sproull and Patrick D. Larkey (Greenwich, CT: JAI Press, 1985); Robert K. Yin, *Case Study Research* (Beverly Hills: Sage Publications, 1984); and id., "The Case Study as a Serious Research Strategy," *Knowledge: Creation, Diffusion, Utilization* 3 (September 1981): 97–114.

83. Karl A. Ericsson and Herbert A. Simon, *Protocol Analysis: Verbal Reports as Data* (Cambridge, MA: MIT Press, 1984).

84. K. Anders Ericsson and Herbert A. Simon, "Verbal Reports as Data," *Psychological Review* 87 (1980): 215–251.

85. Panel Session, "Using Protocol Analysis," American Society for Information Science Meeting, San Diego, CA, 22 May 1989.

86. Gammack and Young, "Psychological Techniques," 105–112.

87. Kamran Parsaye and Mark Chignell, *Expert Systems for Experts* (New York: John Wiley and Sons, 1988), 342–346.

88. H.M. Brooks and Nicolas J. Belkin, "Using Protocol Analysis," in Jennifer J. Kuehn, *Research and Development in Information Retrieval; Sixth Annual International ACM SIGIR Conference* (New York: ACM, 1983), 31–47. See the Autumn 1980 special issue of *Applied Linguistics,* ed. John McH. Sinclair, which provides a western European perspective on discourse analysis.

89. Johnson, "What Kind of Expert," 82.

90. Parsaye and Chignell, 341.

91. Gammack and Young, 109.

92. See, for example, Michelene T.H. Chi, P.J. Feltovich, and Robert Glaser, "Categorization and Representation of Physics Problems by Experts and Novices," *Cognitive Science* 5 (1981): 121–152.

93. Charles A. Cutter, *Rules for a Printed Dictionary Catalogue,* 4th ed. (Washington, DC: GPO, 1904); reprint ed., *Charles Ammi Cutter: Library Systematizer,* ed. Francis L. Miksa (Littleton, CO: Libraries Unlimited, 1977), 53ff and 205ff.

94. Edward Feigenbaum, *Knowledge Engineering: The Applied Side of Artificial Intelligence.* Memo HPP-80-21 (Palo Alto: Stanford University Artificial Intelligence Lab, 1980).

95. James F. Brul and Alexander Blount, *Knowledge Acquisition,* Artificial Intelligence Series (New York: McGraw-Hill, 1989).

96. John Walters and Norman R. Nielsen, *Crafting Knowledge-Based Systems: Expert Systems Made Realistic* (New York: John Wiley and Sons, 1988).

97. John Weckert and Craig McDonald, *Workbook: Libraries and Expert Systems* (Wagga Wagga, Australia: Charles Sturt University, Riverina School of Information Studies, 22–24 July 1990), 11.

98. H. M. Brooks, "Expert Systems in Reference Work," In *Expert Systems in Libraries*, ed. Forbes Gibb (London: Taylor Graham, 1985), 36–49.

99. Ibid., 37.

100. Dana E. Smith and Steve M. Hutton, "Back at 8:00AM; Microcomputer Library Reference Support Programs," *Collegiate Microcomputer* 2 (November 1984): 289–294.

101. Cherie B. Weil, "Classification and Automatic Retrieval of Biographical Reference Books," M.A. thesis, University of Chicago, 1967; Brooks, "Expert Systems in Reference Work;" and Samuel T. Waters, "Answerman, the Expert Information Specialist for Retrieval of Information from Library Reference Books," *Information Technology and Libraries* 5 (September 1986): 204–212.

102. James Parrott, "Expert Systems for Reference Work," *Microcomputers for Information Management* 3 (1986): 155–171.

103. Ibid.

104. Karen F. Smith, "Robot at the Reference Desk," *College and Research Libraries* 47 (September 1986): 486–490.

105. Weil, "Classification and Automatic Retrieval," 3.

106. Parrott, "Using Expert Systems in Reference Work," 7.

107. Smith, "Robot," 486.

108. Waters, "Answerman," 204.

109. Edward R. Reid-Smith, "Expert Systems as a Learning Tool for Student Librarians," paper presented at the Libraries and Expert Systems Workshop and Conference, Wagga Wagga, New South Wales, Australia, 24 July 1990.

110. Students have commented on expert systems in library and information science curricula; see Deborah Henderon, Lauren Mayer, Pamela Monaster, "Rules and Tools in Library Schools," *Journal of Education for Library and Information Science* 30 (Winter 1989): 226–227. See, also, Renate C. Lippert, "Refinement of Students' Knowledge While Developing Expert Systems," Ph.D. dissertation, University of Minnesota, 1988.

111. Reid-Smith, "Expert Systems," 1.

112. See Jack A. Chambers, "The Effects of Educational Software on Learning and Motivation," in *Facilitating Academic Software Development* (N.p.: EDUCOM, 27 July 1987), 23–48.

113. Lippert, "Refinement," abstract.

114. Effy Oz, "A Study of Improvement in Decision-Making Skills Through the Use of Expert Systems," D.B.A. dissertation, Boston University, 1990.

3

The Feasibility of Expert Systems

3.1

3.1

The Problem Domain

Successful expert (or knowledge-based) systems (KBS) development work depends on one's understanding the nature of the problem. To define the domain and profitable areas for development, this chapter draws upon work in operations research, mathematics, linguistics, and philosophy.

The previous chapter discussed the problem domain without trying to define the terms. According to Ackoff,

> by a *problem* we mean a situation that satisfies three conditions: first, a decision-making individual or group has alternative courses of action available: second, the choice made can have a significant effect; and third, the decision maker has some doubt as to which alternative should be selected. There are three kinds of things that can be done about problems—they can be *resolved, solved,* or *dissolved.* . . . To *resolve* a problem is to select a course of action that yields an outcome that is good enough . . . To *solve* a problem is to select a course of action that is believed to yield the *best possible* outcome . . . To *dissolve* a problem is to change the nature, and/or the environment, of the entity in which it is embedded so as to remove the problem.[1]

Within the reference domain, the decision-making individual is the reference librarian. Often, she has many choices (in, e.g., sources) that can be employed in coming to a conclusion or recommendation. Reference librarians do not always know the best sources to recommend. Based on the extensive literature review about the quality of reference service, librarians appear to *resolve* information problems more often than they solve or dissolve them.[2] Also, according to Cartwright, a domain can be understood in four different ways, as a: (1) simple problem, (2) compound problem, (3) complex problem, and (4) metaproblem.[3] Each of these particular understandings places limits on analysis and subsequent actions.

Following this classification scheme, some critics[4] would argue that KBS development work is impossible. Indeed, it is, if one understands the domain as infinite (i.e., open ended), incomplete, unknown, or totally incalculable. Such an understanding would be classified as a metaproblem. Some views of reference work might fall into this category. For instance, reference work might be said to be closed ended in the sense that it takes only an inquirer, a reference expert, and reference sources, but these "factors" are still incalculable.

In other cases, the variables may be knowable, but not measurable. In this instance, the domain would be classed as complex (and, hence, might be more appropriately solved with a blackboard system). Or, one could argue that the reference work domain is a compound problem in which some variables are calculable but others are unknown.

Finally, the domain can be understood one additional way: as a goal-directed system. For our purposes in this and subsequent chapters, the reference domain will consist of inquirers' information problems and solutions. Specifically, the problem (denoted as P) is expressed as an inquirer's question (denoted as q) based on his information need. The solution has a set of answers (denoted as a) contained in reference sources. The intervention, suggesting or recommending a source, is goal directed. Being goal directed is another domain attribute that suggests a KBS approach would be worthwhile. In Figure 3.1, this domain is represented as the function of questions

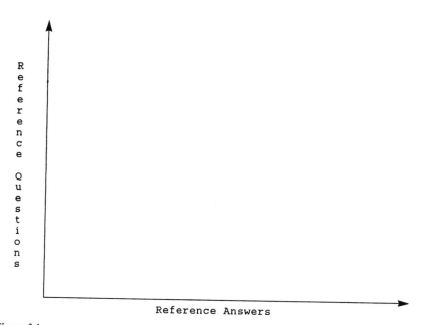

Figure 3.1
The Reference Problem-Solution Boundaries

and answers. Another obvious domain characteristic is that reference work is a large search space. This, too, is promising.

The reference domain can be expressed mathematically: namely

$$P = P(q,a), \text{ where } P = \text{problem}, q = \text{question and } a = \text{answer.}$$

"To put this in more general terms, if any problem (P) is defined as

$$P = P(x_1, x_2, x_3, \ldots, x_n),$$

where x_n represents the nth variable in terms of which the problem is defined, then any solution (S) to that problem must similarly be capable of expression as

$$S = S(x_1, x_2, x_3, \ldots, x_n).$$

Thus, the way in which a problem is defined determines the nature of its solution."[5]

In other words, if q is a finite number and a is also a finite number (meaning that the researcher can calculate the number of reference questions for a particular period and the number of reference books consulted), then reference work can be said to be well structured and precise. Understood as a simple problem, reference work becomes an excellent candidate for further analysis and action. Specifically, the analysis can be rational and comprehensive while the action can be optimized (i.e., *solved*). Yet, nothing said should imply that either of these tasks will necessarily be easy ones. Nonetheless, much of the history of KBS development work is based on understanding the domain as a simple problem.

3.1.1 Sublanguage Considerations

Another potentially productive way to identify appropriate domains for KBS development would be to look at the language being used in those areas. Any area of work can be divided into matrix language and core language.[6] Those areas within reference work that have a core language (i.e., jargon or technical terms) might serve better as appropriate KBS development sites than those areas that can be readily understood by the public. In a variation on this theme, Simon has identified what he calls semantically rich domains.[7] Examples of core language (i.e., semantically rich or sublanguage) within reference work are terms such as information-seeking behavior, question negotiation, reader/user/client, or verification.

There is an interesting parallel in the history of earlier artificial intelligence (AI) efforts. Initially, AI labs started work on what they called general problem-solving schemes. Researchers, however, did not have much success until they switched to projects in narrow domains such as chess playing, specific diseases, oil exploration, or computer configuration. The same situation applies in librarianship; the field is not likely to see *general* KBS. In fact, KBS developers have avoided this difficulty by focusing on reference work that does have a special sublanguage.

3.1.2 Philosophical Approaches

Questions and their answers are a specific domain within reference work. Drawing upon the literature of philosophy, notably applied modal logic, questions are technically called interrogatives or interest-expression systems. Answers are known as a statement, a sentence, or an assertion. Collectively, questions and answers represent a dialogue or contract. As Harrah points out, the central notion behind this domain is that of *interest:*

> an interest is represented as a set consisting of the area of interest, the things that satisfy the interest, and things that partially satisfy the interest. Knowing the latter two is knowing the interest.[8]

Questions show an interest or an "irritation" that presupposes some knowledge. Often questions are not as simple as they appear and may contain presuppositions.[9] For instance, the question "How does UCLA rank among library schools?" presupposes that UCLA and its library school exist and that there are rankings of library schools. According to philosophers, such a question is considered "risky," because although presuppositions do convey information, the quality of the answer is dependent on these presuppositions. Usually, the inquirer is responsible for the truth of these presuppositions. An example of a "safe" question might be, "Do the letters UCLA stand for anything?" It presupposes little.

Being a practical field, reference librarianship has paid little attention to the theoretical types of questions. Still, it is possible to build a calculus of questions (see Table 3.1). Such an approach could serve as an alternate hypothesis to the one presented in Chapter 5. Besides safe and risky ques-

Table 3.1
Rudimentary Calculus of Opening Questions

Category	Type of source(s)
Who	Biographical, directory, bibliography, catalog
Where	Atlas, directory
What	Dictionary, encyclopedia
How much	Statistical source, government publication
When	Encyclopedia, yearbook, newspaper
Why	Encyclopedia, handbook

tions, a theory of question types could draw from the following list (though it may not be a mutually exclusive one): (1) categorical or binary questions that require either a yes or no answer, technically called a one-place truth-functional question; (2) hypothetical or conditional questions; (3) pseudo-questions;[10] (4) which/who questions, where the class is specified; (5) pure or qualified what questions (e.g., "What is glass?" where the context is specified); (6) whether questions; (7) noun questions; (8) interrogative proadjectival phrase-type questions.

As for answers, Harrah has argued it is an "information matching game."[11] Conversely, Wittgenstein observed "When the answer cannot be put into words, neither can the question be put into words. The riddle does not exist. If a question can be framed at all, it is also possible to answer it."[12] Similarly, questions can be classified as (1) simple, direct, or perfect;[13] (2) deliberative;[14] (3) sufficient; (4) incomplete or partial;[15] (5) evasive;[16] or (6) unanswerable.[17]

3.1.3 Boundary Considerations

Reference work is not monolithic nor is it just devoted to question answering. Reference work is a collection of highly interrelated, yet distinct activities, each of which could be used as the focal point for developing a KBS. The following discussion addresses several domains related to question answering for which KBS development would be appropriate.

3.1.3.1 Collection Development

Professionals devote a fair amount of time in reference departments to collection development work as they try to keep their collections up-to-date.[18] Ideally, a KBS that recommends titles in the domain of general reference work also could keep track of those titles most frequently recommended and therefore serve as a purchase order support system when it comes time to think about which new editions to buy. A much more sophisticated system might even "read" the professional literature and alert the reference librarian to those books that would be appropriate for the library's reference collection. At the very least, a KBS could automate the gathering of reference statistics by keeping a log of its transactions.[19]

3.1.3.2 Locational Information

Many reference questions, as many as 40 percent in some libraries, are directional in nature. The Information Machine, a menu-driven orientation to library services, policies, procedures, and facilities, developed by the University of Houston and offered through the AMIGOS Bibliographical Council, is a significant development in trying to reduce the burden created by these kinds of questions.[20]

3.1.3.3 Library Use Instruction

Some users, especially students, need instruction in the use of the library. In some libraries, such as school libraries, reference librarians may spend most of their time in this activity; elsewhere it can still account for 20 percent of a professional's time. Yet, these legitimate questions are being handled increasingly in groups because it is more cost efficient. Nonetheless, a KBS could take over much of this task. Ralph Alberico, formerly of James Madison University, has proposed to undertake work in this area.

3.1.3.4 Referral

Ethically speaking, when a question cannot be answered it must be properly referred to someone or some place else that can answer the question (see Chapter 4). A KBS could automate much of what public librarians call their local resource index or serve as a directory-type source of information.

3.1.3.5 Interlibrary Loan

Interlibrary loan is yet another activity, with its complex decision making, that seems ripe for KBS development work. Professional decisions involve bibliographical verification and the selection of appropriate borrowing libraries. No doubt, actual success in this domain will depend in large part on how ill structured or well structured the problem domain is. Thus far, several agencies have examined interlibrary loan protocol with an eye toward KBS development including Mexico, Craig Robertson at the University of Vermont, and International Library Systems Corporation of Vancouver, British Columbia.

3.1.3.6 Answering Reference Questions

The preceding five activities are not central to the discussion of reference work per se. Nonetheless, that discussion serves to remind readers that there are many other potentially rich areas awaiting investigation. In the future, we might see a single KBS that combines all these activities.

Thousands of reference librarians answer tens of thousands of questions daily. They help in the educational process of students; they help those who are merely curious about something; they serve as consultants in the research process; and they can provide expert advice about which sources to read or consult. The level of activity is staggering; some library systems could be answering 10 million questions or more per year.

At the lowest level, the questions asked are elementary or basic, consisting of fact-type questions; what is sometimes called ready-reference work. Such questions may account for 20 to 50 percent of the questions asked. The intermediate-level reference question involves relationships between things, persons, or events and often requires value judgments to be made. These questions account for 5 to 10 percent or more of the total questions asked. The third and highest level includes both elementary- and intermediate-level questions; it is the kind of composite question likely to be asked by someone, such as a teacher, who must explain something to someone else.[21] Such questions may account for another 10 percent of the total.

Another consideration in designing a KBS is whether it should point to a source versus answering the answer directly.[22] This distinction is recognized in professional practice as the difference between reference and information service (in information science parlance, the latter is called information retrieval). The primary advantage of the latter approach to service is that the user's request is immediately satisfied. Yet, there are several barriers to such a KBS approach: the massive storage requirement; only a part of the knowledge base would ever be used; and the immensity of this large-scale task. Therefore, in the near future, only small- to intermediate-sized systems are likely.

Another important design consideration is the number of reference source types or formats to cover in a KBS. Chapter 1 reveals that certain formats are considered central to general reference work: atlases, bibliographies and catalogs, biographical sources, dictionaries, government publications, and indexes. Less consensus exists about the centrality of audiovisuals, directories, pamphlets, statistical sources, and yearbooks.

If one takes this approach, a closely related concern appears. Are the boundaries of these formats predictable? Take, for example, dictionaries and encyclopedias. Do encyclopedia dictionaries belong to the former or latter category of reference materials? Do any rules exist to help sort out the difference? The notion of a fuzzy set appears relevant here. Even within reference formats with clear boundaries, some members or tools appear to be more central than others; these are called prototypes by psycholinguists. Chapter 5 will address these concerns in detail.

3.1.3.7 Assisting with Online Information Retrieval

Within general reference, another closely related domain for the development of KBS is the promising area of online information retrieval. Parenthetically, some writers include user-friendly interfaces and front-end devices as part of KBS but these are better understood as gateways or database access software. In fact, online searching is an interesting example in which applied logic has taken the form of a formal query language. A KBS module(s) could contain the heuristics related to:

• the decision to go online or use CD-ROM reference tools

Identifiable heuristics include: (1) the need for a comprehensive search over a considerable period; (2) the need to supplement or expand a search through printed sources; (3) the need to extend the search to sources the library does not own, but that are accessible online; (4) the need to answer

complex questions that require the ability to combine one or more search terms; (5) the need for current information; and (6) the convenience of machine sorting and printing of citations.[23]
- the conversion of natural language into searchable terminology

Developers could identify the heuristics related to the identification of distinct concepts, the determination of the correct search terms for those concepts, and the relationships (hierarchical, nonhierarchical) between those concepts.
- the selection of the appropriate online vendor

Having decided which system vendor is best (or at least available), the KBS module could seamlessly link to the online system and automatic logon could begin.[24]
- the selection of the appropriate database(s)

Based on the terminology, selection of a relevant database that is also related to specific systems is the next step. Once this step is completed, the KBS could seamlessly link to the online system and automatically logon.
- the construction of an effective online search strategy

Strategies are sequences of actions. Step-by-step heuristics can be identified related to the appropriateness of truncation, expansion, and/or/not searches, use of parentheses for multiple terms, field limiting (on descriptors or identifiers), positional/proximity/adjacency operations, and formatting of search results (e.g., in alphabetical order by journal title for easier retrieval). KBS could advise about searching controlled vocabulary (when user needs dictate increased precision, currency, or when added specificity is desired) versus searching free-text (when control terms do not describe natural language concepts and when user needs greater flexibility), as well as such basic search strategies such as "citation pearl building."[25]
- the modification of the searching process (including high relevance searches vs. high precision searches)
- the techniques to broaden or narrow search results

In reviewing the literature on searching, Harter and Peters have classified many heuristics used by searchers.[26] Called Project MONSTRAT, Belkin and Windel have examined searcher/client interaction in this area,[27] while Cornelia Yoder has focused on user characteristics in her doctoral dissertation.[28] All this basic research has its application to KBS development work.

3.1.3.8 Reader's Advisory Work

In public libraries about 5 to 10 percent of the reference questions asked are of an advisory nature, while in school libraries, the figure may be even higher. This type of reference work should be as fully valued as answering fact-type reference questions. Yet, Pierce Butler has observed that "librarians, without being fully aware of their attitude, hold a strong conviction that somehow reading for information is nobler than reading for emotional experience."[29]

KBS development work in this area splits into two groups: reader's advisory for adults and for younger readers. Of the two, KBS work on children's reading of fiction may be easier; at least we see more systems available for them. At present, there are several such systems: Book Whiz from Educational Testing Service, Book Brain from Oryx Press, and Good Reads, as well as two earlier prototypical systems called Computer Pix and Byte into Books (see Chapter 9 for more details).

As for adult fiction reading, booksellers generally need ask only two questions before making a recommendation: What have you read and liked? or What kind of fiction do you like? A successful expert advisory system in this area will have to be more subtle. For instance, the development work at Del Mar Technologies has tried to characterize the reader's emotional experience among seven dimensions including age, gender, and thematic interest.

3.1.3.9 Other Applications in Advanced, Subject Reference

While the primary focus of this book is general reference, the boundaries are definitely extendible. In fact, it is not really clear where general reference ends and subject reference begins when one considers the findings in Chapter 5. Therefore, it is worth mentioning the host of other applications being developed for advanced, subject reference work. The paradigm and heuristics for learning this kind of work may be different, but it is not at all clear yet.

In the broad area of the social sciences, several efforts are under way, but business has received the most attention. Interested readers should consult Chapter 8 for detailed analysis of Conceptual Analysis of Business (1984), Gateway to Information (1986), ABLE (1987), Expert Advisory System for Reference and Library Instruction (1987), Research Advisor (1987), and TomeSearcher (1988). One of the most advanced thinkers in the business field is Eloisa Yeargain of UCLA's Management Library.

Politics and government information have been addressed by: POINTER, 1984; GDRA, 1988; and proposed by Ralph Alberico. Other social science applications include: education (Research Advisor, 1987), economics (Research Advisor, 1987), law (Pronto, 1989, and Reference Advisory System, 1989), and patents (Patent Information Assistant, 1987).

The pure and applied, physical, and natural sciences seem equally well covered. For instance, agriculture, including horticulture and aquaculture, is represented by: PLEXUS (1983), Answerman (1986), AquaRef (1986), REGIS (1989), and NAL's ornamental horticulture (1990). Examples from the life sciences, nursing, medicine (notably cancer research), and public health include: Cansearch (1982), LOOK (1987), and Reference Advisory

System (1989). Systems devoted to computer science, electrical engineering, information technology, and material science include: TomeSearcher (1988), Reference Advisory System (1989), REX (1989), and Project Mercury (1988). Chemistry is covered by CHEMREF (1987).

The humanities field is least well covered. Of the two systems, one is a prototype and the other is still a proposal: Technical Writing Assistant (1987) and a system for helping in the field of literary criticism (proposed by Alberico).

In summary, many prototype KBS are under development in university and public libraries throughout the United States, Canada, New Zealand, Israel, and Great Britain. One might ask, though, what is the a priori likelihood of successfully developing such a system?

3.2
Likelihood of Successful KBS

From the outset, for any KBS to be viable: (1) the solution must be valuable and (2) management must want a solution, according to Stefik.[30] Writing in 1985, Waterman listed fourteen specific criteria for determining whether KBS development work was appropriate, justified, or even possible.[31] Clustering around nature, complexity, and scope, his fourteen items are listed below seriatim (see, also, Table 3.2). Immediately following each of Waterman's questions are my personal evaluations. My response range is: no; no, probably not; yes, to some degree; maybe so; probably so; yes, indeed; or yes, absolutely. Then, there are domain-specific comments relating these questions to reference work. Finally, each response has a confidence factor assigned to it. To some degree, of course, these confidence factors are arbitrary. This kind of precision does not occur in everyday life.

1. Does the Task Require Common Sense?

To some degree, yes. Common sense includes an enormous amount of general, contextual information. Truly expert systems must deal with this kind of knowledge and, thus far, it has been difficult to build it into existing systems. Reference librarians can often assume a great deal about an inquirer's question. For instance, they probably know that "UCLA" is a major university on the west coast of the United States or that "John" is usually a male's name.

While successful reference librarians will draw upon sound practical judgment (i.e., common sense), their expertise is primarily the product of intensive training (most often represented by the M.L.S. degree) and long experience, perhaps ten or more years in the field. In other words, the Mudge method or Hutchins heuristic is not likely to occur to the person coming in off the street. Instead, common sense probably would suggest using the closest book to answer a user's query or that one should use a big book for difficult questions because the question is more likely to be in a big book than in a small book. It might be appropriate to assign a confidence factor of 80 to this criterion.

2. Does the Task Require Cognitive Skills Only?

Yes, indeed. Reference work is not primarily a physical task, it is an intellectual one. While it may be useful to walk with the inquirer to confirm that the predicted source contains the answer, the job is not primarily physical. Physical height may be handy to reach reference works on the top shelf, but it is not a primary requirement of the task. Nor is physical strength per se, although it is necessary on occasions to handle unabridged dictionaries, atlases, or any oversized volume effectively. Of course, in a pinch, the user could do this part of the job and will when they work independently of the librarian. For that matter, robotics, another part of AI research, may eventually find an application here.[32] Let's assign a confidence factor of 95 to this criterion.

3. Can Experts Articulate Their Methods?[33]

Probably so. As discussed in the previous chapter, the knowledge base is composed of facts and rules. The declarative knowledge is public knowledge in the sense that it is readily available to anyone who is interested. However, perhaps only 20 percent of the knowledge base is public. The other 80 percent is private knowledge.

As discussed in Chapter 2, there are knowledge elicitation techniques to help get experts to explain what they do. Assign a confidence factor of 85 to this criterion.

4. Are the Experts Genuine?

Yes, absolutely; there are some genuine experts. Given the long history of reference quality studies demonstrating about 50 percent accuracy, however, many reference librarians may not be highly competent. Furthermore, the field needs to identify those they think are competent, proficient, or even outstandingly expert. To a limited extent, the field does know who is competent. For example, in making referrals, librarians are explicitly identifying who they respect and who they believe can answer the inquirer's question. So, let's assign a confidence factor of 100 to this criterion.

5. Do the Experts Agree?

Maybe to probably so. Most of the KBS development work to date has been with a single domain expert. Hence, few developers or even researchers, for that matter, have wrestled with this question. None of the systems discussed in Chapter 8 present a validated knowledge base in the sense that more than two have agreed on the system's recommendations. Chapter 5, however, presents research findings for the first time that answer this question. For the moment, assign a confidence factor of 75 to this criterion.

6. Is the Task Difficult?

No. Human reference librarians have been undertaking this task for nearly a century. If it is too difficult it may be an impossible task, for human or computer. On the other hand, if the task is too simple it may not be worth investing the time and money in developing a KBS. Assign a confidence factor of 90 to this criterion.

7. Is the Task Poorly Understood?

No. Again, reference librarians have been answering questions for about one hundred years now. Nonetheless, as Chapter 2 points out, they may not be able to articulate how they do it. Assign a confidence factor of 90 to this criterion.

8. Is a High Payoff Involved?

Yes, absolutely. Echoing Stefik's concern, one might consider the extraordinary number of questions asked in reference departments and think about the savings in staff time, if they could be freed from the routine questions. Assign a confidence factor of 100 to this criterion.

9. Is Expertise Being Lost?

Yes, absolutely. Reference departments experience turnover due to several reasons including (1) promotions, (2) resignations, and (3) retirements. Having a KBS present that contains that vital knowledge would be protecting the department's knowledge base. Assign a confidence factor of 100 to this criterion.

10. Does the Task Involve Symbol Manipulation?

Yes, absolutely. Reference work is symbolic manipulation. A reference librarian must be able to understand the inquirer's question, decide on an appropriate action, retrieve the requested information, and communicate the results to the inquirer. Each of these steps involves symbol manipulation. Assign a confidence factor of 100 to this criterion.

11. Is the Task Heuristic?

Yes, absolutely. Despite the particular implementations of KBS in reference work, which appear as algorithmic decision trees, there is no evidence that humans work algorithmically. Rather, it seems they have rules of thumb that are good enough to cover the various situations they encounter. Assign a confidence factor of 100 to this criterion.

12. Is the Task Too Easy?

Probably not. The average reference question takes two to five minutes to answer. The expert reference librarian, however, has studied this field for a year or two in graduate school and has several years of practice before becoming truly competent. Assign a confidence factor of 90 to this criterion.

13. Does the Solution Have Practical Value?

Yes, absolutely. Answering inquirers' questions is not only a worthwhile effort, it is the profession's *raison d'être*. Assign a confidence factor of 100 to this criterion.

14. Is the Task of Manageable Size?

Yes, indeed. Some reference collections are extensive, but finite nevertheless. Thus far, the prototypes developed for reference work have contained less than 50 rules and 3000 tools (see Chapter 8). Hence, they are considered small systems. Based on findings presented in Chapter 5, however, it may require more than 1500 rules to begin to model the reference process adequately. An unanswered research question is, On how many titles do reference librarians really operate?[34] Assign a confidence factor of 95 to this criterion.

Adopting Waterman's fourteen questions, UCLA's Anderson Graduate School of Management's Professor Clay Sprowls wrote a KBS to advise on KBS. Using the confidence factors assigned to each of the criteria listed above, the resulting advice is that KBS development in reference work is: (1) possible (at the 75 percent confidence level), (2) justified (at the 100 percent level), and (3) appropriate. ESGUIDE's advice is that development is go (75) or maybe go (90). In other words, the reference domain is limited in scope, the task is not too complex, and the nature of the problem is appropriate to a KBS approach, so we should see some successful KBS.

3.3

Graduate Instruction in KBS

Given the importance of KBS in professional practice, it makes sense that it is a subject that should be covered in schools of library and information science. One can debate whether it should be a free-standing course or

Table 3.2
Likelihood of Successful ES in Reference Work

Question	Answer	Confidence level
1. Common sense?	To some degree, yes.	80 percent
2. Cognitive skills?	Yes, indeed.	95 percent
3. Articulate experts?	Probably so.	85 percent
4. Genuine experts?	Yes, absolutely.	100 percent
5. Do experts agree?	Maybe to probably so.	75 percent
6. Is task difficult?	No.	90 percent
7. Task poorly understood?	No.	90 percent
8. High payoff?	Yes, absolutely.	100 percent
9. Expertise lost?	Yes, absolutely.	100 percent
10. Symbol manipulation?	Yes, absolutely.	100 percent
11. Task heuristic?	Yes, absolutely.	100 percent
12. Task not too easy?	Probably not.	90 percent
13. Practical value?	Yes, absolutely.	100 percent
14. Manageable size?	Yes, indeed.	95 percent

whether it should be incorporated into existing courses. The point, though, is whether the subject is covered at all.

Teaching KBS in the United Kingdom library schools has been summarized recently.[35] In early 1990, Sue Hutton in the Department of Library and Information Studies at Loughborough University surveyed United States library and information teaching practices. Until her report appears, though, it may be worth mentioning that several schools offer KBS in their curricula: William S. Cooper teaches the topic at the University of California, Berkeley; William E. McGrath at SUNY, Buffalo;[36] Glynn Harmon at the University of Texas, Austin;[37] and myself at UCLA.[38]

Some course offerings view KBS simply as another tool, part of their student's vocation skills, familiar with its use (i.e., how to use one and how to elicit knowledge for prototyping systems), while other schools see KBS as part of their student's professional skills (i.e., students understand its proper function). KBS is a valuable addition to the curriculum because it encourages and sharpens students' analytical and systematic thinking about the reference process, whether they actually implement a KBS or not.

Among the set of practical purposes, United States course objectives intend to prepare students for an immediate job market as end users of KBS, as consultants, developers, or marketers of such products. Schools that have offerings in this area are likely to graduate students who can successfully compete in the job market.

3.4

Philosophical and Ethical Issues

Finally, the existence of KBS or prototypes has raised design considerations as well as ethical issues about their role in reference work and the provision of information.

3.4.1 Assistant, Advisor, or Colleague?

Early developers of these new decision support systems adopted the AI term "expert system," but as time passed, their initial optimism suggested in this phrase faded, especially as they recognized that their prototype systems were not as intelligent as they had hoped they might be. Obviously, no one would seriously think of trying to play music with one of the powerful chess-playing programs. Similarly, one might want to have dictionary-type questions answered, but a biographical source prototype system will not answer such questions. In actuality, librarians have been cautious about formally referring to their systems as expert—only Drexel University and James Madison University are using the phrase "expert system" to describe their work.

Without a doubt, the small prototypes that do exist could assist the reference librarian with some of the basic, fact-type questions that they are asked. Perhaps it would be more appropriate to refer to these *modest* systems as assistants (James Parrott, Bruce Harley, and Patricia Knobloch have used this term for their systems); some writers such as Jeff Fadell are rightly referring to their initial prototypes as toy systems or throwaways. Other writers are beginning to back off the unrealistic claims of microcomputer-based expertise and are talking more realistically about reference *advisory* systems for this reason. The work at Goucher College, Northwestern's Science and Technology Library, San Diego State University, and CalPoly Pomona use the term "advisor." Medium-sized systems, covering all reference formats, certainly will be able to advise on a wider range of questions. Eventually we may even see systems that might take the place of reference librarians in most question-answering situations, but right now that possibility is far in the future. Such a system should qualify as brilliant. The point is that the aspirations or hopes of developers have not yet been met in reality. It does not mean the task is impossible, just that it will take some profound thought about how a reference librarian does such a remarkable job of answering almost any question put to her.

3.4.2 Ownership of Knowledge

The appearance of KBS is also causing us to think about intellectual property rights. The question of who owns the knowledge or the KBS is not always clear-cut. In the former situation, it could be argued that the knowledge belongs to the entire profession or at the very least the interviewed experts during the course of development. If the system is developed in a university setting, then that institution may claim ownership. On the other hand, work supported by government contracts may not be copyrightable at all.

The creator of Answerman, Samuel T. Waters, who worked for the National Agricultural Library, advocated making the software "freely available to others so that the knowledge bases are readily accessible to all."[39] Diana Woodward expressed similar concerns in her 1988 ASIS Mid-Year presentation, "Proprietary Expert Systems: A Threat to Intellectual Freedom" in Ann Arbor, Michigan.

In any event, the owner of KBS software is its creator. Those individuals who wish to protect their rights should consider filing for trademark, copyright, trade secret, and patent.[40] Trademark offers protection of the name of KBS programs. KBS code might be protected as a trade secret, so that library employees agree to protect the information by signing a security agreement. Similarly, a patent might protect a library's investment from someone independently developing a similar system. Finally, the name of the KBS might be trademarked for protection.

3.4.3 Liability and Warranties

Yet another question is, Who is responsible for the recommendation of a KBS? What claims are being made by the developers of KBS? Generally, shrink-wrap provisions are legally binding contracts that limit liability. Although there is not much published in the popular press, law suits are another potential area of difficulty.[41]

Libraries may not be buying KBS; rather, they may be contemplating building their own. Despite the fact that libraries might be considered to have deep pockets (behind the public library is the city government and behind the academic library is the university, and behind some of them, the state government), courts have not entertained the notion of consequential damages.[42] Librarians would do well to check that their insurance policies cover such matters, but there do not appear to be great legal risks in KBS development.

3.4.3.1 Standard or Normative Practice

Could the library be held liable for not using an KBS? In this case, one should distinguish between malpractice and mispractice. Malpractice is willful and intentional; decidedly, most reference librarians are not in this category, which is not to imply that bad practice does not occur. Alternatively, from time to time, any librarian may commit mispractice due to forgetfulness (i.e., the misapplication of rules of thumb) or lack of experience (e.g., unfamiliarity with a subject area). Of course, the occurrence of this event should suggest that inexperienced librarians work under direct supervision and legitimately decline to answer questions in some areas due to their lack of competence. So, what about a KBS? Should it be used without professional supervision?

These are some of the most thorny questions that reference department heads and staff must consider, if they choose to develop defensible KBS for general reference work.

Endnotes

1. Russell L. Ackoff, "The Art and Science of Mess Management," *Interfaces* 11 (February 1981): 20–21. Ackoff also asserts that "we experience . . . large and complex sets of interacting problems, *dynamic systems of problems* . . . [which] we refer to . . . as *messes*" (p. 22).

2. Kenneth Crews, "The Accuracy of Reference Service: Variables for Research and Implementation," *Library and Information Science Research* 10 (July–September 1988): 331–355.

3. T.J. Cartwright, "Problems, Solutions and Strategies: A Contribution to the Theory and Practice of Planning," *AIP Journal* 39 (May 1973): 179–187.

4. Hubert and Stuart Dreyfus, for example, in *Mind Over Machine: The Power of Human Intuition and Expertise in the Era of the Computer* (New York: Free Press, 1986). Their article, "Why Expert Systems Do not Exhibit Expertise," *IEEE Expert* 1 (Summer 1986): 86–90, is a briefer statement.

5. Cartwright, p. 182. It is tempting to speculate on the psychology of problems. I believe that many people remain apathetic as long as domains are defined as metaproblems. Once they see solutions, usually derived from simple problems, the path to action is more straightforward.

6. Richard Kittredge and John Lehrberger, *Sublanguage: Studies of Language in Restricted Semantic Domains*. Foundations of Communication. Berlin: W. de Guyter, 1982.

7. Simon, 1978.

8. D. Harrah, "Erotetic Logistics," In *The Logical Way of Doing Things,* ed. K. Lambert (New Haven: Yale University Press, 1969), 3–21.

9. See R.G. Collingwood, *An Autobiography* (Oxford: Oxford University Press, 1939) and J.F. Post, "A Defense of Collingwood's Theory of Presuppositions," *Inquiry* 8 (1965): 332–354.

10. See Rudolph Carnap, *Scheinprobleme in der Philosophie* (Frankfurt: Suhrkamp, 1966).

11. D. Harrah, "A Logic of Questions and Answers," *Philosophy of Science* 28 (1961): 40–46.

12. Ludwig Wittgenstein, *Tractatus Logico-philosophicus* (London: Routledge and Kegan Paul, 1921), par. 6.5.

13. G. Stahl, "The Effectivity of Questions," No. 3 (1969): 211–218.

14. J. Wheatley, "Deliberative Questions," *Analysis* 15 (January 1955): 49–60.

15. M.J. Creswell, "On the Logic of Incomplete Answers," *Journal of Symbolic Logic* 30 (1965): 65–68.

16. J.J. Katz, "The Logic of Questions," in *Logic, Methodology and Philosophy of Science III,* ed. B. van Rootselar and J.G. Staal (Amsterdam: North Holland, 1968), 463–493.

17. Moritz Schlick, "Unanswerable Questions," *The Philosopher* 13 (July 1935): 98–104.

18. Mark Johnston and John Weckert, "Expert Assistance for Collection Development," in *Libraries and Expert Systems,* ed. Craig McDonald and John Weckert (London: Taylor Graham, 1991), 70–87, and id., "Selection Advisor: An Expert System for Collection Development," *Information Technology and Libraries* 9 (1990): 219–225.

19. Several systems already do so; see, for example, Online Reference System (1984), Pointer (1984), and AquaRef (1986).

20. Jeff Fadell and Judy E. Myers, "The Information Machine: A Microcomputer-based Reference Service," *The Reference Librarian* 23 (1988): 75–112.

21. For an elaboration of these levels, see Pierce Butler, "Survey of the Reference Field," in *The Reference Function of the Library,* ed. Pierce Butler (Chicago: University of Chicago Press, 1943), 1–15.

22. Another issue involves what happens when a system is designed to answer a question directly, bypassing and, hence, superseding the traditional sources. How will accuracy of such a system be assured?

23. Anne B. Piternick, "Decision Factors Favoring the Use of Online Sources for Providing Information," *RQ* 29 (Summer 1990): 534–544.

24. Several such systems already exist; see, for example, CanSearch (1982), Patent Information Assistant (1987), and LOOK (1987).

25. Steve Harter of Indiana University has developed an *advisory* system called "Online Search Analyst."

26. Stephen P. Harter and Anne Rogers Peters, "Heuristics for Online Information Retrieval: A Typology and Preliminary Listing," *Online Review* 9 (October 1985): 407–424.

27. Nicolas J. Belkin and G. Windel, "Using MONSTRAT for the Analysis of Information Interaction," In *Representation and Exchange of Knowledge as a Basis of the Information Processes,* ed. H.J. Dietschmann, pp. 359–382 (New York: Elsevier North-Holland, 1984).

28. Cornelia M. Yoder, "An Expert System for Providing On-line Information Based on Knowledge of Individual User Characteristics," Ph.D. dissertation, Syracuse University, 1986.

29. Butler, 6.

30. Mark Stefik, 1985.

31. Donald A. Waterman, *A Guide to Expert Systems* (Reading, MA: Addison-Wesley Publishing Company, 1985), Chapter 11.

32. Robotics work in libraries is still in its infancy. The automatic delivery of documents is being tested in the town library building of Bordeaux-Meriadeck, France and in the university library at California State University, Northridge.

33. Another matter, largely a political one, is whether experts are *willing* to articulate their methods.

34. Expert systems development work might reveal how many titles are actually used; I would hypothesize it is something like 80/20—80 percent of the questions are answered using 20 percent of the available titles.

35. Margaret O'Neill and Anne Morris, "Expert Systems: The United Kingdom's Educational Approach," *Computer in Libraries* 9 (November 1989): 14–18.

36. McGrath first used a shell, 1st-Class, in teaching LIS515, "Sources of Information and Services in Science/Technology" during 1987. Writing of his experience he says "Of 60 or 70 students I exposed to ES, fewer than 10 took it as serious material for library reference. And of those, perhaps 3 or 4 could see its major potential. . . . They are not interested in creating new knowledge; they are interested only in learning what is already known—undoubtedly because the degree gives them a ticket to a job. . . . So it looks like expert systems will be confined to the domain of doctoral students here" (Bill McGrath to Richardson, 18 June 1990).

37. Harmon taught LIS385T.6, an "Expert Systems" seminar, at the University of Texas during the Fall term of 1989.

38. John Richardson, "Toward an Expert System for Reference Service: A Research Agenda for the 1990s," *College and Research Libraries* 50 (March 1989): 231–248, but especially 241. See also, Deborah Henderson, Patricia Martin, Lauren Mayer, and Pamela Monaster, "Rules and Tools in Library School," *Journal of Library and Information Science* 29 (Winter 1989): 226–227.

39. Waters to Richardson, 15 April 1988.

40. Recent reports in the September 1991 issue of *InfoWorld* suggest that corporations are applying for patent more often than copyrights. Nonetheless, the U.S. Copyright Office publishes many useful information pamphlets such as Circular 61, "Copyright Registration for Computer Programs" (October 1989). Otherwise, a good, relatively nontechnical starting place is M. J. Salone, *How to Copyright Software,* 3d ed. (Berkeley, CA: Nolo Press, 1989). A common situation is also covered by William T. McGrath, "Computer Programs and Independent Contractors: Who Owns the Copyright," *BASIS* 16 (February/March 1990): 11–13.

41. Richard Greenfield of the Library of Congress' Special Projects Office has collected several hundred citations to legal cases that may be applicable to expert systems software.

42. Gray, 1988.

Two

Problems

4

Modeling the Reference Transaction

The Reference Transaction

Chapter 1 introduced the three dimensions of the reference paradigm. This chapter elaborates on one of those dimensions, the reference process. In particular, this chapter develops a paradigm of that process based on more than 70 research studies. Such a model is necessary to create a viable expert system for general reference work. The literature, however, is quite rich in descriptive articles, several analytical models, and even some flowcharts. Yet, we do not know all the component parts of the process nor which is the optimal model of those presented. Thus far, no one has thoroughly synthesized all that we know about the process by evaluatively reviewing the previous research[1] literature.[2] In that respect, this chapter extends the teaching and learning paradigm by describing and analyzing the research literature as well as some of the textbook presentations.

By way of additional justification, there is a need for a testable model. "(1) A model acts as an aid for instruction in the reference process; (2) a model of the reference process can be used to learn about the process; and (3) a model can allow predictions to be made about the effects of variables on the process."[3] A model of the reference transaction would allow LIS educators as well as reference librarians to teach a systematic approach to the process. Finally, any extant expert systems application can also be judged against this model.

4.1.1 Theoretical Constructs

Much of the research literature adopts, either implicitly or explicitly, a systems analysis approach or an input-process-output-feedback (IPOF) model. The influence of the Shannon–Weaver communication model is also evident by 1962. Graphically, these models are usually represented by line drawings and less often, but more recently, as a flowchart or flowsheet, a technique or method whereby detailed charting of the steps in the process takes place. Despite the fact that the flowcharting technique was developed between 1915 and 1920 to study manufacturing processes, it has found a more general applicability. Nevertheless, it does involve some distortions of reality by treating the reference interview as a discrete process rather than the continuous process that it is. In that respect, a flowchart represents reality as crisp rather than fuzzy. The model also assumes that the process is linearly progressive and composed of simple rather than complexly interdependent steps.

Finally, in reference research, most of the literature has focused on the user inputs, especially the psychological components, and the reference materials necessary for an output (i.e., a recommendation of a source). Relatively little attention has been devoted to the "activity . . . that transforms input data flow into output data flow."[4]

4.2
Literature Review of Reference Work

The following section provides a chronological review of the major work that has been conducted on the reference transaction process. Many scholars, especially Robert Taylor and Gerald Jahoda, have played an important part in advancing our understanding of the different steps in the question–answering process.

4.2.1 Mary De Jong (1926)

DeJong's 1926 analysis is one of the earliest studies of public library reference questions to be categorized by the inquirer's characteristics. The author reports on one month's inquiries at the Appleton Public Library: (1) study clubs (13 hours and 45 minutes to answer 20 questions); (2) general public (13 hours and 30 minutes to answer 29 questions); (3) students (2 hours and 25 minutes); (4) teachers (2 hours); and (4) other (39 reference questions at main desk and 12 questions over the telephone). Thirty–one hours were spent with questions that took more than 10 minutes to answer.[5]

4.2.2 James Wyer (1930)[6]

As mentioned in the first chapter, Wyer is the first author to write a reference textbook. In his book, he identifies the three essential elements of the paradigm: ". . . the reference question completely and satisfactorily answered involves three factors: inquirer, reference librarian, sources or materials."[7] His presentation suggests a straightforward linear process without many complications.

Wyer focuses on one of those dimensions, specifically the characteristics of successful reference librarians. By surveying thirty-eight eminent librarians, Wyer found twenty-seven mental traits important to success in reference work. In order of importance, his respondents identified: intelligence, accuracy, judgment, professional knowledge, dependability, courtesy, resourcefulness, tact, alertness, interest in work, memory, mental curiosity, interest in people, imagination, adaptability, perseverance, pleasantness, cooperativeness, system, health, initiative, industriousness, speed, poise, patience, forcefulness, and neatness.[8]

4.2.3 Edith Guerrier (1935)[9]

In her study, Guerrier found that thirty-three branch libraries in major metropolitan areas reported an average of 20 percent of their time being spent answering reference questions. Her other findings give insight into the relative utility of various reference formats and specific titles. Analyzing 1000 questions asked at these branches, Guerrier found that 50 percent could be answered using (1) encyclopedias; (2) dictionaries; (3) atlases; (4) *World Almanac;* (5) *Statesman's Yearbook;* (6) *Reader's Guide;* (7) *Who's Who in America;* (8) *Who's Who,* and (9) debate and quotation books.[10] She found that a list of 80 plus reference titles answered another two-sixths of the questions ($N = 333$) and the final one-sixth had to be answered with other titles.

4.2.4 Faith Hyers (1936)[11]

Participating as part of Guerrier's study, the Los Angeles Public Library and its then 48 branches collected one week's worth of questions. Hyers's analysis reveals that 50,000 reference questions were asked during that period, averaging 11 questions per minute per 12-hour day. Using a tripartite scheme of bread-and-butter questions, technical or businesslike questions, and cultural questions, Hyers concludes: (1) that individual differences exist among reference librarians in terms of the sources consulted to answer the same question; and (2) that there is a difference in knowing the subject and knowing the literature (i.e., the reference formats and their relative importance) of the subject. She also implicitly questions whether "the library should be able to answer any and every question."[12]

4.2.5 Carter Alexander (1936)

At one time, Alexander's 1936 article was one of the most frequently cited studies of the reference process. A detailed stepwise approach to searching for the answer to an inquirer's question, this article represents one of the earliest analytical statements about the process. Alexander identifies six steps in the transaction:

> "I. Find out precisely what the question really is.
> II. Decide which kind of library materials is most likely to have the answer to the inquiry.
> III. Decide which items in a given kind of library materials are most likely to have the answer, in order of likelihood.
> IV. Locate the chosen items.
> V. Search in the chosen items in order of likelihood until the answer is found or you are sure it cannot be found there.
> VI. If the answer is not found by the foregoing, go back over the previous steps and take next most likely sources."[13]

The first step consists of two general procedures: "find out what the inquirer intends to do with the answer to his question" and "examine the question to see what clues to its answer it carries."[14] It helps, he suggests, to classify the question into one of seven distinct types: (1) fact type including meaning type of fact, numerical or statistical type of fact, historical type of fact, exact wording type of fact, and proper name type of fact; (2) how to do type; (3) trends type; (4) supporting evidence type; (5) "all about" type; (6) evaluation of reference type; and (7) duplication of previous work type. By recommending analysis by type of reference format and then specific source within type (see Steps II and III), his technique foreshadows the shift to the proceduralist approach articulated by Isadore Mudge and popularized by Margaret Hutchins.

4.2.6 Margaret Hutchins (1937, 1944)[15]

As a proceduralist, Hutchins makes an important distinction by differentiating between the clarification (i.e., question negotiation) and classification (a mental analysis technique) steps. In the former, the reference librarian may need to clarify the inquirer's question further. For instance, "if the request seems peculiar a start may be made by restating it in a different way and asking if that is what is meant or would be satisfactory."[16] Note that she is recommending a closed-ended question (i.e., one that requires a yes or no response) for this step in the clarification process.

Mentioning Wyer's earlier list of mental traits, Hutchins reorders the list, in presenting her top six: (1) memory; (2) imagination; (3) perseverance; (4) judgment; (5) accuracy; and (6) suitability to the reader.[17]

4.2.7 Elizabeth Stone (1942)[18]

In summarizing several methods of evaluating reference service, Stone encourages reference departments to compile questions that could not be answered. Such lists would be helpful in evaluating the reference collection, especially the identification of additional sources. Apparently, she did not consider the need for better training in answering questions or for better tools, per se.

4.2.8 Dorothy Cole (1943)[19]

Cole collected 1026 questions from 14 public libraries in the Chicago area as well as in St. Louis and Billings, Montana. She analyzed these questions in four ways: by Dewey subject areas, inquirer's characteristics, time period of query, and level of complexity. Cole found that the social sciences, useful arts, and history accounted for 72 percent of the questions asked.[20] Her occupational analysis indicated that students asked the most questions (N = 356, 35%), followed by unknown occupations (N = 248, 24%), professionals (N = 210, 21%), shopkeepers and salesmen (N = 61, 6%), and clerks and stenographers (N = 59, 6%).[21] As for time periods, most inquiries concerned the immediate year (N = 196, 19%), followed by the twentieth century (N = 539, 53%), modern era (N = 153, 15%), middle ages (N = 12, 1%), ancient times (N = 20, 2%), no single period (N = 99, 10%), and future events (N = 7, 1%).[22] Cole's complexity analysis yielded the following results: (1) fact-type questions (N = 565, 55%); (2) general information about subjects (N = 200, 20%); (3) how-to information (N = 105, 10%); (4) supporting evidence (N = 85, 8%); (5) historical (N = 35, 3%); (6) trends (N = 25, 2%); and all others (N = 11, 1%).[23] She concludes her thesis with a list of actual sources used in answering the 1026 reference questions.

4.2.9 Raymund Wood (1952)[24]

Based on his reference experience and on an analysis of actual questions, Wood asserted that clarification is often harder than finding the actual source to answer the question. It is a rare instance that the real question is asked immediately. Often, two or three exchanges are needed to define the reference question. He concluded with four illustrative examples of question negotiation.

4.2.10 Jack Delaney (1954)[25]

Other researchers have included the work of Delaney in their literature reviews, although his article does not appear to be based on research or even first-hand reference experience. It is not documented; there are no footnotes or other references. Furthermore, the article does not even appear to be based on informed personal opinion; his position was identified as that of Order Librarian. No experience in reference work is claimed or presented.

Nevertheless, he focuses on the question negotiation process and offers "some interviewing errors common to librarians, [and] then we will consider twelve rules to help the library interviewer." These 12 commonsense rules about interviewing are not so numbered but can be sorted out in his brief narrative. These rules include: "[1] find out what it is the patron wants. What he wants may not be what he asks for. . . . [2] The skill comes in finding out what the patron needs and what is best for him. . . . [3] help the patron get what he wants or needs. . . . [4] Get to know as many steady patrons as possible because the more you know about a patron, the more effective your interview will be. . . . [5] Place your desk where you can get a maximum of privacy. . . . [6] put yourself in the other fellow's place. . . . [7] Keep your prejudices to yourself as much as possible. . . . [8] If you are at ease, it will do much toward helping the patron feel the same way. . . . [9] Allow time enough for the patron to say what he must to make his needs clear, but do not let him waste time or wander on the subject. . . . [10] make your questions short and do not put them in compound sentences. . . . [11] Beware the 'halo effect.' That is, do not judge a patron's social, intellectual, or financial level on his appearance, dress, or manners. . . . [and 12] The interview is most effective, not in getting facts but in giving away the attitude of the speaker."[26] His article raises an interesting ethical and philosophical question about needs versus wants.[27]

4.2.11 David Maxfield (1954)[28]

In one of the earliest efforts to do so, Maxfield draws upon the vast psychological literature, arguing for "more careful attention to . . . the individual person"[29] and that the reference transaction be viewed as part of the "counseling process."[30] Maxfield identifies four factors at work in the successful reference transaction: (1) acceptance and the importance of "suspending judgment"; (2) understanding using "tact and patience"; (3) communication built on asking "questions"; and (4) collaboration in the reader's efforts.[31]

4.2.12 Paul Breed (1955)[32]

After identifying the discrete steps in the general reference process, Breed categorizes the decision-making knowledge needed to accomplish each step according to a five-part scheme: (1) knowledge associated with a liberal arts education; (2) knowledge associated with library specialization (including experience); (3) personal knowledge; (4) knowledge gained in the search process; and (5) knowledge associated with subject specialization. Breed found that 81 percent of the decisions with his discrete steps required knowledge associated with library specialization.

4.2.13 Mary Francillon (1959)[33]

Francillon provides valuable, and some of the earliest quantitative, information on the type of reference questions asked. Based on a sample of 956 reference questions asked in a special library between January and early December 1959, she categorized them into seven different types of questions, which she identified as A through G (see Table 4.1). Three of her categories (i.e., types E and F; D; and C) include a mixture of different formats. Despite the fact that she used a mixed classification scheme, one can reconstruct the relative use of various reference formats (see Table 4.1). This data reveals the relative importance of certain formats. As such, it

Table 4.1
956 Questions Categorized by Reference Format[a]

Rank order of reference formats (type)	Number	Percentage
1. Library catalog (E and F)	462	48.3
2. Directories, encyclopedias, handbooks (C)	218	22.8
3. Indexes (G)	150	15.7
4. Bibliographies, catalogs, indexes (D)	49	5.1
5. Biographical sources and quotation sources (A)	40	4.2
6. Dictionaries (B)	37	3.9
Total	956	100.0

[a] Based on a statistical manipulation of Francillon's (1959) Table 1.

might serve as an indication of which formats to emphasize in schools of library and information science as well as which ES modules to bring up first.

4.2.14 Wallace Bonk (1960, 1961, 1963, and 1964)[34]

Starting in February 1959, Bonk asked other basic reference instructors in the United States about the reference titles they covered in class. He found that "all 25 schools agreed on only five titles out of a total of 1,202": *Encyclopedia Americana, Encyclopedia Britanica, World Book, New English Dictionary,* and *Funk and Wagnall's New Standard.*[35] Overall, his survey of faculty found 50 percent agreement on 115 titles.[36]

Desirous of a greater consensus on the core titles to be taught in library schools, he surveyed 1090 secondary school libraries, public libraries, and college and university libraries to find the best titles based on actual use; he received 1079 usable returns. In actuality, reference librarians reported their perceptions of vital, recommended, and peripheral titles as well as titles not owned. Statistical manipulation of his data (calculating the mean scores and standard deviation for each format) reveals the most important formats along with the single title originally reported as most vital (see Table 4.2).

Interestingly, Bonk initially thought that "reference method" was more important than specific titles, but changed his mind several years later and started arguing that the reference core course's emphasis on technique and method ought to shift to principles, purposes, and policies, and, furthermore, that instructors should "extend the range of titles as we drop away concern for pestiferous minutiae."[37]

Table 4.2
Rank Order of Reference Formats[a]

Ranking of vital + recommended	Most vital title
1. Handbooks	*Bartlett's*
2. Geographical materials	*Shepherd's Historical Atlas*
3. Biography	Kunitz, *20th Century*
4. Yearbooks	*World Almanac*
5. Government publications	*Statistical Abstract of U.S.*
6. Dictionaries	*Webster's 2nd*
7. Encyclopedias	*Encyclopedia Americana*
8. Indexes	*Reader's Guide*
9. Bibliography	*Books in Print*
10. Serials	*Ayer's Directory*
11. Directories	*Official Congressional Directory*
12. Audiovisual materials	*Educational Film Guide*

[a] Statistical analysis of Bonk's (1963) study, pp. 172–179.

4.2.15 James Perry (1961, 1963)[38]

Originally circulated in mimeograph form during 1961, Perry published the now-familiar four stages of query formulation as:

Q0 = some ideal "best" query to obtain information to deal with a given problem or situation

Q1 = the mental conception developed by some person as to needed information

Q2 = the statement of a query by a person without regard to a given IR [information retrieval] system

Q3 = the statement of a query by a person with regard to a given IR system.[39]

The necessity of querying an IR system follows from his assumption that "Needed information = Information in mind + Information to be acquired."[40]

4.2.16 University of Michigan (1961)[41]

One of the earliest and most rigorous studies of perceptions from the other side of the reference desk comes from the Survey Research Center of Michigan faculty members. Respondents rated service on a three-point scale: excellent (54%), good (37%), and poor (only 1%). Quality must be seen from the user's point of view. Earlier studies of the Los Angeles Public Library,[42] Columbia University,[43] Indiana University,[44] and the New York Public Library[45] found similar high levels of reader satisfaction.

4.2.17 Robert Taylor (1962)[46]

Perhaps the most sophisticated presentation yet of the inquirer's formation of a question, Taylor's work draws upon Shannon's Theory of Information, especially the concept of noise, and popularizes the earlier work of Perry. He also discusses question input, answer output, and the role of interim feedback. In passing, Taylor also points out that "filtering for the answer spectrum" involves a relevance judgment on the part of the inquirer.

Specifically, question formation based on the inquirer's informational need may be characterized as having four levels that move progressively from a kind of Platonic ideal question, which is psychological, abstract, complex, diffuse, ill defined, inchoate, and ambiguous to a logical, more concrete, rigid, focused, and simplified state:

Q1 = the actual, but unexpressed, need for information (the *visceral* need)
Q2 = the conscious within-brain description of the need (the *conscious* need)

Q3 = the formal statement of the question (the *formalized* need)
Q4 = the question as presented to the information system (the *compromised* need).[47]

His article ends with a set of research questions and a plea to include the inquirer in the design of information retrieval systems, such as reference work and expert systems.

4.2.18 Allan Rees and Tefko Saracevic (1963)[48]

Originally presented as a conference paper, this article is a descriptive statement of the ten "evolutionary steps" in question asking and answering. Despite the fact that it contains no explicit statement of methodology (except that analysis of reference questions is analogous to subject analysis of documents), this piece is the most comprehensive and detailed description of the entire reference transaction to date. Furthermore, the authors are the first to represent it graphically with boxes, dotted lines, and solid lines with arrows.

The ten steps are: (1) information problem and need; (2) initial formulation of question; (3) analysis by searcher; (4) negotiation between question analyst and questioner; (5) definition of question; (6) enumeration of concepts to be searched; (7) translation of search concepts into indexing language; (8) selection of search strategy; (9) conducting of search; and (10) formulation of alternate search strategies.

Acceptable answers or responses from the librarian will be based on:

1. What the questioner needs . . .
2. What he thinks he wants . . .
3. What he wants . . .
4. What he is prepared to read . . .
5. How much of what he gets he is prepared to read . . .
6. How much time he is willing to devote to it all . . .
7. In what sequence he would like to read what he gets . . .
8. What value he will attach to what he gets . . .[49]

4.2.19 Jesse Shera (1964)[50]

Shera appears to have read Taylor's 1962 article and heard Rees and Saracevic's 1963 ADI paper, and based part of his work on theirs without explicitly identifying his sources. However, the first half of his article is clearly original and devoted to establishing the proper role of decision theory and library automation in reference work, for instance, "the conviction that automation can raise the intellectual level of the reference librarian does not imply a belief that a machine can make a literature specialist out of a simple button pusher."[51]

The second half of his article proceeds from an explicit assumption:

> The fullest utilization of the potential of automation does necessitate a thorough study of the total reference process—from the problem that prompts the asking of a question to the evaluation of the response—for the very simple and obvious reason that machine simulation of that process cannot be accomplished without an understanding of the process itself.[52]

He goes on to describe the "complex associative series of linkages, or events" in the process, which he views as a "communication flow." Echoing Taylor's work, one of his contributions is the explicit graphical recognition of the role of feedback in the process, or what he terms the "evaluation of pertinence" to the information need as well as the "evaluation of relevance" to the inquiry (i.e., its linguistic expression).

4.2.20 Robert M. Hayes and Gary Carlson (1964)[53]

This work is highly optimistic about the possibility of understanding human search behavior because the authors believe it is "really quite regular;"[54] so, it is unfortunate that the literature has largely ignored this work up until now. Carlson proposes a computer simulation that then could be compared with human searching. He observed three librarians—one with four years experience, one with one year, and another who had just started work; hence, there is some question whether they should have been considered expert librarians when two of them were, in fact, advanced beginners. Nevertheless, this study is important because it examines what "librarians do, *not* what they *should* do."[55] Using protocol analysis, one section of this report, "human search strategies," details the protocol of a search and then flowcharts it, while another part of the report flowcharts the process in much greater detail. Their work draws attention to the importance of considering the time and effort involved in the reference transaction: "at each branching point, these strategies serve to limit the search effort by providing estimates of the effort involved in following a particular choice and the likelihood of its leading to a satisfactory result."[56]

4.2.21 Charles Bunge (1967, 1970)[57]

For his doctoral work, Bunge began to inquire into the relationship between professional education and performance on the reference desk. He hypothesized that professionally trained reference librarians would outperform (based on the proportion of questions answered and the time it took) untrained staff members.[58] Studying nine pairs of participants with one to twenty years of experience in seven different libraries, he found that the trained reference librarians were faster and more efficient than other staff.[59] Among professionals, experience correlated with performance ($r^2 = .417$).[60] Age alone and elapsed time from degree did not appear to be statistically significant predictors of success in the reference transaction.

Later, Bunge abstracted some information from his dissertation and made it more accessible by publishing his flowchart of "the major decisions and actions taken by the librarians in answering relatively simple 'fact' type questions."[61]

4.2.22 Herbert Goldhor (1967)[62]

Following up an earlier study of a single public library,[63] Goldhor submitted in writing ten test reference questions to "the person in charge" at twelve public libraries in the Minneapolis area. Despite the fact that librarians took about 20 minutes per question on average (based on five libraries reporting the total time taken), the accuracy rate was only 51 percent correct. Along with Bunge's research, readers will recognize the now-familiar 50 percent rule.

4.2.23 The University of the State of New York (1967)[64]

In a multiple-year study of public libraries, the Division of Evaluation found multiple reasons for poor performance despite strong local resources:

1. inadequate awareness of collection
2. trouble with technical questions
3. acceptance of anything printed
4. unawareness of other community resources
5. lack of interviewing to clarify questions.[65]

Nonetheless, reference librarians answered 70 percent of the questions correctly based on an inference drawn from the report's Table II.

4.2.24 Robert Taylor (1967, 1968)[66]

This study is one of the most highly cited sources in the reference field. In the first part of his article, Taylor repeats his description of James W. Perry's four needs (i.e., Q1–Q4) almost verbatim. Taylor does provide an interesting chart of the prenegotiation decisions by the inquirer. However, the significant contribution to our understanding of the actual reference transaction is his detailed analysis of the process of question negotiation.

Based on personal interviews with twenty special librarians, he found five "filters," which he defines as: (1) determination of subject; (2) objective and motivation; (3) personal characteristics of inquirer; (4) relationship of inquiry description to file organization; and (5) anticipated or acceptable answers.[67] The second filter is the most important because it often reduces search time substantially and determines what constitutes an appropriate response.

4.2.25 Gerald Jahoda et al. (1968, 1974, 1975, 1976, 1977, 1980, and 1981)[68]

In their earliest work, Jahoda and Culnan studied 26 science and chemistry libraries for one month, but found only 47 unanswered questions. The reasons given for not answering the question were categorized as: (1) no reference tool published to answer the question; (2) reference tool published but not in library; (3) existing reference tool not sufficiently up to date; (4) existing tool does not have adequate index; (5) existing tool does not have the information listed in a way to answer question; (6) answer probably in library—no time to answer; (7) question outside the scope of the library; (8) question not properly negotiated; and (9) other.[69] This study echoes Stone's 1942 recommendation.

Latter research suggests that this failure to answer the question was due to three general reasons: (1) 45 percent of the questions were unanswered because of reference tool limitations (categories 1,3,4, and 5); (2) 29 percent of the questions were unanswered because of library limitations (categories 2 and 7); and (3) 25 percent of the questions were unanswered because of personnel limitations (categories 6 and 8).[70] Hence, Jahoda and Culnan recommend studying unasked questions in the future.

By 1974, however, Jahoda was pessimistic about the success of machine searching in general reference work in contrast to Hayes and Carlson. Nevertheless, he identifies nine steps in the machine searching process based on his analysis of 28 general reference questions in science and technology:

1. Selection of indexable information
2. Level of answer
3. Selection of types of reference tools to search
4. Types-of-reference-tools search sequence
5. Type of answer
6. Size of answer
7. Types of access points to search

    8. Selection of specific titles of reference tools
    9. Specific titles search sequence[71]

In discussing point 4, he astutely observed that "Reference librarians have general guidelines but no specific rules for determining search sequence of types of reference tools."[72] Chapter 5 of this book addresses this concern.

    In his 1976 publication, Jahoda identifies eight situations when question negotiation may be necessary. For example,

    1. The real query may not be asked.
    2. Librarian is unfamiliar with the subject of the query.
    3. Ambiguity or incompleteness of query statement.
    4. Amount of information needed is not specified.
    5. Level of answer is not specified.
    6. The query takes more time than you can spend on it.
    7. Answer to query is not recorded in the literature.
    8. Language, time period, geography, or type of publication constraints need to be added to query statements.[73]

Using 23 science and technical reference librarians, Jahoda's 1977 work rediscovers Hutchins's heuristic, but goes on to evaluate the reference process as a simpler six-step model: (1) message selection; (2) selection of types of answer-providing tools; (3) selection of specific answer-providing sources; (4) selection of search headings; (5) answer selection; and (6) negotiation and renegotiation.

    Working with Judith Braunagel, Janice Fennell, Nice Figueiredo, Sims Kline, Miguel Menendez, Herbert Nath, William Needham, Afarin Shahravan, Lee Shiflett, and Vicki West, he developed and tested classroom modules in three reference courses, revising the modules based on faculty and student comments. His Table 2 provides a flowchart modeling the reference process; Table 4, a useful tool-descriptor matrix of knowns and wanteds; and table 5 identifies 12 formats that Jahoda thinks librarians consistently use.[74]

    Finally, Jahoda and Braunagel developed a checklist for determining whether questions are truly answerable based on: (1) clarity, (2) specificity, and (3) freedom from overly restrictive constraints such as language, time period, and geography.[75]

4.2.26 Edward Jestes and David Laird (1968)[76]

    Jestes and Laird conducted a self-study of their own reference desk activities at the University of California, Davis. Only 21 percent of desk time was spent with user or on the user's question.[77] Furthermore, they found that only 12.5 percent of the questions asked required professional training. Hence, they argue that the library should hire students to handle the more basic questions.

4.2.27 Norman Crum (1969)[78]

Accepting Taylor's four needs as originally expressed, Crum points out that users present themselves at different Q stages. The librarian's responsibility is to work back through these stages to the informational need or problem.

In the process, there are: (1) physical, (2) personality, (3) psychological, (4) linguistic, and (5) contextual barriers. He hypotheses that the worst place to transact the interview is behind the reference desk; Crum recommends interviewing in the inquirer's territory. At the very least, though, it is a proactive, even aggressive, reference policy. Although he does not provide an itemized list of each barrier, he indirectly suggests some; for instance, personality barriers might include coolness, indifference, and withdrawal, while informal contacts, direct assignment, and wise choice of locations would reduce other barriers.

Finally, Crum recommends a second interview, a review process to check the results, as a kind of quality control assurance, just before the end of the transaction.

4.2.28 John Lubans (1971)[79]

Focusing on the inquirer's recognition of the library as a possible source of information, Lubans surveyed nearly 3000 undergraduate college students in 1968. He found 8 percent nonusers and 37 percent occasional users of the library. Among all undergraduates, nonuse decreased during their four years in college. However, a two-year follow-up still found a large number of nonusers, so Lubans conducted an interview with 20 of these students. He found: (1) 45 percent still nonusers, (2) nonusers had used other types of libraries, (3) 57 percent said that librarians were "helpful and effective," but (4) most would ask faculty for guidance first.[80] Oddly, Lubans's abstract contains ten ways to convert nonusers into users based on information originally published in the Darnell Institute of Business newsletter (see section on inquirer below).

4.2.29 Patrick Penland (1971)[81]

Influenced by Maxfield's work, Penland starts an entire school of thought regarding cross-disciplinary borrowing of concepts and concerns, that is, the field of counseling, or social service generally, which has developed relevant interviewing techniques.

4.2.30 Bernard F. Vavrek (1971)[82]

Using content analysis on a set of 300 questions (i.e., 150 initial and then 150 negotiated questions), Vavrek establishes a significant difference between the number of elements in the inquirer's opening question (Taylor's Q_4) versus the negotiated question. According to Vavrek's scheme, questions can contain up to nine elements: (1) personal or corporate references; (2) geographical references; (3) time/space references; (4) subject descriptors; (5) form of publication requested; (6) level of analysis requested; (7) specific title references; (8) number references; and (9) behavioral descriptors (i.e., motivational need). In fact, opening questions have 2.7 elements on average, while negotiated questions have 3.7 elements; indeed, the point of question negotiation is to elicit more information, and only 26 percent of the questions had the same number of elements after negotiation.

Vavrek found that initial questions commonly contained three elements: subject descriptors (56.7% of the time), form of publication (48.7%), and level of analysis (36%). After negotiation, subject descriptors increased (68.6%) as did level of analysis (52%). However, dramatic changes occurred in three other elements: behavioral descriptors increased 7.75 times (from $N = 4$, 2.6% to $N = 31$, 20.6%) and time/space references doubled (from $N = 11$ or 7.3% to $N = 22$ or 33%), while form of publication actually decreased. The latter finding can be interpreted to mean that the requested informational package is not as important as the information content of the recommended package.

4.2.31 Geraldine King (1972)[83]

Focusing on the question negotiation process, King is influenced by Gallup's "Quintamentional Plan of Question Design" and F. W. King's adult education material, which encourage "general open-ended questions and [then] proceeds to closed specific questions."[84] King hypothesizes that open-ended questions help clarify the informational need in the inquirer's mind and provide more clues than do closed-ended questions. At the end of her article, she recommends that novices use the "'why' form of open-ended questions because the question 'why' facilitates understanding the request and the supplying of the information."[85] Although King calls closed-ended questions, "the tools of cross examination,"[86] one assumes that later in the classification process, closed-ended questions are more productive in confirming the likely match of potential formats with the inquirer's question.

4.2.32 F.S. Stych (1972)[87]

In order to find "a logical basis for some of the choices and decisions which reference workers are called upon to make,"[88] Stych hypothesizes about the factors that will influence the librarian's question negotiation and subsequent search strategy. Strongly reminiscent of Taylor's five filters and Vavrek's structural elements in opening reference questions, Stych suggests four primary and five secondary factors: (1) subject field; (2) time; (3) space; and (4) language; as well as (5) level of inquiry; (6) amount of information required; (7) time available for search; (8) languages searcher can handle; and (9) languages acceptable to the inquirer.[89] Stych attempts to rank order the top three: subject, space or language, and time. He believes that subject field is especially important in factual questions; that geographical factors are significant in political and literary history; and he suggests consulting works published in the country of the inquiry's origin but, obviously, not consulting works published before an event has occurred.

4.2.33 Mary Jane Swope and Jeffrey Katzer (1972)[90]

In their survey of library users, Swope and Katzer found that 41 percent had questions, but fully 65 percent of them would *not* approach librarians. They conclude:

> Since it is not the user, but the library and librarians who are being called upon ever more frequently to justify their budget in terms of services provided, the burden of responsibility falls ever more heavily on librarians to make whatever changes are necessary to communicate a different message to their potential users.[91]

4.2.34 Carol Kronus (1973)[92]

Adopting a sociology of education perspective, Kronus succinctly reviews prior research, pointing out that much of it is based on simple correlations and hence confounded because of the nonindependence of variables. Thus, she argues the need for a more sophisticated approach, such as multiple regression and factor analytic studies.

Drawing upon a representative sample of 1019 Illinois residents, she found that all of the 14 variables previously identified by researchers resulted in mild correlations. However, Kronus found that use of public libraries in her regression and factor analytic study was dependent on three things, in order of importance: education (number of years and future plans), family life cycle (marital status, family size, and employment status), and urban residence. All told, she could explain about 20 percent of the variance.

Finally, Kronus found that age, gender, and ethnicity were not statistically significant factors in public library usage when intervening variables were controlled.

4.2.35 Helen Gothberg (1974)[93]

Gothberg reviews the extensive speech communications literature related to verbal and nonverbal transactions. She notes that Carl Rogers believed that empathy, warmth, and genuineness (or congruence) facilitated helping relationships and that Albert Mehrabian found that "total liking" of a person consisted of seven percent verbal liking plus 38 percent vocal liking plus 55 percent facial liking.[94]

Hence, she decided to study two reference librarians, one competent and the other expert, at the Weld County Public Library in Greely, Colorado using a two-by-two factorial design, where the librarians role-played immediacy and nonimmediacy (defined as directness and intensity measured by physical distance and body, especially head orientation and eye contact). She used Liebig's refinement of Frank and Anderson's instrument to rate user satisfaction.

Gothberg found that the "user was more satisfied with the reference interview when the reference librarian displayed immediate communication as opposed to non-immediate communication."[95] It is interesting that users were not more satisfied with the actual information transferred.[96]

4.2.36 Elaine Jennerich and Edward Jennerich (1974, 1976, 1980, 1981, and 1987)[97]

Using a rating sheet developed during her doctoral work, Jennerich suggested a five-point Likert scale of poor-to-excellent evaluating the reference librarian's nonverbal interviewing skills: (1) eye contact; (2) gestures; (3) relaxed posture; (4) facial expression as well as verbal skills; (5) remembering; (6) premature diagnosis; (7) reflect feelings verbally; (8) restate or paraphrase comments; (9) open questions; (10) encouragers; (11) closure; and (12) opinions, suggestions.[98]

In discussing the ideal characteristics of reference librarians, the Jennerichs identify 11 attributes: (1) sense of humor; (2) dedication or commitment;

(3) genuine liking for people; (4) good memory; (5) imagination; (6) creativity; (7) patience; (8) persistence; (9) energy; (10) stamina; (11) ability to jump quickly from one subject to another.[99]

4.2.37 James Benson and Ruth Maloney (1975)[100]

Benson and Maloney's goal is "to analyze the [reference] search process, isolating the pertinent elements that make up a search and identifying the many decision points in the search process."[101] Their three-element model reflects the 100-year-old paradigm identified in Chapter 1 of this book: (1) the query, (2) bibliographic bridge, and (3) system.[102]

According to them, the query consists of three components: (1) type (known item, further subdivided by fact, document, or bibliography vs. subject, further subdivided by general, specific, or research); (2) language (vocabulary); and (3) parameters (limitations). The "bibliographic bridge" consists of six steps: (1) clarify the query; (2) establish the search parameters; (3) identify the system; (4) translate the query; (5) conduct the actual search; and (6) deliver the information.

One of their most important contributions is recognition that "failure to locate requested information may be system-related or searcher-related."[103] In the case of a searcher-related failure, failure analysis may consist of:

1. Looking for an expected answer, with failure to recognize what is actually found.
2. Modifying the query to accommodate the searcher's prior knowledge of the system(s).
3. Misunderstanding the query.
4. Relying upon the accuracy of the query.
5. Relying upon the accuracy of the information within the system.[104]

To avoid these situations, Benson and Maloney recommend "a series of questions [which] can be applied to guide in the analysis: (1) Do I know what I am looking for? (2) Am I sure I have not found it? (3) At what points did I make decisions? (4) Taking each decision identified in order, were there alternative approaches I might have taken? (5) Having made the decision, did I proceed properly in following through on the decision made?"[105]

4.2.38 Laura Boyer and William Theimer (1975)[106]

Following Jestes and Laird's 1968 study recommending the use of students at reference desks, the authors surveyed a representative, stratified sample of 150 academic libraries to understand their local practices. Based on a return rate of 75 percent, they found that "in 69 percent of the reporting libraries, nonprofessionals *are* used at the reference desk."[107]

A later study of a single library confirms that nonprofessionals can handle at least 62 percent of the questions asked,[108] while two other library studies found significant differences in professionals and nonprofessionals' capabilities.[109]

4.2.39 Theodore Peck (1975)[110]

Peck assumes that reference librarians and counselors share similar tasks and that the former can learn from the latter. Drawing on the counseling psychology work of Delaney and Eisenberg as well as Krumboltz and Thoresen,[111] Peck hypothesizes that certain characteristics of the reference librarian are especially important for successful transactions. According to his informed personal opinion, the three most important attributes are: (1) empathy, defined as the "ability to understand how his client feels,"[112]; (2) attentive behavior, including good eye contact, proper body position such as a pleasing smile, leaning forward, and open hands; and (3) content listening, defined as "the process of asking questions and repeating to the patron his question in his own words or similar terminology"[113] includes paraphrasing. Nonattentive behavior, notably body positions, includes stiffness (and hence aloofness or disinterest), and slouching or slumping may equate as boredom or fatigue.

4.2.40 Virginia Boucher (1976)[114]

Defining nonverbal communication as "the exchange of information through nonlinguistic signs,"[115] Boucher proposes "to explore the implications of non-verbal communication, particularly body movement, for the library reference interview."[116] Drawing on the nonverbal communications research of Darwin, Birdwhistell, Ekman et al., Scheflen, Harrison, and Key, Boucher implicitly hypothesizes that reference librarians fall into either a preoccupation mode or an availability mode that influences question receipt and subsequent success in the reference interview. Boucher identifies six characteristics of the preoccupation mode: "[1] Arms across chest [2] Downward gaze so no eye contact possible [3] Frown of concentration, firm mouth [4] Hands busy with books, papers, pencils, telephone [5] Turned or leaning away, head bent down [and 6] Behind desk," and then seven characteristics of the availability mode: "[1] Arms relaxed—not covering up body [2] Eyes ready to contact those who enter [3] Smile of greeting, relaxed mouth, eyebrows lifted in attention [4] Hands relaxed [5] Leaning forward, head up [6] Willingness to leave desk [and 7] Head nods . . . of positive reinforcement."[117]

4.2.41 Ronald Powell (1976, 1978)[118]

This study focuses on reference materials. Testing 60 reference librarians on 25 questions out of a set of 50 real, fact-type, ready-reference questions, Powell hypothesized that with a larger collection, reference librarians would be able to answer a larger number of questions.[119] Performance (i.e., percentage of questions answered correctly) was significantly related: (1) nonlinearly to size of collection with diminishing returns at over 3500 reference titles, simple $r = .52$; (2) to librarian's perceived adequacy of reference collection, .50; (3) to librarian holding a professional degree; and (4) to the librarian's having taken a number of reference and bibliography courses, .25.[120] Although age and professional experience were not statistically significant in determining success, the number of substantive reference questions received per week was ($r = .52$).[121]

4.2.42 Mary Jo Lynch (1977, 1978)[122]

Examining the verbal aspects of the reference interview, Lynch seeks to answer three questions: (1) How often does the librarian negotiate the inquirer's initial question and does the frequency vary by (a) type of transaction? (holdings, substantive, or moving) or (b) when the librarian is less busy? (fewer than 11 questions per hour); (2) What information is sought?; and (3) Does the librarian use open- versus closed-ended questions?[123]

She found that the level of negotiation did vary by type of transaction: 35 percent of the holdings transactions were negotiated, 53 percent of the substantive, 78 percent of the moving, while the overall average was 49 percent of the time. She did not answer the second part of the first question.[124]

Using content analysis reminiscent of Vavrek's work, Lynch did find significant differences in her study of question negotiation. As for open versus closed questions, Lynch found that librarians used open-ended questions only 8 percent of the time while closed-ended questions were asked 90 percent of the time. Furthermore, only 13 percent of the initial or original questions required a major reformulation to discover the real question; however, if librarians are not using open-ended questions, she argues that they may be answering the initial, but not real, question in the case of substantive and moving transactions. Directional questions are probably what they appear to be.

In summary, Lynch found that reference librarians did not negotiate questions most of the time, and when they did, they used closed-ended questions, which do not elicit much additional information from the inquirer.

4.2.43 Marcia Myers (1977, 1980, 1983, and 1985)[125]

Based on responses to telephone queries in a stratified random sample of 40 southeastern academic libraries during 1977, Myers found a 49 percent (±1.5) accuracy at the 95 percent confidence level with 12 test questions, but "there was also evidence that even when the library owned the appropriate source, staff members either did not consult, did not know how to use, or misinterpreted the information given in the source. Additionally, staff members infrequently volunteered the source of their response."[126]

Librarians at universities did better than those at four-year colleges with graduate degrees, who did better than librarians at four-year colleges, who, in turn, did better than librarians at two-year colleges (which is really an indirect measure of the library's size). Those institutions with more than 85,000 volume collections or more than 10,000 volume reference departments did the best. Hours open (an indirect measure of commitment to service), especially those open more than 80 hours, also correlated strongly with high-quality service. Implications are that LIS instructors need to teach novices and advanced beginners how to exploit the library's resources to the fullest.

4.2.44 Mollie Sandock (1977)[127]

Studying a stratified random sample of every student enrolled during the Fall 1975 term at the University of Chicago, the author hypothesized that many students were unaware of such library services as reference. Based on telephone interviews, she found that 38 percent did not know where the reference department was located; other knowledge of other services ranged from 33 to 65 percent. Upon closer inspection, she discovered that most of these students who did not know the location were: (1) freshmen; (2) graduate students in the sciences; and (3) students in their first quarter of study at the University of Chicago. Hence, she concludes that a publicity campaign is necessary to ensure that such potential users are aware of reference department services. A similar study of Lake Forest College students is reported in the next decade.[128]

4.2.45 Thomas Eichman (1978)[129]

Drawing upon the Shannon–Weaver model of communication as modified by D.K. Berlo, Searle's speech acts, Leech's functional view of language, and Heilprin's threshold of stability, Eichman focuses on the inquirer's opening reference question. He hypothesizes that ease of access explains why inquirers ask their colleagues first; in passing, he also mentions Taylor's work on this point.

Eichman points out that several preparatory conditions must be present for a successful reference transaction; first, the inquirer's belief and sincerity, followed by the librarian's confidence. "The [inquirer's] speech act counts essentially as an attempt to elicit information from the hearer [the librarian]."[130] In other words, in order for the inquirer to ask a question, he must have confidence in the librarian's ability to respond and the librarian must be empathetic throughout the exchange in order to maintain the inquirer's confidence.

Using Leech's five functions of language (i.e., the expressive, phatic, informational, aesthetic, and directive), Eichman argues that the inquirer's initial question must be general because it must perform several functions, notably the expressive, phatic, and informational at once. Then,

> if the librarian is also careful not to include in the initial response anything seriously challenging the motivational or other emotional aspects of the inquirer's opening speech act, the librarian's initial response rephrasing the proposition will also help satisfy the expressive function of the inquirer's speech act.[131]

In summary, Eichman's work lays a foundation of a reference readiness theory and helps explain that the inquirer's initial phrasing of the question is often quite general due to the phatic function of language.

4.2.46 James Rettig (1978)[132]

After a moderately extensive review of the literature and a general lament about the literature merely describing the process rather than presenting a theoretical or conceptual approach that would explain why things proceed the way they do during the reference transaction, Rettig proposes the necessity of adding feedback and background noise into any model of the reference process.

While he raises the question "how message-receiving ability relates to the ability to provide the level of service a patron wants" without answering it, he does relate effectively how Wyer's three levels of service (conservative, moderate, and liberal, or Rothstein's minimum, middling, and maximum) should vary according to the inquirer's information need. He observes that ALA's RASD's "A Commitment to Information Services" affirms his view.[133]

4.2.47 Marcia Bates (1979)[134]

Her objective was "to focus on and use the strengths and flexibility of human thinking processes" in order to identify short-term tactics used in four categories: monitoring, file structure, search formulation, and term.[135] Monitoring tactics include: (1) check; (2) weigh; (3) pattern; (4) correct; and (5) record. File structure tactics encompass: (1) bibble; (2) select; (3) survey; (4) cut; (5) stretch; (6) scaffold; and (7) cleave. Search formulation tactics consist of: (1) specify; (2) exhaust; (3) reduce; (4) parallel; (5) pinpoint; and (6) block. Term tactics entail: (1) super; (2) sub; (3) relate; (4) neighbor; (5) trace; (6) vary; (7) fix; (8) rearrange; (9) contrary; (10) respell; and (11) respace.[136]

In her article on idea tactics, Bates identifies seventeen tactics based on a review of relevant literature: (1) think; (2) brainstorm; (3) meditate; (4) consult; (5) rescue; (6) wander; (7) catch; (8) break; (9) breach; (10) reframe; (11) notice; (12) jolt; (13) change; (14) focus; (15) dilate; (16) skip; and (17) stop.[137]

Like much of the previous professional literature, this work is based on "my own experience and thinking, from the literature, and from the comments of colleagues and students"; in other words, another armchair reflection of the reference process.[138] No explicit research methodology is presented so that the study could be replicated by someone else. Although her work can be considered brilliant, synthetic, and intuitively correct, it has not yet been rigorously tested or validated to show that these tactics are actually used as suggested by Neill (1984). As a facilitation and teaching model that may lead to testable hypotheses, it remains provocative, nonetheless.

4.2.48 John Larsen (1979)[139]

Following in Bonk's footsteps, Larsen surveyed the 63 accredited LIS programs, receiving usable responses from 31 schools. "Three additional schools do not discuss reference sources by type, format, or specific title, devoting the basic reference course to 'the communication process.' "[140] The total number of titles presented to graduate students ranged from 61 to 615; the mode was 160; median, 229; and mean, 243.

A statistical manipulation of Larsen's table to match Bonk's is impossible, so Table 4.3 is ordered according to the largest number of titles in each format presented in library schools. "In the present survey, seven titles were listed by all thirty-one schools. They included two encyclopedias, *New Encyclopedia Britannica* (fifteenth edition), and *World Book Encyclopedia;* two biographical sources, *Current Biography* and *Dictionary of American Biography;* two indexes, *New York Times Index* and *Reader's Guide to Periodical Literature;* and one yearbook, *World Almanac.*"[141]

4.2.49 Elaine Rich (1979)[142]

Written from a computer science perspective, Rich raises the issue of how reference librarians can effectively use stereotyping behavior (i.e., "clusters of characteristics") based on a handful of visual cues (e.g., age, clothing, and gender) and aural cues (e.g., geographical origin and "self-assurance") from the inquirer.[143] Stereotypes are similar to scripts, frames, and schemas. Her work has led to a new field called user modeling, which distinguishes systems based on a canonical user or a truly individual user.

4.2.50 Thomas Childers (1980)[144]

Continuing his long-term interest in the evaluation of reference service, Childers reports on a 1977 study of 1110 unobtrusive queries by proxies at 57 public libraries in Suffolk County, New York. He included five types of test questions requiring: (1) factual information; (2) bibliographical infor-

Table 4.3
Most Frequently Taught Formats and Titles[a]

Format with most titles	Most frequently presented title
1. Encyclopedias	*Encyclopedia Britannica*, 15th ed.
2. Yearbooks	*World Almanac*
3. Biography	*Current Biography*
4. Indexes	*New York Times Index*
5. Serial publications	*International Periodical Directory*
6. Bibliography	*Books in Print*
7. Dictionaries	Murray, *Oxford English Dictionary*
8. Geographical materials	*Columbia-Lippincott Gazetteer*
9. Directories	*Encyclopedia of Associations*
10. Audiovisual materials	*Media Review Digest*
11. Government publications	*Monthly Catalog of U.S. Pub's*
12. Handbooks	*Statistical Abstract of U.S.*

[a] Modified from Larsen (1979), Table 2 and 3 combined.

mation; (3) local government agency information; (4) further negotiation (which he called "escalator" questions); and (5) referral to nonlibrary resources.

He presents eight major findings: (1) an actual answer was offered 56 percent of the time; (2) 84 percent of these answers were correct or mostly correct; (3) 16 percent were wrong or mostly wrong; (4) only 17 percent of the time neither an answer nor a referral was given; (5) 66 percent of the referrals were to nonlibraries; (6) 66 percent of the nonlibrary referrals were correct; (7) 67 percent of the time librarians made no attempt to probe escalator-type questions; and so (8) only 20 percent got to the third and final step of these questions.

Childers raises issues such as when is it appropriate to negotiate further; when or how soon does one refer; how responsible is the library for its answers or referrals; and what constitutes a correct, mostly correct, or wrong answer. He also includes two brief, but informative, examples of failure to deal responsibly with legitimate reference questions.

4.2.51 Linda Morgan (1980)[145]

Intrigued by architectural influences on reference service, Morgan examined user preferences for reference desks versus counters. She found that 72 percent preferred the counter, even waiting there when the reference desk was free.

4.2.52 Nancy Van House DeWath (1981, 1984)[146]

If for no other reason, this study is noteworthy for its methodological use of a panel of experienced reference librarians from outside the study area (i.e., California) to judge the quality of responses; they found that 79 percent were complete and correct, 15 percent mostly correct, one percent partially correct, two percent incorrect, and four percent yielded no answer. Test questions were mostly fact-type or broad requests, like requests for pictures or instructions. The average cost per reference question was $31, but this and other factors, such as time, were not correlated with correctness.

4.2.53 Marilyn White (1981, 1983, and 1985)[147]

In her earliest work, White found that pauses or the "pacing" of the reference interview significantly influenced the inquirer's responses. She found that either no pauses or pauses of more than ten seconds had a negative influence on eliciting more information from the inquirer; the former meant that the inquirer could not get a word in edgewise, while the latter signaled lack of interest or termination of the transaction on the part of the reference librarian.

For her 1983 work, White draws upon human cognitive information processing and Minsky's concept of frames from AI research. She relates information about the role of memory, notably that the brain can remember only about seven items (cf. Vavrek's work on the number of elements in a typical reference question); that there is short-term memory loss after 30 seconds; transfers to long-term memory take five to ten seconds; and simple question recognition may take two to five seconds. She believes that reference librarians use Minsky's frames to classify reference questions[148] and are involved in a pattern-matching process.

White accepts Taylor's basic model, but illustrating it with three examples, she goes on to postulate a more complex interaction between Q1, Q2, Q3, and Q4 than the simple linear relationship that has previously been thought to exist.[149] In particular, White argues that the librarian's motivation to move back to Q1 from Q4 is based on a concern for possible errors that may have crept in, while Q2 and Q3 may be influenced by the inquirer's problem-solving skills and knowledge of information sources.[150]

Extending her original work, White proposes to evaluate the reference interview by looking for seven content topics: "(1) the problem behind the question, (2) the subject of the question, including its relationship to other areas, (3) the nature of the service to be provided . . . , (4) the internal constraints affecting the client's actual use of information . . . , (5) external constraints affecting use . . . , (6) prior search history, and (7) some assessment of the probability of a successful search,"[151] and eleven indicators of good form: "(1) a positive, helpful attitude, (2) the absence of behavior that develops defensiveness in the client . . . , (3) the use of open questions when appropriate, (4) the use of probing or follow-up questions when necessary, (5) the use of closed questions when possible, (6) minimal interference in the flow of information for extraneous comments . . . , (7) sensitivity to the client's frame of reference . . . , (8) good, attentive listening, (9) a final summary . . . stating the characteristics of the acceptable answer, (10) use of other appropriate techniques of interviewing, and (11) no distracting personal mannerisms. . . ."[152]

4.2.54 Peter Hernon and Charles McClure (1983)[153]

Studying the reference service given in academic government document depository libraries in the northeast and southwest, Hernon and McClure found extraordinarily low success rates. Overall, only 37 percent of their unobtrusive questions were answered correctly, but that figure drops even lower when the day (3% on Saturday and Sunday) or time of day (15% in evening vs. 42–43% during the morning or afternoon) is taken into consideration. Six factors including staff size, volumes held, depository items selected, and budget did not show any statistically significant relationship to accuracy.

4.2.55 Esther E. Horne (1983)[154]

In an experimental design, Horne studied the "inquiry process" or the "need 'to know'" of 198 LIS students asked to frame questions based on a text. Conceptually, she posits two types of questions (open or Kendon's "unsaturated" vs. closed or his "saturated") and two types of acceptable answers: finite versus infinite alternative (based on Belnap and Steels' work; see Chapter 3). She hypothesized that the number of questions would vary directly or inversely with the information need. She found that "questioning behavior, while *idiosyncratic,* does present a pattern and a trend occurring within the constraints of a 'closed' problem situation."[155]

4.2.56 S. D. Neill (1984)[156]

Based on Lynch's and Dewdney's[157] transcriptions of reference transactions, Neill illustrates three different types of memory devices: (1) semantic memory, "which organizes things into lists and categories;" (2) episodic memory, which "points to the importance of experience and the usefulness of specific episodes;" and (3) schematic memory, organized spatially or temporally rather than categorically, is based on prior experience and subsequent expectations.[158] AI researchers such as Minsky and Schrank and Abelson have drawn heavily on this third category for their own work.

Neill asserts that the initial inquiry "will be more general than the question the patron has in mind."[159]

4.2.57 Ethel Auster and Stephen Lawton (1984)[160]

One of the most sophisticated statistical studies of the reference process, this confirmatory study of White's earlier work involved a factor analysis of the types of questions (open vs. closed), length of pauses (none or moderate), extent of inquirer's prior knowledge of the query, and the importance of the information problem as perceived by the inquirer.

Their findings indicate that the reference librarian's use of open questions leads to an inquirer learning more as well as higher satisfaction. However, they also found that long pauses (i.e., ten seconds or more) had a negative effect on quality but that it might be due to their difficulty in training reference librarians to adopt this type of behavior. Finally, "those having a greater need for information are harder to satisfy than are those who have a lesser need."[161]

4.2.58 Charles Patterson (1984)[162]

Patterson attempts to answer Jahoda's 1981 questions about the necessary versus merely desirable traits for successful reference librarians. He believes the following traits are necessary: outgoing personality, logical mind, inquiring mind, and effectiveness on the job,[163] and the following seven are desirable ones: good memory, judgment, imagination, thoroughness, orderliness, persistence, and accuracy.[164] He believes that some, if not all, of these are unteachable, however. Rather, it is the instructor's responsibility to identify students with these innate traits and encourage them to go into reference work.

Another Jahoda question is whether students should know specific titles when they may be going into widely varying types and sizes of libraries. Patterson's informed opinion is that they should know specific titles, but he begs the rest of the question—whether the list of titles should vary by type and size of library.

4.2.59 Kathy Way (1984, 1987)[165]

In a telephone survey of two academic law depository libraries during different times of the day, Way found that sources were cited 74 percent of the time. Although the success rate was highest for MLS/JDs (75%), there was no statistically significant difference between them and MLS holders (69%) or nonprofessionals (53%). This fact may be due to the nature of the test questions, which were basic, fact-type questions that did not require the advanced, subject skills of the MLS/JD librarians.

4.2.60 Ralph Gers and Lillie Seward (1985)[166]

With help from the University Research Foundation of the University of Maryland, the State Division of Library Development and Services in Maryland conducted a major study of inquirer perception of quality reference service. Using a modified version of the Crowley–Childers' test,[167] a set of 40 questions was asked in 60 branch libraries in 22 counties.

Findings indicated a statewide average of about 55 percent accuracy. Further analysis indicated that quality could be improved by: (1) getting the facts through an increased level of question negotiation; (2) setting the tone by the librarian communicating a higher interest level (e.g., more eye contact); (3) giving the inquirer more information by the librarian indicating an increased comfort level in the process (e.g., attentive comments, asking relevant questions); and (4) asking more follow-up questions (e.g., "does this completely answer your question?").[168] Oddly, they found that accuracy increased only slightly during high demand (i.e., busy) periods. The fourth behavior was observed only 12 percent of the time, yet this one step "may be the single most important factor in the interview."[169]

Interestingly, eighty-seven percent of the reference questions asked in Maryland public libraries could be effectively answered with just seven titles: (1) *World Almanac;* (2) *Information Please Almanac;* (3) *World Book Encyclopedia;* (4) *Stevenson's Home Book of Quotations;* (5) *Reader's Guide to Periodicals;* (6) *Motor's* or *Chilton Auto Manual;* and (7) an unabridged dictionary.[170]

4.2.61 Brenda Dervin and Patricia Dewdney (1986)[171]

Based on thirteen years of empirical research, Dervin and her coauthor propose that the inquirer's information need can be characterized as an attempt at "sense-making" that is "situationally bound."[172] Specifically, they propose a tripartite model of information need that is composed of a situation, a gap or stoppages, and uses. Interviews with 17 public librarians about troublesome reference interviews substantiate Taylor's second filter (motivation and use objective) as the most important one, although without explicitly saying so or referring to his work at this point.[173]

Although they identify the reference librarian's three options of closed, open, and neutral questions, they warn against the first because "all closed questions involve [a possibly premature] judgment already made by the librarian of what is relevant to the user."[174] Instead, they provide a set of illustrative neutral questions for use in negotiations and strongly recommend these as opposed to leading, but open questions, although they do not use the term "leading" in their article.

In her doctoral study of 24 reference librarians in three Ontario public libraries, Dewdney found that the inquirer's initial satisfaction was already high, and that satisfaction with those librarians trained in Dervin's neutral questioning and Jennerich's microcounseling skills actually decreased over time. However, those librarians trained in neutral questioning were rated higher on premature diagnosis, use of open questions, and closure.

4.2.62 Joan Durrance (1986)[175]

Assuming that users of reference services are the best judges of quality service, Durrance and graduate students conducted 429 personal interviews with library users of three mid-west academic libraries as they left the reference department during the morning, afternoon, evening, and weekends hours (the interviews, however, were weighted toward afternoons and evenings). Her objective was to examine factors affecting the client–librarian relationship. Her variables included: (1) "user knowledge of staff differentiation"; (2) recognition of staff members (including "the ability to identify library staff members by name"); (3) inclination to ask questions (including "the inclination to look for particular staff"); and (4) inclination to avoid staff members; and (5) "inclination to return."[176]

She found that: (1) 84 percent of the users thought that staff differences existed, but most did not know with any certainty; (2) more than half of the users used appearance (e.g., older) or environment (e.g., behind the desk) clues to establish to which category a staff member belonged; (3) "only 10 percent of all users look for particular staff," which the author interprets as a lack of a true client–librarian relationship;[177] (4) most users had no criteria by which to select a librarian (including appearance, expertise, and personal knowledge); and (5) reasons given for avoiding certain staff included "negative style of the staff member, based on past experience or perception . . . [or] past experience unrelated to expertise."[178]

4.2.63 Roma Harris and Gillian Michell (1986, 1987)[179]

The purpose of this experimental design (a $2 \times 2 \times 2 \times 2 \times 2$ fully crossed design) was to determine the effect of gender, appearance, and verbal and nonverbal behavior on the assessed quality of reference service where videotaped actors played the parts of librarians and users. The judges were 320 male and female users of a medium-sized public library randomly assigned to watch one of sixteen videotapes.

Most viewers of the tapes found high levels of perceived competence in the "librarians" regardless of level of warmth or "inclusiveness" displayed. Gender differences emerged; male librarians were perceived more competent if they were inclusive but not warm while female librarians were judged more competent when they were warm regardless of their inclusiveness. Female users wanted librarians who were less inclusive than male users.

While reference librarians may count other attributes such as professional expertise and knowledge of the library's collection highly, the users' judgment of the professionalism and competence of the reference librarian seem to depend more on communication skills: warmth and inclusiveness.

Their carry-on study asked a total of 64 male and female librarians from different types of libraries to view a subset of the same videotapes. Then comparisons were drawn between the two groups of users and librarians. The authors found that: (1) "the librarians were harder to please than the library patrons with respect to competence in the reference interview"; (2) "female librarians who watched the tapes in which low inclusion was demonstrated gave lower perceived warmth ratings than the male and female patrons who watched the same condition," suggesting to the authors that female librarians may be out of touch with user reactions or that they have higher performance standards; (3) librarians, regardless of gender, thought the librarian who showed more warmth to be more competent, leading the authors to conclude that "the demeanor of the librarian toward the patron during the reference interview may be just as important as competently retrieving information;" other differences were based on the librarian's type of library and location.[180]

Their most significant conclusion is that female librarians differ in their helping styles; they value "inclusiveness" and a teaching role in reference work, while female library users prefer warmth rather than being included.[181] This serious conflict warrants further research.[182]

4.2.64 Jo Whitlatch (1987, 1990)[183]

Studying 257 reference transactions from five academic libraries in northern California, the author tested a model with eight independent variables including service orientation, feedback, and type of assistance, while the dependent variables included librarian, user evaluations of service rendered, and the user's success in finding the necessary material. Overall, her most significant conclusion is that the librarians' evaluation of service quality could substitute for the users' evaluation in 83 percent of the cases because their evaluations were the same or lower than the users' (echoing Harris and Gillian).

4.2.65 George Hawley (1987)[184]

The objective of this Rutgers doctoral dissertation was "to identify factors that influence library referral."[185] Referral includes in-house as well as out-of-building referrals to individuals, libraries, and other organizations. Structured interviews were conducted with 34 librarians (22 women and 12 men) at five academic and five public libraries in the northeast.

His findings support Childers's finding that libraries infrequently provide referral, only about 17 percent of the time.[186] Otherwise, his findings are purely descriptive; he identifies many possible factors but does not provide a metric for measuring these factors or their interactions. Nonetheless, individual factors influencing referral include: extent of training and experience; knowledge of outside resources and their strength (especially interaction with faculty for academic librarians); efficiency; equity; achievement motivation; empathy; tact; and independence. Factors related to the user or client are: physical; mental attitudes about distance and about travel information; attitudes about travel safety; monetary costs; and feedback (e.g., none, little, much, and organized). Institutional factors include: interaction with the director; interaction with coworkers; activity level at reference desk; strength of collection; and the availability and use of referral tools. Factors related to the referral individual, library, or organization include: helpful outside resources; ambiguous or unhelpful outside resources; and institutional policies toward outsiders.

4.2.66 Prince George's County Memorial Library System, MD (1990)[187]

Dedicated to the notion of continuous improvement of reference quality, this library system took the 1985 Maryland findings to heart, started a series of staff workshops, and has worked hard to improve reference quality. By 1990, three of the 19 branches could report 95 percent accuracy in unobtrusive studies of reference service using a modified Childers–Crowley methodology; in fact, surveyors found an "unusual uniformity in the staff use of reference behaviors, and that the PGCMLS staff projected an image of cordiality, competence and professionalism in responding to their survey questions over the telephone." Overall, the 19 branches averaged 77.4 percent accuracy, while more than half the branches were above 80 percent accurate.

4.3
Elements in the Reference Transaction

As described in the preceding section, the reference transaction is a complex process based on (1) "the number of elements in the system" ($N = 44$); (2) "the attributes of the elements;" (3) "the number of interactions among the elements" ($N = 5$); and (4) "the degree of inherent organization."[188] Yet, a model of the reference transaction, realized as a flowchart, can be deduced from the preceding review of nearly 100 pieces of research literature (see Figure 4.1).[189] The following section discusses the research results topically according to the reference process or flow.

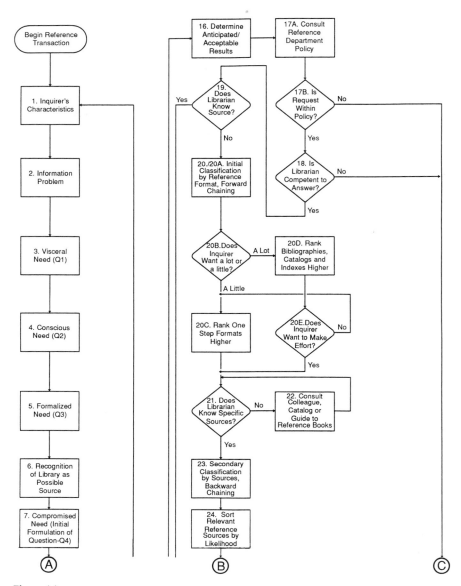

Figure 4.1
A Flowchart Model of General Reference Transactions. Copyright © 1995
by John V. Richardson, UCLA GSE&IS.

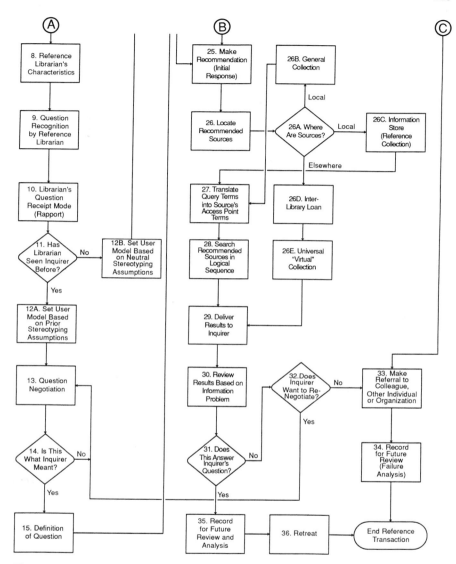

Figure 4.1 (Continued)

4.3.1 The Inquirer/User

Much of the recent work has focused on this dimension of the paradigm. And the work draws on psychological and linguistic research; this emphasis may be due to Noam Chomsky's influence. In any event, there is a great deal of interest in this element of the paradigm. Although Neill (1984) presents a good model of the user/inquirer and Dervin and Dewdney (1986) have developed a good model of the inquirer's information problem, a more sophisticated approach could draw upon motivational theories, especially the work of Frederick Herzberg, David McClelland, Abraham Maslow, and Victor H. Vroom.[190]

Perhaps the time has come to move beyond Taylor and Perry's work and to make a more searching examination to reach a deeper understanding of the inquirer's query process and hence provide the basis for a true information *science*. Fulfilling, or at least satisfying,[191] the inquirer's need is the reason we have reference service. Our status or respect as a field will take care of itself if we take care of fulfilling the user's need.

4.3.1.1 Inquirer's Characteristics

In the preceeding sections, the inquirer has been characterized by 16 variables including age, gender, education, educational plans, income, occupation, ethnicity, marital status, urban–rural residence, family size, employment status, county size rank, geographical mobility, college preference, reading skill, and clusters of factors such as socioeconomic status (notably, education, income, and occupation).

The inquirer has been studied in different settings. As for public library usage, Kronus (1973) establishes the influence of education, family life cycle, and urban residence. Further, Taylor (1962) reminds us to ask of scientific workers: "what is the inquirer's status in the organization, has he been in the library before, what relationship does his inquiry have to what he knows, what is his level of critical awareness?" Sandock (1977) and Durfee (1986) also found college student users unaware of services.

All these contextual variables, what might be termed "personal frames of reference," determine the specific type of information problem (see below). Similarly, Eichman (1978) points out that the attitudes, social system, and cultural attributes of the inquirer are significant factors in determining the information problem and especially the phrasing of the inquirer's opening question.

Rich (1979) suggests that the user should be able to modify the system to suit themselves. Her work also recommends that reference librarians build user models, based on stereotyping based on such factors as those sixteen mentioned above, which can then trigger certain responses.[192] Indirectly, Neill (1984) proposes that such an inquirer schema is operating as part of the reference librarian's memory.[193]

In any event, more research could be undertaken to develop and to make such operative models explicit.

4.3.1.2 Information Problem

Rees and Saracevic (1963) provide a good working definition: "An *information problem* is the 'motivational source' of the formulation of a question."[194] Taylor (1962) points out that "in the first place we are assuming that the need for information is something distinct and traceable."[195] It is an "area of doubt" to use Taylor's terminology. Shera (1964) suggests that the inquirer will judge the relevance and pertinence of the librarian's response against the original information problem and its characteristics.

In the most sophisticated work to date, Dervin and Dewdney (1986) offer a sense-making model by seeking universals in the inquirer's movement through time–space. This physical or cognitive movement (also referred to as "the situation") can be stopped by what they call gaps or "lack of sense," which is highly suggestive of Taylor's phrase, "area of doubt".[196] The inquirer's movement beyond this area or gap is termed their hoped-for "uses" of the desired information. A neutral statement such as, "Tell me how this problem arose" would get back to the situation.[197]

Finally, Rettig (1978) argues that the inquirer's information problem is what should cause the reference librarian's service philosophy to vary among Wyer's so-called levels of service (i.e., conservative, moderate, liberal or what Rothstein terms minimum, middling, or maximum).[198]

4.3.1.3 Visceral Need (Q1)

Simply put, Perry and Taylor's Q1 is what the inquirer needs. Initially, question formation begins as a result of the "conscious and unconscious need for information not existing in the remembered experience of the inquirer."[199] At this point, however, the question is unexpressed; Crum (1969) argues it is physiologically based. Parrott (1988) simply calls it a "vague disquiet."[200] Today, cognitive psychologists would refer to it as subsymbolic knowledge.

White (1983) argues that "the librarian's initial emphasis on moving back toward Q1 rather than moving from Q3 to Q4 is dictated in part by concern about errors that may have crept into the question as it went through the early stages."[201]

Auster and Lawton's (1984) contribution is to demonstrate that the greater the inquirer's need, the harder it is to satisfy.[202]

4.3.1.4 Conscious Need (Q2)

According to Perry (1961) but quoting Taylor, "the next form of need is the conscious mental description of an ill-defined area of indecision."[203] In other words, it is still within-brain (or neural), but it is what he thinks he needs. It appears to exist symbolically. Dervin and Dewdney (1986) suggest that asking a neutral question such as "What are you trying to do in this situation" would be helpful to get at the conscious need.[204]

4.3.1.5 Formalized Need (Q3)

Drawing upon Perry, Taylor (1968) defined the formalized need as the inquirer's "properly qualified and rational statement of his question."[205] This level of need is what reference librarians often call the real question; it is real, concrete; it is what he wants. Much of the time, though, the reference interview can focus on the transition from Q3 to Q4, according to White.[206]

4.3.1.6 Recognition of the Library as a Possible Source

One can categorize inquirers according to a tripartite scheme: (1) library reference service users, (2) potential users, and (3) hard-core nonusers. Swope and Katzer (1972) found users had legitimate library questions, but 65 percent would not approach the librarians. Use of the library's reference department is based on: (1) the inquirer's awareness, including recommendations from friends or acquaintances or public awareness campaigns; (2) prior experience, either positive or negative; and (3) ease of access, best stated by the principle of least effort (i.e., the inquirer's proximity).[207]

Lubans (1971) found that student nonusers may be using another library, but that they prefer to consult a faculty member in any event. He cites nine reasons for nonuse of the library's reference service: (1) does not know it exists (or does not know your brand); (2) can't find it; (3) doesn't need it; (4) doesn't understand it; (5) doesn't expect good service; (6) had trouble in the past; (7) doesn't trust it; (8) uncompetitive value; and (9) prefers another.[208]

Jahoda and Culnan (1968) recommend that reference librarians focus on unasked questions, although such questions may not constitute a particularly large number.[209] Nelson, however, argues that 50 percent of the population is unaware of library services including reference. Studies by Sandock (1977) and Durfee (1986) seem to confirm this finding.

4.3.1.7 Compromised Need (Q4)

The compromised need is the linguistic expression, a question, as presented to the librarian. Rees and Saracevic (1963) refer to this need as the "initial formulation of [the] question,"[210] while Shera (1964) calls it "the inquiry."[211] Although the formalized need and the compromised need are sometimes the same, it appears to be a rare event based on Vavrek's 1971 research.[212] He has discovered that the initial question can have up to nine elements, but most often the opening phrasing has few elements, perhaps two or three at most; in other words, it is expressed quite generally. Eichman (1978) has explained the general nature of the opening question is due to the necessity of "expressing something about the speaker and establishing a channel to the other's mind."[213]

Undoubtedly, the real question is modified to some degree based on the inquirer's expectations as well as the librarian's characteristics. In any event, while it is what he says he wants, the librarian must avoid the temptation to give him what he says he wants because it is nearly always "more general than the question . . . in mind," according to Neill (1984).[214]

4.3.2 The Reference Librarian

Research has identified many of the reference librarian's mental habits, traits, or characteristics needed for successful service. The psychological processes operating during the reference interview, especially question negotiation, are fairly well understood. Yet, little research has examined the reference librarian's methods of problem solving and decision making after this question clarification phase (see Chapter 5 for a solution). Bates (1979) is one of the few to identify the more specific idea and search tactics that might be involved, but these have not been tested.

4.3.2.1 Librarian's Characteristics

Perceptual research has found that the inquirer does not know who is serving him, but makes judgments based on appearance or image[215] as well as previous experience with the staff member, library, or even another institution.[216] Such a finding leads to the idea of name or position tags to identify reference librarians as such.[217]

Although most textbook writers have ignored this element, Wyer identified twenty-seven characteristics of successful reference librarians; Thomas et al., fifteen; Jennerich and Jennerich, eleven; Patterson, ten; Hutchins, six; Katz, five; and Peck, three. The consensual core list of mental traits contains six characteristics: (1) imagination, (2) perseverance, (3) judgment, (4) professional knowledge, (5) good memory, and (6) speed.[218]

The importance of education, specifically broad subject knowledge, must be considered according to Stych (1972), although Breed (1955) found that the professional knowledge associated with library specialization including on-the-job experience was more valuable in general reference work. The SUNY system (1967) found the subject questions (i.e., technical ones) more difficult. Similarly, Benson and Maloney (1975) and the SUNY system study argue for the importance of in-depth knowledge of the collection. Way (1984) found that advanced technical degrees were not helpful in answering basic, fact-type questions.

Other research by Bunge (1967) and Powell (1976 and 1978) about experience per se is equivocal; Bunge says it is a factor, Powell says no.

Both agree that the reference librarian's age is not a significant factor in successful transactions.

Crum (1969) encourages reference librarians to think of ways to communicate: (1) warmth, (2) interest, and (3) approachability. In fact, warmth is strongly linked to the inquirer's perception of the reference librarian's professionalism and competence.[219] Further, Harris and Michell (1986 and 1987) point to differences between female librarians and female users regarding the desired degree of inclusiveness.

4.3.2.2 Question Recognition and Receipt Mode

White's 1983 research suggests that question recognition may take two to five seconds.[220] The inquirer is looking for more than "courteous recognition" or "empty sincerity."[221] As Crum (1969) put it, "the customer has full confidence that the librarian's attention and interest are focused on meeting his needs."[222] This confidence is communicated by nonverbal cues: posture and expression. Reference department policies about not reading at the desk are motivated by this necessity.

The reference librarian can be in either of two modes upon recognition of the inquirer's question: what Boucher (1976) calls preoccupation versus availability.[223] Maxfield (1954) indicated that reference librarians should (1) suspend judgment, (2) build understanding using tact and patience, and (3) communicate and collaborate with the inquirer.[224] According to Gothberg's 1974 findings, the inquirer is more satisfied when the reference librarian is in the availability mode. "Availability" can be considered as demonstrating immediacy rather than nonimmediacy behavior.[225] Peck warns against "non-attentive behavior."[226]

Other researchers have shown that length of time on the reference desk is a significant intervening factor in determining in which mode inquirers encounter reference librarians; without a doubt they found that time on the desk strongly effects reference accuracy.[227] Time of day as well as day of the week were significant factors in Hernon and McClure (1983).

4.3.2.3 Have You Seen the Inquirer Before?

A good internal question for the reference librarians to ask themselves is "have I worked with the inquirer before?" If the answer is yes, the reference librarian can recall certain things useful in establishing the inquirer's potential need. Librarians should remember to maintain a warm and inclusive style, based on research by Harris and Michell (1986 and 1987).

4.3.2.4 User Modeling and Stereotyping Assumptions

To establish a reliable user model, Rich (1979) points out that one can draw upon visual cues such as age, clothing, and gender as well as aural cues (for instance, geographical origin or self-assurance); these data all provide useful stereotyping cues or triggers.[228]

If one has not worked with the inquirer before, then Rich suggests setting middle-of-the-road values and then asking the appropriate questions in order to establish a valid user model. Neill's 1984 work "points to the value of experience and the usefulness of specific episodes" in shaping inquirer and librarian expectations just prior to question negotiation.[229]

4.3.2.5 Question Negotiation

Crum (1969) defined question negotiation as "a process of iterative reformulation and refinement of the initial question."[230] The objective of this process is to extract as many clues from the inquirer as possible so that the librarian can ascertain "what the inquirer intends to do with the answer to his question"[231] and learn possible sources of the answer, while establishing good rapport and putting the inquirer at ease. Although negotiation may not always be necessary, Jahoda has identified eight situations when it is appropriate.[232]

The entire process can be highly structured in practice; it has been analyzed in more detail than other processes in the transaction. Early on, Wood (1952) recognized that the clarification process is more difficult than the classification process because inquirers do not often state the real question and two or three exchanges may be required before discovering the information need; King's 1972 work suggests that open-ended questions would be better than closed-ended ones while Dervin and Dewdney's 1986 research tends to prove that neutral (i.e., nonleading) questions are the best ones to ask in order to get to the real question (i.e., the visceral need).[233] Auster and Lawton (1984) demonstrated that inquirers are more satisfied and learn more when reference librarians use open-ended questions.

Working backward all the way to the information problem, the importance of open-ended questions, such as "What do you intend to do with this information?"[234] or "To your knowledge what will probably be the most fruitful area in which to search?" or "I'm sorry, but this subject means nothing to me. Will you please tell me more?"[235] becomes paramount (as does persistence), according to Taylor and to Crum. These kinds of questions simplify the reference librarian's task, which is to work backward through the so-called "five filters" of Taylor to the earliest stages of the question. As Eichman (1978) points out, the utility of obtaining specific information during question negotiation is a narrowing strategy.

Unfortunately, several studies including those by Lynch (1977) and Childers (1980) have found that questions are not negotiated as much as they should be. Finally, Morgan's 1980 work suggests that users would prefer to approach librarians at the counter to do the question negotiation.

4.3.2.6 Is This What You Meant?

Asking "Is this what you meant?" or some closed-ended variation of this question is a good way to end the question negotiation process and proceed to the next step. This simple question builds feedback into the system.

4.3.2.7 Definition of the Question/Negotiated Question

As a result of the question negotiation process, the reference librarian achieves clarification of the informational need. Indeed, the inquirer's initial question may change due to feedback from the librarian and ultimately the question may be cast in terms that the information system can deliver (i.e., the compromised question in its fullest sense). Taylor suggests that "We redefine the problem to match the search strategy."[236]

Vavrek's 1971 research indicates that the negotiated question often has significantly more elements in it than did the initial question; in other words, the real question is more complex. In these situations, Bates' monitoring tactic to record the question seems appropriate. Even so, some questions may not be answerable according to Jahoda and Braunagel.[237]

4.3.2.8 Determining Anticipated/Acceptable Answers

Writers have used different terms to describe this part of the process, including such terms as constraints, filters, limitations, and parameters. Rees and Saracevic (1963) found eight restrictions on acceptable answers.[238] Based on his empirical research, Taylor (1968) found five filters operating in answering questions; his fifth and last was "anticipated or acceptable answers."[239] Because these are not strictly the same, the suitability of the librarian's response should really be determined by the inquirer's need (i.e., Q1).

Rees and Saracevic (1963) suggests that the range of acceptable answers is based on the inquirer's expectations related to quantity, effort, sequencing, and value of the information.[240] Similarly, Jahoda (1974) found that type, size, and level of answer were significant in determining acceptability.[241]

Among other limiting factors, Stych (1972) identifies language[242] while Benson and Maloney (1975) discuss the effect of pertinence, relevance, and precision on search parameters.[243] Finally, White suggests it is worth paying close attention in "lengthy interviews to the . . . characteristics of the acceptable answer."[244] The risk is not answering the real question, which is, of course, unacceptable. In checklist fashion, Jahoda and Braunagel (1980) have pointed out that not all questions are even answerable, especially if the negotiated question is not clear, specific, or free from unreasonable constraints.[245] White (1985) recommends communicating the probability of a successful search to the inquirer.[246] She also recommends that in lengthy interviews, the reference librarian be explicit regarding her understanding of "the characteristics of the acceptable answer."[247]

4.3.2.9 Consult Reference Department Policy

Early on, Wyer recognized that departmental policies vary. He categorized their service as: minimum, moderate, and liberal. Some departments have explicit rules about not answering certain kinds of questions; for instance, questions relating to crossword puzzle games or newspaper competitions.

4.3.2.10 Is Reference Librarian Competent to Answer?

This ethical question should be silently asked by the reference librarian. Obviously, librarians range from advanced beginners to competent, proficient, and highly expert, depending on the type of question. If the librarian decides not to answer it, then she should refer the inquirer to another librarian.

4.3.2.11 Do You Know A Source?

An experienced or well-practiced reference librarian knows many specific sources and can go directly to them in answering the inquirer's question, thus bypassing some steps in the idealized process. Neill (1984) addresses the role of episodic memory as a device that reference librarians are employing in order to accomplish this task, but it is important not to rely on one's own memory in recalling an actual answer; an appropriate specific source should be used and cited by title, according to Gers and Seward (1985), to be completely correct.

Myers' work (1977 and onward), however, suggests that even when a library owns appropriate sources, the supposedly competent staff does not consult them or know how to use them, or misinterprets the information within the sources. Interestingly, Way (1984 and 1987) found that law librarians did cite their sources 74 percent of the time. By contrast, novices, advanced beginners, and, less frequently, competent reference librarians will not know a specific source and, hence, will have to go through the subsequent steps to obtain a source that is likely to answer the inquirer's question.

4.3.2.12 Classification of Question by Format

Traditionally, librarians have categorized questions according to type: (1) directional, (2) instructional, (3) ready-reference, and (4) extended reference.[248] The first kind probably does not require professionally trained librarians, but the last two certainly can.[249] And when the reference librarian does not immediately know a title that will answer the inquirer's question, a more complicated decision-making process can be invoked.

The best articulation of such a search strategy was originally suggested by Isadore Mudge and explicitly articulated by her student and disciple, Margaret Hutchins (1937 and 1944). Carter Alexander (1936) also recommended the same classification approach about the same time. That is, the reference librarian classifies the question into one or more of the familiar reference formats. Jahoda's later research confirms that reference librarians do use this particular process to answer questions.[250]

Guerrier's 1936 national survey found that encyclopedias, dictionaries, atlases, and yearbooks were used most often. Two decades latter, Francillon's 1959 empirical work revealed a different frequency (notably catalogs, directories, encyclopedias, handbooks, and indexes). About the same time, a larger sample of librarians reported using handbooks, geographical materials, biographies, and then yearbooks.[251] Most recently, Larsen's 1979 study shows that novices are introduced to more encyclopedias than yearbooks than biographies than indexes. Based on work presented in Chapter 5 of this book, the frequency appears to have changed yet again. And, furthermore, the process appears to be based not just on an analytic knowledge of formats but also on an implicit weighting of confidence factors as well.

Other researchers have tried to categorize questions by type (see Alexander, 1936, and Cole, 1943), time period (Cole, and Vavrek, 1971, as well as Stych, 1972), language (Stych, and White, 1983) and subject. Significantly, Vavrek's research found that the number of time and subject elements in the negotiated question increased as a result of the reference librarian's questioning. According to Cole (1943), general reference questions tend to fall into the social sciences and then useful arts (i.e., science and technology) and history. In any event, one of Powell's major findings in 1976 is that quality reference service depends on receiving substantive reference questions frequently.

4.3.2.13 Forward Chain on Formats

As a monitoring tactic, Bates (1979) recommends following a regular pattern to keep the search on track. The regular or normal pattern (according to Hutchins and Mudge) is to make an initial analysis by format, whereupon the reference librarian may find several formats that will potentially answer the question.

Work by Bonk (1960) and others demonstrates that several formats are used quite frequently. White talks about these formats as frames, scripts, or schema, while Neill's work reveals that librarians are drawing upon semantic and schematic memory to accomplish this part of the decision-making task.

4.3.2.14 Do You Want a Little or a Lot?

The amount of information the inquirer desires will influence the selection of certain formats as will the time and/or effort the librarian and inquirer want to devote to the search, according to Hayes and Carlson (1964). Hence, while questions such as "Do you want a little or a lot?" and "How much time do you have?" could be asked earlier as part of the question negotiation process, they must be asked also at this point because the answer will make a difference in which formats to pursue further.

4.3.2.15 Rank One-Step Formats Higher

Some types of sources, such as dictionaries, directories, encyclopedias, handbooks, and yearbooks are self-contained, in that the answer lies within the particular source. This kind of one-stop shopping is convenient when the user wants a simple, straightforward answer.

4.3.2.16 Rank Bibliographies and Indexes Higher

Bibliographies and indexes can generate many citations, including those that are not relevant or pertinent to the inquirer's informational need. By contrast to encyclopedias, which provide broad coverage of topics, they have little or no depth. Hence, such two-step sources are more appropriate when the user wants more information and is willing to spend the time to find the answer.

4.3.2.17 Do You Want to Make the Effort?

Although a search through some two-step sources may be successful in the end, these searches take time and effort. Hence, the librarian needs to know whether the inquirer really wants to undertake this task. To do otherwise, making an assumption about the inquirer's willingness, may result in unnecessarily poor service.

4.3.2.18 Now Do You Know Specific Sources?

The next step is to select potentially relevant titles within each of the previously identified formats, according to Hutchins (1937 and 1944) as well as Jahoda (see his eighth step). At this point, the classification process may have jogged one's memory about specific sources. Hyers (1936) mentions individual differences among reference librarians in their utilization of tools to answer the same question, which would indicate that reference librarians do have favorite reference tools. This situation may be playing a role in Bonk's 1960 study of the most vital, recommended, and peripheral reference tools.

Novices are introduced to a range of tools in nearly every school of library and information science, averaging 243 titles according to Larsen's

1979 article. The apparent consensus among librarians and faculty is that students should know: (1) *Webster's* or *New English Dictionary*, (2) *Encyclopedia Britannica* or *World Book*, (3) *World Almanac*, (4) and *Reader's Guide*. If advanced beginners know just these canonical titles, they can probably answer many, if not most ready-reference, fact-type questions in many libraries.

4.3.2.19 Consult Colleague

If the librarian does not know a specific source, then they should consult the catalog, an appropriate source such as *Guide to Reference Books*, or their colleagues.

4.3.2.20 Backward Chaining on Reference Sources/Tools

As will be discussed in detail in the next chapter, the object of backward chaining is not to eliminate any potentially relevant titles within the identified formats. A static evaluation function must be performed; in other words, librarians should rank order the most to least probable sources and work down the list.

4.3.2.21 Sort Relevant Reference Sources/Tools by Likelihood

Indeed, Alexander (1936) suggested searching sources "in order of likelihood." Hayes and Carlson (1964) draw a similar conclusion from their flowcharting of reference librarians during actual searches.

4.3.2.22 Make Recommendation (Initial Response)

At this point, the preliminary results of the reference librarian's decision making can be communicated with the inquirer. The communication process includes assuring the inquirer that the reference librarian does, indeed, know a source or sources that will most likely answer the question.

4.3.2.23 Locate Recommended Sources

Librarians decrying the inconsistent location of reference sources suggests that physical space serves as a memory device. Preliminary in-progress research by Bunge and Murfin found higher user satisfaction when the reference librarian searched with them rather than merely pointed to the sources.[252] For an extended discussion, see below under "The Reference Materials/Sources."

4.3.2.24 Translate Query Terms into Source Access Point Terms

Most of the research clearly identifies this step as one of the major ones in the reference process. For instance, Rees and Saracevic's seventh step is the "translation of search concepts into indexing language," whereas

Jahoda's seventh step is "types of access points to search," and Benson and Maloney talk about "translating the query."

Having read Carlson's conclusion about the importance of translating ("Here the lesson is very clear: humans should scan over a reference document before making any detailed searches"[253]), Bates generalizes that the reference librarian needs to survey or scan the reference book first to establish appropriate access points and then terms. In the latter case, Bates's term tactics (specify, reduce/exhaust, and parallel) are likely to be helpful. These tactics seem especially well taken when the reference librarian is dealing with a less familiar title or topic.

4.3.2.25 Search Recommended Sources in Logical Sequence

In a simplified model, Jahoda identifies this search as the final step in the process, while Rees and Saracevic as well as Benson and Maloney merely refer to this step as conducting the search. Once again, Bates helpfully suggests the idea tactic of rescue—essentially, if you think the answer is in a source, it probably is—go back and double check it.

4.3.2.26 Deliver Results to Inquirer

In Benson and Maloney's 1975 model, delivery of the information is the last step. There is a philosophical distinction between strict reference service that points or refers to a source and information service that gives the actual answer and cites a source to verify it. Once again, the inquirer's information need should determine the type of service rendered within the boundaries of departmental policy.

4.3.2.27 Review Results (Follow-up)—Does This Answer Your Question?

This necessary iterative feedback loop has been identified and discussed by Shera and Taylor, among others. Carlson reported that reference librarians indicated their own satisfaction with search results, but Crum believes reference librarians can assure quality control only by confirming their own sense of satisfaction with that of the inquirer's.

The "judgment to terminate a search is usually a very arbitrary thing" according to Carlson. There are ironies as one of Taylor's 1968 librarian subjects pointed out; ". . . it may be somewhat frustrating at times when you know you haven't gone far enough, yet they are satisfied." Generally, the decision to terminate a search should be in the hands of the inquirer, but with the advice and consent of the reference librarian.

Shera (1964) points to the role of pertinence and relevance in the inquirer's assessment of satisfaction. Unfortunately, Gers and Seward (1985) found that this behavior (i.e., asking follow-up questions such as "Does this completely answer your question?") was evidenced only 12 percent of the time in their study of nearly two dozen libraries. Yet, when reference librarians did use such a closed-ended question, their accuracy rates increased dramatically.

Finally, satisfaction with reference service is higher among users than among librarians, according to Harris and Michell (1986 and 1987).

4.3.2.28 Do You Want to Renegotiate?

The reference librarian must ask and receive an answer to this question. Assumptions may lead to lower quality of service. If the situation develops where the inquirer would like to renegotiate, then the librarian must return to that step (see 4.3.2.5).

4.3.2.29 Make Referral

Reference librarians should feel free to say that they do not know, but it appears unethical to stop there. Yet, referrals are rarely made, according to Gers and Seward (1985) and Hawley (1987). Childers (1977) found that when made, nonlibrary referrals were correct 66 percent of the time. Daniel has identified the possible role of apathy in the reference librarian's decision not to refer. Jahoda found that there may be no printed source that contains the answer to the inquirer's question because the title is not owned, the librarian cannot think of one, or the answer simply does not exist yet.

If no printed source is available to answer the inquiry, the librarian should refer the inquirer to another collection, individual, or organization. The 1967 SUNY system study found, however, that librarians were "unaware of other community resources." Thus, reference librarians should remember to make in-house referrals first.[254] In this case, questions such as "Whom have you talked to?" or "Do you know X?" and "Do you want to talk to X or should I?" could be useful. Stone (1942) recommends keeping a list of unanswered questions.

Dervin and Dewdney (1986) recommend pauses or pacing the interview so that premature diagnosis (such as unnecessary referrals) do not occur. But even when referral is justified, the fact that there is no directory of expert reference librarians makes effective referrals more difficult.

4.3.2.30 Failure Analysis

Thirty years of studies reporting 55 percent accuracy in reference service suggest the need for failure analysis. One can ask what is the consequence of failure? Despite reportedly high levels of inquirer satisfaction, reference librarians run the risk of user dissatisfaction and ignorance.

Crum (1969) has identified five barriers to successful reference transactions; they are: (1) physical, (2) personality, (3) psychological, (4) linguistic, and (5) contextual barriers. More simply, Benson and Maloney (1975) dichotomize failure as either system related or searcher related. In an empirical study, Jahoda listed in declining order the reasons for failure: (1) questions unanswered because of reference tool limitations; (2) questions unanswered because of library limitations; (3) questions unanswered because of personnel limitations. Although Jahoda ranks searcher-related failures as less significant, Benson and Maloney describe five reasons why that kind of failure may have occurred and provide five questions to ask in order to avoid this failure.

Gers and Seward's 1985 study found a range of "answers:" (1) correct answer and source; (2) correct answer but no source; (3) source where answer can be found; (4) partial answer and source; (5) partial answer but no source; (6) internal directions, lead to correct answer; (7) internal directions, do not lead to correct answer; (8) no answers, external directions; (9) incorrect answer; (10) no answer, no directions.[255]

4.3.2.31 Record Question and Answer for Future Review and Analysis

Unlike chess players, few reference librarians have bothered to take the time to record interactions in detail. Hence, they deny the reference department valuable information about inquirer's needs and wants, details about question negotiation, the subject content of reference questions, the type of sources used, and the actual sources used. Significantly, they lose the ability to improve their service performance.

4.3.2.32 Retreat

This step ends the formal part of the reference transaction. Although there does not appear to be any reported research on this topic, the use of encouragers such as "Come back again, soon" are obviously appropriate.

4.3.3 The Reference Materials/Sources

Historically, reference librarians have accepted the classification of reference sources by format. But even then, there has been a high level of specificity rather than abstractions based on the sets of tools. Similarly, ALA *Booklist Guidelines* promote the attention to detail, although one could argue the knowledge gained is useful in determining confidence levels for various tools. The field may be searching for a way to state confidence levels; perhaps, a statistical approach would be useful.

4.3.3.1 Consult Colleague, Guide to Reference Books, and/or Catalog

Failing specific knowledge of titles, the reference librarian must consult the library's catalog (either card, microfiche, or online), and the Library of Congress's *Subject Headings,* if necessary, or a standard source such as *Fundamental Reference Sources* or ALA's *Guide to Reference Books.*

4.3.3.2 Information Store/Reference Collection

Prior research indicates the existence of a core reference collection, probably consisting of several hundred titles. Jahoda and Culnan (1968) found that 29 percent of unanswered reference questions was due to an unowned source or being outside the scope of the library's collection policy.[256]

However, several studies have collaborated that only a handful of titles actually need to be used in practice and, furthermore, that one source, the *World Almanac,* may answer 57.5 percent of the reference questions being asked in some libraries.[257] At the other extreme beyond 3500 reference titles, Powell (1976) found there was a diminishing rate of return in successfully answering fact-type, ready-reference questions.[258]

4.3.3.3 Local Collection

According to Childers, as well as Benham and Powell, total collection size was a weak factor in successfully answering reference questions.[259] This finding is due to the fact that ready-reference, fact-type questions do not require extensive collections beyond the reference department.

Referral, in the case of reader's advisory, is appropriate here.

4.3.3.4 Interlibrary Loan and the Universal Collection

Often, the use of bibliographies, catalogs, and indexes will identify sources not in the local collection. In that case, referrals will need to be made to the interlibrary loan (ILL) department. As part of measuring output, the ACRL and other groups are examining the ILL fill rate.[260]

4.3.4 Background Noise

The communications literature on which many of the reference research articles are based usually defines noise as interference, distortion, or errors in the process. Yet, most of the reference transaction literature ignores sources of noise. Researchers have not reported investigations of this element in the process. Because reading is a serious enterprise, reference librarians have tried to keep distractions to a minimum with the familiar, if stereotypical, "Shh!"

4.4

Conclusions

The preceding sections have established a secure model of the reference transaction based on numerous research findings. Over seventy years, however, the character of that literature has changed. Initially, it was purely descriptive and then it shifted to a more analytical approach to the reference process in the mid-1960s. After the works of Bunge, Childers, and Crowley, the literature becomes more sophisticated, taking on unobtrusive measures and adopting random sampling as standard procedure. Until the mid-1970s, however, little of the research was quantitative; they missed a certain precision. Now, fortunately, studies regularly appear that use descriptive statistics, at the very least.

Thus, the flowchart model presented in Figure 4.1 is based on an increasingly secure research foundation. I hope that this flowchart will be adopted as the standard model of the reference transaction, modified as new research demands, of course. Expert systems work can adopt this model.

At this point, the author's thinking resonates with something Lowell Martin said in 1974: "more attention has been paid to preparation for performance than to performance itself."[261] It is time for action. I believe that, ultimately, quality is defined by the user of reference services. I hope, too, that more libraries will adopt the position of continuous improvement of reference service.

Endnotes

1. A few articles included herein are not truly research based. Some, such as Delaney, have been included because they are frequently mentioned by other authors writing about the reference process, while other pieces, such as Hayes and Carlson, have been largely ignored in previous reviews. Furthermore, several single institution studies have been omitted because there are doubts about either the methodology or the generalizability of the findings in those studies.

2. Earlier review articles include: Gerald Jahoda and Paul Olson, "Analyzing the Reference Process," *RQ* 12 (Winter 1972): 148–156; Charles A. Bunge, "Interpersonal Dimensions of the Reference Interview: A Historical Review of the Literature," *Drexel Library Quarterly* 20 (Spring 1984): 4–23; F.W. Lancaster, "Factors Influencing the Effectiveness of Question-Answering in Libraries," *The Reference Librarian,* no. 11 (Fall–Winter 1984): 95–108; Ronald R. Powell, "Reference Effectiveness: A Review of Research," *Library and Information Science Research* 6 (January–March 1984): 3–19; Terence Crowley, "Half-Right Reference: Is It True?" *RQ* 25 (Fall 1985): 59–68; Peter Hernon and Charles R. McClure, "Quality of Data Issues in Unobtrusive Testing of Library Reference Service: Recommendations and Strategies," *Library and Information Science Research* 9 (April–June 1987): 77–93; Kenneth D. Crews, "The Accuracy of Reference Service: Variables for Research and Implementation," *Library and Information Science Research* 10 (July–September 1988): 331–355; and Maloy Moore, "The Reference Interview: A Review," MLS Specialization Paper, UCLA, November 1988.

3. Maloy Moore, "Proposal for MLS Specialization Paper," undated, paraphrasing Gerald Jahoda and Paul E. Olson, "Analyzing the Reference Process," *RQ* 12 (Winter 1972): 148.

4. Jerry Fitzgerald, Ardra Fitzgerald, and Warren D. Stallings, Jr., *Fundamentals of Systems Analysis* (New York: Wiley, 1987), G22.

5. Mary DeJong, "Where Does the Reference Librarian's Time Go?" *Wisconsin Library Bulletin* 22 (January 1926): 7–8.

6. James I. Wyer, *Introduction to Reference Work* (Chicago: American Library Association, 1930).

7. James I. Wyer, *Reference Work; A Textbook for Students of Library Work and Librarians* (Chicago: American Library Association, 1930), 96.

8. Ibid., 234–238.

9. Edith Guerrier, "The Measurement of Reference Service in a Branch Library," *Bulletin of the American Library Association* 29 (September 1935): 632–637.

10. Ibid., 632.

11. Faith H. Hyers, "Librarians: Savants or Dilettantes?," *Pacific Bindery Talk* 8 (February 1936): 87–89.

12. Ibid., 87.

13. Carter Alexander, "The Technique of Library Searching," *Special Libraries* 27 (September 1936): 230–238; reprint ed., *How to Locate Educational Information and Data: A Text and Reference Book* (New York: Columbia University Teacher's College, 1941), Chapter 30.

14. Ibid., 231.

15. Margaret Hutchins, "The Artist-Teacher in the Field of Bibliography; An Application of Modern Educational Theories and Techniques to the Teaching of the First-Year Library School," *Library Quarterly* 7 (January 1937): 99–120, and *Introduction to Reference Work* (Chicago: American Library Association, 1944).

16. Id., *Introduction,* 25.

17. Ibid., 32–34.

18. Elizabeth O. Stone, "Methods of Evaluating Reference Service," *Library Journal* 67 (1 April 1942): 296–298.

19. Dorothy E. Cole, "An Analysis of Adult Reference Work in Libraries," M.A. thesis, University of Chicago, September 1943.

20. Ibid., 28.

21. Ibid., 31.

22. Ibid., 35.

23. Ibid., 37.

24. Raymund F. Wood, "What Exactly Do You Wish to Know?" *California Librarian* 13 (June 1952): 213, 245.

25. Jack Delaney, "Interviewing," *Wilson Library Bulletin* 29 (December 1954): 317–318.

26. Ibid., 318.

27. Suppose a person asks for "that new psychology book by L. Ron Hubbard." Considering the tension between advice and information, should the reference librarian reply by: (1) verifying the title and indicating its location by call number in the library's stacks, and reminding the person to come back, if s/he has any trouble locating it; or (2) informing the person "that competent psychologists deplore the study of dianetics, but that there are plenty of general psychology texts here if that is what the patron is trying to find" (p. 318)? Maybe Rule 12 applies.

28. David K. Maxfield, *Counselor-Librarianship; A New Departure,* Occasional Papers, No. 38 (Urbana, IL: University of Illinois Library School, March 1954), and id., "Counselor Librarianship at U.I.C.," *College and Research Libraries* 15 (April 1954): 161–166, 179.

29. Maxfield, *Counselor,* 8.

30. Ibid., 12.

31. Ibid., 15.

32. Paul F. Breed, "An Analysis of Reference Procedures in a Large University Library," Ph.D. dissertation, University of Chicago, 1955.

33. Mary Francillon, "Information Retrieval: A View from the Reference Desk," *Journal of Documentation* 15 (December 1959): 187–198.

34. Wallace J. Bonk, *Composite List of Titles Taught in Basic Reference by 25 of the Accredited Library Schools* (Ann Arbor, MI: University of Michigan Department of Library Science, 1960); id., "Core Curriculum and the Reference and Bibliography Courses," *Journal of Education for*

Librarianship 2 (Summer 1961): 28–33; id., *Use of Basic Reference Sources in Libraries,* Cooperative Research Projects, No. 1584 (Ann Arbor, MI: University of Michigan Department of Library Science, 1963); and id., "Core Reference Course," *Journal of Education for Librarianship* 4 (Spring 1964): 196–208.

35. Bonk, "Core Curriculum," 29.

36. Bonk, *Composite List.*

37. Compare Bonk, "Core Curriculum," 30 with Bonk, "Core Reference," 196, 206.

38. James W. Perry, "Defining the Query Spectrum—The Basis for Designing and Evaluating Retrieval Methods," Mimeograph, 1961, and id., "Defining the Query Spectrum: The Basis for Developing and Evaluating Information-Retrieval Methods," *IEEE Transactions on Engineering Writing and Speech* 6 (September 1963): 20–27.

39. Ibid., 22.

40. Ibid., 23.

41. University of Michigan, Survey Research Center. *Faculty Appraisal of a University Library* (Ann Arbor: University of Michigan Library, 1961).

42. Los Angeles. Bureau of the Budget and Efficiency. *Organization, Administration and Management of the Los Angeles Public Library* (Los Angeles: The Bureau, 1949–1950), vol. 3, 49.

43. Maurice Tauber et al., *The Columbia University Libraries: A Report on Present and Future Needs* (New York: Columbia University Press, 1958), 164.

44. Donald Coney et al., *Report of a Survey of the Indiana University Library for Indiana University* (Chicago: American Library Association, 1940), 70.

45. W.C. Haygood, *Who Uses the Public Library: A Survey of the Patrons of the Circulation and Reference Departments of the New York Public Library.* Studies in Library Science series. (Chicago: University of Chicago Press, 1938).

46. Robert S. Taylor, "The Process of Asking Questions," *American Documentation* 13 (October 1962): 391–396.

47. Ibid., 392; citing J.W. Perry's "Defining the Query Spectrum—The Basis for Designing [*sic*] and Evaluating Retrieval [*sic*] Methods," N.p., Mimeographed, 1961.

48. Allan M. Rees and Tefko Saracevic, "Conceptual Analysis of Questions in Information Retrieval Systems," in *Automation and Scientific Communication, Topic 8: Information Storage and Retrieval; Annual Meeting of the American Documentation Institute, Part II* 1 (1963): 175–177.

49. Ibid., 175.

50. Jesse Shera, "Automation and the Reference Librarian," *RQ* 3 (July 1964): 3–7.

51. Ibid., 5.

52. Ibid.

53. Robert M. Hayes, *The Organization of Large Files—Introduction and Summary; Part 1 of the Final Report on The Organization of Large Files,* NSF Contract C-280 (Sherman Oaks, CA: Hughes Dynamics, Advance Information Systems Division, 30 April 1964), and Gary Carlson, *Search Strategy by Reference Librarians; Part 3 of the Final Report on the Organization of Large Files,* NSF Contract C-280 (Sherman Oaks, CA: Hughes Dynamics, Advance Information Systems, 17 March 1964).

54. Carlson, 28.

55. Carlson, 5.

56. Hayes, 61.

57. Charles A. Bunge, "Professional Education and Reference Efficiency," Ph.D. dissertation, University of Illinois, 1967; reprint ed., *Professional Education and Reference Efficiency,* Research Series No. 11 (Springfield, IL: Illinois State Library, 1967); and id., "Charting the Reference Query," *RQ* 8 (Summer 1969): 245–250.

58. Bunge, "Professional," 20.

59. Ibid., 56, 58–60.

60. Ibid., 72.

61. Bunge, "Charting," 245.

62. Herbert Goldhor, *A Plan for the Development of Public Library Service in the Minneapolis-Saint Paul Metropolitan Area,* with a chapter by Wesley C. Simonton. Minneapolis: Department of Education, Library Division, 1967; reprint ed., Washington, DC: ERIC Document Reproduction Service ED 1977, 1967.

63. Id., "Reference Service Analysis," *Illinois Libraries* 42 (May 1960): 319–322.

64. *Emerging Library Systems: The 1963–1966 Evaluation of the New York State Public Library Systems.* (Albany: The University of the State of New York, State Education Department, Division of Evaluation, 1967).

65. Ibid., 39–42.

66. Robert S. Taylor, *Question-Negotiation and Information-Seeking in Libraries,* Studies in the Man–System Interface in Libraries, Report No. 3, Grant Number AF-AFOSR-724-66 (Bethlehem, PA: Lehigh University, July 1967), and id., "Question-Negotiation and Information Seeking in Libraries," *College and Research Libraries* 29 (May 1968): 178–194.

67. Ibid., 183.

68. Gerald Jahoda and Mary Culnan, "Unanswered Science and Technology Questions," *American Documentation* 19 (January 1968): 95–100; Gerald Jahoda, "Reference Question Analysis and Search Strategy Development by Man and Machine," *Journal of the American Society for Information Science* 25 (May/June 1974): 139–144; id., "Progress Report: The Process of Answering Reference Questions—A Test of a Descriptive Model," Contract/Grant Number OEG-0-74-7307 (Tallahassee: Florida State University, 1975); reprint ed., *Instruction in Negotiating the Reference Query,* Document Reproduction Service, ED 111 421, August 1975; id., *The Process of Answering Reference Questions; A Test of a Descriptive Model,* Office of Education, Bureau of School Systems, Library Research and Demonstration Branch, Grant Number G007500619 (Tallahassee: Florida State University School of Library Science, January 1977); reprint ed., (Bethesda, MD: ERIC Document Reproduction Service, ED 136 769, 1977); id., Judith Braunagel, and Herbert Nath, "The Reference Process: Modules for Instruction," *RQ* 17 (Fall 1977): 7–12; Jahoda and Judith S. Braunagel, *The Librarian and Reference Queries: A Systematic Approach* (New York: Academic Press, 1980); and Jahoda, "Some Unanswered Questions," *The Reference Librarian* 1/2 (Fall/Winter 1981): 159.

69. Jahoda and Culnan, 100.

70. Charles A. Bunge quoting Elin Christianson in his Research in Reference column entitled, "The Reference Query," *RQ* 8 (Spring 1969): 210.

71. Id., "Reference Question Analysis," 140–143.

72. Ibid., 141.

73. Id., *Reference Process,* 51–56.

74. The 12 formats are: (1) atlases and maps; (2) biographical sources; (3) card catalogs and union lists; (4) dictionaries; (5) encyclopedias; (6) guides to the literature; (7) handbooks, manuals, and almanacs; (8) indexes, bibliographies, and abstracts; (9) monographs and texts; (10) nonbiographical directories; (11) primary publications (dissertations, etc.); and (12) yearbooks.

75. Jahoda and Braunagel, *The Librarian,* 116–124.

76. Edward C. Jestes and W. David Laird, "A Time Study of General Reference Work in a University Library," *Research in Librarianship* 2 (January 1968): 9–16.

77. In public libraries the actual time spent at the reference desk may be much smaller, on the order of 6–8 percent, according to an earlier study by Emma Baldwin and W.E. Marcus, *Library Costs and Budgets: A Study of Cost Accounting in Public Libraries* (New York: Bowker, 1941), 142.

78. Norman J. Crum, "The Librarian–Customer Relationship: Dynamics of Filling Requests for Information," *Special Libraries* 60 (May/June 1969): 269–277.

79. John Lubans Jr., "Nonuse of the Academic Library," *College and Research Libraries* 32 (September 1971): 362–367.

80. Ibid., 365–366.

81. Patrick Penland, *Interviewing for Counselor and Reference Librarians,* preliminary ed. (Pittsburgh, PA: University of Pittsburgh, 1970).

82. Bernard F. Vavrek, "Communications and the Reference Interface," Ph.D. dissertation, University of Pittsburgh, 1971; reprint ed., *Communications and the Reference Interface* (Pittsburgh, PA: University of Pittsburgh, 1971), especially 74–95.

83. Geraldine B. King, "The Reference Interview: Open and Closed Questions," *RQ* 12 (Winter 1972): 157–160.

84. Ibid., 157.

85. Ibid., 158.

86. Ibid., 159.

87. F.S. Stych, "Decision Factors in Search Strategy: Teaching Reference Work," *RQ* 12 (Winter 1972): 143–147.

88. Ibid., 146.

89. Ibid., 144–145.

90. Mary Jane Swope and Jeffrey Katzer, "Why Don't They Ask Questions?" *RQ* 12 (Winter 1972): 161–166.

91. Ibid., 166.

92. Carol L. Kronus, "Patterns of Adult Library Use: A Regression Path Analysis," *Adult Education* 23 (Winter 1973): 115–131.

93. Helen M. Gothberg, "User Satisfaction with a Librarian's Immediate and Nonimmediate Verbal–Nonverbal Communication," Ph.D. dissertation, University of Denver, August 1974.

94. See also Adrian L. Van Kaam, "Phenomenal Analysis: Exemplified by a Study of The Experience of 'Really Feeling Understood'," *Journal of Individual Psychology* 15 (1959): 66–72, where he found that 99 percent of his subjects expressed "feeling satisfaction" at the time of being understood. Karen K. Dion, E. Berscheid, and E. Walster have pursued the stereotyping inherent in "facial liking" in what has become an ISI classic citation, "What is Beautiful is Good," *Journal of Personality and Social Psychology* 24 (1972): 285–290.

95. Gothberg, 70–71.

96. Ibid., 72.

97. Elaine Z. Jennerich, "Microcounseling in Library Education," Ph.D. dissertation, University of Pittsburgh, 1974; id. and Edward J. Jennerich, "Teaching the Reference Interview," *Journal of Education for Librarianship* 17 (Fall 1976): 106–111; Elaine Z. Jennerich, "Before the Answer: Evaluating the Reference Process," *RQ* 19 (Summer 1980): 360–66; Edward J. Jennerich, "The Art of the Reference Interview," *Indiana Libraries* 1 (Spring 1981): 7–18; and Elaine Z. and Edward J. Jennerich, *The Reference Interview as a Creative Art* (Littleton, CO: Libraries Unlimited, 1987).

98. Jennerich, "Teaching," 108.

99. Id., *Reference Interview,* 28–30.

100. James Benson and Ruth K. Maloney, "Principles of Searching," *RQ* 15 (Summer 1975): 316–320.

101. Ibid., 316.

102. Ibid., 317.

103. Ibid., 320.

104. Ibid.

105. Ibid.

106. Laura M. Boyer and William C. Theimer, Jr., "The Use and Training of Nonprofessional Personnel at Reference Desks in Selected College and University Libraries," *College and Research Libraries* 36 (May 1975): 193–200.

107. Ibid., 195.

108. See Jeffrey W. St. Clair and Rao Aluri, "Staffing the Reference Desk: Professionals or Nonprofessionals?" *Journal of Academic Librarianship* 3 (1977): 149–153.

109. See Egill A. Halldorsson and Marjorie E. Murfin, "The Performance of Professionals and Nonprofessionals in the Reference Interview," *College and Research Libraries* 38 (September 1977): 385–395.

110. Theodore P. Peck, "Counseling Skills Applied to Reference Services," *RQ* 14 (Spring 1975): 233–235.

111. Daniel J. Delaney and Sheldon Eisenberg, *The Counseling Process* (Chicago: Rand McNally, 1972) and John D. Krumboltz and Carl E. Thoresen, *Behavioral Counseling: Cases and Techniques* (New York: Holt, 1969).

112. Peck, 233.

113. Ibid., 234.

114. Virginia Boucher, "Nonverbal Communication and the Library Reference Interview," *RQ* 16 (Fall 1976): 27–32.

115. Ibid., 28.

116. Ibid., 27.

117. Ibid., 31, 29.

118. Ronald R. Powell, "An Investigation of the Relationship between Reference Collection Size and Other Reference Service Factors and Success in Answering Reference Questions," Ph.D. dissertation, University of Illinois, 1976, and id., "An Investigation of the Relationships between Quantifiable Reference Service Variables and Reference Performance in Public Libraries," *Library Quarterly* 48 (January 1978): 1–19.

119. Ibid., 4.

120. Ibid., 10–11.

121. Ibid.

122. Mary Jo Lynch, "Reference Interviews in Public Libraries," Ph.D. dissertation, Rutgers University, 1977, and id., "Reference Interviews in Public Libraries," *Library Quarterly* 48 (April 1978): 119–142.

123. Ibid., 119, 125, 126.

124. Others have attempted to deal with "busyness"; see Michael Halperin, "Waiting Lines," *RQ* 16 (Winter 1977): 297–299, and *Deskline: A Service Desk Simulation Program* by Alan Kaye (1990).

125. Marcia J. Myers, "The Effectiveness of Telephone Reference/Information Services in Academic Libraries in the Southeast," Ph.D. dissertation, Florida State University, 1979; id., "The Accuracy of Telephone Reference Services in the Southeast: A Case for Quantitative Standards," in *Library Effectiveness: A State of the Art*, ed. the American Library Association. Forward [*sic*] by Bruce A. Miller (Chicago: American Library Association, 1980), 220–233; reprint ed., id. and Jassim M. Jirjees, *The Accuracy of Telephone Reference/Information Services in Academic Libraries: Two Studies.* (Metuchen, NJ: Scarecrow Press, 1983); and Myers, "Check Your Catalog Image," *The Reference Librarian,* no. 12 (Spring–Summer 1985): 39–47.

126. Ibid., 222. A good, recent example is Barbara Berliner, Melinda Corey, and George Ochoa's *The Book of Answers; The New York Public Library Telephone Reference Service's Most Unusual and Entertaining Questions* (New York: Prentice Hall Press, 1990), which, while giving answers, does not cite sources.

127. Mollie Sandock, "A Study of University Students' Awareness of Reference Services," *RQ* 16 (Summer 1977): 284–296.

128. See Linda J. Durfee, "Student Awareness of Reference Services in a Liberal Arts College Library," *Library Quarterly* 56 (July 1986): 286–302, who found the percentage of correct answers about specific services ranged from 51 to 74 percent with an overall average of 65 percent.

129. Thomas L. Eichman, "The Complex Nature of Opening Reference Questions" *RQ* 17 (Spring 1978): 212–222.

130. Ibid., 216.

131. Ibid., 219.

132. James Rettig, "A Theoretical Model and Definition of the Reference Process," *RQ* 18 (Fall 1978): 19–29.

133. Ibid., 25.

134. Marcia J. Bates, "Information Search Tactics," *Journal of the American Society for Information Science* 30 (July 1979): 205–214, and id., "Idea Tactics," *Journal of the American Society for Information Science* 30 (September 1979): 280–289.

135. Id., "Information," 205.

136. Id., "Idea," 208.

137. Bates, "Idea," 282.

138. Id., "Information," 208.

139. John C. Larsen, "Information Sources Currently Studied in General Reference Courses," *RQ* 18 (Summer 1979): 341–348.

140. Ibid., 341.

141. Ibid., 343.

142. Elaine A. Rich, "Building and Exploiting User Models," Ph.D. dissertation, Carnegie Mellon University, April 1979.

143. Ibid., 3.

144. Thomas Childers, "The Test of Reference," *Library Journal* 105 (15 April 1980): 924–928.

145. Linda Morgan, "Patron Preferences in Reference Service Points," *RQ* 19 (Summer 1980): 373–375.

146. Nancy Van House DeWath, *California Statewide Reference Referral Service: Analysis and Recommendations* (Rockville, MD: King Research Inc., 1981); reprint ed. (Washington, DC: ERIC Document Reproduction Service ED 206 311, 1981), and Nancy Van House and Thomas Childers, "Unobstrusive Evaluation of a Reference Referral Network: The California Experience," *Library and Information Science Research* 6 (1984): 305–319.

147. Marilyn D. White, "The Dimensions of the Reference Interview," *RQ* 20 (Summer 1981): 373–381; id., The Reference Encounter Model," *Drexel Library Quarterly* 19 (1983): 38–55, and id., "Evaluation of the Reference Interview," *RQ* 24 (Fall 1985): 76–84.

148. For an example of a biographical reference frame set, see White, p. 42.

149. Ibid., 45, Figure 1.

150. Ibid., 44.

151. Ibid., 78.

152. Ibid.

153. Peter Hernon and Charles R. McClure, "Testing the Quality of Reference Service Provided by Academic Depository Libraries: A Pilot Study," in *Communicating Public Access to Government Information,* ed. Peter Hernon (Westport, CT: Greenwood Press, 1983), 109–123, and Charles R. McClure and Peter Hernon, *Improving the Quality of Reference Service for Government Publications* (Chicago: American Library Association, 1983).

154. Esther E. Horne, "Question Generation and Formulation: An Indication of Information Need," *Journal of the American Society for Information Science* 34 (January 1983): 5–15.

155. Ibid., 15.

156. S. D. Neill, "The Reference Process and Certain Types of Memory: Semantic, Episodic, and Schematic," *RQ* 23 (Summer 1984): 417–423.

157. Patricia Dewdney, "Query Negotiation in Public Libraries: A Content Analysis of Filtering Techniques Used by Reference Librarians in the Process of Clarifying the Inquirer's Information Need," unpublished paper, School of Library and Information Science, University of Western Ontario, 1982.

158. Ibid., 417–418, 422.

159. Ibid., 421.

160. Ethel Auster and Stephen B. Lawton, "Search Interview Techniques and Information Gain as Antecedents of User Satisfaction with Online Bibliographic Retrieval," *Journal of the American Society for Information Science* 35 (March 1984): 90–103.

161. Ibid., 98.

162. Charles D. Patterson, "Personality, Knowledge and the Reference Librarian," *The Reference Librarian* 9 (Fall/Winter 1983): 167–172; reprint ed., *Reference Services and Technical Services: Interactions in Library Practice*, ed. Gordon Stevenson and Sally Stevenson (New York: Haworth Press, 1984).

163. Ibid., 167 and 169.

164. Ibid., 167.

165. Kathy Ann Way, "Measurement and Evaluation of Telephone Reference/Information Service in Law School Depository Libraries in the Greater Los Angeles (CA) Area: A Quantitative Study," M.L.S. Specialization Paper, UCLA, 1984, and id., "Quality Reference Service in Law School Depository Libraries: A Cause for Action," *Government Publications Review* 14 (1987): 207–219.

166. Ralph Gers and Lillie J. Seward, "Improving Reference Performance," *Library Journal* 110 (1 November 1985). 32–35; also reported in Mary A. Hall, "Reference Services: How Well Do We Do What We Do?," Prince George's County Memorial Library System *Staff Newsletter,* 5 March 1985, 2, as well as "Reference Services: How Well Do We Do What We Do?," *The Unabashed Librarian,* No. 54 (1985), 3.

167. See Terence Crowley and Thomas Childers, *Information Service in Public Libraries: Two Studies* (Metuchen, NJ: Scarecrow Press, 1971), especially pp. 30, 51, 98, 111–112, 140.

168. Ibid., 35.

169. Gers and Seward, 34.

170. Ibid., 32.

171. Brenda Dervin and Patricia Dewdney, "Neutral Questioning: A New Approach to the Reference Interview," *RQ* 25 (Summer 1986): 506–513, and Patricia Dewdney, "The Effects of Training Reference Librarians in Interview Skills: A Field Experiment [originally reported as in progress with the title: "User Satisfaction with the Public Library Reference Interview"]," Ph.D. dissertation, University of Western Ontario, August 1986.

172. Dervin and Dewdney, 507.

173. Ibid., 508.

174. Ibid., 508.

175. Joan C. Durrance, "The Influence of Reference Practices on the Client–Librarian Relationship," *College and Research Libraries* 47 (January 1986): 57–67.

176. Ibid., 59, 59, 64, and 64, respectively.

177. Ibid., 64.

178. Ibid., 65.

179. Roma M. Harris and B. Gillian Michell, "The Social Context of Reference Work: Assessing the Effects of Gender and Communication Skills on Observers' Judgement of Competence," *Library and Information Science Research* 8 (1986): 85–101, and id., "Evaluating the Reference Interview: Some Factors Influencing Patrons and Professionals," *RQ* 27 (Fall 1987): 95–105.

180. Ibid., 99 and 99–100, respectively.

181. Ibid., 103, 104.

182. Interested readers might pursue lines of thought presented in Deborah Tannen, *You Just Don't Understand: Women and Men in Conversation* (New York: William E. Morrow and Company, 1990).

183. Jo Bell Whitlatch, "Client/Service Provider Perceptions of Reference Service Outcomes in Academic Libraries: Effects of Feedback and Uncertainty," Ph.D. dissertation, University of California, Berkeley, 1987, and id., "Reference Service Effectiveness," *RQ* 30 (Winter 1990): 205–220.

184. George S. Hawley, *Referral Process in Libraries: A Characterization and an Exploration of Related Factors* (Metuchen, NJ: Scarecrow Press, 1987).

185. Ibid., vii.

186. Ibid., 26; see Thomas Childers, *Information and Referral: Public Libraries* (Norwood, NJ: Ablex, 1983).

187. "Branches' Unobtrusive Survey Results Up From Last Year," *PGCMLS Staff Newsletter* 18 (9 May 1990): 1, 5.

188. Roger J. Volkema, "Problem Complexity and the Formulation Process in Planning and Design," *Behavioral Science* 33 (October 1988): 293.

189. A flowcharting approach assumes a linearity and a procedural programming language.

190. The following sources are particularly worthwhile: Frederick Herzberg, Bernard Mausner, and Barbara B. Snyderman, *The Motivation to Work,* 2d ed. (New York: John Wiley and Sons, 1959); David C. McClelland, *Human Motivation* (Morristown, NJ: General Learning Press, 1973); Abraham H. Maslow, *Motivation and Personality*, 3d ed., rev. Robert Frager (New York: Harper and Row, 1987); and Victor H. Vroom, *Leadership and Decision- Making* (Pittsburgh: University of Pittsburgh Press, 1973).

191. Note the distinction: fulfilling means solving the user's information problem, while satisfying means resolving the user's information need. The former is preferable.

192. Rich, 3.

193. Neill, 421.

194. Rees and Saracevic, "Conceptual Analysis," 175.

195. Taylor, "The Process," 392.

196. Dervin and Dewdney, 507.

197. Ibid., 509.

198. Rettig, 25.

199. Taylor, 1962, 392.

200. Parrott, "Simulation of the Reference Process," *Reference Librarian* 21 (1988): 197.

201. White, 44.

202. Auster and Lawton, 98.

203. Taylor, 182.

204. Dervin and Dewdney, 509.

205. Taylor, 182.

206. White, 55, note 10.

207. Additional confirmation of these facts is provided by Joan C. Durrance, "The Influence of Reference Practices on the Client–Librarian Relationship," *College and Research Libraries* 47 (January 1986): 57–67, especially 65.

208. Lubans, 362.

209. Jahoda and Culnan, 95–100.

210. Rees and Saracevic, 175.

211. Shera, 6.

212. Vavrek, 1971, 95–100.

213. Eichman, 220.

214. Neill, 421.

215. In "The Librarian: From Occupation to Profession," *Library Quarterly* 31 (October 1961): 313, William J. Goode reported that the inability of library users to distinguish clerks from librarians was a serious problem; in related research on undergraduates, they could not tell the difference either, but these same students thought that librarians: 1) sat behind desks, 2) were older, 3) more knowledgeable, and 4) more competent; see Peter Hernon and Maureen Pastine, "Student Perceptions of Academic Librarians" *College and Research Libraries* 38 (March 1977): 129–139. Users reported using appearance as the major criterion for categorizing a library staff member as professional; see Durrance, "The Influence," 60.

216. Differential gender evaluations by observers have been reported; see Roma M. Harris and B. Gillian Michell, "The Social Context of Reference Work: Assessing the Effects of Gender and Communication Skills on Observers' Judgements of Competence," *Library and Information Science Research* 8 (January–March 1986): 85–101, although Frances Benham and Ronald Powell found no significant gender differences in the accuracy of answered questions; see their *Success in Answering Reference Questions* (Metchuen, NJ: Scarecrow Press, 1987).

217. Joan C. Durrance, "Reference Success: Does the 55 Percent Rule Tell All," *Library Journal* 114 (15 April 1989): 31–36, but especially 34.

218. As for the importance of speed (i.e., the total time required to answer a question), Charles Bunge found that professionals performed "significantly more efficiently" than untrained clerks and students; see his "Professional Education," 58–60.

219. Harris and Michell, 94–95.

220. White, 40.

221. John R. Searle, *Speech Acts: An Essay in the Philosophy of Language* (New York: Cambridge University Press, 1969), especially 66–67.

222. Crum, "The Librarian–Customer," 273.

223. Boucher, 31.

224. Maxfield, 15.

225. Gothberg, 70–71.

226. Peck, 234.

227. Frances Benham and Ronald Powell, *Success in Answering Reference Questions* (Metchuen, NJ: Scarecrow Press, 1987), and Nancy Birch, Maurice P. Marchant, and Nathan M. Smith, "Perceived Role Conflict, Role Ambiguity, and Reference Librarian Burnout" *Library and Information Science Research* 8 (January–March 1986): 53–65.

228. Rich, 3.

229. Neill, 417–418.

230. Crum, "The Librarian–Customer," 270.

231. Alexander, 231.

232. Jahoda, *Reference Process*, 51–56.

233. Interested readers might also benefit from consulting the counseling, the psychology, and the oral history literatures.

234. Taylor, "Question-Negotiation," 192.

235. Crum, "The Librarian–Customer," 273.

236. Taylor, "Question-Negotiation," 186.

237. In an earlier chapter, we have seen that this position varies from that of Wittgenstein, who believed that an askable question was also answerable.

238. Rees and Saracevic, 175.

239. Taylor, 183.

240. Rees and Saracevic, 175.

241. Jahoda, "Reference Question Analysis," 141–142.

242. Stych, 144–145.

243. Benson and Maloney, 318.

244. White, 78.

245. Jahoda and Braunagel, *The Librarian*, 116–124.

246. White, "Evaluation," 78.

247. White, "Evaluation," 78.

248. Jeffrey W. St. Clair and Rao Aluri, "Staffing the Reference Desk: Professionals or Nonprofessionals," *Journal of Academic Librarianship* 3 (July 1977): 149–153.

249. Most reference questions are not of extended duration; 27.9 percent of reference questions require one minute or less, while 81.5 percent require 5 minutes or less, according to work by Peter Hernon and Charles R. McClure, "Unobstrusive Reference Testing: The 55 Percent Rule" *Library Journal* 111 (15 April 1986): 37–41.

250. Jahoda, "Reference Question Analysis," 140–143.

251. Bonk, *Use,* 172–179.

252. Charles A. Bunge and Marjorie Murfin, "Wisconsin-Ohio Reference Evaluation Project," in progress.

253. Carlson, 35.

254. Bunge and Murfin found higher rates of success when reference librarians did so; see their "Wisconsin–Ohio Reference Evaluation Project," in progress.

255. Gers and Seward, 33.

256. Jahoda and Culnan, 98–99. Similarly, Goldhor's 1967 study reported that librarians knew a source that would answer the question, but it was not owned.

257. Gers and Seward, 32.

258. Powell, "An Investigation," 9.

259. Thomas Childers, "Telephone Information Service in Public Libraries: A Comparison of Performance and the Descriptive Statistics Collected by the State of New Jersey," Ph.D. dissertation, Rutgers University, 1970; reprint ed., *Information Services in Public Libraries: Two Studies,* by Terrence Crowley and Thomas Childers (Metuchen, NJ: Scarecrow Press, 1971), and Frances Benham and Richard R. Powell, *Success in Answering Reference Questions* (Metuchen, NJ: Scarecrow Press, 1987), 133.

260. Nancy Van House, Charles R. McClure, and Beth Weil, *Output Measures for Academic and Research Libraries* (Chicago; American Library Association, 1990; Van House, Mary Jo Lynch, Charles R. McClure, Douglas Zweizig, and Eleanor Jo Rodger, *Output Measures for Public Libraries,* 2d ed. (Chicago: American Library Association, 1987); and Mary J. Cronin, *Performance Measurement for Public Services in Academic and Research Libraries* (Washington, DC: Association of Research Libraries, 1983).

261. Lowell A. Martin, "Commentary," *Library Trends* 22 (January 1974): 408.

5

The Development of a Knowledge Base for Expert Systems in Reference Work[1],[*]

5.1

The Knowledge Base

> Knowledge without appropriate procedure for its use is dumb, and procedure without suitable knowledge is blind.
>
> —Herbert Simon, 1977

The successful reference transaction is a complex intellectual task, yet many of its elements are evident upon thoughtful scrutiny (see Chapter 4). Obviously, reference questions can be answered by using a variety of reference formats, such as dictionaries or encyclopedias.

Knowledge of formats is somewhat public. For example, Sheehy's *Guide to Reference Books* (10th ed., 1986) that contains nearly 14,000 titles is available to anyone, if they know this one title exists. Knowing when to use these sources, however, is private knowledge carried in the heads of

[*] A more modest version of this chapter appeared as "The Logic of General Reference Work: Basic and Intermediate Level Knowledge" (1991 ALISE Research Paper Prize Winner); reprint ed., in *Libraries and Expert Systems; Proceedings of a Conference and Workshop Held at Charles Sturt University-Riverina, Australia, July 1990,* edited by Craig McDonald and John Weckert (London: Taylor Graham, 1991), pp. 7–16. © 1991 by Taylor Graham and contributors.

150

practicing reference librarians. Furthermore, while the recommended source or sources for the inquirer to consult are also public, the actual reasoning involved in the professional's decision-making process is unclear. Without a doubt the process is a nonmonotonic, multiple-choice classification task. The intellectual task depends on a more complex psychological process than mere memorization and rote recall of specific titles.[2]

A study that examines this decision-making process would be useful to several groups including (1) reference librarians, (2) reference instructors in graduate schools of library and information science responsible for teaching novices, and (3) those involved in the basic training of paraprofessionals. Having the so-called "compiled knowledge of experts" would allow reference faculty to move students from novices to advanced beginners much more rapidly. Findings from such a study also would interest a fourth group, expert system knowledge engineers. In order to proceed, these knowledge crafters must have a secure knowledge base on which to build an expert system for general reference work. Implications for professional practice would include better success rates in the accuracy of question answering and higher efficiency in the reference environment.

5.1.1 Theoretical Structure

Such a study can be decomposed along three dimensions: (1) the reference service domain; (2) the unknown; here, the reference professional's subordinate (sometimes called surface)- and their basic (also known as intermediate)-level knowledge; and (3) the theoretic methodology used to solve for the unknown.

5.1.1.1 The Reference Domain of Question Answering

Along structural lines, reference work is not monolithic. Many activities take place within reference service, including collection development, interlibrary loan, staff training, and general administrative duties. This chapter, however, explores the logic behind the reference librarian's decision-making process related to fact-type, ready-reference questions. As mentioned earlier, question answering can be characterized as a complex, nonmonotonic,[3] multiple-choice classification task, where the reference librarian must choose among many different formats and select the one that fits best. Then the task becomes a choice among specific sources to arrive at the correct "tool of choice."

5.1.1.2 Professional Knowledge

The knowledge necessary to do this task is both private and public; and it involves both basic and subordinate levels of abstractions as well.

Technically, this chapter recognizes *several* levels of knowledge: surface, intermediate, and deep.[4]

An expert librarian knows many facts about reference formats (notably their attributes) and specific sources (specifically their distinctive features by comparison and contrast). Some of this knowledge is public in the sense that it is written down; for example, Sheehy's *Guide* contains many of these facts. Yet, other knowledge about when to use these sources is not codified and is, therefore, largely private.

According to Kelly, to make sense out of what they experience, individuals including reference librarians hierarchically structure their knowledge in meaningful ways. In particular, they build patterns or templates, called constructs, and try them on for size. With more experience, the repertoire of constructs grows. These constructs are then systemized into finite groups of constructs that possess subordinate and superordinate relationships. "Those construction systems which can be communicated can be widely shared."[5]

For reference librarianship, the surface knowledge is a heuristic knowledge of specific, concrete tools used by reference librarians to do their job. These "tricks of the trade" deal with specific strategies—when to consult certain sources, often called the "tools of choice." Perhaps the reason that research on this front has progressed slowly is that the subordinate-level rules are private knowledge that is usually learned during the first years on the job. With on-the-job experience, an advanced beginner in reference work begins to understand the discriminant rules that distinguish various reference tools within a particular format.

The intermediate level has general strategies—when to consult a particular format (i.e., a type of source or class of information) such as dictionaries or encyclopedias. Such knowledge is public and often learned in the early years of one's elementary and secondary education.

Although potentially out of scope for the present chapter, there is yet another level called deep knowledge. This level concerns the transmission of knowledge and involves deep knowledge structures. A study of deep reference librarianship probably would involve motivations, desires, wants, and beliefs involved in the reference interview, or even more generally, any informative communication.

Potential long-term benefits of research on this deep level, using first-order logic such as predicate or symbolic logic and probably modal logic, could lead to the first principles of an information science. Yet, such statements, technically called axioms, definitions, and laws are likely to be general and abstract.[6] It probably would be more like a sociology of science, or knowledge, and therefore of less immediate interest to practitioners. What is lacking to advance study at this level is a good concept or theory of motivation; call it a "reference readiness theory." In the remainder of this chapter, this deeper level will be ignored.

5.1.1.3 Theoretic Methodology

Based on an extensive review of the reference literature, I have identified what must be called the "Hutchins's Heuristic." Writing in her textbook, *Introduction to Reference Work* (1944), Margaret Hutchins states:

> The study of reference books [is] . . . not, however merely a multiplication of books, but types of books, with a training of the power to analyze a question or problem and connect it, first, with the proper type of book and, second, with the right individual book.[7]

Although she never explicitly articulated them, her heuristic operates on the following assumptions:

1. Cognitive efficiency is achieved by maintaining a small, finite set of constructs called reference formats.
2. All reference books can be classified into a small number of reference formats (e.g., atlases, dictionaries, encyclopedias).
3. Each format is a natural category based on experience.
4. These reference formats cover all the general reference questions that are asked as well as all the reference tools that exist.
5. Cognitive effectiveness is achieved by classifying reference questions by format and then by specific sources (i.e., tools of choice) within each format.

5.2

Objectives and Research Question

The purpose of this chapter is threefold:

(1) to elicit and explicitly identify the subordinate-level rules for selecting specific sources to answer fact-type, print-based, ready-reference questions;
(2) to elicit and explicitly identify the basic-level rules and general strategies related to selecting formats or classes of information; and
(3) to hypothesize about the decision-making process involved in answering fact-type, ready-reference questions.

The underlying research question that prompted this study can be stated as "How are fact-type questions answered by expert reference librarians?"

5.3

Hypotheses

Expanding on Margaret Hutchins' pioneering work, a provisional hypothesis may be stated:

> H1: Reference librarians answer inquiries using the general strategy of forward-chaining and classifying the inquirer's question into one of several formats and by the specific strategy of backward-chaining by selecting a certain source or "tool of choice" based on a distinctive feature analysis of the tool.[8]

The advantage of this hypothesis is that it recognizes a reductive transformational process: the reference librarian's complex multiple-choice classification decision is converted into a manageable task that should be wide but somewhat shallow.[9]

5.4

Methodology

There is a threefold path that leads to results—a validated knowledge base. While most of the rules are private knowledge, held in the heads of practicing reference librarians, some of this knowledge is only implicitly discussed in the open literature. In Chapter 1, the exhaustive historical analysis of reference textbooks disclosed some of this knowledge, while a rigorous review of the research on the reference transaction presented in Chapter 4 revealed more knowledge.

As a next step, this knowledge was written down and collated. Then, using a form of Aristotelian induction by simple enumeration, I added my procedural knowledge of how to do reference work, based on seventeen years of library experience. These two steps resulted in a rudimentary knowledge base about reference question answering. Third, that resultant knowledge base was validated using direct observation of 300 reference interviews and protocol analysis[10] with twenty-four expert professional reference librarians serving as domain experts, averaging about two experts per format.[11]

This method assures the reader that the findings discussed below represent not only what other writers say reference librarians should do, but also what they themselves say they do as well as what they do in practice.

5.5 ———

Findings

Reference textbook authors commonly cover eight to thirteen formats. In alphabetical order, the set of 12 reference material formats addressed here are: abstracts/digests; atlases/gazetteers/maps; bibliographies/catalogs; biographical sources; dictionaries; directories; encyclopedias; government publications; handbooks/manuals; indexes; statistical sources; and yearbooks.

5.5.1 Reference Formats

There is good reason to emphasize these formats. The essential reference task is to classify the inquirer's question into one of the known reference formats.[12] The point of this classification process is to reduce the possible search space (see Figure 5.1). Classification by format places boundaries on the otherwise open-ended problem[13] of finding a title that contains the

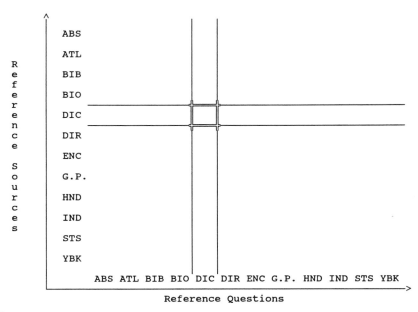

Figure 5.1
The Reference Search Space Boundaries (as illustrated by dictionaries).

answer to the inquirer's question. This powerful technique reduces the search space by a power of 144 (i.e., 12 × 12) to 1.

Reference work has been thought of as a seamless whole in the past. Yet, analysis reveals that professionals in many fields "chunk" their knowledge.[14] Therefore, it is important to examine this whole-part division to understand how the reference process proceeds. As such, reference formats are chunks of knowledge and represent an intermediate level between the deep and surface knowledge of reference work.

Such professional knowledge must be well organized at this level. And this basic level is well organized for several reasons: "ease of perception, memory, learning, naming, and use."[15] Further, it is likely that the reference librarians have created these categories based on a gestalt perception of the tools. Then, too, a kind of cognitive economy or efficiency could also be said to be operating here; "what one wishes to gain from one's categories is a great deal of information about the environment while conserving finite resources as much as possible."[16] Several formats—almanacs, handbooks or manuals, statistical sources, and yearbooks—all share certain features in common. In fact, they seem so similar and appear to have so few differences that it is tempting to group them together as "factbooks." Yet, librarians name them as separate groups,[17] which raises the next point.

Among the different formats there appear to be graded versus clear boundaries. For "factbooks," the boundary conditions are not as readily apparent. Encyclopedic dictionaries are another example in which the boundaries are vague and somewhat fuzzy. On the other hand, some formats have clearer boundaries; for instance, few would mistake an atlas for a

Table 5.1
Prototypic Focal Tools within 12 Reference Formats

Format	Prototypic/focal tool
1. Abstracts	ERIC's *Resources in Education*
2. Atlases	*Times Atlas of the World*
3. Bibliographies	*National Union Catalog*
4. Biographical sources	*Who's Who in America*
5. Dictionaries	*Webster's Third New Int'l.*
6. Directories	*Encyclopedia of Associations*
7. Encyclopedias	*Encyclopedia Britannica*
8. Government publications	*U.S. Government Manual*
9. Handbooks/manuals	*Physician's Desk Reference*
10. Indexes	*Reader's Guide; PAIS Bulletin*
11. Statistical sources	*Statistical Abstract of the U.S.*
12. Yearbooks	*World Almanac and Book of Facts*

dictionary. In other words, each of the formats appears to contain central and noncentral members.

Each format contains central members called prototypic tools. Prototypic tools are those reference sources that are not only central members of their respective format but are exemplars or focal tools for that format. Table 5.1 reveals the exemplary titles that can stand for the entire class of reference sources. It should not be assumed, however, that these specific titles are the most frequently used or somehow always the "best" reference tools in a particular situation.

5.6
Basic-Level Knowledge

This section covers the basic-level knowledge about 12 formats. These formats are listed in straight, alphabetical order.[18]

The decompiled knowledge of reference experts is represented as IF–THEN production rules (see Table 5.2 and subsequent tables, pp. 158–164). The left-hand column of the table presents a situation that may be encountered during the reference dialogue; the right-hand column specifies the recommendation of expert reference librarians. The IF–THEN process is forward-chaining in the sense that when two or more formats present themselves as possibilities, the reference librarian must remember them, consider them, and rank order them (formally called a static evaluation function) in the subsequent search process. During structured interviews, the reference experts confirmed that they used the approach just spelled out.

1. Abstracts/Digests

Experts sometimes consider these two sources separately, but here they will be treated together. Inquirers wanting summaries should be referred to this type of source (see Table 5.2). A critique of material, however, will be found via an index. Inquirers not wanting to read material in its entirety

Table 5.2
Basic-Level Rules for Abstracts/Digests

IF (condition)	THEN (conclusion)
Abbreviated version of original	Abstract
Summary of a Publication	Abstract
Critique of publication	Index, book reviews
Contents of periodicals	Index
Newspaper, indexed or not	Digest

Table 5.3
Basic-Level Rules for Atlases

IF (condition)	THEN (conclusion)
Geographical information	Atlas
Location of places (e.g., countries, cities)	Atlas
Description, esp. comparative	Atlas
Distances	Atlas
Historical development	Atlas
Social development	Atlas
Political development	Atlas
More detail, less context	Map, sheet
Origin of place names/location	Gazetteer
Extensive narrative	Guidebook
Distances	Yearbooks
Historical development	Encyclopedias
Social development	Encyclopedias
Political development	Encyclopedias

Table 5.4
Basic-Level Rules for Bibliographies/Catalogs

IF (condition)	THEN (conclusion)
List of books/reports/pamphlets:	
author	Bibliography, author
about the author	Bibliography, national
subject/area literature	Bibliography, subject
annotated list	Bibliography, annotated
best books in subject	Guide to literature
place of publication	Bibliography, national
List of library's holdings (A,T,S)	Catalog, card/online
Location of library's copy	Catalog, card/online
Published list of library holdings	Catalog, printed
Several libraries' holdings	Catalog, union
List of publisher's offerings	Catalog, publisher's
Alphabetical list of words in text	Concordance
List of topics in text	Index, back of book
Additional bibliographic information	
place of publication	Bibliography
publisher	Bibliography
total pagination	Bibliography
cost of an item	Bibliography
Best books	Bibliography, selective
Reviews	Bibliography
Identification; does a book exist?	Bibliography
Verification	Bibliography

Table 5.5
Basic-Level Rules for Biographical Sources

IF (condition)	THEN (conclusion)
Information about people	
especially notables, specialists, socialites,	Biographical source
field of endeavor, work, or occupation	Biographical source/directories
Addresses	Biographical sources/directories
Telephone number	Directories
Individual has published books	Catalog, card/online
Individual has published articles	Indexes, periodical
Individual has oeuvre	Bibliography
Individual, notable; deceased	Newspaper obituary

can profitably be referred to digests, such as the prototypic *Facts on File*. Otherwise, the most frequently mentioned exemplar is ERIC's *Resources in Education* (see Table 5.1)

2. Atlases/Gazetteers/Maps

Experts think of answering "where"-type questions with atlases (see Table 5.3). By contrast, gazetteers are good for origins of place names, while those inquirers seeking extensive narrative information will find guidebooks more useful. The prototypic tool in this category is the *Times Atlas of the World*.

3. Bibliographies/Catalogs

Bibliographies are more universal lists of works than are catalogs that show only the local holdings of a particular library. Nonetheless, they, too, are treated together due to their similarities. Questions such as "Does a book exist?" and attendant bibliographic information are best answered by this format (see Table 5.4). The most frequently mentioned prototypic title in this format is the *National Union Catalog*.

4. Biographical Sources

Who-type questions are readily answerable by this format (see Table 5.5). In fact, such sources exist to satisfy one's curiosity about other individuals. Less frequently, biographical sources are consulted for addresses and telephone numbers; note that there are better sources for this type of information (i.e., directories). Other related types of sources are identified in Table 5.5. *Who's Who in America* was the most frequently mentioned focal tool among biographical sources.

5. Dictionaries

Commonsense knowledge, learned at an early age, tells one to consult this format when looking for information about words. Indeed, these sources are most commonly consulted when a reference question concerns issues related to language or specific words (see Table 5.6). Although many

Table 5.6
Basic-Level Rules for Dictionaries

IF (condition)	THEN (conclusion)
Information about language	Dictionary
Information about words	Dictionary
Brief information about concepts	Dictionary
Extended information about concepts	Encyclopedias
Extended discussion	Encyclopedias
Information about people	Biographical sources
Information about places	Atlases

dictionaries contain nonlexical matter, they should be evaluated first on their lexical strengths. Similar to dictionaries, encyclopedias should be kept in mind when the inquirer wants a more extended discussion of concepts than that found in a dictionary. The most frequently cited focal tool was *Webster's Third New International Dictionary*.

6. Directories

Similarly, commonsense knowledge, but that learned at a later age, suggests that directories will provide information about telephone numbers or addresses (see Table 5.7). Brief but current facts about individuals as well as organizations can be found in directories. More detailed information about individuals, however, would more likely be found in biographical sources. The one title most characteristic of this format was the misnamed *Encyclopedia of Associations*.

Table 5.7
Basic-Level Rules for Directories

IF (condition)	THEN (conclusion)
Current, brief facts about individuals or groups (addresses, affiliations, etc.)	Directories
Current, brief facts about organizations (addresses, officers, functions, publications, etc.)	Directories
Address information on organizations and products (i.e., addresses and purposes)	Directories
Current address for individual	Directories
Recent address for individual	Biographical sources
To locate organizations devoted to cause or special interest	Directories
Affiliations	Directories, association
Detailed information about people	Biographical sources
Verification of names, spellings	Biographical sources

Table 5.8
Basic-Level Rules for Encyclopedias

IF (condition)	THEN (conclusion)
Information about concepts	Encyclopedias
General information	Encyclopedias
Recent information	Encyclopedias
Specific information on topic or person	Encyclopedias
Self-education	Encyclopedias
Quick bibliographic references	Encyclopedias
Major biographical figures	Encyclopedias
Significant geographical features	Encyclopedias
Extended discussions, general	Encyclopedias
Extended discussions, focused	Monograph/bibliography
Extended discussions, technical	Handbook
Current information	Yearbooks/almanac
Information about words (things)	Dictionaries
Images (of people, things, animals, etc.)	Encyclopedias
Recent/current information	Indexes
Bibliographic references	Bibliography

7. Encyclopedias

Knowledge of the commonsense variety tells the librarian there are multiple reasons for consulting an encyclopedia (see Table 5.8). However, encyclopedias exist foremost to summarize what is known. The fact that there are a multiplicity of reasons explains, perhaps, why some reference textbook authors consider encyclopedias the backbone of the reference collection (see Chapter 1). As a format, encyclopedias are closely related to dictionaries in the sense that they expand on basic, definitional information; this observation becomes clearer when the reader compares Tables 5.6 and 5.8. The prototypic tool for this format is the *Encyclopedia Britannica*.

Table 5.9
Basic-Level Rules for Government Publications

IF (condition)	THEN (conclusion)
Authoritative source of information	Government publications
Wide range of material	Government publications
Statistical information	Government publications
Official version	Government publications
Sole source of information	Government publications
Rules and regulations	Government publications
Inexpensive source of information	Government publications

Table 5.10
Basic-Level Rules for Handbooks

IF (condition)	THEN (conclusion)
Narrative information	Handbook
Updated information	Handbook
Narrow, specific information	Handbook
Detailed information	Handbook
Advanced information	Handbook
Current or historical	Handbook
Authoritative	Handbook
Stray facts—curiosities, events, formulas, allusions, statistics	Handbook
Convenient, hand (vs. encyclopedia)	Handbook
Current information	Newspaper
Recent information	Yearbook
Updated information	Yearbook
Broad, general information	Encyclopedia
Statistical information	Statistical compilation

8. Government Publications

Government publications should be consulted when the question concerns the official, governmental version of events or whenever an authoritative source, especially statistical, is needed (see Table 5.9). The focal tool most frequently mentioned was the *U.S. Government Manual* (which also could be classified as a directory).

9. Handbooks/Manuals

A handbook is one of the most frequently consulted types of sources (see Table 5.10). However, more recent or even current (i.e., within the past year) information can be found in other sources (see Figure 5.2). The exemplary title in this format is the *Physician's Desk Reference*.

10. Indexes

As mentioned, recent (i.e., within the past five years) and even more up-to-date information can be found in indexes. Such commonsense knowledge was learned at a relatively early age, whenever one started writing papers in school. Table 5.11 shows that indexes provide access to serial literature (such as periodicals including newspapers, magazines, and journals) covering a wide range of presentation styles from popular to scholarly.

```
         | Recent      Current    Up-to-Date    Last Minute            |
Past     |------------------------------------------------------>| Present
         | Books:      Serials:   Newspapers:   Databases:            |
         | Bib/Cats    Indexes    Digests       Elect. Sources        |
```

Figure 5.2
Timeliness in Relation to Materials and Types of Sources

Table 5.11
Basic-Level Rules for Indexes

IF (condition)	THEN (conclusion)
Current information	Index, serial literature including newspapers
Popular presentation	Index, magazine
Broad/general/widespread interest	Index, magazine
Scholarly presentation	Index, journal
Define or narrow focus of interest	Index, journal or index, magazine
Contents of periodicals	Index, periodical
Specific location of treatment	Index
Trends	Index, retrospective
Event (including deaths)	Index, newspaper
Contents of a book	Index, back of book
Current/up-to-date information	Digests, newspaper
Recent information	Yearbook
Ownership	Library catalog
Location	Catalog, union
Location of who said what	Quotation book/index

The prototypic tool for popular literature is *Reader's Guide,* while the scholarly index is *PAIS Bulletin.*

11. Statistical Sources

When greater precision or accuracy is necessary, a statistical source should be consulted (see Table 5.12). "How much"-type questions fall straightforwardly into this category. Expert opinion reveals that the proto-

Table 5.12
Basic-Level Rules for Statistical Sources

IF (condition)	THEN (conclusion)
Numerical information	Statistical sources
Greater precision, quantitatively	Statistical sources
Greater accuracy, quantitatively	Statistical sources
Tables, graphs, figures	Statistical sources
Statistical methods, comprehensive	Bibliographies/catalogs
Statistical methods, general	Encyclopedias
Statistical methods, focused	Encyclopedia, subject or handbook
Statistical methods, narrow	Handbook
Statistical terminology	Dictionaries; encyclopedias
Vital statistics, individual people	Biographical sources
Socioeconomic statistics, large geographical areas	Encyclopedias, yearbooks government publications
Very current information	Indexes; digests
Work contains the statistical data	Factbooks—almanacs, directories, handbooks, yearbooks (annuals)

Table 5.13
Basic-Level Rules for Yearbooks (Annuals)

IF (condition)	THEN (conclusion)
Current information (esp. stat)	Yearbook
Updated information	Yearbook
Trend data	Yearbook
Past year's developments	Yearbook
Forecasts	Yearbook (almanac)
Recent happenings	Encyclopedia
Broad area	Yearbook
Timeliness	
immediacy, up-to-date	Digest/newspapers
last-minute information	Electronic sources

typic tool for this category of information is the *Statistical Abstract of the United States* (which is also a government publication). Statistical methods per se, however, probably will be found in another kind of source.

12. Yearbooks

If current, rather than merely recent, information is necessary, then experts consult yearbooks including almanacs and annuals (see Table 5.13). Recent information is contained in encyclopedias, while up-to-date information may be more readily available from digests or newspapers. The focal tool for this format is the *World Almanac,* one of the most frequently used reference sources.

The linkages or interconnectedness of reference formats is shown in Figure 5.3. In other words, based on the preceding tables, when an expert identifies one type of source as relevant, then another format also may be relevant. Recall that this mental operation of ranking potential types of

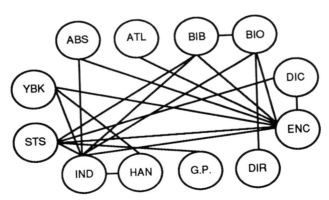

Figure 5.3
Cluster Analysis of Reference Formats

sources is part of the static evaluation function mentioned earlier. However, one format almost stands alone— atlases— while others, such as statistical sources or indexes, are highly linked with several other types.

5.7
Subordinate-Level Knowledge

5.7.1 Specific Reference Sources

Next, the professional's task is to backward–chain from the conclusion to the condition initially presented by the inquirer's formalized need. This subordinate level of a reference librarian's professional knowledge contains the specific reference sources—what reference librarians sometimes call the "tools of choice." Again, the reference task is to classify the question according to certain rules based on a distinctive feature analysis of those tools.

To arrive at a specific source, reference librarians must elicit additional information about the query from the inquirer. Although librarians tend to think of their knowledge as a seamless whole, here they are examining the part within the whole again. In other words, there is another chunk of knowledge that can be represented by explicit declarative and procedural rules. In this section, the discussion about the reference librarian's decision making is arranged alphabetically by format and presented graphically.

1. Abstracts/Digests

These specific sources are covered with indexes due to their similarities (see Figure 5.12).

2. Atlases (including gazetteers/maps)

This category of reference material is one of the most intriguing because it deals with space first and then deeper down the tree it becomes recursive (i.e., involving a pattern within a pattern), dealing with time and then with space again (see Figure 5.4). This self-similarity is an unusual feature of atlases.

At the first-level node, scope of concern, the reference librarian must select either space or thematic interest as the predominant concern of the inquiry. In choosing space, one selects the left-hand node, and moves downward from broadly conceived to more narrowly focused geographical sources. Following the right node at the first level (meaning that the thematic issues are more significant to the inquirer), the branch splits on either physical or cultural concerns (second level). If the latter is chosen, then the selection involves the relevant period again after filtering down through the various aspects of the topic. (see Figs. 5.4B and C).

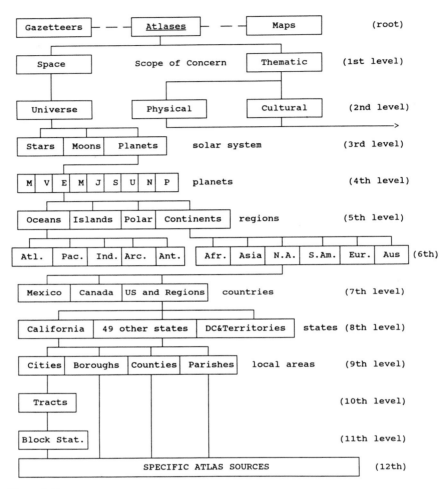

Figure 5.4A
Multiway Tree of Knowledge for Atlases (Space)

The depth of this decision tree (ranging from seven to twelve levels) makes it one of the most complex.

3. Bibliographies/Catalogs

Having decided that a bibliography or catalog is appropriate, the reference librarian must decide next whether the inquiry involves: (1) the physical location of an item that requires the use of a catalog, (2) author or title verification, or (3) subject (see Figure 5.5). The second and third levels involve matters of time and space. These two matters are persistent elements of inquiries across formats.

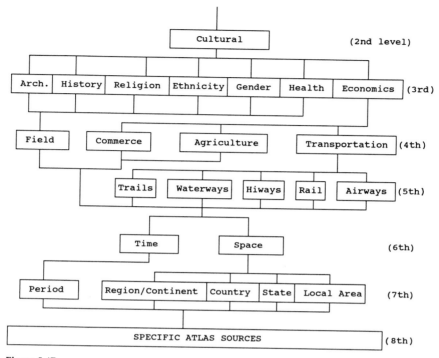

Figure 5.4B
Multiway Tree of Knowledge for Atlases (Thematic)

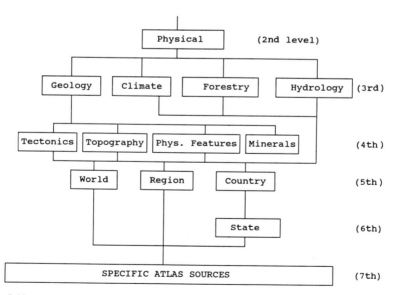

Figure 5.4C
Multiway Tree of Knowledge for Atlases (Thematic)

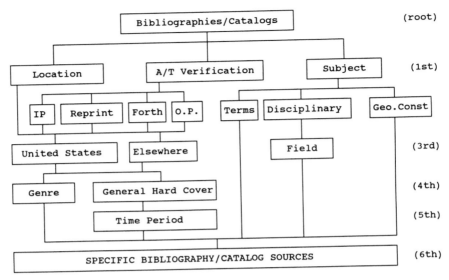

Figure 5.5
Multiway Tree of Knowledge for Bibliographies/Catalogs. A, Author; T, title; IP, in print; Forth, forthcoming; O.P., out-of-print; Geo. Const., geographical constraint.

If the author or title is in doubt, then the issue becomes whether the work in question is out-of-print, in print, reprint, or forthcoming. Whether the work sought is a product of the United States, elsewhere, or part of a particular field is the third level of the decision tree.

4. Biographical Sources

Biographical questions have at least seven attributes: time, space (moving from broad to narrow; e.g., national, regional), gender, ethnicity, occupational field, amount of information desired (i.e., vital statistics or narrative), and whether a portrait is desired by the inquirer (see Figure 5.6). The more well known the individual is, the more likely the inquirer and reference librarian are to know these attributes. Time and space (specifically, the here and now) are most frequent presuppositions of the inquirer. As a search strategy, space (i.e., American or elsewhere) prunes the problem space most efficiently. Besides the national "who's who" sources, there may be regional ones as well.

If a specific person is named (which is the case 82 percent of the time, based on the analysis of 300 questions asked during this study), then the reference librarian identifies gender using commonsense knowledge. For example, first names ending in an *a, ie,* or *y* have a high probability of being female in the English language. Similarly, commonsense knowledge tells the reference librarian that certain last names are likely to be from a

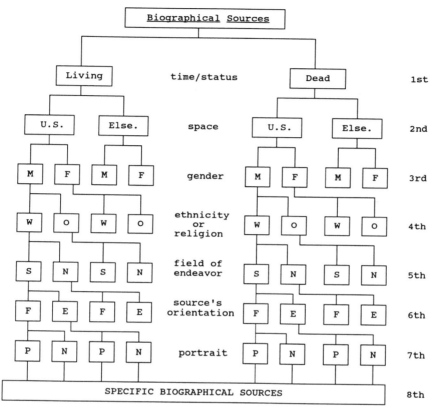

Figure 5.6
Binary Rooted Tree of Knowledge for Biographical Sources. M, Male; F, female; W, white; O, other; S, significant; F, factual; E, evaluative; P, portrait; N, not or none. The right node of levels 2 and 4 are actually multiple choice.

particular place (e.g., Brown, Jones, and Smith are likely to be American or English).

5. Dictionaries

Viewed as a decision tree (see Figure 5.7), the root (i.e., dictionaries) has three branches or nodes at the top: (1) general English language dictionaries, (2) translating (e.g., bilingual) dictionaries, and (3) disciplinary or technical dictionaries. Each node is further subdivided.

The left, first-level node, general English language dictionaries, splits into 16 functional second-level nodes (e.g., spelling, definitions). Theoretically, the middle node, translating dictionaries, should split according to all the living and dead languages in the world; but, only eight are listed. Finally,

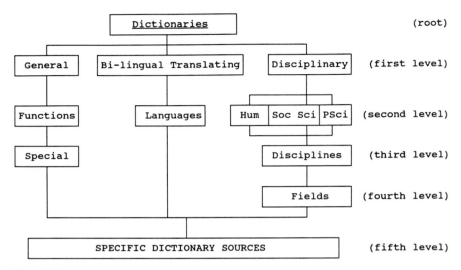

Figure 5.7
Multiway Rooted Tree of Knowledge for Dictionaries

the right node, technical dictionaries, splits into three second-level nodes: humanities, social sciences, and physical sciences. Each of these nodes splits again to specific subject areas, and so on. Eventually, terminal nodes, or the specific reference tools, are reached. Represented as a multiway rooted tree, the knowledge base for dictionaries would have a height of five and a path length of at least 210. This format is one of the most complex!

6. Directories

Directory-type questions demand that the reference librarian accurately distinguish between a question about an individual and a question about an organization (see Figure 5.8). However, the inquirer can combine the individual and the organization in a query (e.g., "I want to know where two particular professors teach—at what specific British university"). In other words, the first level may be connected. Selection of the left node demands that the reference librarian know (or make assumptions) about the geographical scope of the inquiry.

Otherwise, the reference librarian becomes involved in identifying the nature of the particular group or organization in question (i.e., trade or business, professional organization, government, or institution, including schools, libraries, foundations, hospitals, etc.). In either of the two cases, though, the underlying issue is a spatial concern.

7. Encyclopedias

Figure 5.9 looks like Figure 5.7, suggesting that the decision-making process related to encyclopedias is closely related to that of dictionaries. At

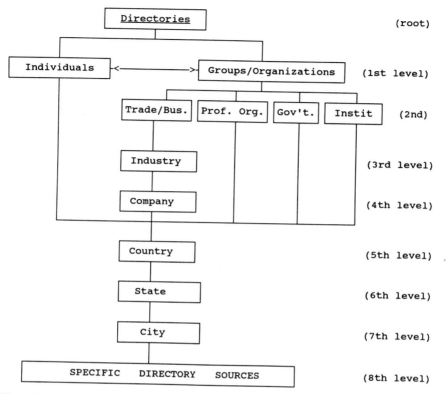

Figure 5.8
Binary Rooted Tree of Knowledge for Directories

the first level, the decision-making structure is the same. In the left node of the second level, there is a departure. Here, the selection of an appropriate encyclopedia demands that the reference librarian make some judgment about the inquirer's age or educational preparation. The figure looks deceptively simple, but it can be exploded to at least 190 branches at the second level, if foreign language is selected.

8. Government Publications

To answer government publications-type questions successfully, the reference librarian must know three things: (1) the level of government, (2) the branch of government, and (3) the publication's issuing agency or provenance (see Figure 5.10).[19]

9. Handbooks

Like many other categories, this one is particularly problematic because publishers misuse the word "handbook."[20] Nonetheless, the decision-making process seems to split based on scholarship (see Figure 5.11); Is the

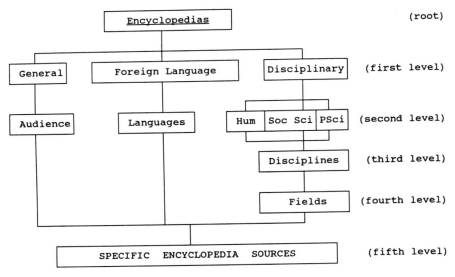

Figure 5.9
Multiway Rooted Tree of Knowledge for Encyclopedias

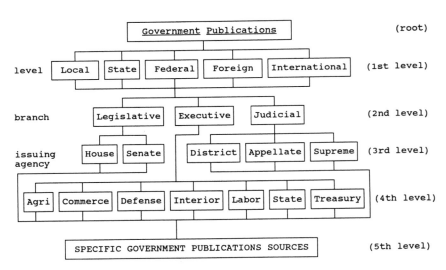

Figure 5.10
Multiway Tree of Knowledge for Government Publications

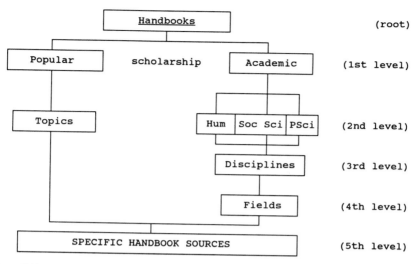

Figure 5.11
Multiway Tree of Knowledge for Handbooks

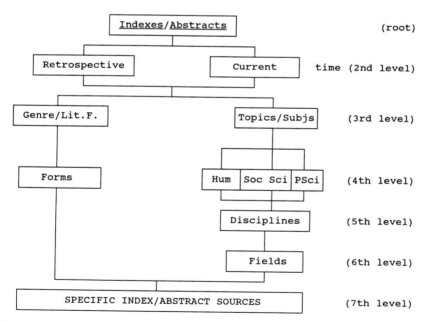

Figure 5.12
Binary Tree of Knowledge for Indexes and Abstracts

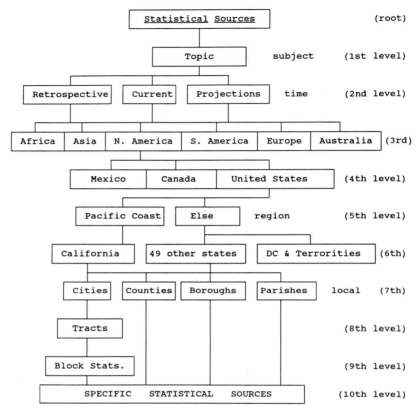

Figure 5.13
Multiway Tree of Knowledge for Statistical Sources

user interested in a popular treatment or a scholarly one? Having made that decision, the reference librarian can move directly to a conclusion. The architectural logic within handbooks does not appear to be particularly complicated.

    10. Indexes (and Abstracts)

    The first question regarding this format is whether the inquirer is seeking current or retrospective information (see Figure 5.12). In that sense, it anticipates the concern as seen in the selection of specific statistical sources. At the second level within this format, especially the right-hand side, this format looks surprisingly similar to several other reference types including dictionaries, encyclopedias, and even yearbooks. If the reference interview's second-level decision takes one down the left side of the tree, then the reference librarian may have to choose from among as many as sixteen

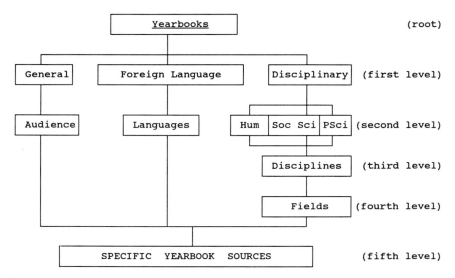

Figure 5.14
Multiway Tree of Knowledge for Yearbooks

different genres such as book reviews, dramas, essays, plays, poetry, proceedings, short stories, as well as speeches and orations.

The right-hand side sorts titles out according to the academic discipline and occasionally field within that. Otherwise, the selection between an index or an abstract depends on whether the inquirer wants a synopsis of the material.

11. Statistical Sources

A statistical reference question usually has three components: (1) subject (first level), (2) time period (level two), and (3) geographic concern (levels three through nine; see Figure 5.13). An illustrative statistical question might be: "I need recent (period) statistics on drunken driving (topic) (where the implied geographical concern is the United States). Depending on the geographical scope of concern, it is possible to provide statistical information for extremely focused areas; in the major cities of the United States these areas are called census tracts and block statistics.

12. Yearbooks

This format is related to encyclopedias (see Figure 5.9) in that it is organized topically, but provides more current information (see Figure 5.14).

The result of the preceeding twelve sections is an explicit conceptual model of the expert professional's knowledge in the reference question-answering domain.[21] Ideally, the architectural structure of the reference librarian's professional knowledge is now clear. The basic level is chunked by format and the subordinate level by the functional aspects of each specific title. The critical decision points are now evident.

Eventually, the entire collection of these logic trees for general and advanced (subject) reference work would serve as an atlas representing the expert's mental world. For the first time, we can map the entire "structure of consciousness" and create a kind of mental geography for this domain. In the meantime, though, novices can now visualize the nontrivial skills of expert reference librarians.

5.8
Implications

Three important implications emerge from this study. First, the actual task characteristics in this narrow area of the reference domain are wide *and* deep in contrast to cognitive psychology studies of other domains. For example, Donald Norman has pointed out that normally a domain's structure should be organized in a wide and shallow fashion so that (1) the task can be performed quickly, (2) without much mental effort, and (3) if the answers have to be only "good enough."[22] This wide-and-deep finding suggests a hypothesis related to the poor quality of reference service, which will be discussed below.

Second, knowing the explicit attributes of the formats increases reference service efficiency. Novices and advanced beginners, not knowing the complete architectural logic of reference work, would take longer to perform their task. Now, however, reference workers anywhere can see the rules related to how these formats are supposed to be used. Now, reference librarians also have content questions to ask during the reference interview. Within each format, certain questions must be asked if reference librarians are to arrive at the correct source.

Yet, the overlap between some formats may contribute to inaccuracies later for those less proficient than the expert librarians in this study. Also, one might speculate that when some reference librarians perform their static evaluation function of the various formats (i.e., the estimate of each format's promise), they may be forgetting to return to those less promising formats when a source within the first format does not contain the expected answer. Therefore, quality suffers.

Third, accuracy in question answering should increase by merely knowing the surface-level rules. Yet, thirty years of reference quality studies show 50 percent accuracy in reference transactions. Evidence from this study suggests that this poor reference quality may be due, in part, to the poor theoretical understanding of the reference process, specifically, the classification aspects of the task. At any rate, the fundamental reference sources can be identified now.

A closely related hypothesis is that the structure of professional knowledge within any format does not simplify the task and, in fact, complicates the reference librarian's work. This finding suggests two previously unidentified reasons for poor-quality reference work. First, reference librarians do not correctly classify the reference question into one of several formats, and second, they do not always ask the correct content questions during the reference interview in order to arrive at the proper source within the selected format.

5.9 Conclusions

There is still work to be done. First, more work needs to be undertaken on the boundary conditions[23] and confidence factors associated with the partitioning of reference books into the set of formats as well as the selection of specific sources. A potentially promising approach might be a graph theoretic of the overlap among reference format attributes. The work thus far has examined the format classification from the point of view that its purpose is primarily for orderly mental storage and retrieval. In other words, it might be possible to discover other relations between and among the different classes of reference books.

The intermediate-level knowledge can be summarized by one principle and one rule. The one principle that underlies all reference work dealing with questions is: All reference questions can be categorized by type of source (i.e., format, class of reference tools, or literature), while the General Reference Rule says: Classify the reference question by type of source and then specific source. Yet, reference librarians do not know the relative frequency of questions by type of format or even how many reference titles are in each format. In other words, why teach some formats to novices if there are few reference questions asked in that category? Posed as research questions and testable hypotheses, these might be promising avenues for future research.

In summary, this chapter has revealed that underlying general reference work a highly structured logic exists. Indeed, there are basic- as well as subordinate-level rules at work in the general reference question-answering dialogue. These results—a properly validated knowledge base—can be used by those interested in improving the quality of reference service via an expert system.

Endnotes ──

1. An earlier version of this chapter appeared as "The Logic of Ready Reference Work: Basic and Subordinate Level Knowledge," in *Libraries and Expert Systems*, ed. Craig McDonald and John Weckert (London: Taylor Graham, 1991), 7–16. A somewhat revised version of this same chapter won the 1991 Association for Library and Information Science Research Paper Competition.

2. This assertion could be tested by asking librarians to recall as many reference titles as possible. It would also be useful to know about differences among novices, advanced beginners, and experts. I would hypothesize that novices cannot name as many titles, or even format attributes for that matter, as can expert professionals.

3. When subsequent information from the inquirer can change the librarian's assumptions about the most promising formats and specific sources, then the decision making can be said to be nonmonotonic.

4. Eleanor Rosch, "Principles of Categorization," in *Cognition and Categorization,* ed. Eleanor Rosch and Barbara B. Lloyd (Hillsdale, NJ: Lawrence Erlbaum Associates, Publishers, 1978), 27–48 and Luc Steels, "The Deepening of Expert Systems," *AI Communications* 1 (August 1987): 10–16.

5. George A. Kelly, *A Theory of Personality: The Psychology of Personal Constructs* (New York: W.W. Norton, 1963), 9.

6. The desire or motivation to be accurate or truthful, for example, or the desire to reduce uncertainty. Obviously, the inquirer is responsible for the truth of presuppositions in the question. Yet, when reference librarians unwittingly accept false presuppositions as true, they have trouble answering the question as posed. For instance, the inquirer wanting biographical information about St. Edmund Hall has confused a place with a person, but will the novice librarian recognize this confusion?

7. Actually a clearer statement can be found in Margaret Hutchins, "The Artist-Teacher in the Field of Bibliography: An Application of Modern Educational Theories and Techniques to the Teaching of the First-Year Library School," *Library Quarterly* 7 (January 1937): 103.

8. An alternative hypothesis would be that the reference librarian's knowledge is actually a statistical probability model based on long-term experience with users' questions and the reference books. In this case, a factor analysis or multiple regression formula might reveal the subtler factors underlying the reference process.

9. Donald A. Norman, *The Psychology of Everyday Things* (New York: Basic Books, 1988), 119–124.

10. Karl A. Ericsson and Herbert A. Simon, *Protocol Analysis: Verbal Reports as Data* (Cambridge, MA: MIT Press, 1984) and Panel Session, "Using Protocol Analysis," American Society for Information Science Meeting, San Diego, California, 22 May 1989.

11. In the first phase of this research, Marie Waters and David Decklebaum of the University Research Library at UCLA have provided dictionary and atlas information, respectively; Nancy O'Neill and Nancy Guidry, reference professionals at the Santa Monica (California) Public Library have provided information about dictionaries along with other formats. For the second phase, experts were identified by Ilene Rockman, editor of *Reference Services Review* and Sandy Whiteley, editor of *Booklist* at the American Library Association. They include: Joan R. Berman of Humboldt State University; Tom Carter of Loyola Marymount University; Winifred F. Dean of Cleveland State University; Marie Ellis of the University of Georgia; Thomas Fry of UCLA; Gary A. Golden of Rutgers University; Clara G. Hoover of Millard South High School (Omaha, NE); Vincent J. Jennings of Hofstra University; Sally Kalin of Penn State University; Arthur Lichtenstein of the University of Central Arkansas; Connie McCarthy of Northwestern University; Josephine McSweeney of the Pratt Institute;

Alan Ritch of the University of California, Santa Cruz; Ed Santa Vicca of Arizona State University; Jim Walsh of Boston College; Sarah Watstein of Hunter College; Lynn Westbrook of the University of Michigan; and Christine A. Whittington of the University of Maine.

12. An interesting and useful study might compare the time it takes a novice to classify a reference question into its proper category versus that of a well-practiced professional and expert librarian. The explicit hypothesis would be that it takes the novice longer than the expert because the former does not know the attributes of each format and/or has not yet organized that information.

13. Following Cartwright's work on problems, this conceptualization would make reference work a metaproblem.

14. A.D. de Groot, "Perception and Memory Versus Thought: Some Old Ideas and New Findings," in *Problem Solving,* ed. B. Kleinmuntz (New York: Wiley, 1966).

15. George Lakoff, *Fire, Women, and Dangerous Things; What Categories Reveal about the Mind* (Chicago: University of Chicago Press, 1987), 38.

16. Rosch, "Principles," 28.

17. Following Rosch's and Tversky's experiments, this point could be tested; for example, reference experts could be asked: "The *Statistical Abstract* is best categorized as (A) a government publication, (B) a statistical source, or (C) a yearbook."

18. Based on a random sample of 300 reference questions asked in a public library, the formats most frequently used (in declining order) were: (1) directories; (2) handbooks/manuals; (3) bibliographies/catalogs; (4) indexes; (5) biographical sources; (6) encyclopedias; (7) government publications; (8) dictionaries; (9) statistical sources; (10) atlases; (11) almanacs; and (12) quotation books.

19. This conceptual framework has been developed elsewhere in more detail. Interested readers might profitably consult my 1986 ALISE Research Paper Competition Prize-winning article, "Paradigmatic Shifts in the Teaching of Government Publications, 1895–1985," *Journal of Education for Library and Information Science* 26 (Spring 1986): 249–266; reprint ed., *Encyclopedia of Library and Information Science,* vol 44, 242–258.

20. Even the Library of Congress recognizes the problematic nature of this group of reference tools by labeling the standard form subdivision "Handbooks, Manuals, *Etc.*" (emphasis added).

21. Alternatively, this structure might be referred to as a theory because the collection of surface- and intermediate-level rules reflects the perceived way of doing reference work.

22. Norman, *Psychology,* 119–125. These specific points about the structure of tasks were also made during his 23 May 1989 American Society for Information Science talk in San Diego, California.

23. Boundary conditions can be viewed from the perspective of chaos theory. It may be that no point serves as the boundary between formats; rather, thresholds exist between the basins (i.e., formats) and within these sets, the focal tools serve as the attractors. Furthermore, a whole alternative hypothesis might be that reference work is a dynamic system (i.e., complex and nonlinear), sensitively dependent on initial conditions. In other words, slightly different initial phrasing of inquiries may lead the same expert reference librarian to different conclusions. Readers interested in pursuing this line of thought might profitably consult James Gleick, *Chaos: Making a New Science* (New York: Penguin Books, 1987), especially pages 44, 103, 169, 170, 179, 219, and 232–233.

6

Evaluative Criteria for Shells

Deborah Henderson, Pamela Monaster Karpf, and Lauren Mayer

The preceding chapter lays out the major elements of the reference transaction in a formal way, that is, as a flowchart model. The reader may now want to consider a machine-based implementation of this model. The choices may be narrowed down to original programming or using a KBS shell. This chapter is for those readers who want to adopt the latter approach. An "expert system shell can be considered as a reasoning system out of which all the knowledge has been emptied. When knowledge about a new domain is entered into the shell appropriately, an expert system is created."[1] Currently there are more than 40 KBS shells available in the market. Yet, the best or most appropriate for developing KBS in the library reference domain have not been identified. There are three basic factors that confound the selection of an appropriate shell for any one domain. First, there are so many shells commercially available, that sheer numbers create an obstacle to selection. Second, these products vary widely in price, quality, and complexity.[2] Finally, shells that are of acceptable quality may be better suited for solving one type of problem in the reference domain than for solving another (e.g., ready reference, bibliographic instruction, directional questions, and staff training). The practicing librarian is unlikely to have either the time or the funding necessary to conduct a comprehensive comparative search among the available shells in order to identify one that will best meet the needs of his library and ultimately the user community. To facilitate such a venture, the authors have articulated a discrete set of forty-eight criteria that will aid librarians, who may be developing their first KBS, in making informed choices and decisions.

6.1

Objectives

Although several authors have articulated evaluative criteria for KBS shells,[3] none have been published for the library reference domain. The goal of this chapter is to produce a list of criteria specifically for the reference domain based on experimentation with several shells and elaboration of existing criteria.

6.2
Scope

6.2.1 KBS Shells

Shells, also referred to in the literature as Expert System Building Tools (ESBTs), or simply "tools," are "software package[s] designed for the creation of specific expert systems."[4] Shells are the preferred development environment for reference applications, since it may be assumed that the typical librarian does not have the level of expertise required to program a KBS in a complex language like LISP or Prolog.[5] Further, much of the recent reference prototyping reported in the literature has utilized a shell-based approach.[6] At the other end of the development spectrum, off-the-shelf varieties are still limited to the specific needs they are developed for and are not widely available for the general reference domain. Recent trends in KBS technology have led to widespread use of personal computer (PC)-based KBS shells. Early KBS technology was inextricably linked with special-purpose programming languages such as LISP and Prolog, which dictated the use of large-scale environments such as mainframes. Although KBS continue to be built using a variety of hardware, "the new reality is expert systems built and/or executed on personal computers."[7] In August 1984, two different software products for constructing KBS on personal computers were released. "For the first time, tools became available to build small knowledge-based systems on widely available hardware without special programming expertise in LISP or Prolog."[8] In short, the trend away from mainframes toward PCs facilitated the availability and use of shells by individuals with no particular artificial intelligence programming training.

Although PC-based tools were initially dismissed as suitable for only small, toylike systems, they are now considered to have reached a level of maturity that has led to their acceptance as a preferred development environment for KBS.[9] Factors in their acceptance are: the relative low cost of PC-based KBS development tools, the ubiquity of PCs themselves, as well as the fact that PC-based expert system shells "have long been appreciated as ideal for exploration and experimentation, particularly for [developers] just beginning to work with KBS technology"[10] (see Table 6.1). For all these reasons, "a shell program will be the development software of choice for most librarians."[11]

Table 6.1
Advantages of Shell-Based Expert
System Development

- Requires little programming knowledge
- Widely available (vs. off-the-shelf systems)
- Lower development costs
- Less time consuming
- Less labor intensive
- Equipment already available in libraries
- Contributes to full utilization of equipment

6.2.2 Reference Domain

"The key factors in determining when it is appropriate to develop an expert system are the nature, complexity and scope of the problem to be solved."[12] The domain of reference service consists of various tasks and activities, such as bibliographic instruction, interlibrary loan, and question answering as discussed in Chapter 3. The task most often implemented using KBS technology is that of question answering, usually at the level of simple, fact-type questions (see Chapter 8).

Certain intrinsic qualities of reference service make KBS development appropriate and they also dictate the choice of an appropriate shell, as "No shell will be perfectly suited to all tasks,...and so long as the task characteristics are known, an intelligent choice of expert system development tools [shells] can be made."[13]

One of the task characteristics of reference is that the solutions to reference queries are heuristic in nature. That is, they require the use of rules-of-thumb to achieve solutions. Second, according to Chapters 1 and 5, the nature of reference service is such that librarians do reference by format, or at least teach by format. In Chapters 1 and 4, as well as elsewhere, Richardson postulates that a reference librarian first mentally categorizes a user's query by type of source (i.e. format)—essentially a pruning activity—and then by specific title(s) within that format.[14] This type of reference activity represents a multiple classification task in that the process itself consists of multiple steps and also because most reference queries may be answered with a recommendation of more than one title. Furthermore, these recommendations may be made with greater or lesser degrees of confidence. Thus, the uncertainty inherent in every recommendation is another characteristic of the task domain, which has bearing on the choice of a shell.

With respect to the scope of the reference domain, the range of reference sources the experts use to solve problems is extensive (Sheehy's *Guide to Reference Books*, 10th edition, 1986, has over 14,000 sources) yet narrow (each individual source can be classified into predetermined formats). Thus, the nature, complexity, and scope of the reference domain justify library reference service KBS applications, and also necessitate the careful selection of appropriate development tools. Although until now the task of question answering has been referred to in a generic sense, in reality, several distinct activities fall under the rubric of question answering. These activities include directional queries, ready-reference or simple fact-type questions, holdings questions (known item searches), and what James Parrott refers to as "complex substantive" queries (those requiring bibliographic verification, subject searches, etc.).[15] Therefore, it is important to note that because every reference department has differing needs and users, they may want to apply a KBS to different aspects of question answering. Thus, a single KBS shell will not meet the needs of all reference question-answering applications in all libraries. Indeed, "the requirements for an expert system shell do not exist a priori but are derived from the uses to which the shell will be put."[16]

6.2.3 Importance of Criteria

Criteria are an important aid in selecting the appropriate KBS shell for individual reference departments. Librarians who may be developing their first KBS will find this discrete set of evaluative criteria a rational alternative to either haphazard selection or extensive individual research. The latter can be overwhelming and is certainly labor intensive. Thus, utilization of this set of criteria will eliminate the need for each prospective developer to "reinvent the wheel" by researching criteria from the perspective of the reference domain. This set of criteria will promote efficiency and economy of effort in the KBS shell selection process. Additionally, the discussion of each criterion will aid the developer in determining those features that will be most useful for their application before actual development begins.

6.3
Method

The following criteria were developed using a combination of hands-on experience with KBS shells, elaboration on existing criteria found in the literature, and knowledge of the reference process and domain. A systematic literature search was restricted to English-language, scholarly materials published within the last ten years whose subject content dealt with KBS shells, not limited to the library domain, and covered the following sources:

1. Dissertation Abstracts International
2. ERIC
3. *Information Science Abstracts*
4. *Library and Information Science Abstracts*
5. *Library Literature*
6. *Medline*
7. ORION (UCLA's OPAC)
8. PsycLIT
9. *Science Citation Index*

6.4
Criteria

The criteria elucidated below are potentially applicable to all reference applications. However, each library's reference department will want to determine the relative significance of each criterion based on its unique needs and individual developer's preferences. The following discussion of the criteria will provide the basis on which the practicing reference librarian may decide what importance to assign each criterion. By combining the criteria outlined below, reference departments will be able to select the KBS shell that will best meet the majority of their needs. The arrangement of criteria is adapted from a logical framework suggested by previously articulated evaluation schema extant in the literature.[17] The nine broad categories are: knowledge representation; inference engine; developer interface; end-user interface; software; hardware; training/company support; documentation; and cost.

6.4.1 Knowledge Representation

Knowledge representation is the method used to encode and store facts and relationships in a knowledge base. The knowledge that may be easily represented by the shell is a key consideration in choosing a shell.[18] The primary methods of knowledge representation in the shell environment are outlined below.

6.4.1.1 Rules
Rules are one mode of representing knowledge and solving problems. A rule is a formal way of specifying a recommendation, directive, or strat-

egy, expressed as IF premise THEN conclusion or IF condition THEN action.[19] Rules establish a relationship among a set of facts. For example:

IF CLOUDY,
THEN TOTE UMBRELLA.

In the application area of reference, the rules attempt to simulate the thought processes the librarian goes through in answering a reference query. For example:

IF SPELLING PROBLEM,
THEN CONSULT DICTIONARY.

Currently, "the rule-based approach to representing expert knowledge is the most common method used in the library/information retrieval field, . . . And the vast majority of KBS development programs for micros employ a rule based schema."[20] KBS shells that employ rule-based schemata include ESIE, Instant Expert Plus, Intelligence Compiler, 1st Class, and Guru.

6.4.1.2 Frames

Another method of knowledge representation is frames, also referred to as "objects" or "units." Frames are self-contained bits of information that may interact with other frames. They are made up of "objects," which are in essence the objects in the expert's world, and "slots," which are filled with attributes of those objects. In a reference application, the objects would be the reference sources and the slots would be filled with the characteristics of those sources. For example,

Object: *Webster's II New Riverside University Dictionary*
Slot: Definitions
Slot: Synonyms
Slot: Etymology
Slot: Pronunciation

Frames may or may not incorporate inheritance, the process by which characteristics of one object are assumed to be characteristics of another. Because the objects of the reference domain—the reference sources—have easily definable characteristics, the concept of organizing knowledge using frames seems intuitively appropriate. It is a fact that reference sources share many characteristics, and may differ in only one attribute. This distinction is what makes specific sources unique and is why a given source would be chosen in one situation and not another.

Frame-based knowledge representation provides the economy and efficiency that make it the representation technique of choice in many areas, though not necessarily in reference work. Although frames have not been widely utilized in reference prototyping, prospective KBS developers are encouraged to consider frames as a viable mode of knowledge representation. As Alberico points out, "expert systems research is a rapidly evolving field and numerous other approaches are being tried. Instead of...rules, we [now] hear about objects, frames and slots."[21] An example of shells that offer a frame-based approach is the Intelligence Compiler. Rules and frames, in effect, use the same pieces of information, the difference being the way in which the knowledge is structured. An additional difference in these two methods is the way in which the inference engine acts upon the knowledge (see Section 6.4.2).

6.4.1.3 Examples

Some tools can generate rules based on real world examples entered by the knowledge engineer/expert. This feature is useful because "Human experts are often able to articulate their expertise in the form of examples better than they are able to express it in the form of rules."[22] In essence, the machine generates the rules for the developer, using induction. These tools are ideal for simple tasks that rely on examples but cannot be used for complex applications.[23] It is interesting to note that a number of existing systems have been built using 1st Class, a shell that utilizes this mode of knowledge representation.[24]

6.4.1.4 Modularity

Modularity is a technique that groups rules. Modules may, in turn, be grouped for easy maintenance and rapid access.[25] A system that provides modularity is appropriate for use in the reference domain because of the easily distinguished formats, such as dictionaries or biographical sources. This method is "desirable in cases where a large number of rules are involved, if the rules can be subdivided into sets."[26] Analysis of the reference transaction could conceivably produce a large number of rules, as well as an enormous number of potential conclusions (equal to the number of reference sources available). In the literature, modularity may also be referred to as "structured rule-based tools."

6.4.1.5 Probabilistic Knowledge

KBS shells may allow the expression of probabilistic knowledge, or the degree to which the knowledge or data is known to be correct. Two types of uncertain knowledge may be represented in a KBS . The first type stems from the incompleteness of information (i.e., it is not that the information is inherently uncertain, but rather that the amount of information is insufficient to solve the problem). The other type of uncertainty arises in those cases in which the knowledge itself is inherently imprecise.[27] The most common approach to expressing uncertainty is through the use of "probability-like numbers attached to facts and rules that indicate either the certainty that the expert has in a rule or the user has in a fact," called certainty, confidence factors, or simply CF.[28] Parenthetically, certainty factors are typically represented by numbers on a continuum between 0 to 100, with CF = 0 meaning absolutely false, CF = 100 meaning absolutely true, and all numbers in between representing the range of inexact certainty.

Because the aim of a KBS is to mimic human decision-making processes, it is important that knowledge be represented in the context of the real world, including all of its uncertainty. Theoretically, then, one would like to have this capability in a KBS shell. In the domain of reference service, confidence factors might be used to rank titles as to the likelihood of their containing the answer to a patron's query, such as in REFSIM, a KBS for general reference developed by James Parrott at the University of Waterloo.

6.4.1.6 Logic

"In the case of [shells], logic commonly refers to a theorem-proving approach involving...substitutions of variables performed in such a way as to make two items match identically."[29] Much of the formerly articulated criteria in the literature discuss logic as both a means of representing knowledge and an inference approach. With respect to the former, "logic representation is based on predicate logic (also known as predicate calculus or standard logic),"[30] and includes facts and rules. With respect to the latter, most shells now incorporate logic into the inference engine, enabling the developer to focus on the surface level of knowledge representation (i.e., rule creation).

6.4.2 Inference Engine / Methods Of Reasoning

The inference engine is that part of the KBS that performs the reasoning function. The modes of inferencing available in a shell are important, because they predetermine the form in which knowledge must be represented (i.e., in the form of IF–THEN rules, frames, or examples).[31] Depending on the intended function of a KBS, some methods of inferencing may be more appropriate than others. Thus, the application domain is a determining factor in the choice of an appropriate inference strategy, and thus of an appropriate shell.

Based on the potential functions of a KBS in the reference domain (i.e., classification, advising, and instruction), backward- and forward-chaining, inheritance, and induction have been identified as the most appropriate methods of reasoning to look for in a shell.[32] "Another important consideration in a tool is the degree of integration of its various features."[33] For example, tools that provide multiple modes of inferencing and allow for simultaneous operation offer greater flexibility to the developer. "Full integration is desirable so that all the tool features can be brought to bear, if needed, on the solution of a single problem."[34]

6.4.2.1 Backward-Chaining

This method of reasoning is often called "goal-directed." This phrase means that the system works backward from the conclusion of the rules to determine if the information provided by the user proves that goal. An example would be:

> *Dictionary of National Biography*
> IF person is male
> and person is dead
> and person is British.

6.4.2.2 Forward-Chaining

This method is sometimes called "data driven." This process occurs when the system sequences from facts to final conclusion. An example would be:

> IF person is male
> and person is dead
> and person is British
> THEN *Dictionary of National Biography*.

6.4.2.3 Inductive Reasoning

This mode of reasoning dictates the use of examples to represent domain knowledge. From groups of examples, the inference engine performs induction and generates rules that universally apply to those examples. The knowledge engineer inputs large numbers of domain examples that constitute the system's information base. To make a recommendation, the tool converts the examples into a rule and determines the order the system will follow when questioning the user.[35] Shells that offer inductive reasoning include TIMM and Arity/Expert.

6.4.2.4 Inheritance

This method of reasoning is most closely associated with the use of frames/objects. "If you think of chaining as the inference strategy that allows a system to determine new facts from the initial data, then inheritance is the inference strategy used by object-oriented systems."[36] An example of this process is as follows:

> Parent> Object: *Dictionary of National Biography*
> Status: dead

Nationality: British
Gender: male
Style: narrative Child>
Object: *Dictionary of American Biography*
Nationality: American

The "child" will inherit all of the attributes of the "parent" unless the slot is restated with a different value. In the example above, the *Dictionary of American Biography* shares the characteristics of status, gender, and style with the *Dictionary of National Biography,* and differs only in the characteristic of nationality. One of the advantages of this mode of inferencing is that it saves time in the development process by allowing more compact representation of information (see Section 6.4.1.2).

6.5

Developer Interface

Developmental facilities are crucial to successful knowledge-base creation, editing and debugging, end-user interface creation, and control. Important features to consider in selecting a shell include five concerns related to knowledge-base creation and five concerns related to knowledge-base editing.

6.5.1 Internal Editor or Extensibility

A shell either should have its own word processing-like facility, or should be extensible to an external word-processing package to aid in the actual creation and inputting of the knowledge base and the rules. Importing and exporting to and from an external word-processing program can extend development time significantly.

6.5.2 Line Entry versus Menu Entry

In some shells the developer must type in line by line the rules and the facts, using the prescribed format, while in others the shell provides a preformatted screen into which the developer simply plugs the information. An example of the former is ESIE and Instant Expert Plus is an example of the latter.

6.5.3 Graphics

Graphics can be valuable in creating the end-user interface. While few KBS development tools currently contain internal graphics packages, many have the capability to interface with external graphics packages (or external text editors with graphics capabilities). If graphics is a feature that the developer desires, it is important to choose a shell that will be compatible with any graphics packages already owned or considered for purchase. Shells that have internal graphics packages are Experfacts and KDS; those with graphics interface capabilities include ART and KEE.

6.5.4 Compilability

A compiler translates English-like knowledge bases into an unspecified internal form.[37] KBS shells that can be compiled run faster than those that cannot, but a compiled system "tends to limit online editing during development."[38] Not surprisingly, Intelligence/Compiler compiles.

6.5.5 Help

Online help or online tutorials are desirable features, and may supplement written documentation (see Section 6.11). One of the more useful features is context-sensitive help, which provides assistance and information directly related to the portion of the shell in which the developer is working. 1st Class is one shell that provides this feature. Additionally, 1st Class HT includes a hypertext interface to guide developers by answering questions and providing information required to build a new KBS knowledge base.[39] Tutorials are useful when they guide the user through the basic steps of development and allow the user to actually construct a prototype. Instant Expert Plus, for example, walks the user through the creation and implementation of a small advisory system.

6.5.6 Knowledge-Base Editing

It is likely that the developer will spend more time editing and debugging the knowledge base than actually creating it. Of course, as new reference sources become available and older sources become outdated, the developer will want the ability to make changes in order to maintain the integrity of the database. According to Gilmore, it is important to have some type of online editor even if the database was created on an external editor or word processor "to maintain the state of the development environment."[40]

6.5.7 Full-Screen Editing versus Menu Editing

The value of having a full-screen editing facility rather than a menu facility is that changes can be made in the database while the developer is creating the knowledge base. If a full-screen editing facility is not available, the developer will have to close the database, select a menu, choose to edit or modify, then get back into the database, and finally, make the changes desired. Instant Expert Plus is one system whose lack of a full-screen editor necessitates this time-consuming process.

6.5.8 Additional Editing Features

These features include: syntax check, spell check, search utility (specific attribute editor that lets the developer identify every reference to any particular attribute contained in the knowledge base), consistency check, global change facility, and graphical representation of the knowledge base.

6.5.9 Explanation Facilities

Most shells provide a facility for the developer to trace the inferencing of the system by invoking the "how" and/or "why" facilities. This feature may be useful in the debugging process. The question "how" elicits information concerning rules or data that has led to a particular conclusion, and "why" elicits information about why the system is asking a particular question. It is unfortunate that most "how" and "why" features simply restate in ungrammatical English what the developer already knows. Therefore, this function proves to be only marginally useful.

6.5.10 Apropos Facility

This facility lists all the knowledge structures that mention a particular attribute so that the developer can see how changing that attribute might propagate a change of behavior in the system (i.e., global effect). The apropos facility also allows a universal search and replace to be performed (i.e., global change).[41]

6.5.11 Saved Cases

Some systems will provide the ability to store and automatically reenter exemplary cases that the developer can then use for modifying or debugging the system. This utility can be a useful aid in the developmental stages of a KBS, by allowing the developer to "run test cases on the system being developed making appropriate modifications... until the system can solve all cases correctly and consistently."[42]

6.6

End-User Interface Creation

6.6.1 Explanation Facility

"Most tools allow a developer to include information that can be obtained by the user if the user asks for more elaborate explanation."[43] "How" and "why" facilities, as discussed above, may also be available to the user, and the developer may have the ability to augment the information presented to the user by these facilities.

6.6.2 Screen Formatting Utilities

Almost all tools have programming facilities that allow the developer to create screens that will be aesthetically pleasing and informative to the end user.

These facilities include: icon editors, window size and window placement, graphics, color, and utilities for specifying screen titles.[44] The developer should keep in mind the audience for whom the system is being developed when choosing a shell, as the ability to create more elaborate or explanatory screens will be more or less important depending on the audience. In the general reference domain, the end user could be either the librarian, the support staff, or the client. The screen appearance will be somewhat less important if the system is intended to be used only by the library staff. On the other hand, formatting utilities will be more important in developing an interface for the client, as they will not only require more instruction and guidance, but also will need it to be presented in a simple and clear manner.

6.6.3 Graphics/Animation Facilities

Currently, few existing tools provide for developing graphics and animation within the tool itself. Therefore, most graphics or animation capabilities will result from interfacing with a graphics package. Because these features can only add to the aesthetic value of a system, they are not essential. However, if the future holds the time and money to add these features, the developer should choose a system that will allow for such expansion.

6.6.4 Control

6.6.4.1 Lockability
The developer may want the ability to prohibit additions and deletions from the database, or to regulate them. While many KBS allow users to input information in the form of answers to questions or suggestions/comments, this data is usually retained only temporarily. If the shell is lockable, user input does not permanently alter the system's knowledge base.

6.6.4.2 Run-Time Version
"When an expert system shell is modified to incorporate a specific knowledge base and to deactivate certain programming features, the resulting system is called a run time system or a run time version."[45] That is to say, what the public sees on their terminal may be a modified version of what the librarian/developer sees on her terminal, although each version is run from the same database. This decision is based on the developer's perception of how much information the user needs to see. Run-time version facility may be an added cost (see Section 6.12).

6.6.4.3 Access Control/Passwords
This feature is similar to lockability in that it restricts access to the database by requiring a password for initial entry into the system. This feature can tie in with run-time versions as well by allowing certain passwords access to particular portions or versions of the database. It is another way of controlling the use of information in the database.

6.7

End-User Interface

Many of the facilities available for developers are also relevant with respect to the end user, although the facilities may appear in modified form to the user.

Ideally, any KBS created for the client as the end user would successfully emulate the human reference interview process. Unless a system can handle natural language responses (i.e., has a significant thesaurus), it will be able to simulate only closed-ended reference queries. Below are some features to consider in terms of what the user will see.

6.7.1 Response to System Queries

This feature refers to the manner in which the user interacts with the system (i.e., answers the questions presented). It does make a difference whether the user is required to answer a question with a "fixed" response ("yes," "no," or multiple choice answer), or whether he may respond with free text or natural language. While free text would be ideal because it simulates the open-ended question in the reference interview paradigm, the developer must anticipate all possible responses (or provide a comprehensive thesaurus), making fixed choices the more viable alternative.

6.7.2 Visual Presentation

Ideally, the shell should allow the developer to create screens or menus for the user that are self-explanatory and easy to use, clear and inviting with not too much text but sufficient information, and that do not require extensive reading of instructions. Graphics are not necessary, but can be a nice feature for the user interface. The developer should bear in mind that some users may be intimidated by overzealous use of graphics and visual aids.

6.7.3 Keyboard Functions

Questions to consider regarding the system's utilization of the keyboard include: Does the keyboard interaction with the shell conform to normal expectations from users? That is, do the arrow keys work as expected, or, for example, do ⟨Enter⟩ and ⟨Return⟩ accomplish the same function?

6.7.4 Multiple and Uncertain Answers

Some shells allow the user to answer "unknown," or to give multiple answers to the system's queries. "If the problem is tightly structured and involves analyzing documents that are always complete, multiple answers and unknown might not be necessary. Most problems involving judgment however benefit from this capability."[46] In short, acceptance of these answers increases the system's overall flexibility. In the reference domain, a user may be asked if she is looking for information about a living or dead person. A flexible system will be able to accept the response, "I don't know," and still be able to provide an acceptable answer.

6.7.5 Initial Pruning/Directed Search

"Initial pruning . . . [allows the user] to direct the line of questioning so that the system need not pursue areas that are felt to be irrelevant or unnecessary."[47] For example, in the reference domain, the user may be directed to encyclopedias or biographical sources without first wading through many questions that do not apply to their reference query. If the user is forced to play "20 questions" each time he approaches the system, it may reduce repeat use. Instant Expert Plus allows the user to "prune" at the beginning of the search because each format may be organized in an individual unit called a "class."

6.7.6 Multiple Conclusions

Another feature to offer the end user is the potential for more than one recommendation. For instance, if two sources could answer a question, the system would be able to provide this information, perhaps with a proba-bility ranking that presents the most likely answer first, and a secondary choice as well. This response could increase user confidence in the system because it would more closely emulate the behavior of an expert librarian.

6.7.7 Help

The "how" and "why" explanation facilities described above can be useful to the user, as well as the developer. In addition, there is the "what if" option. This feature "allows the end-user to select alternative parameter values and observe the effect on the outcome."[48] It is important to note that the system's ability to answer "how," "why," and "what if" queries theoretically enhances the user's confidence in and comprehension of the system's decision-making ability (see Section 6.11).

6.7.8 Fast/Slow Interaction

The speed of execution is largely a function of the programming language in which the shell is written. Except through initial selection of a shell, the developer cannot control the speed of interaction in the system. Speed is largely subjective and becomes important only if it discourages use.

6.8 _____

Software

6.8.1 Programming Language

KBS shells are written predominantly in the languages, PROLOG, C, LISP, and PASCAL. The language the shell is written in is important, since it determines whether the system is compilable (see Section 6.8.4). Programs that are written in LISP are generally more sophisticated. "However, even these tools are now being rewritten in languages such as C to increase speed, reduce memory requirements, and to promote availability on a larger variety of computers."[49] In the majority of cases the language is irrelevant to the immediate concerns of the developer because it is so far removed from their realm of interaction. However, the language will matter if the KBS developer plans to extend the program and therefore needs to be literate in that language.

6.8.2 Extensibility/Links/Hooks

Extensibility allows the developer to expand the shell, either by adding or modifying programming code or by linking with other languages, programs, or databases. An issue to consider is that the program itself can be "locked" by the vendor (see Section 6.8.6).

6.8.3 Embeddability

Embeddable systems are those that can be integrated into some preexisting external environment.[50] "Shells that developers embed in conventional software—shells such as Neuron Data's NEXPERT OBJECT—are the next step in the progression of expert system applications."[51] Embeddability supports data exchange with external databases. It allows the KBS to draw upon other programs, and those programs may be able to draw upon the KBS when necessary. In the reference domain, a KBS could be embedded in a larger database, such as the library's online catalog, acting as an intelligent front end to that database.

6.8.4 Compilability/Speed

A compiler translates English-like knowledge bases into an unspecified internal form. Compiled systems run faster, but compiling "tends to limit online editing during [system] development."[52] Compilability can occur incrementally or in a batch mode. It "reduces the memory requirements and increases the speed of the KBS; [while] incremental compilability speeds development."[53] Development is accelerated through debugging section by section. The domain of reference service and its easily defined divisions of the reference tools by format lend themselves well to modularity. Thus, the ability to create, edit, and compile each module or section separately can save development time in the reference environment.

6.8.5 Run–Time Version

The ability to provide run–time version sometimes requires additional software, which could increase costs (see Section 6.6.4.2).

6.8.6 Lockability

There are two kinds of lockability, that imposed by the vendor and that controlled by the developer. With respect to the former, "most tools on the market are locked, so they may not be tampered with or the code altered. This provides some protection for the vendor while causing some difficulty for the... developers."[54] Thus, vendor protection can make it impossible for the developer to alter the existing program, forcing the developer to work within the constraints of the shell program. With respect to developer-controlled lockability (see Section 6.6.4.1), this feature is also a function of the software. If this feature is desired for the individual developer's reference department, it must be considered when choosing a shell.

6.8.7 Additional Software

In some cases the KBS shell requires the use of additional software programs or packages in order to operate. For example, the PC version of Instant Expert Plus (a shell originally developed for the Macintosh) requires the use of Gem Desktop, a DOS window environment, in order to simulate the mouse facility of the Macintosh. Additionally, "some tools require a separate language to be running on the computer before they will function properly or work at all."[55]

6.9

Hardware

"The [hardware] supported by the various tools [shells] are primarily a function of the language and operating system in which the tools are written, and the computer's memory, processing, and graphics display capabilities."[56]

6.9.1 Memory

An important consideration is the amount of memory required to house and run the system. It is also necessary to take into account the extent of the knowledge base and rule base to be created. An example in which memory capacity becomes a problem is with the shell NEXPERT OBJECT. The memory required for loading this shell is well beyond the limits of the typical PC. NEXPERT OBJECT not only requires two megabytes of RAM memory to run the program itself, but also requires Microsoft Windows, which also uses precious memory.[57] Depending on the extent of the intended system, the developer will want to be aware of the memory requirements of the shell under consideration.

6.9.2 Host PC

Choice of a shell depends on the type of PC available. The majority of the shells are designed for IBM-compatible PCs with a growing number for Apple's Macintosh.

6.9.3 Additional Hardware

Some programs may require additional memory or peripheral equipment. Examples of peripheral equipment are a color monitor or a mouse.

6.10
Training/Company Support

In the library domain, the knowledge engineer and the domain or subject expert are likely to be the same person. Therefore, it is necessary to provide for this individual some kind of training, either in the techniques of knowledge engineering or in the use of the shell. Many shell vendors offer a wide variety of training programs and company support. These include workshops, electronic mail, telephone hotlines, consulting, and documentation. Issues to consider in workshops are cost, course length, and number of people to be trained. The price of workshop attendance may be included in the purchase price of the shell. Electronic mail and telephone hotlines provide ongoing interaction with the trained technicians. In addition to direct vendor support, conferences, seminars, workshops, and courses are offered throughout the country by various independent sponsors or organizations.

6.11
Documentation

Documentation is important. The successful creation of a KBS depends on how well the developer understands and uses the shell to its full potential. Documentation must be readable, that is, clearly written with explanations or cross-references in the text and written at a skill level not above that of the developer. Additionally, the documentation should provide clear, understandable examples, an extensive index with cross-references, a glossary, and updates corresponding to new versions. "Many current tools lack good training, documentation and support programs simply because their developers have spent all of their time developing the product and have not taken the time to explain how to use it. If you are willing to thrash around in the documentation, you can eventually figure out how to use the smaller tools, but the larger tools require good documentation and training."[58]

6.12
Cost

Because libraries are traditionally constrained by budget limitations, cost will unquestionably be one of the major considerations in selecting a shell for KBS development in the library reference domain. Cost of shells ranges from shareware (technically, shareware is freely distributed, but the vendor does expect some nominal payment) to close to $60,000.[59] Potential developers will need to consider not only initial start-up costs, but also "hidden costs" represented in staff time, hardware and software maintenance, and user instruction. There is not necessarily a one-to-one correlation between cost and quality.

6.13

Ranking Of Criteria

Although cost was the last criterion discussed, we believe that it is the most discriminating factor in choosing a shell. Even though many features of a shell may be desirable, it will automatically be eliminated from the pool of potential purchases if it is out of the library's price range. For this reason, the criterion "Cost" is listed first in Appendix A, which is a checklist for the developer to use when evaluating KBS building tools (see Appendix B). Documentation is second on the list because, simply put, a shell without decent documentation renders it virtually unusable. The next three major criteria correspond to essential components of a KBS, namely knowledge representation, inference engine, and interface. The importance of these criteria will be determined by individual developers based on their needs.

6.14

Conclusions

We have tried to identify all relevant criteria for a reference librarian to consider when choosing a KBS development tool (Appendix B). It is important to recognize that no one shell will universally meet the needs of all reference environments and that, conversely, there may be a multiplicity of shells that could potentially satisfy all the needs of one library. Since each library will represent a unique set of needs, it is important to articulate those needs before attempting to evaluate any shells, and then to weigh each criteria accordingly. It is important to keep in mind when choosing a shell that there is an implicit trade-off between flexibility and ease of use. "The simpler tools are shells into which knowledge is inserted in a specific, structured fashion. The more sophisticated tools are generally more difficult to learn, but allow the system developer a much wider choice of knowledge base representations, inference strategies, and the form of the end-user interface."[60] The world of KBS development tools is rapidly evolving. In summary, "the variety of expert system building tools keeps increasing, prices continue to drop, and new features keep getting added to the established tools."[61]

Endnotes _____

1. Kamran Parsaye and Mark Chignell, *Expert Systems for Experts* (New York: Wiley, 1988), 304.

2. William B. Gevarter, "The Nature and Evaluation of Commercial Expert System Building Tools," *IEEE Computer* (May 1987): 27. Also, Brent G. Wilson and Jack R. Welsh, "Small Knowledge-Based Systems in Education and Training: Something New Under the Sun," *Educational Technology* (November 1986): 11.

3. Recent articles by Gevarter, Gilmore, and Harmon et al. (1988) have discussed general criteria for evaluating expert system building tools.

4. Rao Aluri and Donald E. Riggs, "Applications of Expert Systems to Libraries", in *Advances in Library Automation and Networking,* Vol. 2, ed. Joe A. Hewitt (Greenwich, CT: JAI Press, 1988), 6.

5. This statement is based on the fact that entrance requirements for the UCLA Graduate School of Library and Information Science, which according to Dr. Robert M. Hayes are the highest standards in the country, include only one quarter of computer programming (UCLA GSLIS *Announcement* September 1990, 18): "The school has identified three requirements which should be completed by the time students begin the M.L.S. program: . . . (3) A computer programming requirement, met either by completing a college-level course . . . or by passing a proficiency examination administered by the school (most standard languages such as PL/1, FORTRAN, COBOL, PASCAL, and BASIC or database packages such as dBASE3, KNOWLEDGEMAN, and CONDOR are acceptable).

6. The best-known examples are POINTER, an expert system for government documents developed by Karen Smith at SUNY Buffalo; the National Agricultural Library's Answerman, a ready-reference expert system developed by Sam Waters; PLEXUS, a gardening advisor developed at the University of London by Alina Vickery and Helen M. Brooks; REFSIM, a general reference expert system developed by James R. Parrott at the University of Waterloo; and the Searchin' General, an expert system for biographical sources developed by UCLA Graduate School of Library and Information Science, Debbie Henderson, Patti Martin, Lauren Mayer, and Pamela Monaster.

7. William P. Martorelli, "PC-Based Expert Systems Arrive," *Datamation* (April 1, 1988): 56.

8. Wilson and Welsh, 11.

9. Martorelli, 56.

10. Ibid.

11. Ralph Alberico, "Software for Expert Systems: Languages Versus Shells," *Small Computers in Libraries* 8 (July/August 1988): 4.

12. Donald A. Waterman, *A Guide to Expert Systems,* The Teknowledge Series in Knowledge Engineering (Reading, MA: Addison Wesley, 1986), 131.

13. A. Martin and R.K.H. Law, "Expert System For Selecting Expert System Shells," *Information and Software Technology* 30, no. 10 (December 1, 1988): 579.

14. See Chapter five of John V. Richardson, Jr., "The Logic of Reference Work: Basic and Subordinate Level Knowledge," in *Libraries and Expert Systems,* ed. Craig McDonald and John Weckert (London: Taylor Graham, 1991).

15. James R. Parrott, *Using Expert Systems in Reference Services: Course Notes* (Waterloo, ON: University of Waterloo Press, 1989), 11.

16. Ronald Citrenbaum, James R. Geissman, and Roger Schultz, "Selecting a Shell," *AI Expert* (September 1987): 38.

17. Recent articles by Gevarter, Gilmore, and Harmon et al. (1988) have discussed general criteria for evaluating expert system building tools. See Bibliography.

18. Gevarter, 25.

19. Harmon et al., 394.

20. Ralph Alberico, "Knowledge Representation: The Realm of the Possible," *Small Computers in Libraries* 7 (November 1987): 5.

21. Ibid.

22. Gevarter, 27.

23. Harmon et al., 47.

24. Expert systems that have been created using the 1st Class shell include Answerman and Aquaref.

25. Gevarter, 25.

26. Harmon et al., 47.

27. Parsaye and Chignell, 211–212.

28. Harmon et al., 61.

29. Gevarter, 27.

30. Parrott, 23.

31. Harmon et al., 61.

32. Martin and Law, 581–582.

33. Gevarter, 27.

34. Ibid.

35. Harmon et al., 47.

36. Ibid., 61.

37. Bruce Olsen, Bruce Pumplin, and Mickey Williamson, "The Getting of Wisdom: PC Expert System Shells," *Computer Language* 4 (March 1987): 117–150.

38. John F. Gilmore and Kirt Pulaski, "A Comprehensive Evaluation of Expert System Tools," in *Applications of Artificial Intelligence III: Proceedings of SPIE International Society of Optical Engineers in Orlando, FL 1–3 April 1986,* ed. John F. Gilmore (Bellingham, WA:SPIE):2–15.

39. John Pallatto, "Development Shell Gets Hypertext Feature," *PC WEEK* 6, no. 11 (March 20, 1989): 54.

40. Gilmore, 7.

41. Ibid.

42. Ibid.

43. Harmon et al., 61.

44. Gevarter, 7.

45. Harmon, 269.

46. Ibid., 63.

47. Gevarter, 28.

48. Ibid.

49. Ibid., 29.

50. Gilmore, 7.

51. Tom Arcidiacono, "Expert System On-call," *PC Tech Journal* (November 1988): 112.

52. Gilmore, 8. Also, Harmon et al., 64.

53. Gevarter, 29.

54. Harmon et al., 65.

55. Ibid., 64.

56. Gevarter, 29.

57. Jon Lemelin and John Li, "Analysis and Evaluation of Selected Expert System Software Packages," University of California, Los Angeles, Anderson Graduate School of Management [unpublished draft] 1989: 14.

58. Harmon et al., 65.

59. Ibid., 66.

60. Gevarter, 27.

61. Harmon et al., 67.

7

User Interface Issues in General Reference Work

Karen Howell

7.1

The User Interface

The purpose of this chapter is to provide information about user interface design to help librarians: (1) evaluate the user interfaces of expert system applications they plan to purchase; (2) determine whether an expert system shell provides facilities to create interfaces that will meet their end users' needs; and most important (3) design usable systems that bring about the productivity and training benefits promised by expert systems. The chapter first examines the importance of the user interface in an expert system and deals with some misconceptions about designing user interfaces; the chapter then discusses general user interface principles and special considerations about designing the user interface for expert systems. It also makes suggestions for designing the user interface for an expert system in the general reference domain. The chapter concludes with an interface development and evaluation process, and endnotes for help in designing a user interface.

7.1.1 Importance of the User Interface in an Expert System

The user interface design is critical to the acceptance and use of an expert system.[1] No matter how much time and effort is spent making an expert system correct and efficient, if no one can communicate with the system, it is a failure. Expert systems can present several usability problems encountered by users. Users can become overwhelmed with the system's complexity because they cannot see the underlying reasoning processes. Users may not understand what functions the system can and cannot handle. Users may also be skeptical about the validity of artificial intelligence.

Traditional software packages, such as word processors, automate a process. Very rarely do users require the interface to show the internal workings of the word processor or to produce a representation of the algorithms used to format text and print documents. Expert systems, on the other hand, represent an expert's judgment process, rather than the mere implementation of a process. Expert systems often help in the decision-making process, so users are not content with someone else's judgments being promoted as "the answer." Like other human experts, a reference librarian "doesn't just respond to the immediate request of the user, rather he/she aids the user in formulating the problem and generating a plan. He/she aids the user to determine the right questions to ask, how to look for or evaluate possible answers, how to develop or debug an action to achieve goals."[2]

Users of an expert system miss this progression when the user interface does not make its reasoning process visible. Users want to follow along to be sure they will agree. Typical experts in this group would be doctors, lawyers, physicists, managers, and others who are traditionally viewed as experts in their own field.[3] Consequently, users need explanation of the reasoning process by which a conclusion was reached, and display of this reasoning so they can ascertain whether the process agrees with their own judgments.[4]

The user interface gives the user a way to interact with the knowledge base and inference engine. The knowledge base of facts and rules, the global database of facts established through inference or solicited from the user, and the inference engine should be transparent to the user. Because the user interface is the only component of an expert system visible to the user, in essence the user interface *is* the system to the user. Therefore, it becomes very important for the user to be able to query the explanations the system produces in order to validate the answer, to understand the meaning of the answer, and to decide what to do with the answer. A good user interface alone is not enough to assure acceptance.[5] It does play a key role, however, because the user interface allows the user to access the functions of the system in order to carry out the tasks for which the system was designed, with a minimum of errors.[6]

7.1.2 Misconceptions about User Interface Design

Before looking at the user interface literature for general design principles, several misconceptions about user interface design need to be resolved. The first misconception is that user interface design decisions are unnecessary because natural language interfaces, windowing facilities, built-in help, and adoption of graphical user interface standards will eliminate user difficulties.

This viewpoint is based on an assumption that the user interface consists merely of the surface appearance of an application. As this chapter will discuss later, the visual levels of a user interface are only one stage of the design process. Decisions about the conceptual levels of a user interface (task, conceptual models) and testing and errors analysis influence how the dialogue and events are presented to the user.[7]

A second misconception is that the user interface facilities are built into an expert system shell, and therefore librarians are unable to design a user interface. However, this misconception overlooks the importance of text and graphics in the user interface. Practically all expert system shells allow the developer to supply text for opening screens, screen titles, menu choices, help screens, and explanation screens. If the expert system shell allows developers to import graphics, librarians can include computer clip art, graphics, and charts in the user interface.

Many shells use question-and-answer dialogue, and some offer menu and form fill-in interaction styles, so librarians need to understand how to use these tools to create menu options, choose wording, create meaningful sequences of screens, and provide default choices. Moreover, interface styles used in popular software packages tend to become available in expert system development tools eventually. The growing popularity of user-definable environments exemplified by Borland's Sprint, HyperCard for the Apple Macintosh, and ToolBook for Microsoft Windows, is mirrored in hypertext and windows in Knowledge Pro for Windows, windows in 1st-Class Hypertext,[8] and graphical user interface facilities in Level 5 and NEXPERT OBJECT.[9] Also, HyperCard and HyperPAD can be used to create front ends to expert system applications. Now that SuperCard is being supported by Allegiant Technologies, it looks promising.

A third misconception about user interface design is that the primary purpose of a user-friendly interface is to help novices. Further, people may be experts in a subject field but not in a particular computer system. Furthermore, people transfer between computer systems, and constantly move around the continuum of novice and expert. A well-designed user interface makes all classes of users more productive.[10]

A fourth misconception is that user interface design centers on a few key design issues: choice of interface style, method of cursor movement, whether to have online help, and how to deal with multiple windows on a screen. This focus on screen design is too narrow a view of user interface design, which includes both broader cognitive issues as well as more detailed design issues.

Woods and Roth caution that too often questions about user interface design revolve around current technology, rather than cognitive questions. This approach results in debates such as the merits of menus versus command language, or horizontal versus vertical versus pull-down menu systems.

Such questions should be reformulated into questions about what are the demands on the user's memory and cognitive activity and is there too much competition between the amount of memory and cognitive activity required to make a selection, thereby reducing the user's ability to concentrate on domain tasks. Can a person see all currently available or meaningful options or must he/she recall them? When these types of questions are asked, designers can use various technologies to implement designs that perform the same cognitive function.[11]

At the other end of the spectrum, details involved in any broad design strategy can have great impact on the user because their frequency of use is so high. All users face them all the time. For example, what does the ENTER key do? It could acknowledge a message, terminate data entry, move to a new line, supply a default response to a Yes/No question, or give a "do-it" command. A study comparing user performance with a variety of user interface styles concluded that expending time on perfecting the details—crafting a design—is more important than interface style differences. There was no difference due to the use of command, menu, or iconic style interfaces. The factor that made the most difference in usability of systems was their maturity. Systems that had been revised several times, based on user feedback, were the most usable.[12]

A final misconception is the "peanut-butter view of user-interface design."[13] That is, user interface design can be spread on at the end of the system's development. This misconception thinks of user interface design as nothing more than making system messages more pleasing for the user to read. However, the user interface design is inextricably linked with other system development decisions and must be a concern from the conception to the very end of the software life cycle. A wish list of desirable features must be scrutinized to see whether the features will actually be needed by the users. The visible levels of a user interface (the dialogue, events, and presentation) are the last part of what the user gets in a user interface. The most important user interface issues involve invisible elements—conceptual models, task structure, and information flows.[14]

For example, consider the question of the user's information requirements. The expert system could be used as an expert answer giver, a "second opinion" consultation with a colleague, a "what-if" system so the human can test various scenarios, or a training system in which an expert helps novices learn a task, rather than the expert performing the task herself. The interface designer must determine the goals of the system and the user and make sure the interface provides support for these types of interactions. A "definitive expert" system might use traditional data entry techniques with the system controlling the interaction by asking questions to get data it needs in the inference process. A "what if" system might place the user in control, with the interface reactive rather than prerogative.

7.2

Overview of User Interface Design Principles

What issues should librarians be aware of when designing the user interface of an expert system application? This section reviews general user interface principles found in the human–computer interaction literature. General user interface principles can be grouped into three categories: human information processing issues, models of human–computer interaction, and specific user interface design issues.

7.2.1 Human Information Processing Issues

System designers often make decisions based on the capabilities and limitations of available hardware and software, and fail to take into account the strengths and weaknesses of humans. Several important human performance issues and individual differences affect how well a person can interact with a computer system. A knowledge of these issues can guide the designer in allocating functions between computer and human and providing tools to aid efficient human use of the system.

7.2.1.1 Memory

Human memory can be divided into two types: short-term memory and long-term memory. Short-term memory contains the information necessary for a person to focus on the present task. Items such as phone numbers, numbers while doing addition, and new names are held in short-term memory. Other activities, including thinking, talking, or listening, can interfere with a person's ability to retain information in short-term memory. An often-cited paper describes the capacity of short-term memory as seven plus or minus two, or five to nine items of information.[15] The capacity of short-term memory can be increased by combining several similar or related items into one conceptual unit, a process called "chunking".[16] Chunks can vary in size and complexity, based on a person's knowledge and experience. Experts differ from novices in their ability to create, recognize, and recall large and complex chunks.[17]

Items held in short-term memory can be moved to long-term memory by rehearsing the item over and over. Long-term memory is limited not in capacity but by a person's ability to organize and retrieve information. It takes effort to remember something well, and humans remember better when the material being memorized has a meaningful structure.

These characteristics of human memory have several implications for system designers. Humans have difficulty remembering details and keeping track of changing modes. Because short-term memory is limited, users need help in keeping track of variables that change often. To aid users, systems should be designed to remind users of where they are in complicated, long, or nested procedures. Users need prompts telling them "what actions are appropriate in a current mode and how to change modes." Because of long-term memory limits, users also need aids in remembering "meaning, special codes, and clusters of items."[18]

Several methods can be used to relieve memory demands of the user:

> Divide and Conquer. Modularize the task so different
>   parts can be done separately.
> Displays. Display only information that is relevant at
>   the moment to the task.
> Timing. Give ample time to learn and digest information
>   in order to form "chunks" that can be used to get an
>   overview of all the complex information.[19]

7.2.1.2 Learning

The user's primary source of information on which to build a cognitive model of the system is the user interface. In *The Psychology of Everyday Things,* Donald Norman proposes two cognitive models: (1) a design model, and (2) a user model. The system designer creates a design model of the user, the tasks the user desires to accomplish using the system, and the system itself. This design model is given physical form through the system image (the screens, the dialogue mechanism, documentation, instructions, and labels). The user develops a model, through interaction with the system image, of how the system operates and what it can do.[20]

If the user interface does not clearly portray the designer's model to the user, the user develops an inaccurate model of the system. When the user's model matches the designer's model, the user can learn the system more easily because he is able to predict how the system works. When a new situation arises or an error occurs, the user can figure out what is happening and what to do next.[21] Designers should take advantage of the user's ability to learn and his desire to find meaning in the system's behavior. If the designer does not provide users with a model, they are likely to create their own models. This situation is why some users find it difficult to learn a new system, while others are able to modify and extend system capabilities and often use the system in ways the designers did not foresee.[22]

Humans respond to misunderstandings by teaching others. The expert system interface should do likewise. Designers must account for user confusion and design ways to clarify what the problem is so the user can learn more about how the system functions. When an error occurs, the system should try to figure out what the user intended and suggest what to do to respond correctly.[23]

7.2.1.3 Vision

Several characteristics of the human sensory system have important implications for situations where the user's attention is focused on a point where information is to appear. These figures do not count the time it takes someone to move their eyes or turn their head. The minimum time for detecting a visual signal is 50–200 milliseconds (msec). Visual decay time, the amount of time after which someone will forget half the information, is 90–1000 msec. Information retained immediately after presentation (called partial recall), is 7–17 written letters.

Humans can focus on detail in an area spanned by two degrees. If the information presented is more than two degrees away from the focus, the eyes must move to the new target. Typical eye movement time is 230 msec. When the target is more than 30 degrees away from the focus, the head must be turned to establish a new focal point.[24]

These figures result in several suggestions.[25]

1. If two stimuli are meant to be perceived as one continuous stimulus, they must be presented successively in a range of time less than 50–200 msec (the detection time). "Instant" response time will be perceived within 50 msec, the shortest detection time.

2. If several pieces of information must be integrated, the time delay between each piece must be short enough to prevent loss of sensory trace of one piece before the next one arrives. Screen changes or other interruptions in visual displays should not take more than 90 msec, or the user starts to lose track of the connection between the pieces.

3. The limitations of a human's ability to retain information immediately after presentation (partial recall) means that the user will experience overload if the rate of presentation is high and the user cannot control the pace.

4. Restrictions in visual acuity imply that warning and help messages outside of the focal point should last at least 230 msec for eye movement plus 100–200 msec for detection. Long messages or ones that are difficult to understand must remain on screen even longer.

7.2.2 Models of Human–Computer Interaction

The Random House Dictionary defines a model as "a standard or example for imitation or contrast; a representation, generally in miniature, to show the structure or serve as a copy of something." Before leaping into designing the mechanisms for dialogue, a user interface designer should understand why the dialogue takes place and how the interaction modifies the user's image of the system and future interaction with the system. The word "model" is used in this section for two purposes. First, two models of human–computer interaction are examined to show the structure of dialogue between human and computer. Second, the models of human–computer interaction themselves talk about conceptual models that designers and users hold. Donald Norman describes the designer's and user's conceptual models of systems, and Ben Shneiderman proposes a semantic/syntactic model of user behavior.

7.2.2.1 Norman's Seven Stages of Action

Donald Norman's Seven Stages of Action (Norman, 1986, 1988) attempt to answer the question, "How do people do things?" The seven stages a user goes through are:

Stage 1: Forming the goal
Stage 2: Forming the Intention to act so as to achieve the goal
Stage 3: Specifying a sequence of actions that we plan to do, then specifying the first action to take
Stage 4: Executing the action
Stage 5: Perceiving the state of the world
Stage 6: Interpreting the state of the world
Stage 7: Evaluating the outcome

Two gulfs, one of execution, and one of evaluation, result in systems that are difficult to use. The gap between Stage 2, forming an intention, and Stage 3, specifying a sequence of actions, is the Gulf of Execution. How easily can a person translate their intended action into an allowable system command? Often a person has to "work around" the system, rather than perform an action directly.

The Gulf of Evaluation is the result of a gap between Stage 5, perceiving the state of the world, Stage 6, interpreting the state of the world, and Stage 7, evaluating the outcome. How hard is it for the user to determine if the system did what he intended it to do? The gulf is small when the user's mental model of the system coincides with the designer's model and the user can predict how the system will behave. The user's model and the designer's model coincide when the user interface created by the designer clearly communicates the designer's model to the user.[26]

Norman suggests using the Seven Stages of Action as a basic checklist of questions to ask to ensure that the Gulfs of Evaluation and Execution are bridged.[27] How easily can one:

1. determine the function of the system?
2. tell what actions are possible?
3. determine the mapping between intention to physical movement?
4. perform the action?
5. tell if the system is in the desired state?

6. determine mapping from system state to interpretation?
7. tell what state the system is in?

He boils these questions down to four principles of good design:

1. Visibility—by looking, the user can tell the state of the device and the alternatives for action
2. Good conceptual model—designer provides a good conceptual model of the user, with consistency in the presentation of operations and results and a coherent, consistent system image
3. Good mappings—it is possible to determine the relationships between actions and results, between the controls and their effects, and between the system state and what is visible
4. Feedback—the user receives full and continuous feedback about the results of actions

7.2.2.2 Shneiderman's Semantic/Syntactic Model of User Behavior

In the syntactical/semantic model of user behavior (Shneiderman, 1987),[28] users must have three kinds of knowledge to use a system successfully:

1. Syntactical Knowledge of Commands

This is knowledge of the correct structure of issuing commands. Examples of this kind of knowledge are physical actions, such as typing correct keystrokes, pressing a function key, moving a mouse, and other system-dependent implementations of an interface.

2. Semantic Knowledge of Computer Concepts

This is knowledge about the meaning of computer concepts. Examples of this type of knowledge are opening and closing files, moving through hierarchical file directories, constructing a legitimate file name, and other objects and actions needed to manipulate a computer system.

3. Semantic Knowledge of Task Domain

This is knowledge about the meaning of the application and the objects and actions used to carry out a task in the application. If the task is maintaining a bank account, then the objects might be account owner, account name, account balance, and so on; and the actions might be to make a deposit, write a check, transfer money between accounts, and the like. If the task is answering a reference question, then the objects might be patron, reference book, and library building, and the actions might be to, for example, choose a subject field, ask a question, volunteer information, ask for an explanation, or print a map.

Users can concentrate on their tasks when a computer system allows them to operate the system without a high level of syntactical knowledge about command syntax and semantic knowledge of computer concepts. The user can concentrate on questions such as "What can I do with this system?" and "How do I put together the right commands to create a strategy that achieves my goal?"

7.3
Special Concerns of User Interface in Expert Systems

Two user interface topics raised by expert systems are the nature of problem-solving interaction and the locus of control between the user and the system. The cognitive model, semantic level, and syntactic level concepts can also be used to analyze special expert system user interface requirements.

7.3.1 Interactive and Collaborative Problem Solving

People will not seek advice from an expert until it is necessary (see Chapter 4). The human expert then tries to find out what problems the person is having. Expert systems, on the other hand, solve problems that are preselected by the human expert system developer. The developer decides which problems are within the realm of the system's expertise. If the developer predicts the user's problems correctly, then the problem-solving interaction between the user and the expert system is satisfying. However, if the user's problem is not predicted correctly, the user will either have to redefine his problem into something the system can handle, or try to force the system to work around the problem.

It is easier to design an expert system that steers users along a predefined path than it is to design a system that is flexible enough to respond to a variety of problems of different users. Unfortunately, the resulting interaction between the user and the system can be inefficient and frustrating. Waern gives an example of a toxic materials identification expert system that does not vary its interaction with the user, even after receiving numerous clues that he is highly experienced. As a result, the system asks unnecessary questions and gives unsolicited advice in a patronizing tone. An expert trying to identify possible toxic wastes does not need an enormous warning that the chemical he is investigating is highly dangerous. He wants a list of conditions to confirm his preliminary hypothesis, and advice on how to treat the situation.[29] In the same manner, a general reference expert system designed for use by subject experts such as chemistry faculty or graduate students should not use the same interaction as an expert system designed to assist freshman composition students, or an expert system designed for use by librarians at a reference desk. Interactive problem solving should allow flexible interaction based on the user's experience level.

The choice of the inference engine and method of reasoning influences the ability of the developer to create a collaborative problem-solving approach and an understandable user interface. Backward-chaining relies on forming a hypothesis and collecting selective data to prove or disprove it. Forward-chaining relies on collecting observations and forming inferences based on the data. A user who tries to solve a problem with the backward-chaining "hypothesize and test" method will be frustrated by the seeming inefficiency of a forward-chaining system that asks questions in a random order. A user who bases his reasoning on gathering observations will be unable to feed a backward-chaining expert system the hypotheses required. If the user doesn't understand what problem-solving approach the system is using, he will not be able to understand the context in which the questions are asked. Limitations in short-term memory will cause him to lose track of the line of reasoning, and he will be unable to interpret or evaluate the explanations the system produces.[30]

The implication for expert system user interface designers is to match the inference method to the user's style of problem solving. Chapter 4 suggests that expert reference librarians use forward-chaining to determine reference formats and backward-chaining to select reference titles. A general reference expert system should be designed to inform the user that the first set of questions are intended to gather information to form an inference on which type of reference format is likely to contain an answer. Once that portion of the consultation is completed, the expert system should allow the user to ask "what if" questions if the user does not agree with the format suggested. If the user does agree, then the expert system can move to the next part of the consultation (backward-chaining on reference titles) and let the user know the next set of questions is intended to find a specific title within the reference format selected. Including this dialogue within the consultation enhances the quality of interaction and gives a sense of collaborative problem solving.

7.3.2 Locus of Control

The division of labor between the user and the expert system often consists of the system controlling the dialogue and asking questions, the user feeding in answers, and the system solving the problem. There is no evidence thus far that such a Socratic style of dialogue is effective for interactive tutoring.[31] In a study of human expert consultation, the best results were found when the expert shared control of the dialogue with the novice and worked together with him to solve the problem, rather than when the expert simply pronounced an answer.[32]

Baroff and his associates suggest that many users prefer to "enter information in a sequence that suits them, experiment with different values to see how variables are related, and develop an understanding of the underlying model."[33] Hildreth concurs that the trend in expert systems and intelligent retrieval is toward shared decision making, with the system completing some tasks automatically and the user participating at key points in the process.[34] One way users can participate is to volunteer information about the problem to the system. This approach requires both a dialogue style that makes it easy for the user to take over control from the system at any point and also appropriate interfaces (e.g. menus, graphics, etc.) that help the user enter different types of information naturally and efficiently.[35]

Fischer and Lemke cite examples where giving the user more control is not always better. Some examples cited are: manual versus automatic transmission in driving a car; assemblers that manage memory allocations automatically; high-level programming languages and compilers that take care of specific hardware architectures; document production systems that enable users to focus on content instead of format. The amount of user control varies, depending on the users and their tasks, and whether they choose to take control or not. Fischer and Lemke plan to investigate further whether systems should adapt their behavior based on a model of the user and the task or whether systems should be adaptable by the user.[36]

One possibility of giving more control to users is to provide hypertext nodes that allow experimentation and browsing. Alternatively, designers could give more control to the expert system by designing intelligent defaults. Reference librarians may wish to use both options for a general reference expert system. For example, if a common question is "Where can I find articles on subject X?" the expert system could supply default choices that made it easy for the inquirer to find articles published within the last five years in English-language journals held by a library on campus.

7.3.3 Cognitive Model

Some traditional interface design issues must be rethought when it comes to designing expert systems. In an expert system, the mental model is extremely important. It is crucial that a user, particularly a domain expert, believe that the system is reasoning "correctly." If users cannot understand the coverage of the system, the inference processes, and the match to their own reasoning processes, their ability to use the system is diminished and may hinder acceptance of the system. Lehner and Krlj's research suggests that "the quality of a user's interaction with an expert system is affected by how readily he can build a correct mental model of the system."[37] One cognitive factor includes how much consistency there is between how the user structures the problem and tries to solve it and how the expert system represents knowledge and the procedures it uses to solve a problem. If the user's cognitive model of the "reasoning" processes within the system are faulty, then the interaction is likely to leave the user with incorrect assumptions.[38] Mental modeling issues greatly influence interface design when expert systems seek to model the domain, as in "what if," "second opinion," and training expert systems.

The system's ability to "explain" both the reasoning process it uses and how that process is represented by the user greatly affects whether a user can model the expert system's processes accurately. The ability of an expert system to explain its behavior is not something that can be "tacked on" at the end of its design. Explanation must be built into the system throughout. As described above in Section 7.3.1, if a reference system forward-chains to reference formats and backward-chains to reference titles, the system should explain what the purpose of the line of questioning is before the questioning starts. The user should be able to confirm the preliminary hypothesis (suggested reference format) of the forward-chaining, or engage in "what if" questioning at this point instead of waiting till the end of the session. The user should be able to choose when to move to the next step of the consultation, which is to find a specific reference title within the reference format suggested. Thus the interface designer must be involved in the design of the system itself, making sure that the eventual interface will have access to the knowledge necessary to explain the system's behavior. This explanation is critical not only to the end user, but also to the knowledge engineer who tests and debugs the system.

7.4
Suggestions for General Reference Expert System Application

7.4.1 Typical Expert System Session Tasks

It may help the interface designer to view a typical expert system session as a progression of three phases: the beginning, the consultation itself, and the conclusion. At each stage, the user has several questions and tasks that the user interface should support.

7.4.1.1 The Beginning
How does a reference librarian start an expert system session when a user comes to the reference desk with a question? How does the librarian generalize from a specific question to what kinds of reference works might contain an answer? This type of information must be input into an expert system to start a session.

In this stage, a user needs to know:

1. What can this expert system application do?
2. Is this expert system appropriate to use to answer this question?
3. How do I get started?
4. How do I interact with the expert system application? What sequence of commands should I issue?

7.4.1.2 The Consultation

During the actual consultation, the user must find a way to volunteer information to the expert system. If the expert system covers a large or complex problem space, the developers may choose to segment the application into several knowledge bases. In this case, a user must choose which of several knowledge bases within the expert system is the appropriate one to consult. The interface designer must structure the interaction and dialogue between the expert system and the user to support both tasks (volunteering information and making choices).

7.4.1.3 The Conclusion

The conclusion of the expert system session requires the same attention to detail as the consultation itself. The session should be easy to stop. The user should find it easy to start another session. Quitting the expert system shell itself should be simple, but should not use the same mechanism as leaving a session, so a user will not quit by mistake. The user should be satisfied with the results and feel a sense of closure at the conclusion of an expert system session.

7.4.2 General User Interface Design Issues

An interface designer must consider several general issues before making specific design decisions. General issues that influence interface design include the purpose for the expert system, the varying kinds and levels of knowledge potential users possess, and the activities a general reference expert system must support.

7.4.2.1 Purpose of the Expert System

The level of detail, explanation of reasoning, and assumptions of prior knowledge of the user are influenced by the *raison d'être* of the expert system. The expert system might be used to produce an answer, train novices ("experts-in-training"), provide a "second opinion" diagnosis, or classify a fact. The design of the interface can also be shaped by the reason people use the expert system, which might not coincide with the reason the expert system was created. For example, expert systems may be designed to provide answers to well-defined problems, but human experts are often asked to help other experts understand the problem area so they can solve their own problems.[39] This implies the need for a much richer form of dialogue than an inflexible single-thread series of questions and answers.

7.4.2.2 Users

The designer's choice of terminology, phrasing, and screen design is influenced by her knowledge of the potential users of an expert system and their varying levels of knowledge and experience of:

1. domain (the subject of the expertise contained in the system)
2. task (steps to find an answer in a library)
3. library terminology (what do you mean by "citation"?)
4. library and bibliographic control concepts (call numbers, main and added entries, subject headings, controlled vocabulary, indexing)
5. physical organization of the library (floor plans, shelving locations, etc.)
6. specific knowledge of library's collections (special collections, collection strengths, level of collecting in their topic)
7. local library policy (interlibrary loan, circulation)
8. expert system terminology
9. computer concepts
10. the particular system

Potential users could include reference librarians who are familiar with library terminology but might be unfamiliar with the domain (subject matter) of the expert system, and could be unfamiliar with expert system terminology (e.g., goal, rule, frame, parameter, confidence level). A second group of potential users could be paraprofessionals, who may or may not be familiar with library, domain, and expert system terminology. Other categories of users could include students, who might know the domain, but are not familiar with information about library holdings, interpreting bibliographic citations, and methods of searching for materials by subject. The list of potential users goes on: faculty, administrators, researchers, business people, professionals, parents, the general public. The point is to identify the group(s) of potential users and consider what levels and areas of knowledge the group members might possess.

7.4.2.3 Activities

The task of answering questions can be analyzed into several categories of activities. A human expert, the reference librarian, may answer directional queries, ready-reference fact-type questions, holdings questions (item searches), or complex substantive queries requiring bibliographic verification, and subject searching. A hypothetical scenario, based on Chapter 4, is presented below to illustrate how an expert system might be used in one general reference situation, and therefore what specific subtasks the user interface must support.

This scenario illustrates the task of answering a ready-reference fact-type question. The librarian wants to identify a reference source likely to contain the answer or a pointer to an answer.

1. Inquirer comes to librarian with a question.
2. Librarian clarifies the question and determines what would constitute an acceptable answer.
3. Librarian starts the expert system program,
4. chooses an appropriate knowledge base or module, and
5. starts the knowledge base (loads it into memory).
6. Librarian chooses the first level of question so she can provide information. Alternatively the system may allow her to type in a natural language query.
7. Librarian provides information to the expert system. This could be done by selecting menu choices or typing natural language. If the librarian does not know exactly how to do this, or what kind of information the system needs, she could browse through available options with hypertext capabilities.
8. The expert system produces the answer.
9. Librarian asks for an explanation of the answer, that is, how did the expert system arrive at the conclusion?
10. Librarian asks for a printout of the answer and reasoning.
11. Librarian may try another consultation, which could be in the same knowledge base or in another knowledge base.
12. Librarian explains the answer to the client and shows the client how to get the identified book, use the catalog, or search an index.
13. Librarian reminds the client to come back if the answer does not prove satisfactory (feedback).
14. Patron retrieves the book, makes xerox copies of a journal article, fills out an interlibrary loan form, purchases the material, drives to another library, or pursues any of a number of activities.

As this scenario illustrates, the entire task has many activities and is quite time consuming, so the user interface to the expert system must help the librarian work expediently, make options clear so choices can be made efficiently, allow the librarian to try several paths through the knowledge base, back out easily, and support repetitive routine work.

Concentrate on task domain semantic issues at first. At the task domain semantic level, examples of objects and actions are: What can the user do with this expert system? How can he do it? The task domain semantic level of the user interface for expert systems is complicated by the different types of users involved in the expert system development cycle. Expert system development consists of three components: knowledge capture, programming and debugging, and system acceptance by the user community. Each type of user (the domain expert, the knowledge engineer, and the end user) will have different actions he wishes to accomplish, and the user interface must supply different objects and actions that allow each of them to do so. Expert system shells can provide separate interfaces for knowledge capture and end use or a single interface for all functions.

Semantic level decisions include determining what set of functions to make available to the end user and what "commands" (in whatever form—command language, menu, graphics) the system can perform. End users can be provided with a variety of objects and actions to:

1. supply information requested by the expert system;
2. ask "Why?" questions (Why is the expert system asking this question? How will the answer be used? Where is the expert system going with this line of reasoning?);
3. ask "What?" questions (What does this question or option mean? or, How do I select that option or skip this question?);
4. ask "How?" questions (How did the expert system reach this conclusion? What factors did it use? What reasoning did it employ?);
5. ask "Huh?" questions (What does this explanation mean? I don't understand what it says.); the system should be able to answer a vaguely formulated follow-up question;[40]
6. ask "What if?" questions; explore the result of changing the values of different variables (What would happen if I answered this question differently?). This capability is important for exploration and learning;
7. make printouts of the session, including questions and conclusions; users may want to examine the reasoning and develop a view of the whole, not just the single answer. For example, a trainee reference librarian may wish to look over all dictionaries and the circumstances for using each. One practical use for a printout is to keep a permanent record of the reasoning so the user doesn't have to return for another consultation.

Another semantic issue is determining the granularity of a problem-solving task.[41] How do you break a task down into reasonable components? What constitutes one semantic chunk? Section 7.3.1 suggests that one semantic chunk is completing the forward-chaining on reference formats. Other chunks include-backward chaining on reference titles, giving explanations of answers, allowing replays of the session, asking for a printout of results, choosing another consultation or another knowledge base to query, or quitting the system. Within each chunk the task can be further analyzed.

What information belongs together to accomplish a given task? What should go on one screen or menu choice, and what should be broken down into several choices?

Other semantic level decisions revolve around the sequence of presenting:

1. Screens—In what order should you arrange screens?
2. Commands—What sequence of commands and/or menu choices do you want the user to take to accomplish a given task?
3. Answers—How do you present the answer, before or after or without explanation? If there are multiple answers, how do you arrange them?

Designers should answer these questions about the meaning the user interface will convey before designing the final physical structure of the interface. Some other semantic issues are discussed below (see Table 7.1).

7.4.3 General Semantic Design Issues

7.4.3.1 Progressive Disclosure

The interface should not overwhelm the user with every possible option, but make a few major functions clearly visible. The functions should be easy to learn and enable the user to do useful work immediately. Some expert system shells give the developer the ability to define function keys or create menu short-cut keys so that experienced users can access more advanced functions when they need it.

7.4.3.2 Human Performance Limitations

Don't force the user to memorize the names of knowledge bases. Display a list of names to choose from, with explanations of what each one encompasses. This list is especially important at the beginning of the expert system session, when the user has little idea what to expect or how to proceed. VP Expert displays a message, "file not found or disk full, press

Table 7.1
General Semantic Design Issues

- Progressive disclosure
- Human performance limitations
- Navigation
- Feedback
- Response time
- Exploration and recovery
- Consistency

---

enter to resume," which is enough to put the user off. Level 5 gives the user a file selection menu of available files on the current directory.

Display the functions most likely to be used from a particular screen. This can be done by providing onscreen reminders of function key assignments, displaying buttons to click, or highlighting a likely menu choice.

To support short-term memory limitations, the user interface should provide a variety of ways to help the user keep track of the rules being executed, the choices already made, and where they are in the consultation process. The user should be able to see a trace facility of rules fired, both in textual and graphic form. Some expert system shells provide the user with the ability to review all of his previous responses at once for possible changes, then return to the consultation for "what if" investigating.

The interface should allow the user to ask for results in screen, paper, or file formats. Screen format is the most convenient, but paper is easier to scan when the answer is long or complicated. People have difficulty reading an abundance of text on a screen, and some expert system shells do not provide a capability to view a previous screen. Printouts of answers and explanations should contain the date of the consultation, a user-supplied title for the consultation session, and a caution about rechecking answers before accepting the results. Personal Consultant Easy and PC Expert send the results of a consultation to a disk file, so the material can be manipulated and edited before printing or kept for case histories.

7.4.3.3 Navigation

The interface designer should provide flexible navigation, enabling the user to easily move around in the text. The user should be able to move to the beginning, end, and previous page, as well as to the next page when viewing help screens and explanations. For example, Easy Expert does not allow the user to back up when the recommendations are more than one page.

It should be easy to quit the current consultation and start another one, or to quit the current knowledge base and pick a different one to query.

7.4.3.4 Feedback

If something has changed on the screen, provide some visual clue that there is new text to read on the screen.

If an action will take some time to complete, such as loading a knowledge base, then place a message, for example, "Loading knowledge base. Please wait." to assure the user that the system is still working.

7.4.3.5 Response Time

Users tolerate different thresholds of response time depending on what their experience and expectations are. Microcomputer users are accustomed to almost instantaneous response time, while users connected to a time-sharing mainframe system are used to complaining about slow response time. Most reference library expert systems run on a microcomputer, so response time should be within the range of 50–90 msecs to be perceived as instantaneous.[42] People will tolerate longer response time for tasks that they perceive as complex, such as inducing an answer, but will not accept the same delay for tasks such as scrolling. An expert system has little likelihood of being used at a busy reference desk if it is a chore to load the expert system application, choose a knowledge base, and interact with the system. Variations in response times may be caused by the different methods an inference engine uses to induce an answer, the amount of processing used to display a graphical user interface, and the power of the workstation on which the expert system runs.

7.4.3.6 Exploration and Recovery

By making choices visible, user interface techniques such as menus, prompts, and icons can prevent a user from making syntactical errors. However, these techniques do not ensure that users understand what they are doing. For example, two menu choices may appear to overlap or seem contradictory to a user. A pull-down menu may make it simple to choose an option, but the user does not know the implications of choosing one option rather than another. Seeing an option available on a pull-down menu does not mean its significance is obvious. Some researchers suggest providing an "undo" feature to encourage users to experiment and take several paths through a consultation.[43]

The system should be easy for the user to explore various options and easily change his mind. It should not be difficult to recover from mistakes. The user should not be forced to go all the way through a consultation before he can change an answer. The user interface should allow the user to back up one screen at a time, to the beginning of consultation, or all the way out to a menu of knowledge bases.

Some expert system shells allow the user to back up and change just one question in the consultation, so the user can change one answer, without having to repeat the entire question-and-answer dialogue. 1st Class offers this "what if" replay feature.

Some systems allow the user to skip a question, so the user is not forced to answer a question that is not applicable or that he does not have enough information to answer. If the capability to skip a question is not available in an expert system shell, the interface designer should be sure to include "Don't Know" or "Don't Care" options for the user to select.

The interface should be designed to handle incorrect responses to questions or menu choices. If the user is asked, "Is the person an American? Y/N," and the user types "M" instead of "N," will the system stop working or will an explanatory message ask the user to type "Y" or "N"?

7.4.3.7 Consistency

Consistency in the user interface helps the user build an accurate cognitive model of the expert system. Users can predict what the system will do in any given situation and can rely on a few rules to make use of the system. This eads to ease of learning, ease of use, fewer errors, shorter learning time, lower training costs, and feelings of mastery and satisfaction.[44]

7.4.4 Work on System-Dependent Issues Next and Modify Semantic Decisions as Needed

This level of user interface design is concerned with issues such as (Table 7.2):

1. How will the user and the system communicate? How is the dialogue structured?
2. On this screen, how do I best display the possible commands?
3. What do I call the commands?
4. What is the exact sequence of letters, commands, and so on to give directions to the expert system?

7.4.5 System-Dependent Design Issues

7.4.5.1 User Interface Design Styles

Several styles of user interface can be used to structure the dialogue between the expert system and the user. Each style has advantages and limitations in gathering input from the user and displaying instructions, feedback, and recommendations. Although the developer's choice of interface style may be limited by the capabilities of the expert system shell employed, the effectiveness of the interface depends on attention to interface design principles, user feedback, and iterative design more than on mere choice of interface style.[45] Other local variables may affect the choice of interface style: the hardware available, the software package's abilities, memory available, input and output devices, potential users, and their tasks.

Table 7.2
System-Dependent Design Issues

- User interface design styles
- Selection methods and response formats
- Graphics
- Color
- A word about menu design

It is useful to categorize various interface design styles to look at the advantages and disadvantages of each style, although interfaces generally blend several styles. The five primary interaction styles are menu selection, form fill-in, command language, natural language, and direct manipulation.[46]

Interaction Style Comparison

Advantages	Disadvantages
Menu Selection	
Shortens training, reduces keystrokes	Danger of many menus
	May slow down frequent users
Structures decision making	Requires screen space
Permits use of dialogue management tools	Requires rapid display rate
Easy to support error handling	
Form Fill-In	
Simplifies data entry	Consumes screen space
Requires modest training	Requires typing skills
Assistance is convenient	
Shows context for activity	
Permits use of form management tools	
Command Language	
Flexibility; supports user initiative	Difficult to retain
Appeals to "power" users	Poor error handling
Potentially rapid for complex tasks	Requires substantial training and memorization
Support macro capability	
Natural Language	
Relieves burden of learning syntax	Requires clarification dialogue
	May require more keystrokes
	May not show context, unpredictable
Direct Manipulation	
Visually presents task; easy to learn	May require graphics devices
Easy to retain; errors can be avoided	More programming effort until tools improve
Encourages exploration; high subjective satisfaction	Hard to record history or write macros

Many handbooks and articles have been published on the art of designing menus. There are fewer articles on form fill-in, natural language, and direct manipulation styles.

7.4.5.2 Selection Methods and Response Formats

Selection methods are system dependent, and the interface designer is constrained by the variety of interface tools made available by the expert system shell used to develop the application.

Although there is a wide variety of selection mechanisms, the two most popular are keyboard and mouse. Keyboard input is not synonymous with command-language interfaces, just as mouse input is not necessarily associated with direct manipulation interfaces. A direct manipulation interface portrays objects of interest on a screen, allowing the user to point to an object to act upon. This could be done using function keys, arrow keys, a space bar, the ⟨Enter⟩ key, or a mouse pointer.

Direct manipulation is not always the best way to make selections. For long lists of possible choices, the user may want a quicker way to select from the list, such as using the keyboard to type the first letter to go to that part of the alphabet, or typing in the name if he knows it is more efficient.

When designing user response formats, follow standard conventions. VP Expert uses the space bar to go to next page as well as go backward. The ⟨End⟩ key is used to select options instead of the ⟨Enter⟩ key.

Use keys consistently. Level 5 uses F1 to go to the next page instead of using the ⟨Page Down⟩ key or ⟨Enter⟩. F8 is used to back up instead of ⟨Esc⟩. By following standard conventions, the designer helps the user build on previous knowledge and transfer skills from other packages.

Be consistent in naming function keys and in the way they operate. Sometimes Level 5 calls the F8 key "Menu," sometimes it is called "Back." F8 does not always back the user up to the previous step. Sometimes the user backs all the way out to the main menu. Sometimes the F6 key is used for Back instead of F8.

Do not put prompts for function keys that are not valid on the screen. Level 5 places the function key for the "Why?" command on the title screen. If you press it, you get an error message.

Watch which commands you place next to each other. For example, in Level 5, it is too easy to hit the F8 Menu (or Back) key instead of the F9 Help. Do not make it easy to make errors. If there is no prompt to ask if you really mean it, there could be drastic consequences. Bigger consequences should require more attention from the user and more effort to confirm the action.

Allow abbreviations for input. For example, allow the user to type "Y" for "yes." Provide templates for dates and examples to show valid data format (single number, range of numbers, letters, words, single or multiple choices). PC Expert lets you provide templates for user prompts.

7.4.5.3 Graphics

The designer should consider certain questions when deciding whether or not to use graphics. Is the application best served by a graphic or by text? Graphics should clarify, not clutter up a screen. Will graphics capability be available on all workstations on which the application is to run? Will the use of graphics also require the use of a mouse to select a graphic, and if so, will the workstations have appropriate hardware and software to run the application?[47]

In a graphical user interface, icons and symbols are used to associate a function with an easily recognizable idea. The user issues commands by pointing (using a mouse or cursor arrow key) to an object of interest and selecting it. Graphical depiction of functions can present a system model or metaphor that the user understands more easily than a textual description.

Graphics represent a powerful user interface tool, even when an expert system development tool does not provide the capability to create a graphic user interface. Some expert system shells permit the developer to import scanned images or clip art, and the inventive designer can create adequate representations of symbols using the graphic characters in the IBM extended character set.

Graphics can be used to clarify what a question means, especially if the terminology could be ambiguous. Graphics can also be used to show images corresponding to each menu option or condition that the user is observing. Graphics are especially useful for helping the user visualize the structure of the knowledge base and could be placed on title screens to indicate which part of the knowledge base is covered and to help the user visualize relationships between the facts, rules, and objects in the knowledge base. Graphics are valuable in answers and explanations, and can take the place of complicated directions, especially when an explanation involves floor plans, organization charts, campus maps, or forms. Certain domains, such as chemistry, may benefit from presenting labeled illustrations in the answer or explanation. Other domains could conceivably use flowcharts, line graphs, bar charts, pie charts, or scatterplots to illustrate or display data-intensive answers.

Another valuable use of graphics is a system-generated diagram of the inference network, which lets the user look at the ongoing chain of reasoning during the consultation. The connection between the questions the system poses to the user and the hypotheses the system is attempting to prove is more apparent to the user and can provide the rationale that is often missing from the explanations at the end of the consultation.[48]

7.4.5.4 Color

One of the first decisions the designer must make is whether to use color at all. Does the application need color? Will color add any clarity or function to the interface? Will the workstations on which the expert system will run have color monitors?[49]

Color contrast affects how quickly a user can locate information on the screen.[50] Color coding information seems to help users identify information more quickly than items identified by brightness, form, or size. Possible uses for color coding include highlighting instructions, explanations, answers, or other information that the designer wishes to bring to the attention of the user. Using contrasting foreground and background colors can make the answer to a consultation stand out from other text on the screen.

Color can be used to focus the user's attention on the current window. If the expert system must also run on a monochrome system, the developer must select colors with enough contrast that they will be distinguishable on both systems.[51]

Some exploratory work has been done using a trained neural network to help users select color combinations.[52] Perhaps this facility will become available in commercial expert system development tools eventually. The significance of this work is that it shows that even experts have different opinions. Color combinations are hard to select because there are so many interactions possible. The developer needs to allow the user the ability to change the colors, perhaps among preselected color palettes, with one default. When users chose colors themselves in this experiment, they sometimes created problems for themselves because they obscured the important focus points on the screen.

A few guidelines on how to use color are summarized here.[53]

1. The darker colors near the extremes of the spectrum, such as red, blue, and brown make good background colors. Other good background colors are light gray, green, and yellow. Avoid intense reds, blues, purples, or magenta for large solid areas. The brighter colors near the middle of the center of the spectrum, and black, gray, and white produce more legible text.

2. Use blue for backgrounds or in the periphery. People cannot focus sharply on blue, so avoid blue for text, thin lines, small shapes. Avoid adjacent colors differing only in the amount of blue. Edges will appear indistinct.

Avoid red and green in the peripheral area of displays. The periphery of the retina is not sensitive to these colors. Yellow and blue are better periphery colors.

3. Use complementary colors such as yellow and blue, red and green, or cyan and magenta.

4. Avoid pairing colors that are at opposite ends of the color spectrum, such as red and purple. Such color combinations cause eyestrain, because the eye must refocus for the different wavelengths.

5. Limit the number of colors and make sure they are widely separated in the color spectrum. This will reduce the effect of backgrounds or nearby colors changing the hue of a color. For example, a color on a dark background looks lighter and brighter than it does on a light background.

6. Group related screens or screen elements by using the same background color, and use the color consistently throughout the system.

7. Take advantage of meanings traditionally associated with red, amber, and green. For example, use red for alert, yellow for caution, and green for normal in system messages.

8. The brightest and most saturated area of color draws the viewer's attention. The best way to get attention is to use a brightly saturated color such as red, yellow, orange, or green, and to use a color that is different both in hue and brightness from the surrounding areas. Make the most of this effect; do not highlight the caption "Explanation." Instead highlight the actual text of the explanation.

9. Use the least number of colors necessary to enhance the user interface, but no more than four to six discriminant colors. Too much color can overwhelm the user and defeats the purpose of using color to draw the user's attention or group information. Color should enhance the user's ability to use the system, not impress the user with the garishness of the designer's favorite color combinations.

10. Colors change in appearance as the amount of ambient light changes. Be sure to test color choices at the location where the workstation running the expert system is located. The amount of light and glare at a reference desk may cause the designer to change the choice of colors used in the expert system application.

7.4.5.5 A Word about Menu Design
Much of the literature on user interface design focuses on menu design. A few suggestions on how to use menus in an expert system are given. Menus are singled out for discussion because the design issues are similar whether menus are used in a traditional full-screen character-based system or for pull-down menus in a graphical user interface. Both designs require the developers to deal with issues of human memory and learning.

7.5
Possible Uses of Menus in an Expert System

Menus can be used to gather facts and avoid presenting redundant questions to the user. When all knowledge is represented as simple facts, the expert system cannot tell the connection between, "Is the printer on?" and "Is the printer off?" so the system will ask the user both questions. Redundant questions can lead to inconsistent answers. The designer can avoid problems by pulling together all the different values that can apply to an object and presenting them to the user as a menu. When the user chooses one, the other values are assumed false and closed out of query generation. When the expert system needs the value of the fact again, it is held in working memory and the user is not asked for the information again. Level 5 lets the designer group attributes of an object together into a menu of choices.

Menus can also be used to present subgoals at the beginning of the consultation. Then the expert system can apply questions from a pertinent knowledge base, pursue relevant goals, and ignore nonrelevant ones. For example, the user does not need to go through all the questions about dictionaries if he needs to find a quotation.

Menu titles: Every menu should have a title to inform the user what the choices pertain to, and to provide the user and librarian with a common name to use in referring to the screen. The title of the menu should repeat the words of the previously selected menu item to provide the user feedback that the system correctly interpreted his command. In Norman's model, this is bridging the Gulf of Evaluation. When the menu title does not change to show that the user's intention was carried out, the user can experience disorientation. For example, the KDS demo used the same menu title for the first three screens. To start another consultation, the user must return to the third of the screens, but it is difficult to recognize where you are and how to get where you need to be.

Menu items: The most common choice should be listed first on the menu. The menu items should list appropriate choices and include "not applicable" and "not sure" categories.

All menu choices should be reasonable. Do not list 10%, 20%, 30%. This leaves no room for 15%. This could be the same problem with presenting choices to the user. Perhaps the user does not want to pick only one format, for example, journal, because he wants both journals and books, or both dictionaries and encyclopedias. Provide some means of choosing more than one option, or of placing a bookmark so the user can return to the menu and follow a different path. One way to help the user with this is to provide the capability to print out the path selected so far, and to provide a "what if" capability to change just one choice.

7.5.1 Specific User Interface Design Issues

Specific design decisions are influenced by both semantic task domain decisions and system-dependent design capabilities and constraints. This section discusses these issues and then makes specific recommendations for designing user interfaces to general reference expert systems.

As discussed earlier, the knowledge a user must have to operate a computer system can be divided into syntactical knowledge about the structure of issuing commands, semantic knowledge about computer concepts such as using a mouse to point and click, and semantic knowledge about the task domain.

Both the syntactical and semantic computer knowledge are system dependent. The knowledge a user needs to issue commands and to manipulate computer objects and actions depends on the computer hardware (e.g., IBM PC, Macintosh, or a dumb terminal connected to a mainframe computer). A graphical user interface relies on having a pointing device such as a mouse, bitmapped display monitors, and an appropriate operating system.

The semantic knowledge of computer concepts, that is, the objects and actions to operate the expert system, depends on the hardware and software the developers choose to use. To some extent, the designer is limited to the interface tools and underlying computer concepts that are currently available in the expert system shell chosen. Creating a custom expert system can require more resources but provide more flexibility in the interface.

Task domain semantic knowledge is not system dependent, and the developer should concentrate on such issues at the beginning. Once a clear idea of the purpose of the expert system and the desired way of interacting with the system is decided, the designer can move to system-dependent design decisions. (see Table 7.3). Sketching the physical structure of the interface in turn (the screens, commands, words, dialogue) may highlight inconsistencies and conflicts in the original semantic decisions and cause refinement.

Table 7.3
Specific User Interface Design Issues

- Title screen
- Starting the consultation
- Organizing the knowledge base
- Graphics
- Screen layout
- Interaction
- User-defined text
- Vocabulary
- Asking questions
- Presenting answers
- Explanation
- Online help
- Error messages
- Status messages
- Concluding the consultation

7.5.1.1 Title Screen

Some expert system applications allow the designer to create a customized title screen display. Where possible, an expert system application should always have an opening screen that provides the user with enough information about the knowledge base so he can decide whether the expert system is appropriate to use. Many expert system applications launch the user immediately into a question-and-answer dialogue without setting the context. This puts the user in a position analogous to reading a book without ever seeing a cover or title page.

The opening screen should contain the following information:

1. Title of expert system. If a catchy but uninformative name is used, follow the name with an explanatory phrase.

2. Date knowledge base was created and dates of the material covered, so a user can judge when the material was last updated.

3. Authority. What are the names and titles of the domain experts and designers responsible for the information contained in the system?

4. Scope. Tell the user what they can and cannot expect the expert system to cover. What is the domain of expertise contained in the system?

5. Capability. Within the scope, what is the realm of questions that the expert system can answer? What functions are available?

6. Instructions. How to start and use the system; how to ask for help; how to quit. The instructions on how to get started should be easy to understand and easy to find on the screen.

All of the title screen information should be presented in a few concise sentences, not a lengthy essay.[54] Long descriptions are hard to follow, understand, and remember. Fuller instructions can be made available through a menu choice if the user chooses to ask for it, but a first screen full of text is unlikely to be read, and makes it difficult for a user to find the pertinent instructions on what to do next. A clean, well-formatted screen invites users to continue using the system.

7.5.1.2 Starting the Consultation

The user might choose an option from a menu or might type in a query using natural language to start the consultation. In a menu system, which could be implemented either in character-based mode or through a graphical user interface direct manipulation mode, a reference librarian chooses from a list of categories. In a natural language system, the reference librarian must guess which natural language words the system understands. The problem with natural language is the reference librarian has to know the content of the knowledge base. At the very least, the librarian needs to know the first level of choices. What terms can the user type in? What can the expert system do? Natural language may not provide reassuring answers and may actually be less efficient than a menu system for first-time users.

7.5.1.3 Organizing the Knowledge Base

Present a natural way of organizing the knowledge bases so the user can make an appropriate selection. Several methods are explored below.

The instructions on how to get started and how to select a knowledge base to use should be easy to understand and easy to find on the screen. Graphic roadmaps can be used to show the relationships between linked knowledge bases, especially if a user can choose (through direct manipulation or a menu system) to jump to one of the knowledge bases. A user could jump from the top level directly to the journal indexes used in engineering, or to detective novels with a setting in San Francisco.

Use a form fill-in interface to solicit information from the user. For example, VP Expert provides a fill-in-the-blank form field that is linked to a specific variable in the expert system. The form field always displays the current value assigned to the linked variable. You can use the mouse or the keyboard to make an entry into a form field, causing the entry to become the new value for the linked variable. Using one or more rules, the expert system can then examine the entry that was made and add or remove other form fields from the display. For example, if you entered "Married" into a "marital status" form field, a "whenever" rule could cause "spouse name" and "number of dependents" form field to appear. In contrast, an entry of "Single" could cause the same form fields to be removed from the display. Similarly, instead of presenting the user with a long question-and-answer dialogue of questions that must be answered Yes or No, present a fill-in-the-blank form, so the user has a choice about the order in which to answer questions, gains a sense of what information the expert system is gathering, can make corrections simply without backing up and re-answering the same stream of questions in lock-step order, and can skip questions that are not applicable.

Some systems provide the capability to subdivide the knowledge base into multiple rule sets. The developer can turn off variable rule sets based on the information obtained from the user, which makes the rules more efficient for the inference engine and more understandable for the user (prevents asking unnecessary questions). Use this feature when there are differences in the types of questions you might ask about each subdivision. This feature can be implemented in the interface with form fill-in or with selectable graphical icons representing subdivisions.

Knowledge implies an understanding of a process or of relationships. A human can know both how to do something and how to explain it to someone else. That's knowledge, not simple data or algorithms. To produce the same sense of explanation in the expert system, the designer should include text that explains how a domain is segmented into several knowledge bases and what determines the chaining between the knowledge bases.

You can use propositions to which the user must answer Yes or No to establish the truth or falsity of the statements. Such binary Yes/No questions can lead to redundant questions and inconsistent facts. Another way to handle this situation is to group the set of propositions and facts to be established into a dynamic menu item presentation, so the user can both recognize (rather than recall) appropriate values, and be guided in the semantic organization of the facts. If the expert system does not allow the ability to deal with variables, then the developer cannot deal with information in a range. For example, the sequence of questions, "Do you want electrical engineering? Y/N," "Do you want mechanical engineering? Y/N," is tedious and can elicit redundant and inconsistent answers.

The system can automatically phrase a question for you, or you can use variables to state the rule. The developer can phrase the question and supply valid options.

Look at the inference engine. Does it start with the first rule and try to provide it, then go on down the list? If so, then the developer should put preliminary goals at the top. The order implies some logic. Put in Help text for that question and in the explanation text for the conclusion. The system can show the user his progress during the consultation and display interim conclusions along the way. The user then knows when the system passes each major hurdle and receives a sense of closure along the way.

1st Class optimizes the order in which questions are asked, so the fewest questions need to be asked to arrive at an appropriate recommendation. Unfortunately, this order may not be the order in which an expert or novice naturally thinks about the problem to be solved. The optimization may pick factors with values that discriminate and eliminate more possibilities. This behavior depends on data already in the knowledge base. Presumably if the knowledge base is modified or updated, the reasoning path could change, which could disconcert a regular user of the expert system application.

7.5.1.4 Screen Layout

Galitz[54a] and Tullis[54b] provide specific guidelines. The expert system shell can provide facilities that make it easier to create readable usable screens.

Does the shell allow the developer to customize titles of screens?

Is it easy to see how the text will be formatted on the screen? Or is the text cluttered with embedded formatting characters and quotation marks?

Is it easy to switch between editing and user mode?

Does the expert system provide an automatic page-numbering function for your text screens? (e.g., Page # of #). This is useful so you know how much there is to read, and where you are in the explanation.

Can the user recognize that the screen has changed? In one demo, the window size and position of the help screen remained the same after a second help screen was requested, so the user did not perceive that the help text had already changed.

7.5.1.5 Interaction

If the interface uses a menu system, the designer should make the menu choices reflect the natural categorization of the domain. This has the effect of making the problem-solving process proceed in a natural manner, as well as teaching users unfamiliar with the domain the semantic constructs of the domain. When a menu item is selected, place the item's words at the top of the next screen, to help the user maintain a sense of where he is headed.

Give the user some control over the consultation. For example, on menu choices, provide options for "Don't know" and "Don't care" so the user is not forced to make inappropriate choices. Allow the user to back out if he made a wrong choice. The choice could be wrong in intent or wrong in execution, and the expert system should support both. The user should be able to move one level back, return to the beginning of the consultation with the current knowledge base, or back all the way out to the beginning of the expert system session. Hypertext can be used to satisfy the needs of both beginning and advanced users. Novice users could follow paths to read definitions of terms used in questions, answers, or explanations; domain experts can find detailed and technical explanations.

7.5.1.6 User-Defined Text

Whether or not the expert system shell chosen allows the interface designer to create a graphical user interface, a character-based menu and function key interface, or a straight question-and-answer text interface, all tools give you the option of writing text. Most expert system shells allow developers to create title screens, customize questions, provide a list of valid options for the user to choose from, display intermediate screens whenever a "chunk" of reasoning has been concluded, provide system help and message screens, and provide explanation screens that reveal metarules as well as individual rules of the reasoning process. These features can be used to reduce syntactic load and semantic computer considerations, so the end user can concentrate on exploring the semantic task.

7.5.1.7 Vocabulary

The intended audience and the information expected from the expert system affect the developer's choice of vocabulary. The developer must aim the vocabulary of the system at the knowledge level of the intended audience. Too often the domain expert has a tendency to use vocabulary that is unfamiliar to the nonexpert end user. If the end user perceives the vocabulary to be too technical, the expert system becomes useless; on the other hand, explaining fundamental concepts the user already understands leads to an inefficient interaction and an impatient user.

If the expert system is designed for use in general reference, then library jargon such as "bibliographic citation" can be used without definition. If the target audience is undergraduate students, then library jargon should be avoided or at least defined when used. Even when developers expect other librarians to use an expert system, there is the question of subject specialty. If the expert system covers a subject area about which not all librarians are familiar (such as law, medicine, engineering), subject area jargon should be avoided or defined at the point of use.

Several shells offer features to help the developer supply definitions or elaborations of concepts that might be unclear to end users. Knowledge Pro for Windows and 1st Class HT provide a hypertext facility. KDS supplies an automatic data facility and graphics. (See Appendix B for more examples.)

Developers should also avoid expert system terminology. After spending hours creating an expert system, there is a tendency to use terms such as "goal," "subgoal," "parameter," "value," and "consultation" in directions and explanations. To an uninitiated user, the question "What goal do you want to solve?" does little to demystify the "magic" of expert systems. The choice of terminology must depend on the knowledge level of the end users.

A second approach to fitting vocabulary to the potential audience is to look at the information the user expects from the expert system. If the purpose of the expert system is to provide information, then the conclusions of a consultation should be phrased as information. If the expert system is action oriented, then the system should provide specific directions to the user. An action oriented expert system could tell the user how to get to the science library, how to check out books, how to read a call number or a bibliographic citation, or how to fix CD-ROM or printer problems. There could be places where information and directions are mixed, such as a recommendation that explains what ILL is and how to initiate a request.

7.5.1.8 Asking Questions

The purpose of the expert system affects how you choose and phrase the conditions that define factors pertinent to the case. For example, diagnostic and classification expert systems rely on an end user's observations, so choose conditions that emphasize observable facts, and enhance the questions with graphics and messages to help the user make his decision. Leave a "Don't know" option for the user. The following example illustrates why this option is necessary. An expert system that asks the user if the person being classified is English, American, or African-American makes two assumptions: (1) that the user knows the answer, and (2) that the choices listed cover the universe of possibilities. If the user does not know, and there is no "unknown" choice, the user must either make an inappropriate choice or abandon the expert system session.

If the purpose of the expert system is to select products, then the system should allow the user to choose a "Don't care" option. An expert system that helps a manager select potential candidates for interview might ask whether the candidate should have at least two years of college education. If the user does not think the answer to that question is important, the user should be able to skip the question or choose a "Not important" option. The phrases used to describe the user's choices should be tested with end users in order to ensure they understand the conditions and how to respond to the questions. Help screens and graphics may be necessary supplements to the text.

Some expert system development tools give the developer the option to make an answer mandatory for certain questions. If the developer chooses to force the user to answer a question, the developer must be certain that the options provide viable answers for the user to select; otherwise, provide a "Don't know" option. A mandatory answer is useful if the inference engine cannot make reasonable inferences without that information. Easy Expert allows the user to skip a question if she doesn't know the answer.

Some expert system shells automatically generate the wording of the question from a fact, while others (such as Level 5) permit the developer to associate customized question text with a fact. The latter option produces questions that sound more polished, can be longer, and that could include graphic characters. The customized question text represents the facts in a form that makes sense to the user.

Easy Expert gives the developer a fill-in-the-blank form for question text, explanation text, menu choices, and feedback (if a menu choice is selected). This feature associates all the information about a question in one place so the developer can see if the question and help text make sense.

Provide help to interpret the meaning of a question. Provide examples, explanations, definitions about the menu choices (e.g., what does RPM mean?). Hypertext could be useful here.

Provide help to tell the user what a valid form of the answer could be and supply an example of a reasonable range of values. What is wanted, a single number, a range of numbers, a date, or words? Give a template to show the format desired, or give examples of the correct format.

Graphics can be used to allow the user to select the level of certainty required for the answer, or to show the level of certainty associated with the answer provided. Pictures can also be used to give the answer itself.

Some examples of icons available in expert system shells are control chassis, reset switch, lights, dials, and on/off switches. Graphics are most understandable when they are accompanied by labels or captions.

7.5.1.9 Presenting Answers

How specific should the answer text be? A biographical expert system could conceivably provide any of the following answers, ranked from least specific to most specific.

1. Recommend a biographical source
2. Recommend a biographical source on American scientists
3. Recommend *American Men and Women of Science*
4. Recommend *American Men and Women of Science,* vol. 5, 237

Highly specific answers require more IF–THEN cases, which in turn require more time to develop and test the application, and require more time to maintain the system (make updates, additions, corrections). All cases in the system should result in approximately the same level of specificity.

The order of presentation can make a difference in how acceptable an end user finds the expert system's conclusion. If there are several possible answers, save the end user's time by presenting the most likely answer first. Bielawski and Lewand[55] say they chose to present the explanation of the reasoning first, then the specific recommendation, so the user could understand the recommendation better. Some packages present the specific recommendation and wait for the user to initiate the request for how a conclusion was reached.

Some systems allow the end user to augment the explanation based on individual rules with a metaexplanation based on metarules. Metarules, or rules about rules, may provide more information on the choice of rules followed, give strategic knowledge about why the rules were used, and the order they were followed in, so the answer can be more understandable.

Don't assume the consultation was successful. In the text of the explanation, suggest ways to get another answer if the user disagrees with the expert system. A message could direct the user to try another path through the expert system, or consult a reference librarian.

Provide the user with a choice of output formats—screen displays, printouts, and disk output. Individuals differ in learning styles, and some people do better looking at answers and explanations on paper, while others don't want to wait for a printout before seeing an answer and want to see it first on screen to decide how useful the answer is. The printouts of the answer and the logic that produced it should be formatted to present the answer and logic in a clear graphic way. Sometimes tables are clearer than a textual explanation.

If the answer contains procedures, include all necessary information to interpret the procedures, or describe where to get that information. For example, if the answer is a journal index, show the user where the index is located in the library with a floor plan, map, or location of reference room.

Provide explanations that are more than English translations of rules. Explain why the rules were chosen and executed in the order they were. John Black and his associates conducted an empirical study comparing four kinds of instructions in an online tutorial that required the subjects to infer procedures from the instructions. (1) The general-to-specific version presented instructions as general rules, from which the students were expected to infer how to apply the rule in the given context; (2) The explanation-to-specific version supplied information about the functional organization of the program in addition to general rules; (3) The specific-to-specific condition gave an example of the use of a command, from which the student was to infer how to apply the command in a slightly different context; (4) The control version gave explicit instructions. The best performance on a posttest consisting of realistic tasks was obtained from the general-to-specific and explanation-to-specific conditions.[56]

The language should be appropriate to the level of the user's knowledge, experience, intelligence, role, and intent. Hypertext can be an effective way to present material for a heterogeneous group of users. For example, if the system is designed for novices, experts can view short-cut commands or detailed material via hypertext links. Conversely, if the system is designed for experts, novices can read explanations of basic terms and concepts embedded in hypertext nodes.

7.5.1.10 Explanation

Explanation text tells the user how the conclusion was reached. Some research has been conducted, but there is no clear conclusion on how best to provide explanation.[57] Clancey discusses the question of how to explain the "outside" logic of the order of the rules. Perhaps the developer needs to provide this reasoning in the explanatory text. Otherwise, the user cannot see how the rules are related to each other, and may feel that he is missing some of the complex combinations of IF-THEN conditions possible. Visualization may help. Level 5 allows multiple pages of explanatory text and graphic information as well as references from the known factors of the current session. The explanatory text describes how the rules were selected and how the conclusion was inferred from the rules by displaying a summary of all intermediate as well as final conclusions. This process helps the user see what the reasoning was, and also permits the system to display a message saying "Insufficient information available to reach a conclusion," if there is not enough information. For classification expert systems, where the number of answers is small, but there are many ways to reach them, the explanation should tell the user how he reached that solution, because he may have reached it several different ways, and the user may want to recheck the logic used to reach the same conclusion based on different input.

1st Class lets you have a decision tree, but the tree does not explain how the expert system inferred the conclusion. KDS gives you an unpolished printout of rules with an asterisk next to the ones from which the expert system drew inferences. Easy Expert has a metarecommendation feature that explains the explanation. This feature is not as useful as it might be, because it is not integrated into the consultation. The user must make a separate menu choice from the main menu after he asks for the explanation of the conclusion. Texas Instruments's Personal Consultant Easy, though no longer sold, allows the developer to control the order in which rules are tried in the inference process. Metarules supply information on how best to apply the other forms of knowledge, particularly rules. So, Personal Consultant Easy can make the expert system try rules most likely to be useful during the majority of consultations, and dynamically change the order in which the rules are tried during a particular consultation based on information received during the consultation.

The explanation text should be adapted to the context of the current session. The text associated with the conclusion of a rule can contain the values that caused the rule to fire. For example, Level 5 allows the system to display this explanation: "Proposal was not acceptable because (fact name, format) is too long a time frame for a consumer capacity project. Consumer capacity projects can be funded only if duration is six months or less." (Fact name) shows the value of the fact. This capability is sometimes called sentence masking or a finessed form of natural language.

PC Expert keeps track of how parameters are established during the consultation. A parameter is a named item that represents a fact in the problem domain. The parameter takes on values during the consultation, determined by asking the user a question, using rules to infer the value, obtaining the value from a file, database, or spreadsheet, or using a default value. How the value was determined should be incorporated into the review screen or explanation process. PC Expert enables the developer to create a custom natural-language-like explanation by writing the explanation text and the parameter values at the conclusion of each rule to a text file. At the end of the consultation, the file is displayed to the user.

Some systems allow the developer to indicate a confidence level with the explanation. Rather than displaying the confidence level in parentheses at the end of the explanation, include the percentage in the explanation. Instead of:

"Your illustration is found in the *American Heritage Dictionary*. (70%)"

Display this:

"There is a 70% possibility that your illustration can be found in the *American Heritage Dictionary*."

or group percentages into ranges and substitute English-language phrases:

"There is a strong possibility that your illustration can be found in the *American Heritage Dictionary*."

Users often do not find probabilities useful because the values, whether numerical or verbal, do not explain why the expert assigned that magnitude. One solution is to have the domain experts justify why a probability value was assigned, store the justification in the knowledge base, and use it to construct the explanations.[58]

Personal Consultant Easy makes it easy for the user to ask for an explanation. After showing the conclusions, the system displays a prompt to press <Enter>. The expert system shows a menu of available commands: Continue, How, Print Conclusions, Review, Save, Playback, File, or Quit. The choices are listed in the order most likely to be useful.

7.5.1.11 Online Help

The developer can supply help text for what each option means. This is true whether the interface style is a simple question-and-answer dialogue, or a menu selection system. The help text explains to the user why the question is being asked. Personal Consultant Easy lets the user ask "Why?" repeatedly until he reaches the beginning of the logic tree that controls the consultation. The expert system can display help text automatically when an option is selected or wait until the user requests help.

Help messages should display instantaneously or the user will be reluctant to use the help feature. The text should show an example, rather than just listing algorithmic syntax. It should tell you what a valid form of answer could be and a reasonable range of values. Should the user input a number, a range, or specific words? Provide examples as well as templates. Help text can be updated more readily if the text is kept in a separate text file rather than with the programming rules. Finally, help text should address both syntactical and semantic problems. The help in Easy Expert talks about what function keys do, but does not explain how to use the functions during the session.

Other ways to use help include user-defined help and system messages, context-sensitive help, online tutorials, user guides, and installation instructions. (Level 5 gives the developer the capability to create these.)

7.5.1.12 Error Messages

Error messages should be specific to the situation. If the user does not enter a correct knowledge base name, VP Expert displays a message "file not found or disk full, press enter to resume" message. This error message conflates two conditions—file not found and disk full—which are not necessarily related in the end user's mind. A second problem with this error message is that the text does not tell the user how to recover from the error. The user is no wiser about the correct format for a knowledge base name, and does not know what knowledge bases are available. A better message would be "A rulebase is a filename of 8 characters, followed by a period, followed by k," and the best response would be to list the available knowledge bases, allowing the user to choose from them.

Many error messages sound more like place holders than active explanations. For example, Level 5 displays, "That key is not active. Please, try again," which sounds friendly, but does not provide any other directions. The message would be more useful if it suggested which key the user should try next or listed which keys were valid choices.

7.5.1.13 Status Messages

Use status messages to provide feedback to the user, especially when the action selected may take some time. For example, if the user must wait for a knowledge base to be loaded, display a message, such as "loading filename ... please wait," or "one moment please ...," so the user knows that the system is active and responding.

If the system uses toggle switches to set options, then the interface should indicate whether a switch is on or off. One demo, XXXPERT (a shareware package), lets the user turn the trace of rules on or off, but the user cannot tell what the status is after giving the command. The user will not know (1) whether the command had taken effect, and (2) whether the result was what he intended. In terms of Norman's model, the user encountered the Gulf of Evaluation. The physical state of the system did not enable the user to determine how well his expectations and intentions have been met.

7.5.1.14 Concluding the Consultation

Deliberate inconsistency in the interface may be useful here.[59] For example, the ⟨Esc⟩ key could back up one screen at a time until the top level is reached. Then the interface could require "E" for Exit or "Q" for Quit so the user does not leave the application without meaning to. If ⟨Esc⟩ is used to quit the expert system application, then a message should ask the user to confirm if he wants to quit.

7.6
Development Process

This section lists steps for librarians to take in the user interface development process.

7.6.1 Commit to an Iterative Design Process

The human–computer interaction literature does not give minute details. So, along with the above suggestions and guidelines, and the journal articles, proceedings, and conferences suggested, designers need to commit to a process of iterative design and empirical testing with intended users early in the expert system development cycle. The Bellcore Artificial Intelligence team, through their experience developing five expert systems, concluded that the most difficult and time-consuming issues in development were not artificial intelligence issues, but the user interface and integration with conventional systems, and recommended that these issues be dealt with early in the development life cycle. Eliciting expert knowledge from the domain experts was necessary, but an actively involved and informed user community, which can be achieved through iterative design, is necessary for success.[60]

Developers should gather feedback from users as soon as they have enough facts in a knowledge base to answer several questions, rather than waiting until they have finished testing the rules. They may find that user interface testing will change the organization of the rules, and this should be discovered early in the process. User interface development should go on at the same time as expert system development because the user interface design will interact with the logic, reasoning method, ordering of rules, and deep system organization. These interactions must be identified early so developers can organize the way screens and questions are presented to the user.

7.6.2 Set Measurable Usability Goals

Specific measurable usability goals help the developers know when the design is successful, which parts of the interface still need work, and provide a way to determine whether design modifications result in the desired improvement. Usability goals provide a way of knowing when to stop.

7.6.3 Focus Early and Continuously on Users and Their Tasks

Who will be the users? What will the users do with the expert system? What are the kinds of tasks, how often is each done, what is the user trying to accomplish, what are likely errors? The user interface design process is greatly influenced by whether the designers have clear answers to these questions. Gould and Lewis emphasize that "open decisions about the intended users reflect slipperiness, not flexibility."[61] If no homogeneous group emerges as the user group, then the system will have to be tailored and tested for several groups, and design trade-offs may be required.

Information should be displayed in a form that matches the user's mental representation. For example, display months in temporal order, not in alphabetical order. Before designing the interface, the designer must assess the users' cognitive representation. Then display should contain many clues to show the user the intended relations among the displayed items. For example, "causal or directional relations should be indicated with lines or arrows, whereas groups of units, commands, or labels that are related should be spatially clustered and graphically set off from unrelated items by lines, boxes, etc."[62]

7.6.4 Allocate Tasks between Human and Expert System

List human strengths and weaknesses and computer strengths and weaknesses. Decide where the application can take advantage of human and computer strengths, and design mechanisms to support human and computer weaknesses. The list below is a sampler to get the designer started.

Human strengths
- recognizing temporal and spatial patterns
- extracting concepts from noisy data
- making inferences
- assessing similarity of objects on many dimensions

Human weaknesses
- remembering details (limited capacity)
- keeping track of changing states

Computer strengths
- remembering details
- keeping track of changing states
- calculating

Computer weaknesses
- recognizing temporal and spatial patterns
- extracting concepts from noisy data

7.6.5 Consult Guidelines for Advice

Developers can find useful information in user interface guideline manuals, provided they are aware of certain limitations. Often, specific advice is based on research that is restricted to certain applications (text editing) or domains (automobile safety, aerospace, banking, insurance), and the results may not be generally applicable. Sometimes the research tests do not reflect real user tasks. For example, measuring the time it takes a user to find a randomly appearing image of a disk on the computer screen may not be a good predictor of the amount of time it takes a user to find a specific menu item on the screen. Sometimes guidelines clash. For instance, keeping a command structure consistent may cause a conflict with keeping the interface flexible, and both may hinder simplicity.

Guidelines do not give much advice on where, when, and how to use them, and on how to apply them in a particular situation. The guidelines generally will not tell you whether you should use a pop-up dialogue window to display a prompt or eliminate the need for the prompt by redesigning the screen. Guidelines should be used along with empirical testing and iterative design to craft a user interface design that matches the local situation.

In their landmark article, Gould & Lewis[63] show empirically that software designers do not follow good design principles. A second article in 1987[64] shows that even professional user interface designers are not able to get a system right the first time. These articles make a strong argument for the need for user feedback and iterative design.

Nevertheless, guidelines often provide the only formal collection of specific suggestions that a designer can consult. Several guidelines provide a good starting point for design.

7.6.6 Draw Up Own Guidelines Document

A guidelines document tailored to the local environment enables the developer to maintain consistent tone, terminology, specificity, knowledge, and understanding of the organization of the knowledge base. Much of this information may seem obvious to today's developers because of their intense involvement in designing the system, but the real value of the document is to maintain the design philosophy for future system enhancements, educate new development team members in case of turnover or additional staff, and provide background material for staff and user documentation.

7.6.7 Create Prototype and Modify It

Look for a programming environment that permits developers to experiment with various designs and implement an initial prototype rapidly and incrementally. The prototype should be designed by starting with cognitive and semantic decisions, and then designing syntactic interface level.

Prototypes should be tested early in the development process so developers can discover blind spots, modify the designs quickly, and retest the designs. Gould (1987) says the team revised the user manual 200 times and tested the design with 150 people. His paper lists many techniques to prototype rapidly, including paper and text, screen design tools, and videotaping.[65] Iterative design and testing should be continued until users meet usability goals or the team runs out of time. This process will bring to light some expert system design questions that need to be resolved now, rather than when the system is first released to the public.

7.6.8 Get Empirical Evidence about Effectiveness

Gather both quantitative measures and qualitative comments to direct the modifications to the prototype. A good manual to use for evaluating the interface is Ravden's *Evaluating Usability of Human–Computer Interfaces: A Practical Method*. The book is exactly what the title says: a practical method, complete with checklists.[66] Other useful reading is an article by Good et al. on usability engineering and setting specific goals.[67]

7.7

Sources of Information on User Interface Design

Designers make false assumptions about people. Gould and Lewis, in a landmark and often-cited paper, presented empirical data showing that design principles are not always intuitive to designers. Their evidence indicates that identifying specific, potential problems in a human–computer dialogue design is difficult. There are several sources of information to guide user interface designers:

1. Guidelines documents (several are listed under 2 below)
2. Published literature: Journal literature and conference proceedings. Association for Computing Machinery, Special Interest Group on Computer–Human Interactin. *Bulletin. Proceedings.*
   Behavior and Information Technology
   Communications of the ACM
   Human Factors
   International Journal of Man–Machine Studies
3. Conferences and association meetings
4. Scientific approach to design user interface for expert systems, accomplished through usability labs and user interface testing which conduct:
   a. controlled experiments
   b. observational and thinking aloud studies of user behavior

c. look at different user communities and expert system programmer tasks: what support or tools do they need to do their job?
d. and measures for each user community:
1. measurements of learning time
2. speed of performance on bench mark tasks
3. rate and distribution of errors
4. retention over time for a variety of user communities
5. subjective satisfaction scales and informal comments to provide insight into the problems users experience

7.7.1 Prototyping Tools

The most important characteristic of a prototype tool is that the designer can make changes to the interface quickly. Tools vary in sophistication
and cost. Listed below are several possibilities:

- paper and pencil
- paint or draw programs
- Dan Bricklin's DEMO program
- HyperPAD
- HyperCard
- SuperCard
- ToolBook

The *Human Factors* journal carries advertisements for more sophisticated prototype programs, some with online user interface advice.

7.8

Conclusions

The user interface is crucial to the acceptance of an expert system, and
its design should not be left to the end of the development process. The
design of the interface, like the design of the logic of the expert system,
should involve end users and iterative development. Summarized below are
the user interface issues discussed in this chapter.

1. The user interface is vital to usability and therefore the acceptance
of an expert system knowledge base.
2. The user interface is more than the built-in visual objects and interface style an expert system shell gives you.
3. Not all users are alike. Important human performance issues and
individual differences affect how well any user can use a system.

4. The user interface must be designed to meet the needs of the users and their tasks.

5. No design is right the first time. User interface testing is crucial to perfecting user interface design.

6. Commit to early testing by intended users and use results to design iteratively.

7. Set measurable usability goals.

8. Iterative design depends on a commitment to modify a design and on good user interface development tools that allow rapid prototyping

Currently, expert systems are of benefit to several audiences: "expert-in-training"—the novice librarian; experts but not in the domain of the expert system; and end users. However, two trends open the possibility of widening the audience that can use expert systems profitably:

1. Interest in creating an intelligent user interface. Intelligent interfaces can be applied to expert systems themselves to make user–computer interaction easier and more efficient. For instance, an intelligent user interface can contain expert knowledge of the application domain; the expert system development tool; the different tasks the user might want to carry out; the user's level of competence with the system; his model of how the system works; his goals, needs, expectations, assumptions; and preferred method of interaction. This information could be obtained by asking the user questions at the beginning of the session or by the system directly inferring it from the user's online behavior. Such a system could check whether a user's input makes sense in the current context rather than merely check whether the input is a legal value.[68]

2. Trend toward integrating expert systems into traditional data processing. Hendler talks about an expert system running on a separate machine, needing a separate password, and users with no time to learn how to use it. Librarians can identify with that situation. The future lies in integrating expert systems into the user interface of other applications such as OPACs or online searching systems. Answerman at NAL is the beginning of that vision.

The payoff for librarians to invest time in designing the user interface is in making the expert system more usable, so that stored knowledge can be put to use. When expert systems cease to be a trendy technology, we can see where the enduring uses of expertise can be applied to information systems. As information networks become larger and encompass more types of information (e.g., the Internet, the proposed National Research and Education Network, local databases, multiple bibliographic database files), we will need to embed our expertise about navigating through huge seas of information into user interfaces to the virtual library.

Endnotes _____

1. Alison Kidd, "Human Factors Problems In The Design And Use Of Expert Systems," in *Fundamentals Of Human-Computer Interaction,* ed. Andrew Monk (New York: Academic Press, 1984), 237–247; Alison L. Kidd and Martin B. Cooper, "Man–Machine Interface Issues In The Construction And Use Of An Expert System," *International Journal Of Man–Machine Studies* 22 (January 1985): 91–102; Mike Coombs and Jim Alty, "Expert Systems: An Alternative Paradigm," *International Journal Of Man–Machine Studies* 20 (January 1984): 21–43; John M. Carroll and Jean McKendree, "Interface Design Issues For Advice-Giving Expert Systems," *Communications of the ACM* 30 (January 1984): 14–31.

2. D. M. Woods and E.M. Roth, "Cognitive Systems Engineering," in *Handbook of Human–Computer Interaction,* ed. Martin Helander (Amsterdam: Elsevier Science Publishers, 1988), 19.

3. For a study of military officers' reaction to an expert system in the decision-making domain, see Robert R. Mackie and C. Dennis Wylie, "Factors Influencing Acceptance of Computer-Based Innovations," in *Handbook of Human–Computer Interaction,* ed. Martin Helander (New York: Elsevier Science Publishers, 1988), 1081–1106.

4. James Hendler and Clayton Lewis, "Introduction: Designing Interfaces For Expert Systems," in *Expert Systems: The User Interface,* ed. James A. Hendler (Norwood, NJ: Ablex, 1988), 3.

5. M. Lynne Marcus, "Power, Politics, and MIS Implementation," *Communications Of the ACM* 26(1983): 430–444, proposes the theory that system design interacts with the context of the organization. Resistance to a new system occurs in the context of political struggles. Changing individuals or fixing technical features will have little effect on resistance.

6. Mike Jones, "Man–Machine Interface Design For Expert Systems," in *Structuring Expert Systems: Domain, Design, and Development,* ed. Jay Liebowitz and Daniel A. De Salvo (Englewood Cliffs, NJ: Yourdon Press, 1989), 88.

7. Tom Carey, "Position Paper: The Basic HCI Course For Software Engineers," *SIGCHI Bulletin* 20 (January, 1989): 15.

8. John Pallato, "Developer Shell Gets Hypertext Feature," *PC Week,* March 20, 1989, 59.

9. Milam W. Aiken and Olivia R. Liu Sheng, "NEXPERT OBJECT," (software review) *Expert Systems* 7 (February 1990): 54–57.

10. Henry Ledgard, "Misconceptions in Human Factors," *Abacus* 3 (Winter 1986): 21–45.

11. Woods and Roth, 3–34.

12. John Whiteside et al., "User Performance With Command, Menu, and Iconic Interfaces," in *Proceedings CHI '85: Human Factors In Computing Systems* (New York: Association For Computing Machinery, 1985), 185–191.

13. John Gould et al., "The 1984 Olympic Message System: A Test Of Behavioral Principles of System Design," *Communications of the ACM* 30 (September 1987): 759.

14. Carey, 15.

15. G. A. Miller, "The Magical Number Seven Plus Or Minus Two: Some Limits On Our Capacity To Process Information," *Psychological Review* 63 (1956): 81–97.

16. H. A. Simon, "How Big Is A Chunk?" *Science* 183 (1974): 482–488.

17. Wilbert O. Galitz, *Handbook Of Screen Format Design,* 3d ed. (Wellesley, MA: QED Information Sciences, 1989), 17.

18. Judith S. Reitman, W.B. Whitten II, and T. M. Gruenenfelder, "A General User Interface For Entering And Changing Tree Structures, Nested Menus, And Decision Trees," in *Proceedings of NYU Symposium on User Interface Design* (Norwood, NH: Ablex, 1985): 223–241.

19. Yvonne Waern, *Cognitive Aspects Of Computer Supported Tasks* (New York: John Wiley & Sons, 1989), 210.

20. Donald A. Norman, *The Psychology of Everyday Things* (New York: Basic Books, 1988), 189–190.

21. Norman, 1988, 70–71.

22. Gerhard Fischer and Andreas C. Lemke, "Constrained Design Processes: Steps Towards Convivial Computing," 1–58, in *Cognitive Science And Its Applications For Human–Computer Interaction,* ed., Raymond Guidon, (Hillsdale, NJ: Lawrence Erlbaum, 1988), 2, 6–7.

23. Reitman et al., 228–229.

24. Waern, 20. She compiled the figures from data given by psychological investigations reported by Stuart K. Card, Thomas P. Moran, and Allen Newell, in *The Psychology Of Human-Computer Interaction* (Hillsdale, NJ: Lawrence Erlbaum, 1983).

25. Waern, 20–22, 27.

26. Norman, 189–190.

27. Ibid., 48–53.

28. Ben Shneiderman, *Designing The User Interface: Strategies For Effective Human–Computer Interaction* (Reading, MA: Addison-Wesley, 1987).

29. Waern, 194–195.

30. Ibid., 196–197. Waern cites an experiment showing that incompatibility between the user's approach (forward-chaining) and a decision support system's approach (backward-chaining) led to the decline in performance quality of between 30 and 60%.

31. John M. Carroll and Jean McKendree, "Interface Design Issues For Advice-Giving Expert Systems," *Communications of the ACM* 30 (January, 1987): 15.

32. Coombs and Alty, 21–43.

33. James Baroff, Roland Simon, Francie Gilman, and Ben Shneiderman, "Direct Manipulation User Interfaces For Expert Systems," in *Expert Systems: The User Interface,* ed. James A. Hendler (Norwood, NJ: Ablex, 1988), 123.

34. Charles R. Hildreth, *Intelligent Interfaces And Retrieval Methods For Subject Searching In Bibliographic Retrieval Systems* (Washington, DC: Library of Congress, 1989), 51–52.

35. Kidd, 237–247.

36. Fischer and Lemke, 6–7.

37. Paul E. Lehner and Mary M. Krlj, "Cognitive Impacts Of The User Interface," in *Expert Systems: The User Interface,* ed. James A. Hendler, (Norwood, NJ: Ablex, 1988), 307–318.

38. Ibid., 307.

39. Coombs and Alty, 21.

40. Johanna D. Moore, "Responding To "Huh?": Answering Vaguely Articulated Follow-Up Questions," Proceedings of the CHI '89 Conference, 91–96.

41. It has been suggested that a coarser grain of analysis could allow more fluent and understandable dialogue with the user than a microscopic grain of analysis that focused more on the organization of the knowledge base. Carroll and McKendree, 18.

42. Waern, 20.

43. Fischer and Lemke, 30–31.

44. Jakob Nielsen, ed., *Coordinating User Interfaces For Consistency.* San Diego: Academic Press, 1989, 2–3.

45. Whiteside et al., 185–191.

46. The following taxonomy of user interface styles is summarized from Ben Shneiderman, "We Can Design Better User Interfaces: A Review of Human–Computer Interaction Styles," *Ergonomics* 31 (May 1988): 699–710.

47. Mike Jones, 106–107.

48. Kidd and Cooper, 98.

49. Mike Jones, 111.

50. Robert R. Sanchez and Allen L. Nagy, "Interaction of Color and Luminance Differences for Optimal Visual Search," *Society for Information Display Digest* 20 (1989): 296–299. One limitation of this experiment is that the conditions did not approximate a real-world environment or task.

51. Mark K. Jones, *Human–Computer Interaction: A Design Guide* (Englewood Cliffs, NJ: Educational Technology Publications, 1989).

52. Gitta B. Salomon and James Chen, "Using Neural Nets to Aid Color Selection," *Society for Information Display Digest 20 (*1989): 326–329.

53. Mike Jones, 110–113; Gerald M. Murch, "Colour Graphics—Blessing or Ballyhoo?," Computer Graphics Forum 4 (1985), 127–135; Wilbert O. Galitz, Chapter 10, Color in Screen Design, *Handbook of Screen Format Design,* 3d ed. (Wellesley, MA.: QED Information Sciences, Inc., 1988), 203–218; David Travis, *Effective Color Displays: Theory and Practice* (Academic Press, London, 1991).

54. Patricia Wright and Fraser Reid, "Written Information: Some Alternatives To Prose For Expressing The Outcomes Of Complex Contingencies," *Journal Of Applied Psychology* 57 (2) (1973): 160–166. Wright and Reid give suggestions for when to use bureaucratic prose, flowcharts, list of short sentences, or a two-dimensional table to give operating instructions or written instructions. Subjects following instructions written in bureaucratic prose fared the worst in time, errors, or both.

54a. Galitz, Wilbert O. *Handbook Of Screen Format Design.* 3rd ed. Wellesley, MA: QED Information Sciences, 1989.

54b. Tullis, Thomas S. "A System For Evaluating Screen Formats." *Proceedings of the Human Factors Society 30th Annual Meeting,* pp. 1216–1220. Santa Monica, CA: Human Factors Society, 1986.

55. Larry Bielawski and Robert Lewand, *Expert Systems Development: Building PC-Based Applications* (Wellesley, MA: QED Information Sciences, Inc., 1988).

56. John B. Black, J. Scott Bechntold, Marco Mitrani, and John M. Carroll, CHI '89 Conference Proceedings. "On-Line Tutorials: What kind Of Inference Leads To The Most Effective Learning?," 81–83.

57. William J. Clancey, "The Epistemology Of A Rule-Based Expert System: A Framework For Explanation," *Artificial Intelligence* 20 (May 1983): 215–251; W. Swartout, "XPLAIN: A System For Creating and Explaining Expert Consulting Programs," *Artificial Intelligence* 21 (September 1983): 285–325; and Michel Dubas, "Expert Systems In Industrial Practice: Advantages and Drawbacks," *Expert Systems* 7 (August 1990): 150–156.

58. Kidd and Cooper, 99.

59. Wendy A. Kellogg,"The Dimensions Of Consistency," in *Coordinating User Interfaces For Consistency,* ed. Jakob Nielsen (San Diego: Academic Press, 1989), 14–15.

60. Adam Irgon et al., "Expert System Development: A Retrospective View Of Five Systems," *IEEE Expert* 5 (June, 1990): 25–41.

61. John D. Gould and Clayton Lewis, "How To Design Usable Systems," in *Handbook of Human–Computer Interaction,* ed. Martin Helander (Amsterdam: North-Holland, 1988), 757–790.

62. Reitman et al., 223.

63. Gould & Lewis, 1985.

64. Gould et al., 1987.

65. Gould et al., 1987.

66. Susannah J. Ravden, *Evaluating Usability of Human–Computer Interfaces: A Practical Method.* (New York: Halsted Press, 1989).

67. Good, Michael; Spine, Thomas M.; Whiteside, John; and George, Peter. "User-Derived Impact Analysis As A Tool For Usability Engineering," in *Proceedings CHI '86: Human Factors In Computing Systems,* 241–246 (New York: Association of Computing Machinery, 1986).

68. Kidd, 245-246.

Three

Progress

Whatever you say, the plan was splendid; it was simple and clear, you couldn't conceive of a better one. There was only one drawback to it; how it could be put into effect was totally unclear.

—Lewis Carroll

No one yet has succeeded in inventing an automaton to answer all the wise and foolish questions asked by the American public.

—Louis Shores, 1937

The popular conception of automation as applied to the work of the reference librarian suggests a mechanical marvel from which accurate and authoritative answers to questions will be disgorged in immediate response to a push of the proper button.

—Jesse Shera, 1964

8

A Review of KBS Applications in General Reference Work

In addition to discussing what is feasible in KBS terms as we did in Chapter 3, it may be equally useful to consider what has been done in the reference field already. However, many of the reports of KBS are scattered throughout the literature, appearing in diverse places. And, of course, there are other systems that have not been reported before.

Therefore, the purpose of this chapter is to identify the prototype and commercial KBS in the field of general reference work and critically review them based on evaluative criteria developed in Chapters 4, 5, 6, and 7. Arranged in chronological order and alphabetically within each year, this chapter presents 56 known prototype KBS for reference work. Each system is described and analyzed in detail, many for the first time. The concluding assessment is also the first independent evaluation for most of these systems. Notably, this chapter omits some systems by request such as Bruce Bennion's chemistry KBS work but includes such systems as the Information Machine (1987) and PRONTO (1989), which are not strictly speaking KBS, but useful prototyping efforts, nevertheless. The chapter concludes with a prototypic KBS and a state-of-the-art discussion.

Automatic Retrieval of Biographical Reference Books (1968)

Project staff: Cherie B. Weil, MA Student, University of Chicago
Thesis advisor: Victor Yngve
Domain expert: Weil
Development platform: Mainframe, batch processing
Programming language: COMIT, a list-processing language
Library environment: University

Specific domain: 234 Biographical Reference sources
Reasoning: Rule based; backward-chaining
Size of system: Small; 6 rules and 234 tools
User interface: Socratic
Special features: Characterized sources based on living/dead, nationality, sex, occupation, religion, race, memberships, and date

Testing/Evaluation: 14 test questions; 71.4% accuracy

Published reports: Cherie B. Weil, "Classification and Automatic Retrieval of Biographical Reference Books," MA thesis, University of Chicago, September 1967, and id., "Automatic Retrieval of Biographical Reference Books," *Journal of Library Automation* 1 (December 1968): 239–249.

Estimated development time/Cost: $990

Perceived benefits: "Freed to perform tasks less easily mechanized, there are not enough reference librarians who have perfect recall of their collections."

Availability/Cost: Program code appended to thesis

REFSEARCH (1971)

Project staff: Institute of Library Research, University of California, Berkeley

Principal investigator: M.E. Maron, Professor of Librarianship

Project coordinator: Ralph Shoffner, ILR

Conceptual approach: Mary Whouley and Edith Darknell, RA, UCB School of Librarianship

Programming: Allan Humphrey, Katsuhiko Kurano, and Rodney Randall, ILR

KB analysis and encoding: Howard White with assistance of Patricia Stewart and Ruth Warheit

Development platform: IBM 360/40 and Sanders 720 CRT and keyboard

Programming language: DISCUS (CAI programming language)

Library environment: Library school CAI

Specific domain: 144 general reference works (about 790 volumes)

Special features: Categorizes reference works according to 15 "channels" or distinctive features: fields, nonliving objects, products, human procedures, concepts, natural processes, living objects, art works, corporate bodies, words, places, persons, events, dates, and eras. Reference questions are further characterized by "qualifiers." White writes "categorizes reference works and reference questions in a common language, the use of which simulates a reference librar-ian's thought processes in converting a question into a search strategy for one or more plausible sources in which the answer may be found."

Testing/Evaluation: 20 test questions appended. Also used in Mrs. Raynard Swank's "General Reference" course, UCB School of Librarianship

Published reports: Joseph C. Meredith, "Reference Search System (REFSEARCH) Users' Manual," (Berkeley, CA: Institute of Library Research, April 1971); reprint ed., Bethesda, MD: ERIC Document Reproduction Center, ED060918 (124 pp.), and id., "Machine-Assisted Approach to General Reference Materials," *JASIS* 22 (May/June 1971): 176–186; Howard D. White and Diana Woodward, "A Model of Reference Librarians' Expertise: Reviving Refsearch on a Microcomputer," in *Expert Systems in Libraries,* ed. Rao Aluri and Donald E. Riggs (Norwood, NJ: Ablex Publishing Corporation, 1990), 51–63; see note on page 63 of Aluri and Riggs.

Funding: DHEW OEG 1-7-071085-4286

Estimated development time/Cost: 18 months (15 December 1968–30 June 1970)

Perceived benefits: "tireless reiterative ability"

Availability/Cost: ERIC Document Reproduction Center

GRUNDY (1979)

Project staff: Elaine Rich, PhD candidate, Carnegie Mellon University

Dissertation committee: George Robertson, Jon Bentley, Susan Fiske, and Raj Reddy

Domain expert: Clark Thompson
Development platform: DEC20
Programming Language: LISP
Library environment: Public
Specific domain: Adult fiction (novels)
Reasoning: "Pattern matching. Each book is described as a feature vector. Each user is also represented as a similar vector (as a result of the user modeling process). So a pattern matcher that knows the relationship between book vectors and readers vectors tries to find the closest match."
Size of system: 66 books, 153 words that could trigger sterotypes, 90 stereotypes, and code to implement the matching and the updating of the stereotypes
User interface: Simple natural language and socratic questions
Special Features: Stereotyping triggered by gender, genre, and prior reading habits. Can adapt its recommendations based on user's reaction to annotations.
Testing/Evaluation: "When books were recommended at random, 47% were judged good by the user. When the user models were used as a basis for selection, 72% were judged good. The user population

$[N = 20]$ was all drawn from the university community and the books were generally 'intellectual' fiction."
Published reports: Elaine Rich, "Building and Exploiting User Models," PhD dissertation, Carnegie-Mellon University, 1979 (193 pp). Id., "User Modeling via Stereotypes," *Cognitive Science* 3 (1979): 329–354; id., "Users are Individuals: Individualizing User Models," *International Journal of Man–Machine Studies* 18 (1983): 199–214; Id., "GRUNDY: A System that Exploits User Models for Retrieval," in *Intelligent Library and Information Systems,* ed. Roy Davies (Chichester: Ellis Horwood, 1986).
Funding: DARPA Order No. 3597 supervised under F33615-78-C-1551. Additional Xerox funding.
Estimated development time/Cost: 12 person months; $20,000.
Perceived benefits: "The system never went into production use. Its contribution was in showing that user models can help and can be built using stereotypes."
Availability/Cost: Dissertation, UMI Order Number 79-25024

Reference Librarian Enhancement System (REFLES, 1979)

Project staff: Roger C. Palmer and Kathleen T. Bivins
Research assistants: David Haynes and David Abels
Development platform: Radio Shack TRS-80
Programming language: Basic Level II
Library environment: College library and University engineering library
Specific domain: Fact-type questions related to library schedules, policy, equipment, and locational or directory information
Reasoning: Pattern matching of indexed records via thesaurus
Size of system: Small
User interface: Menu driven
Special features: Browsing of thesaurus records
Testing/Evaluation: 2 trial environments
Published reports: Bivins and Palmer, "RE-

FLES: A Proposal for a Microcomputer-Based Database for Fact Retrieval and Search Strategy Development," *ASIS Proceedings* 1979, 58–65; "A Microcomputer Alternative for Information Handling: REFLES," *Information Processing and Management* 17 (1981): 93–101; and "REFLES: An Individual Microcomputer System for Fact Retrieval," *Online Review* 4 (December 1980): 357–365.
Funding: UCLA GSLIS Research Assistance and equipment
Estimated development time/Cost: Proposal, December 1978; Development, Spring and Summer 1979 through Summer 1980
Perceived benefits: Fast retrieval of nonprint information; ease of access and maintenance; enhancement of reference librarian status

Availability/Cost: A planned commercial version running on an Alpha-Micro 100 announced as available from Documentation Associates was cancelled in 1982.

Computer Pix (1981)

Project staff: Wayne Oakland (MI) Library Federation, 33030 Van Born Road, Wayne, Michigan 48184

Project director: Silva Makowski, Coordinator, YA Services; formerly, Kaye Grabbe, Chairperson of YAS Committee

Development platform: Offline computer

Library environment: Public Library

Specific domain: Reader's advisory for ages 13 through 18 (junior and senior high grades); 1000 fiction titles

Reasoning: Pattern matching of 5 simple questions asked of young adults (YAs) with book's attributes based on a librarian-developed 14-item checklist, "Interest Inventory Sheet"

Size of system: Small; 7 rules and 1000 titles

Special features: Books characterized by (1) genre (story type); (2) plot subject; (3) main character (male; female; nonhuman; machine); (4) geographical setting; (5) time period; and (6) reading level.

Testing/Evaluation: For Computer Pix '82—"weeding old titles . . . clarifying some of the terms used in the pilot." Currently, "adding new titles on an annual basis."

Published reports: "Computer Matches YA's and Books," *American Libraries* 13 (January 1982): 88.

Perceived benefits: "Instant, high appeal reader's advisory for teens, who are notoriously hard to motivate!"

Availability/Cost: History and description of its development; phone (313) 467-5341 or fax (313) 326-3025.

REFLINK (1981)

Project staff: Kathleen T. Bivins and Lennart Eriksson

Development platform: ABC-80 microcomputer

Programming language: ABC-80 Basic

Library environment: University

Specific domain: Ongoing research in specific field; bibliographic instruction; and personal reference files

Size of system: Small

User interface: Menu driven

Published reports: Bivins and Eriksson, "Reflink: A Microcomputer Information Retrieval and Evaluation System," *Information Processing and Management* 18 (1982): 111–116 and "Reflink: A Microcomputer Information Retrieval System," 73–80, in *National Online Meeting, Proceedings—1981*, ed. M.E. Williams and T.H. Hogan (Medford, NJ: Learned Information, 1981).

Perceived benefits: "assumed that a microcomputer-based system was the most cost-effective means of providing individualized data bases for reference service in a library."

CANSEARCH (1982)

Principal investigator and co-PI: A. Steven Pollitt

PhD committee members: Karen Sparck Jones, Michael F. Lynch, Barry Barber

Developer (i.e., Programmer/Analyst): Pollitt

Domain expert: Oncology Information Service, University of Leeds/MEDLAR Indexing Manuals

Development platform, Initial: Research Machines 380Z microcomputer; Final: Prime 750 time-shared minicomputer

Programming language, Initial: Micro-PROLOG; Final implementation: Portable Prolog, a Prolog interpreter written in PASCAL.

Library environment: Special

Specific domain: 60K cancer therapy related documents drawn from MEDLINE

Reasoning: Rule based; blackboards

Size of system: Small

User interface: Hierarchical menu; touch terminal

Testing/Evaluation: 40 test queries by 11 doctors. "[On occasion] doctors using CANSEARCH were able to outperform the intermediaries. . . ."

Published reports: A. Steven Pollitt, "A Search Statement Generator for Cancer Therapy Related Information Retrieval," *Proceedings of the 6th International Online Information Meeting* (Oxford: Learned Information, 1982), 405–413; id., "End User Touch Searching for Cancer Therapy Literature: A Rule-Based Approach," *Sixth Annual International ACM SIGIR Conference on Research and Development in Information Retrieval, SIGIR FORUM* 17 (1983): 136–145; id., *An Expert Systems Approach to Document Retrieval: A Summary of the CANSEARCH Research Project.* Technical Report No. 86/6 (Huddersfield, England: Department of Computer Studies and Mathematics, 1986); id., "A Rule-based Systen as an Intermediary for Searching Cancer Therapy Literature on MEDLINE," in *Intelligent Information Systems: Progress and Prospects,* ed. R. Davies (London: Ellis Norwood, 1986); id., "An Expert Systems Approach to Document Retrieval," PhD Dissertation, Huddersfield Polytechnic, 1986; id., "CANSEARCH: An Expert Systems Approach to Document Retrieval," *Information Processing and Management* 23 (1987): 119–138; id., "Intelligent Interfaces to Online Databases," *Expert Systems for Information Management* 3 (1990): 49–69.

Estimated development time/Cost: 1982 through 1986

PLEXUS (1983)

Project staff: Central Information Service of the University of London

Semantic categories and search strategy: B.C. Vickery

Semantic categories: Eric Coates

Development platform: Sirius I microcomputer with 850KB memory and 20MB external disk

Programming language: 10,000 lines of Turbo-Pascal

Library environment: Public library

Specific domain: Gardening, horticulture, and related aspects

Reasoning: Forward-chaining

Size of system: Intermediate; 1000 rules

User interface: Natural language

Special features: User modeling based on familiarity with system, job related, length of experience, familiarity with resources, prior advice-seeking activities, and user's geographical location

Testing/Evaluation: Phase 2

Published reports: A. Vickery, H.M. Brooks, B. Robinson, and B.C. Vickery, *Expert System for Referral: Phase I. Final Report* (London: British Library Research and Development Department, 1986); H.M. Brooks, "Expert Systems in Reference Work," 36–49, in *Expert Systems in Libraries,* ed. Forbes Gibb (London: Taylor Graham, 1986); A. Vickery and H.M. Brooks, "PLEXUS—The Expert System for Referral," *Information Processing and Management* 23 (1987): 99–117.

Funding: 4-year British Library Research and Development

Estimated development time/Cost: Early 1983 to May 1987; 40 person months over 20 months

Perceived benefits: "free intermediaries and reference librarians from routine and mundane questions."

Availability/Cost: Commercial version; see Tome Searcher (1988)

Reference and Information Station (1983)

Domain expert: Dana E. Smith, Purdue University

Programmer/Analyst: Steve M. Hutton

Development platform: IBM and Apple with minimal memory and one disk drive

Programming language: Applesoft Basic and authoring software

Library environment: University

Specific Domain: Directions and general information on library services and equipment; specific examples of library resources (including indexes, newspapers, periodicals, biographical sources, dictionaries, encyclopedias, government sources, company information) with detailed information, call numbers and location.

Reasoning: Production rules

Size of system: Small

User interface: Menu driven

Special features: When idle, uses mandala graphic display to catch user's attention. Statistical summaries of use intended as management decision purposes. Included suggestion box for name, phone number, and question

Published reports: Smith, "Reference Expert Systems: Humanizing Depersonalized Service," *Reference Librarian* 23 (1989): 177–190 and Smith and Hutton, "Back at 8:00AM: Microcomputer Library Reference Support Programs" *Collegiate Microcomputer* 2 (November 1984): 289–294.

Perceived benefits: Compliment to traditional services; ability to refer routine questions to machine. Captures information on the "lost" user who does not interact with reference staff

Availability/Cost: Operational

Byte into Books, Version 2.1 (1984; 1986 release; 1989)

Project staff: New Britain Public Library, Connecticut

Principal investigator and co-PI: Laurel Goodgion and Diana Norton

Project director: Laurel Goodgion

Developer (i.e., Programmer/Analyst): Peter Chase, Director of Plainville Public Library, Connecticut

Domain expert: Staff of the New Britain Public Library's Children Department

Development platform: Apple IIe

Programming language: Compiled Basic

Library environment: Public

Specific domain: Reader's advisory; more than 500 Children's books for third through fifth grade (ages 7–14)

Reasoning: Boolean search logic

Size of system: Small; 5 rules and 520 book records

User interface: Menu

Special features: Books characterized by: (1) 24 subject areas; (2) gender appeal; (3) popularity factor (high, average, or special); and (4) reading level (Grade 1 through 8). Title recommendations accompanied by one or two sentence annotations. Students stereotyped by: (1) reading ability; (2) enthusiasm

for reading; and (3) preferred reading interests. Subject/Title index and database listing. Generates reports on usage, subject, and subject/grade analysis

Testing/Evaluation: "it certainly motivated children to borrow more books . . .," "Microcomputer Software," *Booklist* (July 1987): 1693.

Published reports: Laurel Goodgion, "Byte into Books," *Library Journal* 111 (May 1986): LC6–LC8; Laurel Goodgion, "BYTE INTO BOOKS: Operator's Manual" (New Britain, CT: Children's Department, n.p.)

Funding: $7000 LSCA grant through Connecticut State Library

Estimated development time/Cost: One year; $7000

Perceived benefits: "To make reading attractive"

Availability/Cost: Used in about 139 libraries; $99.95 for three diskettes (Librarian's Disk; Patron Disk; and Data Disk) from CALICO (Computer Assisted Library Instruction CO, PO Box 15916, St. Louis, MO 63114; 24-hour telephone: (314) 863-8028

Conceptual Analysis of Business Information Needs (1984)

Project director: Eloisa Gomez Yeargain, Head of Public Services/Reference, UCLA Management Library

Domain expert: Yeargain

Development platform: PC and PC compatibles

Programming language: C-based

Shell software: VP-Expert

Library environment: Public, academic, and corporate

Specific domain: Business

Reasoning: Binary, rooted trees; forward-chaining

Size of system: Small

User interface: Menu driven

Special features: Uses widely recognized business information concept at its core

Testing/Evaluation: Extensive public presentations

Published reports: Nevada Library Association, 1984 Annual Conference; Southern California Association of Law Libraries, 15th Annual Institute (1987); and American Library Association, 1987 Annual Conference, Business Reference Services Discussion Group.

Funding: Private funding

Perceived benefits: Satisfies initial-level need for business reference at libraries without a business specialist or to supplement existing staff

Availability/Cost: Prototype in development

DEBIS, Distributed Expert-Based Information System (1984)

Project staff: Rutgers University 1984 and 1987 Workshops attended by computer and library and information scientists

Domain experts: Distributed

Programming language: Logic Programming (MU-Prolog); blackboards between functional models

Specific domain: Online, computer-based text documents including AIList Digest documents

Project: KIWI-KIRA, Denmark

Project: MONSTRAT, City University of London (Brooks)

Project: I3R by

Project: CODER by Edward A. Fox

Models: Monstrat composed of 10 functions including problem state, problem mode, user model, problem description, dialogue mode, retrieval stategy, response generator, input analyst, output generator, and explanation. I3R composed of request model, domain knowledge model, user model, document representation, and browsing model

Size of system: Large

Testing/Evaluation: MONSTRAT tested at City University, London

Published reports: Nicholas J. Belkin et al.,

"Distributed Expert-Based Information Systems: An Interdisciplinary Approach," *Information Processing and Management* 23 (1987): 395–409; Helen M. Brooks, "The Functions of an Information System: The MONSTRAT Model," paper presented at Workshop on Distributed Expert-Based Information Systems, Rutgers University, March 1987; Roger M. Thompson, "An Implementation Overview of I3R," paper presented at Workshop on Distributed Expert-Based Information Systems, Rutgers University, March 1987; W. Bruce Croft and R.T. Thompson, "I3R: A New Approach to the Design of Document Retrieval Systems," *JASIS* 38 (1987): 389–404; Edward A. Fox, "Development of the CODER System: A Testbed for Artificial Intelligence Methods in Information Retrieval," *Information Processing and Management* 23 (1987): 341–366; and Robert K. France and Edward A. Fox, "Knowledge Structures for Information Retrieval: Representation in the CODER Project," *Proceedings IEEE Expert Systems in Government Conference* (McLean, VA: IEEE, 1986), 135–141.

Funding: Monstrat by ESPRIT

Fiction Advisor—The Bookseller's Assistant (1984)

Project staff: Del Mar Group Inc.

Project director: Harold M. Kester, CEO

Domain experts: "over 18,000 users [i.e., readers] from all walks of life and reading patterns"

Platform: American Research IBM PC XT clone with 75MB hard drive; printer; bookstore version: $8500 machine, rented to sites

Programming language: Lattice C ported to Microsoft C

Environment: Large retail bookstores

Specific domain: Reader's advisory; adult fiction—"310 most popular English language authors as determined by Publisher's Weekly and other reading lists, such as Anthony Burgess's 'Book of Reading Lists.' There are approximately 1500 Book titles represented or about five per author."

Reasoning: Statistical knowledge model; users asked about their gender, movie and TV show preferences, 23 themes

Size of system: Intermediate; first prototype, 150 authors

User interface: User selects by pressing space bar or typing a letter or number.

Special features: Uses color. User selects favorite author(s) from list of 36 authors organized in 4 screens of 12 authors each. In the latest release, user can further refine recommendations based on 23 themes (adventure, mystery, romance, sex, suspense, violence, horror, spies and intrigue, science fiction, fantasy, power, war, western, sports, history, travel, psychology, family, community and society, politics, religion, supernatural, and humor) using a 1-to-5 Likert scale of awful, poor, so-so, good, and great. In addition, user may be asked to rank authors (like/dislike or no opinion/haven't read), rate 61 movies and TV shows, as well as provide gender information. Prints out recommendations. If not prompted, program times-out and returns to initial screen. Bookstore version, special features: Touch screen. Small percentage of titles accompanied by pictures; the pix files displayed for 5–10 seconds

Testing/Evaluation: Bookstore version, tested at 12 bookstore sites. Surveyed sample; *t*-test; factor analysis.

Published reports: None. 2-page "Instructions for Using Fiction Adviser"

Estimated development time/Cost: $1.25 million. Copyrighted, 1984, 1985, and 1986.

Perceived benefits: "will satisfy your personal reading interests and advise you on a gift selection." Encourages reading and book sales.

Availability/Cost: Britannica Software/Del Mar Technologies, 722 Genevieve Street, Suite M, Solana Beach, CA 92075; (619) 259-0444

Microcomputer Reference Program for Federal Documents (POINTER, 1984)

Project staff: Karen Smith, Documents Department, Lockwood Library, SUNY at Buffalo, Buffalo, NY 14260

Co-principal investigators: Stuart Shapiro, Faculty

Programmer: Sandra Peters, Computer Science student

Domain expert: Smith

Development platform: IBM PC 256K and two disk drives

Programming language: Originally LISP on a VAX; rewritten in Basic (6K lines of code)

Library environment: University

Specific domain: Federal Government Publications

Reasoning: "Problem reduction modeled after reference interview techniques (i.e., using closed rather than open questioning)"

Size of system: Small; 100 rules and 100 tools (130 screens of text)

User interface: Menu driven

Special features: Based on analysis of 1071 queries; Site customizable; printed manual, *POINTER: User's Guide and Reference Manual*

Testing/Evaluation: See published reports.

Published reports: Smith, "POINTER vs. *Using Government Publications:* Where's the Advantage," *Reference Librarian* 23 (1989): 191–205; "Robot at the Reference Desk," *College and Research Libraries* 47 (September 1986): 486–490; id., "Robot at the Reference Desk," 1986 ACRL Research Paper; id., Shapiro and Peters, *Final Report on the Development of a Computer Assisted Government Documents Reference Capability: First Phase* (Buffalo, NY: SUNY at Buffalo, 1984); "POINTER: The Microcomputer Reference Program for Federal Documents," in *Expert Systems in Libraries,* ed. Rao Aluri and Donald E. Riggs (Norwood,

NJ: Ablex Publishing Corporation, 1990), 41–50.
Funding: Council on Library Resources, Faculty/Librarian Cooperative Research Grant, No. 785-B ($3000)
Estimated development time/Cost: 4 months; $6000. Under development from 1984 to February 1987; tinkering since then. 1991 sabbatical plans to expand POINTER "to cover New York, Canadian, and European Community documents."
Perceived benefits: Solution to lack of staff; training tool for student assistants and clerical staff
Availability/Cost: $30 from address above

Online Reference Assistance (ORA, 1984)

Project staff: University of Waterloo Library Task Group including R. David Binkley, Maureen Carter, Gary Draper, Tom Eadie, Mary Ferguson, Linda Leger, Sue Moskal, Susan Routliffe, and James Parrott
Development platform: DEC Pro-350 microcomputer with color graphics monitor linked to VAX VMS operating system
Programming language: Digital Equipment's Courseware Authoring System (CAS); written in Digital Authoring Language (DAL), which is a subset of PASCAL
Library environment: University
Specific domain: 5 functional activities including directional transactions and holdings transactions as well as factual information and literature searches; computer-aided instruction (CAI) interpreting bibliographic references in order to obtain physical item
Reasoning: Backward- and forward-chaining
Size of system: Small
User interface: Menu and subject index
Special features: Color graphics for call number location
Testing/Evaluation: September 1986 to September 1987 in Engineering, Mathematics, and Science library and Arts library

Published reports: Parrott, "Expert Systems for Reference Work," *Microcomputers for Information Management* 3 (September 1986): 155–171; R. David Binkley and Parrott, "A Reference-Librarian Model for Computer-Aided Library Instruction," *Information Services and Use* 7 (1987): 31–38; Parrott, "Online Reference Assistance (ORA): An Expert System for Academic-Library Reference Assistance," in *Expert Systems in Libraries,* ed. Rao Aluri and Donald E. Riggs (Norwood, NJ: Ablex Publishing Corporation, 1990), 109–122; and Parrott, "Reference Expert Systems: Foundations in Reference Theory," in manuscript.
Funding: Digital Equipment of Canada for hardware and software
Estimated development time/Cost: Summer 1984 Task Force appointed through September 1987; cost was staff time; impossible to estimate
Perceived benefits: When a large number of alternatives are present and when quick answers are necessary as well as possible solution to reference crisis
Availability/Cost: No longer operational

Online Reference System (ORS, 1984)

Project staff: William Treat and Janet Chrisman
Project director: Janet Chrisman
Developer (i.e., Programmer/Analyst): William Treat
Development platform: Data Phase Automated Circulation System
Programming language: DataPhase (ALIS II) Automated Circulation System using Meditech Interpretive Information System (MIIS)
Library environment: University

Specific domain: Science reference material
Reasoning: Menu system would lead users to catalog record with annotation to assist in locating needed reference material
User interface: Menu driven
Published reports: J. Chrisman, and W. Treat, "An Online Reference System," *RQ* (Summer): 438–445.
Funding: Faculty Research Grant
Estimated development time/Cost: 6 months
Availability/Cost: Not available

Sci/Tech Book Advisor (1984?)

Project staff: Del Mar Group
Project director: Harold M. Keister
Development platform: PC and CD-ROM player
Library environment: University or college

Specific domain: John Wiley and Sons technical books
Reasoning: Relevance-ranked retrieval
Special features: Table of contents and back-of-the-book indexes

REFSEARCH2: Drexel University Expert System for General Library Reference (1985)

Project staff: Howard D. White, Diana Woodward (deceased, worked on the project from 1985–1986), Il-Yeol Song, Judith Ahrens, Drexel University
Developer (i.e., Programmer/Analyst): Song
Domain expert: White
Development platform: IBM PC
Shell software: Insight, initially; VP-Expert, at present; NEXPERT OBJECT (in future)
Library environment: University
Specific domain: General reference
Reasoning: Backward- and forward-chaining
Special features: Hypertext-based help facility; data stored in dBaseIII+ system
Testing/Evaluation: To follow development
Published reports: White and Woodward, "A Model of Reference Librarians' Expertise: Reviving Refsearch on a Microcomputer,"

in *Expert Systems in Libraries,* ed. Rao Aluri and Donald E. Riggs (Norwood, NJ: Ablex, 1990), 51–63; Diana Woodward, ASIS Mid Year Meeting, 16 May 1988; and "Automation Comes to the Reference Interview," *Library Journal* 111 (1 February 1986): 32.
Funding: Texas Instruments Research Grant; Drexel University Research Scholar Award; and John O. Haas Research Grant
Estimated development time/Cost: Work in progress through 1991/92; about $20,000
Perceived benefits: Runs on any 286 or higher-level IBM PC or compatibles; easy to use; can use dBaseIII+ files; can be customized to fit particular reference collections
Availability/Cost: Not determined as yet

Answerman (1986)

Project staff: Samuel Waters, National Agricultural Library
Development platform: IBM PC with 256K
Shell software: 1st-Class and Fusion
Library environment: Special
Specific domain: Agricultural
Reasoning: Example based
Size of system: Small to intermediate
User interface: Menu driven
Special features: Automatic capture of user feedback; automatic links to external devices such as CD/ROM player and online

systems such as BRS/Dialog files including Superindex and AGRICOLA via Crosstalk script files
Published reports: Waters, "Answerman, the Expert Information Specialist: An Expert System for the Retrieval of Information from Library Reference Books," *Information Technology and Libraries* 5 (September 1986): 204–212.
Perceived benefits: Librarians cannot remember all the relevant sources; free librarians from routine questions; stem "brain drain"

Aquaref Advisor (1986)

Project staff: National Agricultural Library, Aquaculture Information Center (AIC)
Principal investigator and co-PI: Deborah Hanfman and Lee Decker
Project director: Deborah Hafman
Developer (i.e., Programmer/Analyst): Hanfman and Decker
Domain expert: Hanfman
Development platform: IBM PC with 512K
Shell software: 1st-Class
Library environment: Special
Specific domain: Aquaculture
Reasoning: Example based
Size of system: Small
User interface: Menu driven
Special features: Links "to external programs, including bibliographic databases through remote access and CD-ROMS." Links to Aquatic Sciences and Fisheries Abstracts and DIALOG's AGRICOLA
Testing/Evaluation: Based on two years worth

of patron correspondence. 1000 diskettes distributed to users between January and September 1987. Informal evaluation.
Published reports: Deborah Hanfman, "AquaRef: An Expert Advisory System for Reference Support," *Reference Librarian* 23 (1989): 113–133.
Funding: NAL's AIC established in 1985 by congressional mandate
Estimated development time/Cost: 6 months; $35,000, total including $495 for 1st Class; 2 part-time salaries; 2000 diskettes, mailers, and distribution costs
Perceived benefits: "No single librarian or information specialist can be expected to consistently remember the best sources for locating answers on a particular subject."
Availability/Cost: NAL distributed to the public; no longer available due to replacement system, REFIS

Gateway to Information (Ohio State, 1986)

Principal investigator and project director: Virginia Tiefel, Office of Library User Education, Ohio State University Libraries
Project manager: Susan Logan, Automation Office, OSU Libraries

Project staff: Fred Roecker, Office of Library User Education; Carol DeWorth, University Systems
Developer (i.e., Programmer/Analyst): John Salter, three undergraduate students: Clint

DeWorth, Mohammed Khan, and Weimen Shen, and one graduate student: Sanjay Gadkari

Domain expert: Nancy O'Hanlon, Head, Reference Department, OSU Undergraduate Library (6 month leave), James Bracken (Communication), Eleanor Block (Journalism), Chuck Popovich (business), Ted Riedinger (Latin American Studies)

Local consultants: Phil Smith, Industrial Design and Engineering; Sal Abate and Kathleen Davey, Center for Teaching Excellence; Marjorie Cambre, College of Education; Joe Foley, Communication Department

Outside consultants: Evan Farber, Earlham College; Brian Nielsen, Northwestern University; Judy Sandler, University of Delaware; Karen Markey Drabenstott, University of Michigan

Development platform: Gateway Workstation Hardware: Apple Macintosh IIcx, 80M fixed disk, 4MB memory, EtherTalk card; Gateway Workstation Software: Apple's Hypercard, Mitem's MitemView, Apple's MacTCP, and Campus TCP/IP Network (SONNET); CD-ROM Server System Processor: (Intel 80286, 1 MB memory), Novell Netware (IPX), Merdian's CD-NET tower stacks, Microsoft Extensions, and PC Anywhere III

Programming language: HyperTalk

Shell software: Hypercard

Library environment: University

Specific domain: Lower-level undergraduate user instruction and general reference

Reasoning: Hypertext

Size of system: Small; 270 reference titles in print and CD-ROM

User interface: Menu driven

Special features: Analysis of information need by timeliness, narrowness, and length of project. Recommends research strategies using 31 dictionaries; 5 general (including CD-ROM Grolier full text searching) and 82 subject encyclopedias; 70 periodical indexes (including 9 Wilson on CD-ROM);

28 biographical sources; 35 book review indexes; 3 general and 12 specialized statistical sources of local, national, and international data. Information includes title, call number, year, brief description, and OSU locations with current subscriptions. Local facilities by name, location on map, floorplan, and collection profile.

Testing/Evaluation: Over 900 public evaluation forms since September 1989. Demonstration at the Ohio Libraries Information System Conference, 22–23 January 1990; ALAO conference and Ohionet Conferences, both in November 1990

Published reports: Tiefel, "An Expert System for All Seasons;" Brian Nielsen, "Roll Your Own Interface: Public Access to CD-ROMs," *Database* 12 (December 1989): 105–109 and id., "The Gateway to Information: A System Redefines How Libraries Are Used," *American Libraries* 22 (October 1991): 858–860.

Funding: $512,000; U.S. Department of Education: Fund for the Improvement of Post-Secondary Education, $170,725 over three years (1987–1990); Higher Education Act, Title II-D, College Library Technology and Cooperation Grants Program: $115,560 in 1988/89 and $117,558 in 1990. William Randolph Hearst Foundation: $35,000 in 1990; renewable for two more years

Estimated development time/Cost: 1986 to present; January 1990, first public Gateway workstation; 2 unsupervised workstations since July 1990; two more workstations added to Main Library location on 9 October 1990; two more workstations set up in Undergraduate Library on 4 January 1991. Version dates: 2.5 (Summer 1990); currently, version (3.0)

Perceived benefits: Need for intelligent front-end due to overdependence on LCS (online catalog). No more library staff

Availability/Cost: Possible marketing plan; "transferability" may be limited by need to modify narrative

Simulation of the Reference Process (REFSIM, 1986)

Principal investigator: James Parrott

Developer and domain expert: Parrott

Development platform: IBM PC XT compatible with 640K

Programming language: Arity Prolog

Library environment: University library

Specific domain: Bimodal, reference training and consultation on directional and ready-reference type questions

Reasoning: Backward-chaining

Size of System: Small

User interface: Natural language, "fuzzy semantically-driven" parser

Special Features: Reference question-type frames, reference strategy rule base, reference tool database, teaching rule base, student model, mode control; drill-and-practice and socratic method available in training mode

Testing/Evaluation: Never evaluated

Published reports: Parrott, "REFSIM: A Bimodal Knowledge-Based Reference Training and Consultation System," *Reference Services Review* 16 (1988): 61–68; "Simulation of the Reference Process," *Reference Librarian* 21 (1988): 189–207; "Simulation of the Reference Process II: REFSIM, an Implementation with Expert System and ICAI Modes," *Reference Librarian* 23 (1989): 153–176.

Funding: Self-financed—own time and computer

Estimated development time/Cost: October 1986–May 1989

Perceived benefits: Possible solution to reference crisis

Availability/Cost: Operational prototype

System Name: Unknown (1986)

Project staff: Mary Micco and Irma Smith

Domain expert: Dr. Irma Smith, Chatham College, PA

Development platform: IBM AT with hard disk; "networked into the various library databases that are already available."

Programming language: Microprolog with Apes; LISP

Library environment: College

Specific domain: 4 modules for reference work: diagnosis of information-seeking behavior; subject analysis; database design; and graphical interface

Reasoning: Rule based

Size of System: Small; earlier version used *Books in Print, Library of Congress Subject Headings* and name authority list

Special features: User profile based on ordinal scales: (1) reading level; (2) knowledge of topic; (3) familiarity with search system; and (4) stage in research

Published reports: Micco and Smith, "Expert Systems in Libraries: Do They Have a Place?" *Library Software Review* 6 (January–February 1987): 25–28, and id., "Designing an Expert System for the Reference Function Subject Access to Information," *ASIS Proceedings* 23 (1986): 204–210.

Perceived benefits: "to improve service to library users in a variety of ways."

Availability/Cost: "Not yet fully operational."

Automated Business Library Expert; The Electric Librarian (ABLE, 1987)

Project staff: University of North Texas, Department of Business-Administration Business Computer Information Systems and the University Libraries General Reference Services Department

Project director: Maurice G. Fortin, Assistant Director for Public Services

Developer (i.e., Programmer/Analyst): Ten MBA and PhD students of Dr. Richard Vedder (BCIS) worked on developing five prototypes using shell software

Domain expert: Fortin; Ralph Johnson, and Scott Lemmermann

Development platform: IBM XT 8MHz, 640K RAM, 20 MB hard drive, and EGA monitor

Development software: American Programmers Guild's INSET for reformatting graphics (see Special features, below)

Shell software: EXSYS, 1st Class, GURU, Personal Consultant Easy, and Personal Consultant Plus

Library environment: University

Specific domain: Three areas: general business, specific industry, and specific company information

Size of system: 1.5MB

User interface: Menu driven

Special features: Graphical information (floor maps) for directional questions created using Dr. HALO II. Also recorded simple statistics on users.

Testing/Evaluation: Human experts evaluated five prototypes using following criteria: (1) power and flexibility; (2) application development environment; (3) consultation (user) interface; (4) system connectivity; (5) training requirements and documentation; (6) hidden costs; and (7) ease of changing or updating the program. "The system was only used for a four week period in 1989. During that time it operated flawlessly and received excellent comments from users."

Published reports: Richard G, Vedder, Maurice G. Fortin, Scott Lemmermann, and Ralph Johnson, "Five PC-Based Expert Systems for Business Reference: An Evaluation," *Information Technology and Libraries* 8 (March 1989): 42–54; Richard G. Vedder, ed., *Evaluation of PC-Based Expert System Shells*, BCIS Dept. Working Paper, No. WP-88011 (Denton, TX: University of North Texas, 1988).

Funding: Completed as part of class project

Estimated development time/Cost: 14.5 weeks (4.5 weeks learning tools, 6 weeks; total time, one and one-half years

Perceived benefits: "The system would have relieved reference desk personnel from answer[ing] mundane informational/ directional questions as well as simple business reference questions."

Biographical Reference Advisor (BRA, 1987)

Project staff: Goucher College, Decker Center for Information Technology

Principal investigator and co-PI: Robert Lewand, Professor of Mathematics and Computer Science, and Larry Bielawski, Director of Decker Center

Domain expert: Yvonne Lev and Barbara Simons

Development platform: IBM PC

Shell software: 1st Class

Library environment: College

Specific domain: Biographical sources

Reasoning: Forward- and backward- chaining

Size of system: Small; 680 nodes on a total of 85 decision trees

User interface: Menu driven

Special features: Sources characterized by coverage of contemporary versus historical figures; 14 occupations; 12 nationalities; and gender. User need based on format (books, articles, and sketches). Prescription includes title, call number, location, and annotation

Testing/Evaluation: "Student evaluations have been favorable...[yet] students rarely use the system."

Funding: Internal (Goucher College)

Estimated development time/Cost: 5 months; $2500

Perceived benefits: "relieves reference librarians of routine tasks; available during all library hours."

Availability/Cost: Available for public release; send 6 diskettes to Lewand, Department of Mathematics and Computer Science, Goucher College, Towson, MD 21204; telephone, (301) 337-6000

Bookbrain (1987)

Project staff: Barbara Flaxman, Technical Support; Sam Mongeau, Senior Editor; Anne Thompson, Senior Editor and Project Manager

Project director: Susan Slesinger, Vice-President, Editorial

Developer (i.e., Programmer/Analyst): Original Release, Knowledge Access, Inc.; Revisions, Greg Schaefer

Domain expert (annotations): Elizabeth A. Hass, a.k.a. Dr. Rita Book

Platform: Apple II and IBM PC

Programming language: Orignal release, Basic; Apple revision, 6502 Assembly; IBM version, 8088 Assembly

Library environment: School and public

Specific domain: Reader's advisory; fiction books for Grades 1–3, 4–6, and 7–9

Reasoning: Rule based implemented through tables, characteristic weighting

Size of system: Intermediate; 5 characteristic rules and 2200 titles for Grades 1–3; 2400 titles, Grades 4–6; and 1800 titles, Grades 7–9

User interface: Menu driven

Special features: Reader stereotyped by level of difficulty, grade level, reading level, and type of main character. Utilities to add new book entries, add call numbers, write and edit comments, order new books, and suppress and label titles. Keep statistics for librarian and classroom instructor. Toll-free (800) telephone support

Testing/Evaluation: Beta testing at school and public library sites for all levels of program

Published reports: Dudley B. Carlson, "Using *Bookbrain* in the Public Library," *Journal of Youth Services in Libraries* 2 (Spring 1989): 278–279; Charles Parham, "In Search of a Good Book," *Classroom Computer Learning* 9 (October 1988): 68–77; "Computer Software Review," *School Library Journal* 36 (November 1989): 52–53 and 34 (August 1988): 56–57; Patricia Wilson, "Computer Software," *The Reading Teacher* 42 (April 1989): 646–647; "The Electronic Hermit," *Wilson Library Bulletin* 62 (February 1988): 30, 109; Virginia Kalb, "Curriculum Connections: Literature," *School Library Media Quarterly* 18 (Spring 1990): 175–176.

Estimated development time/Cost: Released 1987

Perceived benefits: "Bookbrain is an interactive database for children which provides reader's advisory assistance and experience with database searching."

Availability/Cost: Commercial system; Oryx Press, $195 per level

BookWhiz (1987)

Project staff: Educational Testing Service

Program administrator: Marlene Comer

Developers: Lila Norris and Laurence Shatkin

Programmer: James Misti

Domain experts: 35 identified national experts (school and public librarians, teachers and others) in YA literature

Platform: Apple II

Library environment: School and public

Specific Domain: Reader's advisory; Grades

3–6, 6–9, and 9–12; 1000 books grouped into 8 major genres and 3–6 subcategories

Size of system: Intermediate; 1000 titles in Grade 6–9 module

User interface: Menu driven

Special features: Customizable based on library ownership of titles. Displays up to 50 books, each with two-line annotation

Published reports: Patricia J. Wilson, "Computer Software," *Reading Teacher* 42 (December 1988): 251–252.

Availability/Cost: Commercial system; ETS, $175 per level (Apple) and $195 per level (IBM); demo available

CHEMREF (1987)

Project staff: Craig Robertson, University of Vermont

Domain experts: Department of Chemistry Professors William N. White, Christopher W. Allen, and Karen B. Sentell

Development platform: IBM with 384K

Shell software: 1st Class

Library environment: University

Specific domains: Chemistry—organic, polymer; chemical hazards and safety, and chemical separations

Reasoning: Example and rule based

Size of system: Small (30 small KBs with more than 500 examples)

User interface: Menu driven

Special features: "aims to do more than merely point a user to reference books, treatises or databases. It often offers interpretation of their use, describes their limitations and suggests alternate approaches."

Testing/Evaluation: "in place at the Chemistry and Physics Library and gets staff use."

Published reports: Pending as *RASD Occasional Paper*

Funding: University of Vermont; $395 for software and $600 for training at National Agricultural Library

Estimated development time/Cost: October 1987–present. "Actually, much of the time was my own, at home, so I will estimate it took a certain percentage of my work time for one year, and give it a nominal development cost of $2,800."

Perceived benefits: "Scarcity of human skills and experience"

Availability/Cost: Downloadable subset of CHEMREF via NAL's ALF

Expert Advisory Systems for Reference and Library Instruction (1987)

Project staff: James Madison University (JMU) librarians

Principal investigator: Ralph Alberico

Developer (i.e., Programmer/Analyst): Alberico

Domain expert: Jerry Gill, Business Reference Librarian

Development platform: IBM PS/2 Model 50 which connects to a VAX minicomputer to use the local numeric database (COMPUSTAT) and to an HP computer to use an OPAC (VTLS) and to DIALOG

Shell software: VP-Expert

Library environment: University

Specific domain: Business reference, company and industry information

Reasoning: Rule based, backward-chaining

Size of system: Small; 100 + rules, several hundred lines of code in communication scripts, numerous text files containing explanatory text and bibliographic citations

User interface: Menu driven

Special features: Connects to local and remote online databases, assists the user with a search and then returns to the advisory system consultation

Testing/Evaluation: Extensive; "a prototype

system which has been validated but not yet field tested."

Published reports: Ralph Alberico and Mary Micco, *Expert Systems for Reference and Information Retrieval* (Westport, CT: Meckler, 1990), Chapter 9: "Developing a Microcomputer-Based System."

Funding: JMU Library Budget

Estimated development time/Cost: 18 months for prototype development

Perceived benefits: Addresses "scarcity of reference expertise, an increasing need for specialization..., the inadequacy of existing access mechanisms..., [and] the difficulty of providing instruction when it is needed and where it is needed."

Availability/Cost: "Lack of funding and a job change by the principal investigator effectively stopped development at the prototype phase."

Information Machine (1987)

Project staff: University of Houston Libraries

Project director: Jeff Fadell

Programmer: Judy E. Myers

Domain expert: Fadell, Myers, internal committee

Development platform: IBM PC XT

Programming language: BASICA, then Microsoft Quick Basic

Wordprocessing software: WordPerfect

Library environment: University

Specific domain: Basic library instruction (e.g., finding journals and locating call numbers)

Reasoning: Menu driven

Size of system: Intermediate; 350 screens

User interface: Menu driven

Special features: Opening marque to attract users. Uses color. Headers similar to GEAC online catalog. Statistics on total screens viewed, and total number of system users

Testing/Evaluation: Committee comment and critique; user questionnaire

Published reports: Jeff Fadell and Judy E. Myers, "The Information Machine: A Microcomputer-Based Reference Service," *Reference Librarian* 23 (1989): 75–112.

Estimated development time/Cost: 1985–January 1987; 9 months

Perceived benefits: 1. "to serve those who did not ask." 2. "handles as many queries as a person at the Reference/ Information Desk every hour the Library is open (approximately 5,400 hours/year. At $10/hour, this is worth $54,000/yr."

Availability/Cost: Commercial system; contact, Geri Hutchins, AMIGOS Bibliographic Council, 11300 North Central Expressway, Suite 321, Dallas 75243, or call (800) 843-8482; $245 (AMIGOS members) or $295 (Nonmembers); $10 demonstration disk

LOOK (1987)

Project staff: Gail E. Thornburg, PhD candidate, University of Illinois

Major advisor: Linda C. Smith, UI GSLIS; Charles Davis, Ralf Shaw, Don Krummel; R.S. Michelski, Computer Science

Domain experts: Mitsuko Williams and Elisabeth Davis of Biology Library and William Mischo of Engineering Library; Carla Heister of the Natural History Survey Library and Maria Porta of the Agriculture Library

Development platform: IBM 286 AT customized with 640K RAM memory and 30MB hard disk

Programming language: Aurora 1.0, an expert systems environment

Library environment: Academic life sciences

Specific domain: Online search selection of 18 different databases from Dialog or BRS

Reasoning: Rule based, weighted with 3-stage analysis

Size of system: Small; 91 rule complexes and 18 online databases

User interface: Menu driven

Special features: Reduction, Discrimination, and Confirmation phases by characterizing query by type of search (seven possibilities), 18 general subject areas, five search slants, exhaustiveness (7 options), and 34 more specialized terminologies. Out-of-scope evaluation. Certainty factors. User's Guide. Aurora, the builder, is capable of learning.

Testing/Evaluation:

Published reports: Gail E. Thornburg, "LOOK: Implementation of an Expert System in Information Retrieval for Database Selec-

tion," PhD dissertation, University of Illinois, 1987. 103 pp.

Funding: ONR N00014-82-K-0186; NSF DCR 84-06801; DARPA N00014-K-85-0878; and ISI's Information Science Doctoral Dissertation Fellowship (1985)

Estimated development time/Cost: Approximately 12 months

Perceived benefits: Analysis of the expertise involved in presearch evaluation of a query/search request

Availability/Cost: UMI Order Number 88-03222

Patent Information Assistant (1987)

Project staff: University of Texas Libraries

Principal investigator: Susan B. Ardis, Head of the McKinney Engineering Library, University of Texas, Austin

Project director: Mary Seng

Developer (i.e., Programmer/Analyst): Ben Fang and Ira Carver

Domain expert: Ardis

Development platform: IBM AT with 20MB hard disk, color monitor, 2400 baud modem, and printer

Programming language: C, Turbo Pascal, Basic (all heavily compiled)

Library environment: University

Specific domain: Engineering patents

Reasoning: Ruled based

Size of system: Small

User interface: Branching menu screens; question and answer and function keys

Special features: Seamless dial up access to

Patent Office CASSIS and Dialog's World Patent Index (Files 350 and 351)

Testing/Evaluation: "Tested onsite—the only complaints were over aspects—such as the Patent Office dial up over which we had no control."

Published Reports: Ardis, "Online Patent Searching: Guided by an Expert System," *Online* 14 (March 1990): 56–62.

Funding: Computer from IBM Project Quest

Estimated development time/Cost: the equivalent of one person working full time for one year

Perceived benefits: "The current system was installed in June 1987 and is available to the public 83 hrs a week. It never tires, it is never irritated, and it provides all levels of users with customized instruction."

Availability/Cost: Not available at this time—due to local and USPTO conditions

RESEARCH ADVISOR (1987)

Principal investigator: Kathleen Dunn, Head, Reference Department, California State Polytechnic University Pomona, 3801 West Temple Avenue, Pomona, CA 91768-3090

Domain experts: Engineering and Statistics, Ken Quinn; Law, Laura Smith; Science/Medicine, Carlene Bogle; Business/Company Information, Daniel Hanne; Educa-

tion, Bruce Emerton; Community Services, Karen Harvey; and Economics, Emma Gibson

Development platform: IBM PS/2, 10MB hard disk or hardcard

Shell software: 1st Class

Library environment: University

Specific domain: 8 areas including business

(marketing and advertising, international trade, financial information, specific companies, and career/interviewing information) and engineering (aerospace, chemical and material, civil, computer, electrical, industrial and manufacturing, and mechanical)

Reasoning: Rule based

Size of system: Small; company module, 73 active examples and 40 sources

User interface: Menu driven

Special features: Linked modules using separate menu software; title, call number or physical location

Testing/Evaluation: Fall 1990 survey "to determine who was using it and why they used it. The results suggest that it is often not

effectively used. Students are very confused by too many different computer systems in the library, and therefore it is hard for them to figure out which one best suits their immediate need."

Funding: Kellogg Foundation grant, $5389

Estimated development time/Cost: September 1987–present; $7000, total cost for software and equipment

Perceived benefits: "We intend to keep developing and enhancing our expert systems. They are a critical component of our shift to providing users with more opportunities to help themselves."

Availability/Cost: Write or call Kathleen Dunn at above address

Technical Writing Assistant (1987)

Project staff: Texas A&M University

Principal Investigator and co-PI: Nancy J. Butkovich, Ann S. Moore, and Kathryn L. Taylor

Domain expert: Sharon Dent, English Department Instructor

Development platform: IBM AT compatible

Shell software: Symantec's Q&A

Library environment: University

Specific domain: Undergraduate technical writing students; general reference formats

Size of system: 428 records

User interface: Natural language

Special features: Database provides titles, call numbers, building locations, format type (encyclopedia, handbook, etc.), and detailed subject headings

Testing/Evaluation: User questionnaires—"the Q&A database (Technical Writing Assistant) was well received by the students who used it."

Published reports: Nancy J. Butkovich, Kathryn L. Taylor, and Ann S. Moore, "Imple-

menting an Expert System for Use by Undergraduates," *Proceedings of the Ninth National Online Meeting* (1988): 43–47; Nancy J. Butkovich, Kathryn L. Taylor, Sharon H. Dent, and Ann S. Moore, "An Expert System at the Reference Desk: Impressions from Users," *Reference Librarian* 23 (1989): 61–74; reprint ed., Christine Roysdon, and Howard D. White, ed., *Expert Systems in Libraries* (New York: Haworth Press, 1990), 61–74.

Funding: $250.00

Estimated development time/Cost: "We worked on it an average of about 4 hours a week for 6 months. Actual total time spent (excluding building the database) was probably about two weeks. The database took about 3 weeks to a month to build."

Perceived benefits: Then extant "OPAC did not support subject searching. This database was an attempt to fill that gap, at least as far as the reference collection was concerned."

UCLA GSLIS modules (Fall 1987, Winter 1989, Fall 1989, Fall 1990, Fall 1991, and Winter 1992)

Instructor: John Richardson

Domain experts: 100 graduate LIS students in 41 group projects

Development platform: IBM PC

Shell software: ESIE; EXPERT; and VP-Expert

Library environment: Library School

Specific domain: 12 General Reference Formats including atlases (1 time), bibliographies and catalogs (3 times), biographical sources (5), dictionaries (5), encyclopedias (13), fact books (1), government publications (1), and indexes (8). Rules for selecting formats has been tried four times

Reasoning: ESIE, backward-chaining

Size of system: Small; maximum developed, 100 tools

User interface: Socratic or menu

Special features: General Format module by Ed Pai and the "Searchin' General," biographical module by Henderson, Martin, Mayer and Monaster demonstrated at 1988 ASIS Mid-Year

Testing/Evaluation: Students required to devise their own test questions; Class evaluations; Deborah Henderson, Patti Martin, Lauren Mayer, and Pamela Monaster, "Rules and Tools in Library Schools," *Journal of Education for Library and Information Science* 30 (Winter 1989): 226–227.

Published Reports: Richardson, "Toward an Expert System for Reference Service: A Research Agenda for the 1990s," *College and Research Libraries* 50 (March 1989): 231–248.

Funding: Council on Library Resources, Summer 1986

Estimated development time/Cost: 5 weeks

Perceived benefits: Pedagogical—become more familiar with tools and rules used in recommending titles rather than with traditional teaching methods; students move from novice to advanced beginner more quickly

Availability/Cost: Operational prototype

FNICAID (1988?)

Project staff: National Agricultural Library, Food and Nutrition Information Center

Project director: Holly Irving

Developer (i.e., Programmer/Analyst): Irving

Domain expert: Irving

Development platform: IBM

Shell software: 1st Class

Library environment: Special

Specific domain: Food and Nutrition

Reasoning: Example based

Size of system: Small

User interface: Menu driven

Testing/Evaluation:"a very primitive prototype that went no further because of no funding."

Availability/Cost: Unknown

Good Reads (1988)

Project staff: County of Los Angeles Public Library

Principal investigator and co-PI: Linda Crismond, County Librarian

Project director: Phyllis Young, Collection Services Coordinator

Developer (i.e., Programmer/Analyst): Meg Holliday and Enrique Peña

Domain expert: Harriet Traeger, Fiction Material Evaluator

Development platform: Compaq PC 286-640K, with 20MB hard disk

Programming language: Rbase for DOS and AskSam

Library environment: Public

Specific domain: Adult fiction reading; some

YA and smaller amount of juvenile materials

Reasoning: Boolean logic

Size of system: Intermediate; 4 rules and 8000 titles

User interface: Enter search term, usually subject

Special features: 23 genre, 150 locales, 50 time periods, and 650 subjects (from accident to zen). Succinct, short synopses of titles. Staff and maintenance levels

Testing/Evaluation: Testing in four of the five library regions

Funding: State of California Library Services and Construction Act Grant, $55,200

Estimated development time/Cost: September 1987–. $100,000

Perceived benefits: Librarians may not be the fiction readers they once were; system could support librarian's decision-making process. Interactive system for patrons

Availability/Cost: Under development

Government Documents Reference Aid (1988)

Project staff: Stanford University Libraries

Principal investigator and co-PI: Bruce L. Harley and Patricia J. Knobloch

Project director: Bruce Harley

Developer (i.e., Programmer/Analyst): Bruce Harley

Development platform: IBM AT with 30 MB hard disk

Shell software: Level5

Library environment: University

Specific domain: U.S. local, state, federal, foreign, and international (including UN) government publications

Reasoning: Production rules; backward-chaining

Size of system: Small; 30 rules and 13 reference tools

User interface: Menu driven

Special features: "Both ASCII text files and an external program are directly accessed. The external program, Samson, provides the telecommunications link to Socrates, SUL's online catalog, activated from within GRDA's rule structure."

Testing/Evaluation: Staff evaluation via questionnaire at five sites

Published reports: Harley and Knobloch, "Government Documents Reference Aid: An Expert System Development Project," *Government Publications Review* 18 (January/February 1991): 15–33.

Funding: Stanford University Libraries Payson J. Treat Fund, $1265

Estimated development time/Cost: 4 weeks; $1265, total cost

Perceived benefits: Solve problem of increasing workload; "contributes to the mainsteaming of government documents with SUL; helps train staff providing government documents reference service; supplements existing government documents reference service."

Availability/Cost: "The system is available as Disk #26 from Lloyd Davidson (BITNET: L Davidson@NUACC) for $2.00 or send one disk or interested parties may contact Harley (BHARLEY@CALSTATE.BITNET)."

Information Transfer Associates Dictionary Module (1988–present)

Project staff: John Richardson

Domain expert: Richardson and Marie Waters

Development platform: IBM PC

Shell software: ESIE

Library environment: Academic, public, school, special

Specific domain: Dictionaries

Reasoning: Backward-chaining

Size of system: Small

User interface: Version 1, socratic; version 2–3, menu driven

Special features: Validated knowledge base, using Hutchins's heuristic

Testing/Evaluation: Presentations at ASIS, ALA/LITA, and SLA

Published reports: Richardson, "Toward an Expert System for Reference Service: A Research Agenda for the 1990s." *College and Research Libraries* 50 (March 1989): 231–248; reprinted, "Toward an Expert System for Reference Service: A Research Agenda for the 1990s," in *Expert Systems and Library Applications*; *An SLA Information Kit* (Washington, DC: Special Libraries Association, 1991), 95–112.

Estimated development time/Cost: Version 1, January 1987; version 2, May 1988; version 3, April 1990; version 4, Summer 1991
Perceived benefits: Proof of concept; validated knowledge base
Availability/Cost: Commercially available; $30

Intelligent Reference Systems (IRS) Project: Index Expert and Knowledge Base Management System (1988–1989)

Project staff: Intelligent Reference Systems Committee, University Libraries, University of Houston. IRS Committee members were Charles W. Bailey, Jr. (Assistant Director for Systems), Jeff Fadell (Information Services Librarian), Judy E. Myers (IRS Chair and Assistant to the Director), and Thomas C. Wilson (Computerized Information Retrieval Services Coordinator)
Project managers: Judy E. Myers and Charles W. Bailey, Jr.
Developer (i.e., Programmer/Analyst): Systems Analysis: IRS Committee; DEMO Program II and VP-Expert prototypes, Jeff Fadell; Intelligence/Compiler Prototype, Charles W. Bailey, Jr.; Prolog Prototype: Judy E. Myers; Index Expert: Charles W. Bailey, Jr., with sections by Judy E. Myers; Knowledge Base Management System: Charles W. Bailey, Jr.
Domain experts: IRS Committee
Development platform: Hardware, 12 MHz CompuAdd 212 with 40MB hard disk and EGA monitor; Software, First Prototype: Dan Bricklin's DEMO Program II; Second Prototype: VP-Expert; Third Prototype: Intelligence/Compiler; Fourth Prototype: Turbo Prolog
Index expert: Turbo Prolog
Knowledge base management system: Turbo Prolog
Library environment: University
Specific domain: Indexes and abstracts, electronic and printed
Reasoning: Frame based with backward-chaining

Size of system: Small; 274 frames and 150 indexes
User interface: Menu driven
Special features: Knowledge base is contained in ASCII text files that can be easily modified by reference staff using a word processor. Collects statistics on use
Testing/Evaluation: User testing took place between 17 May 1989 and 6 July 1989; 1615 uses and 51 usable evaluations. Survey results: "86 percent found an appropriate index, 98 percent felt the program was easy to understand, and 57 percent felt the program was definitely helpful (39 percent felt it was somewhat helpful). . . the system was more helpful to undergraduate students than to graduate students."
IRS published reports: Charles W. Bailey, Jr., "Building Knowledge-Based Systems for Public Use: The Intelligent Reference Systems Project at the University of Houston Libraries," in *Convergence: The Proceedings of the Second National Conference of the Library and Information Technology Association*, *October 2–6, 1988*, ed. Michael Gorman (Chicago: ALA, 1990), 190–194; Charles W. Bailey, Jr., Jeff Fadell, Judy E. Myers, and Thomas C. Wilson, "The Index Expert System: A Knowledge-Based System to Assist Users in Index Selection," *Reference Service Review* 17 (Winter 1989): 19–28.
Funding: University Libraries, University of Houston
Estimated development time/Cost: Development work on Index Expert was continued by the IRIS Project's Knowledge Engineering

Group. Total development time was 28 months of part-time effort. Costs include: (1) staff time; (2) $815 software, DEMO Program II, VP-Expert, Intelligence/Compiler, Turbo Prolog, and Turbo Prolog Toolbox; (3) $2537 hardware, CompuAdd 212 with EGA monitor, 40 MB hard disk, and Epson LX-800 printer; (4) $614 furniture/security

Perceived benefits: Assists users with index selection when reference staff are unavailable. Captures, preserves, and makes accessible knowledge about major indexes and abstracts

Availability/Cost: Not being distributed at this time. Inquire about availability

Sci/Tech Advisor (1988)

Project staff: Lloyd Davidson
Development platform: IBM
Shell software: 1st-Class
Library environment: University

Specific domain: Science and Technology
Size of system: Small
User interface: Menu driven

Project Mercury (1988)

Project staff: Carnegie Mellon University and Online Computer Library Center
Development platform: DEC 6000 class VAX machines
Programming language: Prolog
Search software: OCLC's search engine "Newton"
Library environment: University
Specific domain: Artificial intelligence community and computer science. Reference room and reading room
User interface: Users can customize "screen layout to suit their needs and preferences." Interface design based on OCLC research (DIADEM)
Special features: Computer searchable indexes

including AAAI, CMU technical reports, *Computer and Control Abstracts* and *Electrical and Electronic Abstracts*. Modules built to national or proposed standards; interfaces with Library Information System II (LIS II)
Published reports: Nancy H. Evans, Denise A. Troll, Mark H. Kibbey, Thomas J. Michalak, and William Y. Arms, *The Vision of the Electronic Library,* Mercury Technical Report Series, No. 1. (Pittsburgh, PA: Carnegie Mellon University, 1989).
Funding: Pew Memorial Trust and American Association for Artificial Intelligence
Perceived benefits: Addresses "physical storage space for every book, journal, magazine, and newspaper."

Tome Associates's TOME-SEARCHER (1988)

Research director: Alina Vickery
Marketing director: Jerry Horwood
Managing director: C. Mattocks
Development platform: IBM PC 640K, 5 MB hard disk and Hayes compatible modem
Programming language: PASCAL

Library environment: Online searching
Specific domain: INSPEC and other databases covering electrical engineering, computers, and information technology; under development: pharmaceuticals, business, and finance

Size of system: Intermediate; 1500 rules, frames, thesaurus, and dictionary
User interface: Natural language or "free expression" and menu driven
Special features: User profile (encrypted); full-function semantic analyzer
Testing/Evaluation: PLEXUS
Published reports: TOME SEARCHER: A Technical Review of a Knowledge-Based System (London: Tome Associates, June 1988) and *TOME SEARCHER: An Intelligent Interface for Searching and Retrieving Information from Online Databases; A Brief Technical Description* (London: Tome Associates, n.d.)
Estimated development time/Cost: May 1987–
Availability/Cost: Commercial product, February 1988; £495

Videoseller's Assistant (1988)

Project staff: Del Mar Group
Ingram technical Support: Anthony Doulgas
Technical analysis: Patti Farr
Development platform: ARC computer, NEC MicroTouch multisync monitor, NCR printer, and Archive tape derive
Environment: Retail outlet
Specific domain: 15,000 videos; monthly updates
Reasoning: Statistical modeling
Size of system: Intermediate
User interface: Menu driven
Special features: Touch screen with considerable screen typing required. Searchable by director's or star's name, title, 20 broad subjects, and Academy Award winners. Advice mode. Report mode generates use statistics related to gender, age, household income, number in household, frequency of video rental, number of rentals in the past 2 weeks, type of last purchase (personal or gift), frequency desired title was unavailable, and reaction to unavailability; reports available for specific periods of time
Testing/Evaluation: 26 systems including B. Dalton and in Alaska, Book ?
Published reports: Ingram Customer Services, *Videoseller's Assistant User's Manual,* June 1988.
Estimated development time/Cost: Copyrights, 1986 and 1987

Intelligent Reference Information System Project (IRIS, 1989–1991)

Project staff: Intelligent Reference Information System (IRIS) Project, University Libraries, University of Houston
Project management Group: Charles W. Bailey, Jr., PMG Chair and Assistant Director for Systems; Cherie Colbert, Coordinator of Instructional and Electronic Services; Kathleen Gunning, Assistant Director for Public Services and Collection Development; Judy E. Myers, Assistant to the Director; Donna Hitchings, Head of Information Services; and Thomas C. Wilson, Head of Systems
Knowledge engineering group: Judy E. Myers, Chair; Charles W. Bailey, Jr.; Jeff Fadell, Information Services Librarian; Jill Hackenberg, Information Services Librarian; and Thomas C. Wilson.
Electronic publications instruction group: Cherie Colbert, Chair; Ivan Calimano, Manager of the Electronic Publications Center; Carolyn Meanley, Coordinator of Government Documents; and Derral Parkin, Head of Branch Libraries
Research and evaluation group: Kathleen Gunning, Chair; Donna Hitchings; and Kimberly Spyers-Duran, Information Services Librarian
Project director: Robin N. Downes, Director, University Libraries
Project manager: Charles W. Bailey, Jr., Assistant Director for Systems
Developer (i.e., Programmer/Analyst): KnowledgePro prototype, Judy E. Myers; VP-Expert prototype, PDC Prolog prototype,

and Reference Expert program: Charles W. Bailey, Jr.

Domain experts: Knowledge Engineering Group

Development platform: IBM Compatible

Hardware: IBM Token-Ring Local Area Network running Novell Advanced Netware 2.15 with 10 80386SX-compatible workstations

Software: First Prototype, KnowledgePro; second, VP-Expert; third, PDS Prolog; reference expert: PDC Prolog

Library environment: University

Specific domain: Reference materials, printed and electronic

Reasoning: Frame based with backward-chaining

User interface: Menu driven

Special features: Links users to 19 networked CD-ROM databases. Knowledge is contained in ASCII text files that can be easily modified by reference staff using a word processor. Collects statistics on use

Published reports: Charles W. Bailey, Jr. and Kathleen Gunning, "The Intelligent Reference Information System," *CD-ROM Librarian* 5 (September 1990): 10–19; Thomas C. Wilson, "Zen and the Art of CD-ROM Network License Negotiation," *The Public-Access Computer Systems Review* 1 (1990): 4–14; Charles W. Bailey, Jr., "Intelligent Library Systems: Artificial Intelligence Technology and Library Automation Sys-

tems," *Advances in Library Automation and Networking* 4 (1991): 1–23; Charles W. Bailey, Jr., "Communications: The Intelligent Reference Information System Project: A Merger of CD-ROM LAN and Expert System Technologies," *Information Technology and Libraries* 11 (September 1992): 237–244; Kathleen Gunning, et al., "Networked Electronic Information Systems at the University of Houston Libraries: The IRIS Project and Beyond," *Networked Electronic Information Systems* 11, no. 4 (1993): 49–55, 83; Kathleen Gunning and Kimberly Spyers-Duran, "Evaluation of Reference Expert: An Expert System for Selecting Reference Sources," in *Research in Reference Effectiveness,* ed. Marjorie E. Murfin and Jo Bell Whitlatch, RASD Occasional Papers, no. 16. (Chicago: American Library Association, 1993).

IRIS funding: 51%, U.S. Department of Education, College Library Technology and Cooperation Grants Program, Research and Demonstration Grant, $99,852; 49%, University of Houston, $94,710 (estimated)

Perceived benefits: Assists users with reference material selection when reference staff are unavailable. Captures, preserves, and makes accessible knowledge about major reference materials. Advances state-of-the-art in expert systems and CD-ROM networking

PRONTO/PRONTO!! (1989)

Project director: Frederick E. Smith, Faculty Services Librarian, 2211 Law Building, UCLA School of Law Library, 405 Hilgard Avenue, Los Angeles, CA 90024-145802, (213) 825-3960 or ECZ5FES@ UCLAMVS.OAC.EDU

Developer (i.e., Programmer/Analyst): Initial, Ray Ramberg, University of Oregon, Computer Science student

Domain expert: Frederick E. Smith

Development platform: Zenith, IBM compatible

Programming language: Initial, Turbo Pascal 5.0; second version: Turbo C 2.0

Library environment: University

Specific domain: Law library services and staff; general law library user

Size of system: Small; 50 datafiles

User interface: Menu driven

Special features: Initial, calendar of upcoming events, online passwords, directory-type information (faculty, students, and committee appointments). User can add data to their copy. Second version, Animated graphic floor-plan displays of stack and room locations for materials and services; calendar of upcoming events; emergency preparedness information; staff and committee rosters; text display explanations of library materials and services.

Testing/Evaluation: Initial, informally passed out to 15 individuals; few responses—"the best description of the responses: 'tempered enthusiasm'. The most important comment was that it might be very useful if mounted on our Law School LAN. . . . ;" Second version, trial installation scheduled for summer 1991; law school computer operations supportive of project; AI software manufacturer interested in project.

Funding: Intial, none; "strictly a home-grown bootstrap effort." Second version: grant proposals submitted

Estimated development Time/Cost: initial: 100 hours total; 40 hours programming and 60 hours by domain expert. Second version: 200 hours

Perceived benefits: Initial, "this provides a handy source of information for faculty. Also, as far as the other kinds of information (e.g., directories) are concerned, this puts them all in one place, again a convenience to faculty (and library staff)." Second version, "it is anticipated that this project, as a user help station in the library in close proximity to the reference desk, will enable many users who now queue for directional and other lower level assistance to be more self-sufficient. This will also extend hours when such assistance is available. It will also make appropriate referrals to reference librarians. In addition, the directory and activity information will be a convenience and increase the sense of community in the Law School."

Availability/Cost: Interested parties should address their questions to Frederick E. Smith

Reference Advisory System (1989)

Project staff: San Diego State University Library

Principal investigator and co-PI: Robert Carande

Project director: Robert Carande

Developer (i.e., Programmer/Analyst): Robert Carande

Domain expert: Robert Carande, Lilliam Chan, Anne Turhollow, Mary Harris, and Kati Harkanyi

Development platform: IBM AT with 516K, 40 MB hard disk

Programming language: turbo-Prolog

Library environment: University

Specific domain: Reference materials in Materials Science and Engineering; Computer Science; Nursing; Public Health; Journal Indexes in Science/Health subjects; Environmental Issues; and Biology

Reasoning: "Through menu option input, patron asserts facts that describe an information need. The system, taking these facts as true, examines the knowledge base for clauses whose antecedents correpond to

these facts. The consequence of such clauses (which contain bibliographic information) are then accepted as true. The program then returns to the inference engine and uses these consequents to achieve the final goal state (which includes commands to write out the bibliographic information contained in the consequents). The process of reasoning utilizes forward chaining."

Size of system: Small

User interface: Natural language screen then menu driven

Special features: Multiple recommendations with title, imprint, frequency, online availability, SDSU location, and brief annotation

Testing/Evaluation: "Each reference advisory module requests natural language description of need and saves such descriptions along with the menu options subsequently chosen. Among other things, this lets us determine both how many needs would have been met by our module's suggestions and how the patron is interpreting our menu choices."

Published reports: Robert Carande, "Reference Advisory Systems (RAS): Some Practical Issues," *Reference Services Review* 17 (Fall 1989): 87–90, and id., "Reference Advisory Systems Board," *Information Technology and Libraries* 9 (June 1990): 180–184.

Funding: State of California Lottery Funds, $10,000

Estimated development time/Cost: Current multimodule configuration designed and developed between September and January 1989; ongoing modules

Perceived benefits: Quick, simple and easy; cooperative effort in creating custom-designed reference tools

Availability/Cost: Individual reference advisory systems are available free (without the HyperPAD front-end) provided interested parties include floppy disc mailers by writing the domain experts or call (619) 594-4456 for more details

REGIS & REGIS II; REGional Information System for African Aquaculture (1989)

Project staff: National Agricultural Library, Aquaculture Information Center, USDA, National Agricultural Library, 10301 Baltimore Blvd, Room 109C, Beltsville, MD 20705

Project director: Deborah Hanfman

Developer (i.e., Programmer/Analyst): Professors Larry Bielawski and Robert Lewand, Decker Center for Information Technology, Goucher College, Baltimore, Maryland

Domain experts: Robert R. Freeman, FAO Fisheries Information Chief; Dr. Meryl Broussard, Extension Service, USDA; and Deborah Hanfman

Development platform: Microcomputer, EGA graphics, and mouse

Shell software: Knowledge Pro

Library environment: Special

Specific domain: African aquaculture

Reasoning: Hypermedia and decision trees

Size of system: Small; based on a manuscript version of the 60-page document by Benedict Satia, *A Regional Survey of the Aquaculture Sector in Africa, South of the Sahara.* Report No. ADCP/REP/89/36. Rome: 1989.

Special features: Map of Africa using Lotus Freelance Maps; access to CD-ROM version of *Aquatic Sciences and Fisheries Abstracts* as well as DIALOG's online databases

Testing/Evaluation: ". . . audience needed to be clearly defined and limited." ". . . an operational system (as opposed to a prototype such as REGIS at its current stage) would need considerably more complete information to inspire confidence."

Published reports: Scott Mace, "Regis Merges Two Technologies; Hypermedia, Expert Systems More Effective Together than Apart," *InfoWorld* 11 (20 March 1989); "REGIS: Intelligent Documents on African Aquaculture," *Information Alert from NAL,* 21 April 1989; "REGIS: Intelligent Documents on African Aquaculture," *Technology Applications at the NAL,* 21 April 1990; "Refined Aquaculture Computer System Available from NAL," *Information Alert from NAL,* 14 August 1990; Robert R. Freeman and Deborah T. Hanfman, "REGIS: A Prototype Regional Information System for African Aquaculture," International Association of Marine Science Libraries and Information Centers, 15th Annual Conference, Hamilton, Bermuda, 2–6 October 1989. 11 pp.

Funding: Food and Agriculture Organization and United Nations Development Programme

Estimated development time/Cost: Two months

Availability/Cost: $39.95 for the abbreviated version or $49.95 for the full version; both from National Technical Information Service, (703) 487-4650

Reference Expert (REX, 1989)

Principal investigator and co-PI: Yuval Lirov and Viktor Lirov

Domain expert: Reference librarians/bibliographers

Development platform: SUN Workstation

Programming language: AWK and Prolog using standard Quintus Prolog library routines

Library environment: Special

Specific domain: Subject bibliographies

Reasoning: forward- and backward-chaining

Size of system: Medium

User interface: Menu

Special features: Creates customized subject bibliographies from downloaded Dialog searches (using OneSearch)

Testing/Evaluation: Used to derive a subject bibliography on applications of logic programming

Published reports: Yuval Lirov and Viktor Lirov, "Online search + logic programming = subject bibliography: an expert systems approach to bibliographic processing," *Online Review* 14 (1990): 3–12; id., "Logic Programming Applications in Decision and Control—A Subject Bibliography," *Computers and Mathematics with Applications* 20 (1990): 141–179.

Funding: AT&T Bell Laboratories, Holmdel, New Jersey

Estimated development time/Cost: 8 weeks; $20,000

Perceived benefits: "Rex constructs subject bibliographies effectively, quickly, and inexpensively" (p. 8).

Availability/Cost: Contact authors

CONET-IR (1990)

Principal investigator and co-PI: Dania Bilal, Associate Director of Library Services, Clinch Valley College of the University of Virginia and George Meghabghab, Department of Computer Science, Valdosta State College, Valdosta, GA 31698

Domain expert: Dania Bilal

Development platform: IBM and UNIX compatible

Programming language: Brainmaker and Common LISP

Library environment: Academic libraries

Specific domain: General reference query negotiation; information retrieval

Reasoning: Neural Network

Size of system: Intermediate; 2000 nodes

User interface: Natural language; menu

Special features: "Learns to negotiate. Tailors its internal structure to new situations. Understands concepts especially those with different meanings. Can solve problems containing partial information and inaccurate information. Performs associative information retrieval when interfaced with an online catalog."

Testing/Evaluation: Still in the testing phase. Pilot testing will be considered when funds become available

Published reports: George Meghabghab and Dania Bilal, "Application of Information Theory to Query Negotiation: Toward an Optimal Questioning Strategy," *JASIS* 42 (July 1991): 457–462; id., "CONET-IR: Connectionist Network for Information Retrieval: Part 1, Query Negotiation," *Information Processing and Management* (1991), in press.

Estimated development time/Cost: Since March 1990; $500.00

Perceived benefits: "Assists patrons in identifying their true information need prior to accessing an online catalog; assists reference librarians in negotiating subject queries in which they are unfamiliar."

Availability/Cost: Contact Drs. George Meghabghab or Dania Bilal at above addresses or call (912) 333-5787 or (703) 328-0159

HRef (1990)

Project staff: Katherine Webster, University of Texas, Permian Basin, Odessa, Texas

Development platform: IBM PC/XT/AT/PS2 compatible with 256K RAM

Programming software: Hyperties, Cognetics Corporation

Library environment: Academic

Specific domain: General reference

Reasoning: Hypertext

Size of system: Small; 400 links and 40 tools

User interface: Hypertextual. Index of titles and string-searching capability.

Special features: An "article" contains title, call number, and brief annotation of reference work. Program "keeps track of a user's path through the database to prevent him or her from getting 'lost' while using it." Video sequences can be incorporated

Testing/Evaluation: In-house; "other librarians and faculty have used it and offered comments."

Published reports: Katherine Webster, "A Hyperties Reference Database," *Computers in Libraries* 10 (June 1990): 14–15.

Funding: From Library's regular budget

Estimated development time/Cost: Development, probably 40 hours; it takes about 30 minutes to 1 hour to enter information for one book. $300 for software

Perceived benefits: "Same as 'hard to find' file at Reference Desk; saves staff time."

Availability/Cost: "HRef" itself is not for sale

NZRef, New Zealand Reference Advisor (1990– in progress)

Project staff: Alastair Smith, Lecturer, Victoria University of Wellington Department of Library and Information Studies, PO Box 600, Wellington, New Zealand; e-mail: agsmith@matai.vuw.ac.nz

Shell software: Initial, ESIE; second version, EXSYS

Library environment: National Library

Specific domain: 16 Kiwinet databases

Reasoning: Backward-chaining

Size of system: Small; 7 rules and 16 tools

User interface: Menu driven

Special features: "It draws heavily on Jahoda's model of given's and wanted's."

Testing/Evaluation: Demonstrated at September 1991 NZ Library Association Conference. An October 1991 6-page questionnaire has been sent to users; will become basis for MA thesis to be submitted in January 1992

Estimated development time/Cost: One month; earlier version was called KIWI

Perceived benefits: "Useful exercise in encapsulating surface level knowledge in a knowledge base."

Availability/Cost: Write to developer

Plant Expert (1990)

Project staff: National Agricultural Library, Information Systems Division; Goucher College, Department of Mathematics and Computer Sciences

Project director: Pamela R. Mason, Automation Librarian, Information Systems Divison, NAL

Developer (i.e., Programmer/Analyst): Mason and Teresa Sample (NAL); Larry Bielawsaki, Robert Lewand, and Stephan Bennett (Goucher College)

Domain expert: Randall Heatley (Michigan State University Cooperative Extension Service and Ed Gilman (University of Florida Environmental Horticulture) plus advisory committee on 13 experts

Development platform: Phase I and II: IBM PC 286/386 with 40MB drive, color VGA monitor, CD-ROM drive with audio; Phase III: CD-ROM XA drive or DVI drive with add-in board and then Macintosh platform

Programming language: Knowledge Pro (Windows 3.0)

Library environment: Special

Specific domain: Home landscaping; 1200 plants grown in United States

Reasoning: Rule based and object oriented

Special features: Audio pronunciation guide to plant names in Latin and English

Testing/Evaluation: Land-grant university libraries, selected cooperative extension service offices around the country

Published reports: Pamela R. Mason, "Planning a Multimedia CD-ROM," in *National On-line Meeting Proceedings 1–3 May 1990* (Medford, NJ: Learned Information Inc., 1990): 265–271; id. "Ornamental Horticulture on a Multimedia CD-ROM," *CD-ROM EndUser* 2 (July 1990): 46–48; id. "Planning the National Agricultural Library's Multimedia CD-ROM *Ornamental Horticulture*," *Government Publications Review* 18 (March/April 1991): 137–146.

Funding: Cooperative agreements with University of Florida and Michigan State University

Estimated development time/Cost: May 1990–February 1992; 20 months requiring 5 people, part-time

Perceived benefits: CD with national plant database for home gardening

Availability/Cost: Eventually will be available to public

Northwestern University (in progress)

Principal investigator and co-PI: Gilbert K. Krulee and Alex Vrenois, Department of Electrical Engineering and Computer Science and Brian Nielsen, Head, University Library Reference Department (now Assistant University Librarian for Information Services Technology)

Domain experts: Nielsen and Lloyd Davidson, Reference Librarian, Science/Engineering Library

First Prototype:

Development platform: Apple II with 48K memory

Programming language: LISP

Library environment: Dewey Decimal Classification

Specific domain: 36 Reference works

Reasoning: Ruled based, not strictly either forward- or backward-chaining

Size of system: Small; 36 reference tools

User interface: Natural language using template matching on keywords

Special features: Uses "Relative Index"

Second Prototype:

Development platform: IBM

Shell: VP-Expert

Library environment: University Library

Specific domain: Science and Engineering periodicals

Size of system: Small

Third Prototype:

Development platform: IBM

Shell: Knowledge Pro

Published reports: Krulee and Alexander Vrenios, "An Expert System Model of a Reference Librarian, *Software Review* 8 (January–February 1989): 13–15; Krulee and Brian Nielsen, "Intelligent Support Systems for the Reference Librarian," Report given in Toronto, 1989. 19 pp.

Funding: Council on Library Resources, Librarian/Faculty Cooperative Grant Program, $3000 (Krulee and Davidson)

Estimated development time/Cost: About one year for first prototype (1987); second prototype, 1990; third prototype, 1991

Perceived benefits: "when reference desk is busy or closed"

Availability/Cost: Prototype

Question Master (in progress)

Principal investigator: John Richardson

Domain expert: More than two dozen reference librarians throughout the United States

Development platform: IBM AT-compatible 80486 with 4 MB RAM running under Windows 3.x, 110MB hard disk, CD player, and 9600 baud modem

Programming language: Visual Basic

Library environment: Public and university

Specific domain: General reference; 12 formats including abstracts and digests, atlases, bibliographies and catalogs, biographical sources, dictionaries, directories, encyclopedias, government publications, handbooks, indexes, statistical sources, and yearbooks

Reasoning: Backward- and forward-chaining

Size of system: Intermediate to large

User interface: Menu

Special features: Validated knowledge base

Testing/Evaluation: Evolutionary prototyping; based on experience with UCLA GSLIS ESIE modules and ITA dictionary module

Funding: Initial knowledge base secured with UCLA ASCOR funding and Council on Library Resources, Grant No. 8027

Estimated development time/Cost: October 1995–June 1997

Perceived benefits: Validated, comprehensive knowledgebase

The Information Station (1993): based on a KBS formerly called Project ilLUMINAte, a tutorial program.

Project staff: Barbara Kautz, Kay Kane, Celia Hales-Mabry, Shirley Stanley, Julia Schult, Susan Gangl, and Mary Koenig-Loring. Address: 180 Wilson Library, Reference Services Unit, 309 19th Avenue South, Minneapolis, MN 55455

Principal investigator: Celia Hales-Mabry

Project director: Barbara Kautz and Kay Kane

Developer: Barbara Kautz, Kay Kane, Celia Hales-Mabry, Shirley Stanley, and Julia Schult

Domain expert: Barbara Kautz and Kay Kane

Development platform: MacIntosh SE

Programming language: Hypertalk

Shell software: Hypercard

Library environment: University

Specific domain: Wilson Library; University of Minnesota Libraries Resources and access information

Reasoning: Hypertext

Size of system: 9 stacks, comprising approximately 1600K

User interface: Menu driven

Special features: Makes extensive use of hypertext features

Testing/Evaluation: Prose statements by composition students and TAs as class assignments; comment sheets

Published reports: Hales-Mabry, Celia, "Project ilLUMINAte: Learning the Library by Computer," to be published in *The College and University Media Review* 1 (Spring 1994); Hales-Mabry, Celia, "Project ilLUMINAte at the University of Minnesota Libraries," in Edward J. Valauskas and Bill Vaccaro, eds. *Macintoshed Libraries 5.* (Cupertino, CA: Apple Library Users Group, 1992). (Available in print and diskette versions.)

Funding: Project MinneMac (University of Minnesota) for initial Mac SE and ImageWriter printer with accompanying software including Hypercard

Estimated development time/Cost: 1990–1992 (Equivalent of 1 FTE); 1993– (Equivalent of .5 FTE)

Perceived benefits: Solution to shortened hours at the Reference and Information Desks and lack of staff during open building hours

Availability/Cost: Free with 2 HD floppy disks and a self-addressed return mailer

Brill Library Electronic Guide (1994)

Project staff: Susan Hocker, Head Science Librarian, Brill Science Library, Miami University, Oxford, OH 45056 (E-mail: shocker@miamiu.acs.muohio.edu).
Principal investigator: S. Hocker
Project director: S. Hocker
Domain expert: S. Hocker
Development platform: IBM PC, 256K with two disk drives
Programming language: Partially in ASCII
Shell software: 1st Class
Library environment: University Branch Library
Specific domain: Science Branch

Reasoning: Closed question menu system
Size of system: Small (about 30 rules, 25 screens)
User interface: Menu driven
Special features: Graphics—5 maps available for viewing to reinforce locations
Testing/Evaluation: Will test in-house
Funding: In-house
Estimated development time/Cost: 6 months
Perceived benefits: Useful for familiarizing students/H.S. students with locations before using library
Availability/Cost: Request from above address

Pat Ref–Patent Information Resources Guide (1994)

Project staff: Susan Hocker, Head Science Librarian, Brill Science Library, Miami University, Oxford, OH 45056 (E-mail: shocker@miamiu.acs.muohio.edu).
Principal investigator and co-PI: S. Hocker, Carol Gramman, Leona Coffee, students at Louisiana State University Graduate School of Library and Information Science
Project director: S. Hocker
Domain expert: S. Hocker
Development platform: IBM PC, 256K with hard disk
Programming language: Partially in ASCII
Shell software: 1st Class
Library environment: University/public
Specific domain: U.S. and foreign patents
Reasoning: Closed question

Size of system: Small (under 100 rules and screens)
User interface: Menu driven
Special features: Some graphics, maps of patent libraries; applies to any system—Lexis, CASSIS, etc.
Testing/Evaluation: Sent to Patent Depository Librarians for testing
Funding: In-house
Estimated development time/Cost: 1 year
Perceived benefits: Can be handed out to persons unfamiliar with library and unwilling to come for training; can replace expensive training
Availability/Cost: Request from above address or Patent Depository Library

Biological Abstracts Information System (1994)

Project staff: Jerome UpChurch Conley, Brill Science Library. Miami University, Oxford OH 45056 (E-mail: jconley@watson.lib.muohio.edu)
Principal investigator: J. Conley
Developer: J. Conley
Domain expert: Nancy Moeckel, Life Sciences Librarian

Development platform: 433 SX, 4MB RAM, 105MB hard drive
Programming language: Partially in ASCII
Shell software: 1st Class
Library environment: University
Specific domain: Biological Abstracts
Reasoning: Since *Biological Abstracts* is the world's most comprehensive life sciences

index, I am attempting to find ways of making this source easier to use by our library community
Size of system: Small
User interface: Menu driven
Special features: Built-in help screen
Funding: Miami University
Estimated development time: 6 months

Perceived benefits: Tool can be used to supplement the librarian's lectures or any patron can sit down at this user-friendly system and learn how to use *Biological Abstracts* at his/her convenience
Availability/Cost: Free upon request from above address

8.1

Evaluative Summary of Progress to Date

The development curve of KBS in reference was relatively flat for about its first decade, from 1968 until the early 1980s (see Table 8.1). Then, interest started to grow dramatically, and from 1981 onward, the field has seen new systems appear every year. For the moment, peak development seems to have occurred in 1988, when eleven new systems were developed that year, but that could still change.

The initial pioneering work between 1968 and 1981 was done by graduate students or faculty in four universities, notably Chicago, Carnegie-Mellon, University of California Berkeley, and University of California Los Angeles. Everett Roger's now standard diffusion/innovation curve applies here. Following Weil's pioneering 1968 work, early adopters appeared followed by the early majority. We probably have not yet witnessed the late majority, but prototypic ES work appears well established in general reference work.

8.1.1 KBS Staffing

An analysis of Table 8.2 reveals eight common ways of organizing KBS development work. Generally, a librarian or two has undertaken KBS development work in the reference field. Today, team projects may be more typical. Certainly, DEBIS (1984) is an interesting approach to development. Interinstitutional cooperation has not appeared yet.

Even so, it is not clear who is really expert in the subject domain. Most of the systems use self-identified experts. Who has consistently mastered the field and, if they have, where are the standard scenarios that should appear as textbook cases? Are these local experts different from nationally identified experts? No one formally recognizes expertise beyond the ALA-accredited MLS degree.

Table 8.1
Analysis of Expert Systems in General Reference Work, 1968–PRESENT

Control	Date	Project	Staff	Platform	Lang./Shell	Library	Titles	Time-Wks	$ Cost
1	1968	Weil	Student	Main	COMIT	Univ.	234		$990.00
2	1971	REFSEARCH	Group	Main		Lib. Sch	144	72	
3	1979	GRUNDY	Student		LISP	Public	114		
4	1979	REFLES	Faculty	Micro	BASIC	Univ.		60	
5	1981	Computer Pix	Librarian	Main		Public	400		
6	1981	REFLINK	Faculty	Micro	BASIC	Univ.			
7	1982	CANSEARCH	Student	Micro/Main	Prolog	Special			
8	1983	RIS	Librarians	Micro	BASIC	Univ.			
9	1983	PLEXUS		Micro	Pascal	Public		160	
10	1984	Byte into Books	Librarians	Micro	BASIC	Public	520		$7000
11	1984	Fiction Adv	Business	Micro	C	B'store	1500		$1,200,000
12	1984	ORA	Librarians	Micro	Pascal	Univ.			
13	1984	ORS	Librarians			Univ.	1000	13.5	
14	1984	POINTER	Librarian	Micro	LISP/BASIC	Univ.	100	8	$6000
15	1985	Sci/Tech	Librarian			Univ.			
16	1986	Micco	Fac/Libr	Micro	Prolog/LISP	Univ.			
17	1986	Answerman	Librarian	Micro	First-Class	Special			
18	1986	Aquaref	Group	Micro	First-Class	Special		24	$35,000
19	1986	Con. Bus.	Librarian			Univ.			
20	1986	Refsearch2	Faculty	Micro	Insight;VP-E	Univ.	270		$20,000
21	1986	Gateway	Group	Micro-Mac	Hypertalk	Univ.			$512,000
22	1986	REFSIM	Librarian	Micro	Prolog	Univ.			
23	1987	ABLE	Group	Micro	5 Shells	Univ.		14.5	
24	1987	BRA	Fac/Libr	Micro	First-Class	Univ.		20	
25	1987	Bookbrain	Business	Micro	BASIC/Assem	Sch/Pub	6400		$2500
26	1987	BookWhiz	Business	Micro		Sch/Pub	1000+		

#	Year	Name	User	Platform	Software	Setting	Size	Total Hrs	Total $
27	1987	CHEMREF	Fac/Libr	Micro	First-Class	Univ.	500		$2800
28	1987	EASRLI	Librarians	Micro	VP-Expert	Univ.		72	
29	1987	InfoMachine	Librarians	Micro	BASIC	Univ.			
30	1987	NorthWest	Fac/Libr	Micro	LISP/VP/KPro	Univ.			
31	1987	Patent Info							
32	1987	Tech Writ Assist.	Libr/Fac	Micro	Q&A	Univ.		2	
33	1988	InfoTransAssoc.	Faculty	Micro	ESIE	Univ.	60		
34	1988	IRS	Librarians	Micro	VP/IC/Prolog	Univ.		56	
35	1987	LOOK	Student	Micro	Aurora	Univ.	18		
36	1987	RESEARCH ADVISOR	Librarians	Micro	First-Class	Univ.	40		$7000
37	1988	FNICAID	Librarian	Micro	First-Class	Special			
38	1988	GDRA	Librarians	Micro	Level 5	Univ.	13	4	$1265
39	1988	Proj. Merc		Mini		Univ.			
40	1988	Good Reads	Librarians	Micro	RBase	Public	8000		
41	1988	S/T Adv.	Librarian	Micro	First-Class	Univ.			
42	1988	TOMESEARCHER	Business	Micro	Pascal				
43	1988	Video. Assistant	Business	Micro			15000		
44	1989	IRIS	Librarians	Micro	KP/VP/Prolog	Univ.		5	$194,562
45	1989	PRONTO	Libr/Stud	Micro	Pascal/C	Univ.			
46	1989	RAS	Librarians	Micro	Prolog	Univ.			
47	1989	REX	Group	Micro-SUN	Prolog	Special		8	$10,000
48	1989	REGIS	Group	Micro	KnowPro	Special		8	$20,000
49	1990	CONET-IR	Fac/Libr	Micro	BM&LISP	Univ.			
50	1990	HRef	Librarian	Micro	Hypertext	Univ.	40	1	
51	1990	QM	Faculty	Micro	Visual Basic	Univ.	1500		
52	1990	NzRef	Faculty	Micro	ESIE/EXSYS	Special	16		$14,000
53	1990	Plant Expert	Group	Micro-Mac	Hypertext	Special		80	

Mean Year
1986

							Size	Total Hrs	Total $
							35,869	608	2,032,127
						M Avg.::	1708.05	35.764706	135,475.1333

Table 8.2
Expert System Staffing Patterns

Pattern	Number	Examples
Librarians	13	RIS, Byte into Books, ORA, ORS, EASRLI, InfoMachine
Librarian	8	ComputerPix, Pointer, Answerman
Group	7	REFSEARCH
Faculty	6	REFLES, REFLINK, Drexel, ITA, KIWI, Question Master
Faculty/Librarian	6	CHEMREF, Northwestern, TWA
Business	5	BookBrain, BookWhiz, TOME SEARCHER, Video Assistant
Student	4	Weil, GRUNDY, CANSEARCH, LOOK

8.1.1.1 KBS Development Platforms

The preferred development platform is time dependent (see Table 8.1). First efforts were on the mainframe, but shifted to microcomputers in 1979, specifically the TRS80. The widespread availability of microcomputer-based KBS development tools after 1984 aided in this shift. Developers have selected IBM compatibles by a wide margin ($N = 43$), but Apple/Mac is present ($N = 2$; Gateway and Plant Expert) as is the VAX minicomputer ($N = 1$; Project Mercury).

Increasingly powerful workstations should make ES development easier.

8.1.2 KBS Languages/Shells

As for programming languages, Table 8.1 reveals that BASIC in its different versions ($N = 7$) is tied with a fifth-generation AI language, Prolog ($N = 7$). LISP has been used five times, while Pascal has been used four times. Other programming languages include C (twice), COMIT (once), and Assembly (once). The adoption of blackboard systems seems inappropriate because they were designed for "ill-defined, complex applications"[1] because reference work is certainly not the former although it may be the latter. However, the appearance of VisualBasic, an event-driven language, seems destined to speed development work on PCs in the near future.

Several prototyping efforts have used shell software, most notably 1st Class ($N = 7$) after 1984. The National Agricultural Library's efforts, starting with Answerman, have influenced this situation dramatically. In addition, developers have also used VP-Expert ($N = 4$), KnowledgePro ($N = 3$), ESIE ($N = 2$), Insight/Level 5 ($N = 2$), Intelligence/Compiler ($N = 1$), and EXSYS ($N = 1$).

In comparison, the ratio of programming languages to shells is about one to one, favoring programming slightly. Judging from developers' comments, shells seem highly suited to rapid prototyping. Indeed, it can be a good way to learn about KBS with little cost and a short development time.[2]

Of course, the shell approach raises the question whether these systems are throw-it-away versus evolutionary (i.e., incremental) prototypes. With few exceptions (notably, REFSIM, PLEXUS, and IRS/IRIS), most systems seem to fall into the former category. Incidentally, that category includes any system that can be considered a scale model, a mock-up, or a test vehicle. One could conclude that librarians have been learning about KBS at little cost and with short development time. If so, one might ask what it will take to move toward truly KBS in general reference work.

8.1.3 KBS Library Environments

Without a doubt, the preferred library environment for development work is the academic library ($N = 32$), followed by special ($N = 8$), public ($N = 6$), and school ($N = 2$). Again, much of the special library showing is due to the extensive development work at the National Agricultural Library. This situation suggests that academic libraries are more research oriented and willing to invest in the future of ES technology.

8.1.4 Knowledge Base (Reference Formats)

Real knowledge, certainly not commonsense knowledge, is not present in any of the systems thus far. There is no artificial intelligence yet, because expert knowledge is scarce. Hence, the systems seem weak; and we all know that knowledge is power. Perhaps that is a real reason why the 50-plus extant systems are not truly *expert* systems.

With the exception of ITA's dictionary module, none of the systems appear to adopt an explicit model such as the one presented in Chapters 4 and 5. Implicitly, however, many systems are undertaking a modular approach by adopting the reference format as the basis of the modularity. In other words, most systems have a simple, rather than a compound or complex, definition of reference work. Inadequate theoretical knowledge, until that discussed in Chapters 4 and 5, has held the field back.

According to Table 8.3, formats within general reference work include multiple formats ($N = 3$), government publications ($N = 2$), biographical sources ($N = 2$), and dictionaries ($N = 1$). Children and young adult reader's advisory services ($N = 3$) is popular, followed by instruction/services ($N = 3$) and online searching ($N = 2$). In addition, a variety of specific subject domains have been attempted including agriculture, aquaculture,

Table 8.3
Expert Systems in Reference Work

Areas	Examples
General reference work	RefSearch, RIS, ORA, ORS
RefSearch2, Refsim	
Biographical work	Weil, BRA
Dictionaries	ITA
Government publications	Pointer, GDRA
Multiple formats	Gateway, IRS, IRIS
Reader's Advisory Services	GRUNDY, Computer Pix, Byte into Books, Bookbrain, BookWhiz, Good Reads
Social sciences	
Business	Conceptual Analysis, Gateway, ABLE, TOMESEARCHER, Research Advisor, and Expert Advisory System for Reference and Library Instruction
Economics	Research Advisor
Education	Research Advisor
Law	Pronto, Reference Advisory System
Patents	Patent Information Assistant
Physical Sciences	
Agriculture	Answerman
Aquaculture	AquaRef, REGIS
Chemistry	CHEMREF
Electrical Engineering, Computer Science, and Information Technology	Reference Advisory System
Horticulture	PLEXUS, NAL's Ornamental
Horticulture	
Life Sciences, Nursing, Medicine, Public Health	CanSearch, LOOK, Reference Advisory System
Material Science	Reference Advisory System
Humanities	
Technical writing	Technical Writing Assistant

business ($N = 4$), chemistry ($N = 2$), computer science, engineering ($N = 2$), gardening and horticulture, law, nursing, public health, and science and technology. Notably, subject coverage of the humanities is lacking.

For most of these systems, formats, and subject domains, however, the modest knowledge bases have not been formalized or validated. Disappointingly, few even discuss the nature or architecture of the professional knowledge going into their systems. Unfortunately, these systems are designed from the top–down rather than the bottom–up. Furthermore, they define reference work as literally pointing to an answer rather than a direct connection to the source (with some notable exceptions such as Gateway and IRIS) or at least pointing into the contents of the sources.

Much of the problem has been unresolved theoretical issues. For the first time, however, Chapters 4 and 5 present an architectural logic for the basic- and subordinate-level knowledge of expert practitioners. To be fair, of course, the "objective complexity of the situation"[3] may account for some of the prior "failures." But now, perhaps we can move on to more KBS.

8.1.5 Knowledge Representation and Validation

Reasoning has been production rule, followed by example based, and finally frame based. Forward- and backward-chaining has been adopted about equally. The ES developers' assumption, which may be influenced by the adoption of certain PC-based shell software (but remember an equal number are undertaking full programming), is that human expertise can be modeled using Horn Clause axioms (i.e., IF–THEN-type rules). Still, such an approach seems clumsy.

Most systems are small, but several intermediate systems have emerged if you are willing to count the knowledge base of the reader's advisory systems (upwards of 2000 titles, but using only a handful of rules). Most of the small systems are so-called toy or throw-away systems used to learn about the practicality of KBS in reference work. Truly intermediate-sized systems would have more than 500 rules, while large systems have more than 1500. Quite simply, we are still experiencing first-generation KBS, because the available knowledge representation techniques are unwieldy.

Thus far, there are only a handful of evolutionary systems, one at UCLA (ESIE, ITA, and now Question Master) and at the University of Houston (Information Machine, Index Selector, and now IRIS). Even so, these are only the beginning of second-generation systems.

Few systems have been built with validated knowledge bases (Question Master), and furthermore, only a few have been tested for their accuracy (Weil, 1968), or even formally evaluated by users (IRIS) or staff (GDRA). Given the twenty years worth of studies of reference quality, it is not clear why more testing of ES has not been undertaken. After all, the validation methodology is not ill defined (see Chapter 4, note 2). ES developers must make clear how or whether they validated the knowledge base with any rigor. Otherwise, how can they identify defects or predict performance?[4]

The ultimate usefulness of the extant systems must be questioned as well. One must admire Goucher College reporting that their Biographical Reference Adviser simply was not used. What is the true state of other systems?

8.2
User Interfaces Issues

User interfaces have changed over the years from socratic interaction to menu-driven style of interaction; nevertheless, some are natural language systems, notably, PLEXUS and TOME SEARCHER. The now-preferred menu style interaction still means that the system controls the questions and the user enters the answers. As noted earlier, natural language processing is still an extremely complex research area. And, unfortunately, it is still resource intensive, so PC environments are not likely to have this capability for some time. Whichever interaction style is selected, perfecting the details of the particular interface is more important than the differences among styles.

Most of the extant systems depend on the user's syntactical knowledge; physical actions required to use these systems include typing and, less often, touching the screen. The extent of typing ranges from pressing the enter key to accept the anticipated response to typing a single word to an entire sentence. Mouse support, especially for younger and older inquirers, is rare but would require users only to read screen text.

The flow of information in these systems does not seem to be well considered, with few exceptions. The order of screens and menu choices has not been validated.

8.3
KBS Costs, Funding, and Development Time

As for funding, an important role has been played by the United States federal government and one private philanthropic organization, the Council on Library Resources. Equipment manufacturers, Texas Instruments and Digital Equipment Corporation, have supported efforts twice.

Regrettably, little data was available during the data collection phase (see Table 8.1). Nonetheless, reported development time ranges from two weeks to 160 weeks, averaging one week. The conclusion is that most of the reference ES are rapidly developed, prototype, first-generation systems. An analogy is being able only to play tic-tac-toe when we really want to play checkers or chess instead. In other words, we have just started up the S-curve of ES development work. We need to make a serious intellectual investment along the lines of that addressed in Chapters 4 and 5, before true KBS emerge. Based on experience in other fields, if developers define reference work as a simple problem, it will probably take two person-years to build something useful,[5] while forty person-years might result in a reference KBS that could handle more difficult tasks.[6]

The cost also varied dramatically, from well under $1000 to a high of $1.2 million for Fiction Adviser. The mean figure is about $143,000, but is significantly influenced by Ohio State University's Gateway and the University of Houston's half-million-dollar efforts. This latter figure is what libraries should expect to spend, if they want functional systems. Finally, some modest commercial systems have begun to appear, for example, from a token $30 for a single-format module (e.g., POINTER and ITA's Dictionary Module) to $125–$195 reader's advisory systems (e.g., BookBrain or Book-Whiz); the most expensive commercial[7] system is £495 for TOME SEARCHER. One obvious conclusion is that more top administrative support is necessary.

8.4

Toward Design Specifications

Based on an examination of these prototype systems a list of desirable features has been developed. Interested readers should keep in mind the research findings from Chapter 7 as well.

Future systems should make extensive use of color graphics. When idle, the system should use a moving color graphic to attract use and to avoid creating burned-in images on the screen. User feedback should be captured via an electronic "suggestion box" as part of the system. For example, Aquaref asks three questions: (1) "Exactly what was your question?" (2) "Did the system provide information that may be helpful in your research?" and (3) "Do you have any recommendations for improving the system?" in its batch evaluation file. Smith and Hutton included something similar in their KBS.

Other statistical reporting features include (1) total number of users; (2) total screens viewed; (3) pathways and branching through the system; and (4) ranked-order frequency of specific titles recommended. Multiple recommendations should include (1) the title, imprint, and update frequency for serial titles; (2) brief annotation on use, limitations, alternate approaches, and online availability of this title; (3) local call number, physical location with printable map-drawing option, and graphic representation of the source (e.g., the book itself). Along with recommendations, it would be helpful to advise the inquirer about how to use the particular source. The ES should seamlessly link to external devices such as (1) a CD-ROM player and (2) online systems including the catalog and database services. The system must be site customizable based on the ownership of titles, online catalog, and external devices such as CD players and database access.

8.5

Conclusions

In summary, based on an analysis of more than 50 extant systems, the most typical KBS has been built by one or two people (a domain expert and knowledge engineer) using a shell, 1st Class, on an IBM microcomputer for a university reference environment. It is a relatively uninspired system, not based on a theoretical model of reference transactions. The ES claims of "improved decision making; more consistent decision making; reduced decision making; improved training; better use of expert time; improved service levels; rare or dispersed knowledge captured"[8] do not seem justified. Menu driven, it would be a small system for business or government publications. It probably would not have received significant external funding nor have been rigorously tested. To date, Weil (1968), Gateway (1986), and Houston's IRIS (1990) represent the best systems available. It is much easier to create a first-generation prototype than it is to put an operational KBS into place. Yet, we must expend the effort and money to move into second-generation systems if we are to ever have truly KBS in general reference work.

Endnotes

1. Daniel Corkill, "Introducing Blackboard Systems," *AI Expert* 6 (September 1991): 40–47. One exception would be the use of multiple experts to atomize the reference transaction and have specialists in parts of it; perhaps another exception would be the use of multiple, modular knowledge bases.

2. Sharam Hekmatpour and Darrel Ince, *Software Prototyping, Formal Methods and VDM,* International Computer Science Series (Reading, MA: Addison-Wesley, 1988).

3. N.V. Krogius, *Chess Psychology* (Chicago: Alfred Kalnajs and Son, 1972), 5.

4. William E. Perry, *A Standard for Testing Application Software:* Testing Prototypes (Boston: Auerbach, 1988), xxiv. Interested readers should also consult "Software Engineering: A Practitioner's Approach," in R.S. Pressman, *Software Testing and Reliability* (New York: McGraw Hill, 1982), 289–295.

5. Donald A. Waterman, *A Guide to Expert Systems* (Reading, MA: Addison Wesley, 1986).

6. M.J. Abdolmohammadi, "Decision Support and Expert Systems in Auditing: A Review and Research Directions," *Accounting and Business Research* 17 (Spring 1987): 183.

7. Anticipated by PLEXUS and the NAL's work, a commercial group called GardenTech is selling three hypertext gardening knowledge bases; one on trees, another on flowers, and one on bugs.

8. Pamela K. Coats, "Why Expert Systems Fail," *Financial Management* 17 (November 1988): 79.

9

The Future of KBS: Some STEPE Speculations

Where there is no vision, the people perish.

—Proverbs 29:18 (KJV)

As shown in the previous chapter, there are many extant KBS for reference work and even more intelligent systems are likely to appear in the future. These systems have the potential to change the nature of our work. To some readers it may seem that there is a strong temptation to do KBS development work just because it is possible but without considering the constraints or consequences. Thus, reflection on the nature of these constraints and consequences might be worthwhile.

In thinking about the future of KBS for general reference work, five types of contextual uncertainties are readily apparent. To organize this material and the results of a modest Delphi study,[1] this chapter adopts the STEPE model (i.e., Social, Technological, Economic, Political, and Ecological) in attempting to answer the following question: What is the most important constraint or consequence on the further development of KBS? Or, more generally, what will be the nature of the change? The prospects for KBS are summarized in Table 9.1.

9.1
Social Constraints and Consequences

The adoption of KBS in general reference work brings some social risks and rewards. Many risks have been identified already in Chapter 2. This section addresses those same five.

Table 9.1
Prospects for ES in General Reference Work

Constraints/ Consequences	Rating
Social	Mixed
Technological	Promising; more and better
Economic	Generally positive
Political	Mixed
Ecological	Mixed

9.1.1 End Users

This group will benefit the most, if truly KBS emerge, by having enhanced reference or information service. An obvious benefit would be the move to a self-service-oriented reference department. KBS in reference work could always be available for users, even when staff are on break, at lunch, or have gone home. For that matter, such a system could be available as a dial-up service or as an optional part of the library's online catalog. This self-service model seems to be society's preference in many situations.

In addition, computer scientists are also aware that complex systems present another risk. Because such systems are not linear, users simply cannot know how these systems work—and what they do not know, they may not favor. More to the point, they may not want to trust the results or recommendations of a KBS in general reference. System designers should not ignore this confidence issue. How can one evaluate these systems?[2] With the appearance of larger, more complex systems in the future, these systems must be designed to show how they arrived at answers (see design specifications in Chapter 8).

The major constraint in the further development of KBS may be society's acceptance of such systems. The popular press has made it more difficult by its coverage of computer technology and raising hopes.[3]

9.1.2 Reference Librarians

The Delphi study suggested that suppression of professional initiative and increased dependence on machines may be the most important consequences of adopting KBS in reference work. In other words, reference professionals may not believe that they have any reason to master procedural matters such as question negotiation, or declarative knowledge such as the various reference sources, if a machine can do it as well or better. The result might be a kind of de-skilling or shifting of work.

A closely related risk is the potential lack of challenge in the workplace. By shifting the emphasis away from how librarians do reference work to what reference librarians do, Chapters 4 and 5 may present a mechanistic view of reference work. Thus, there would be no room for creativity; as Bernd Frohmann said in the Delphi study, "In the automated world, the worker becomes a machine." Yet, expert knowledge will become that which is *not* widely diffused and codified by definition. Chapters 4 and 5 have made this formerly private expert knowledge, public. Now, the challenge to reference librarians will be to move to a deeper level where KBS have not gone. Certainly, stress may be an unanticipated byproduct of introducing this new technology.[4]

KBS in reference work also may ignore the power of professionals' social customs/traditions in general reference work.[5] For instance, most of the extant systems ignore the established reference paradigm (see Chapter 1). Of course, there are a couple of philosophical approaches to KBS. One is to assume that such systems should work the same way reference librarians do (that is the assumption of Chapter 5); the other approach says that it does not matter how one does development work, since the resultant system reaches the correct answer. An analogy with the adoption of online searching is relevant. Initially, online searching was not accepted behavior, so progressive library administrations introduced it, but outside the regular reference department structure. A separate department handled online searching.

Another constraint on the development of KBS is the so-called knowledge engineering bottleneck, first identified by Edward Feigenbaum. The system developers must have articulate professionals whose knowledge can be coded for the machine. Chapters 4 and 5 have provided some, if not much, of this basic and intermediate knowledge. If the field wishes to move beyond an intermediate stage of KBS development, then the profession must grapple with the task of identifying the real experts who are willing to share their knowledge.

In summary, there are still obvious rewards to introducing KBS. The major one is that professionals would be freed up to do the more interesting and useful tasks that only a human can perform. KBS will most likely influence our social structures; if the reference librarian favors the status quo, then this scenario is undesirable. If, on the other hand, the reference librarian believes that things should change, then perhaps she will welcome further development work. Interested (read astute) librarians ought to learn more about the KBS area by attending continuing education programs offered by the American Library Association (notably LITA), the American Society for Information Science, and the Special Library Association. In addition, some graduate schools of library and information science such as Wisconsin and Illinois offer continuing education programs where practitioners can learn more about KBS development tools.

9.1.3 Reference Department Paraprofessionals

If any group is at risk, this group seems most likely to be superannuated by future KBS. That raises the question, what moral or ethical obligation is present? One solution is to follow the Japanese example of offering lifetime employment to this group or giving this group the opportunity to retrain in the library's related areas. On the other hand, actually answering reference questions is still a small part of most paraprofessionals' responsibilities, so the risk does not seem highly serious for the moment.

9.1.4 Reference Department Heads and Library Directors

Based on the findings of Chapter 8, management must be convinced that the effort is worthwhile because the amount of time and money devoted to these systems has been modest. Support from the top is essential if KBS are to progress any further than these first-generation (i.e., toy or prototype) systems. The fact is that most extant KBS are not impressive. Administrators ought to support team efforts (such as LIS faculty, their students as research assistants, reference librarians as the domain experts, and disciplinary faculty in advisory capacities). If top management is seriously committed to the idea of total quality control,[6] then KBS offer one mechanism to assure consistent, high-quality answers.

9.1.5 Library and Information Science Students and Faculty

LIS faculty can adopt a leadership role. By introducing knowledge-based approaches to the next generation of practitioners, faculty can lead the profession. Indeed, the primary social consequence of introducing KBS into the curriculum is the transfer and advancement of knowledge about the reference transaction. As students, these reference beginners will move much more quickly up the learning curve. Although students probably should never expect to leave graduate school completely competent (in other words, there still is a significant role for on-the-job experience in learning the reference process), they would leave school with a validated mental model of the reference process and a good idea about the actual content questions to ask during the reference interview (i.e., specific structurally related questions that must be asked to arrive at the correct answer). In other words, based on Chapters 4 and 5, they can be taught the architectural logic of doing reference work.

Finally, one would hope that this knowledge-based approach to learning reference work will be more satisfying for students and faculty. This possibility alone should encourage faculty to investigate the utility of a knowledge-based approach to teaching reference work.

In summary, the social structure of professional practice may change with the introduction of KBS into general reference work.

9.2
Technological Constraints and Consequences

KBS have emerged from the artificial intelligence research laboratory, in large part, because of the technological innovation curve. Powerful hardware and inexpensive software are available now. Furthermore, the hardware is increasing in power while it is decreasing in cost. Parenthetically, one might ask where we are on this slope and if, in fact, it is an S-curve. In other words, how long can this or will this situation last?

Unit shipments of workstations have experienced a 54 percent compound annual growth rate between 1988 and 1991.[7] Similarly, there are 13 million home PCs as of 1989 and McCrone Associates estimates that this figure will grow to 30 million by 1994.[8] Peripherals, such as CD-ROM drives are not widespread, however, with an estimated 340,000 in existence worldwide in 1990, according to Infotech.[9] If reference work is to draw upon a large fact base, then CD-ROM drives will need to be more widely available. For instance, one might hope that the next edition of *Guide to Reference Books* (estimated 1995) will be issued on CD-ROM, so that a KBS front-end could make use of its declarative knowledge.

With the coming of the personal computer, the field has witnessed a tremendous growth in KBS development tools (see Appendix B). Despite their inability to provide an explanation why they reach a particular conclusion, neural networks and other machine learning techniques[10] much talked about in the 1950s are appearing as well as hypertextpert systems. Without a doubt, there are tools that will increase productivity when one decides to try a KBS implementation for general reference work.

In addition, it seems reasonable to expect not only expert, but brilliant, systems in the long term, if the requisite time and money is expended. Such systems are ones that will operate at the same level as the top one percent of professionals. These systems could be integrated with other systems to create intelligent systems. Such systems could "read" the professional literature online, generate new rules, make recommendations for when new editions are needed, and suggest additional sources to be added to their knowledge base. In effect, they could automate their maintenance and learn from experience.

In summary, from the purely technological point of view it would appear that the future of KBS is promising.

9.3
Economic Constraints and Consequences

On average, little time and equally modest amounts of money have been expended on developing KBS, as Chapter 8 shows. Hardware is not the constraint, it is the software; the familiar 20 percent hardware to 80 percent software investment ratio probably holds here. While software development tools exist, the field has not built anything of truly great significance beyond mere proof of concept and real promise (such as Ohio State University's Gateway to Information).

An interesting parallel argument with manufacturing and office workers may be appropriate here. Capital investment in the 1970s favored the factory worker (perhaps $25,000 for the factory worker to only $2,000 for the office worker). Then, the office worker began to catch up in the 1980s with the introduction of office automation. One wonders if the same thing does not apply for technical services librarians compared to public services librarians. OCLC and circulation systems are only now beginning to be matched by online systems and CD-ROM searching in public service areas.

Fortunately, extramural funding agencies (specifically, the federal government and one foundation, the Council on Library Resources) have supported KBS proposals. Whether this situation continues will depend on the national economy and agenda. In the short term, budget reductions seem a fact of life. Therefore, the economic constraints seem real and not particularly promising for future developments.

In addition, the Delphi study identified an intriguing long-term possibility. The development of KBS for general reference work might result in the creation of an information product that can be bought or sold (the Information Machine, e.g.). Historically, the library profession has tried to maintain that information is a resource, but here, information is a commodity. If publishers should see strong commercial potential in KBS, then the field might eventually see the inclusion or exclusion of certain reference sources in a KBS because it would have a positive financial impact to recommend solely one's own sources. Obviously, this situation would have a negative economic consequence for other publishers. Competition from other systems is necessary and healthy. It is certain that KBS will have some influence on reference book publishing; if nothing else, KBS will encourage the issuance of CD-ROM products that can be dynamically linked together via CD juke boxes on local area networks.

Finally, a cynic might argue that the development of "user-friendly" systems is an economic threat to the library profession. If these computer-based systems are more approachable and more widely available than human professionals, what will happen? If reference professionals do not exhibit positive verbal as well as nonverbal behaviors, people might no longer prefer people.[11] Perhaps there is room to be optimistic, though; many of the objections raised are probably analogous to those voiced when the safety pin was invented.

9.4 _____

Political Constraints and Consequences

The creation of KBS raises power,[12] legitimacy, and control issues. If the profession identifies or decides who is expert as they, indeed, must do to develop such systems, then this decision is an empowerment for those individuals. In another sense, the creation of KBS might be seen as a "disempowerment," in that "intelligence" shifts from humans to machines in the long term. It is ironic that it has taken the profession so long to look at individuals and their personal responsibility for creating quality reference service, just when responsibility can be given to a machine for consistent high-quality service.

The result affects groups as well as individuals. For instance, consider the relationship between technical services and public services. It can be viewed as a political perspective. In 1960s money went to the former; in the 1990s where will the money go? When will public services receive its "fair share"? If the resources go one place, will the best and brightest follow?

The introduction of technology leads to control issues. With technology, one becomes concerned about the timing, volume, speed, and predictability of events.[13] Recall Table 1.4 from Chapter 1 that showed that speed is an increasingly desirable trait to be found among reference librarians.

One possible long-term control scenario would be the global hegemony of information.[14] For example, eventually multinational information corporations, with interlocking boards of directors, could market KBS to the whole world; the content of systems would be driven by the profit motive (where the system recommends tool X because X is produced by some subsidiary company). The result would be increased centralization of power in the hands of multinational corporations. Dominion, not domination, is the issue.

9.5

Ecological Constraints and Consequences

Be aware and act in an environmentally conscious way is a platitude, yet it may be necessary to change the way we think and act about our environment. First, the environment is changing, and we cannot manipulate it. In other words, there are other information providers besides the 44,000-plus libraries in North America, for example. We cannot change that fact. Second, a library exists in a particular ecological information niche, but that can be manipulated. What a library does locally is a conscious decision. For instance, a library can choose to become involved in KBS work. Doing so might help that library's public image. Rather than talk among ourselves about the sad stereotypical image of a librarian, we should do something about changing it. Adopting expert system technology certainly would differentiate that library from almost all of the other 44,000 institutions. And therein lies an important point: studies of other fields have shown that specific companies can escape competition by differentiation.[15]

Although it sounds suspiciously like a slogan, it may be useful to think globally to succeed locally. Yet, the temptation is to adopt an internal perspective. While many practitioners are inclined to approach matters solely from the library's perspective,[16] users come from other arenas. Indeed, librarians might target the owners of those 13 million home PCs; our KBS might serve as a new outreach to touch the potential millions of users who simply did not know the wide range of sources available at the library.

The library and information environment is changing; it is no exaggeration to say our survival is at stake. Faculty in graduate schools of library and information science must consider this fact, respond appropriately, or face extinction.[17] With aggressive faculty carrying out the needed curricular changes, one might better appeal to and attract those students interested in becoming information resource specialists, knowledge engineers, KBS brokers, and KBS developers.[18]

Finally, some consideration must be given to the raw materials and energy expended in the creation (i.e., manufacturing of computers makes heavy use of hydrocarbons, silicon, and iron oxides), transportation (e.g., gasoline burnt), use, and ultimate disposal of KBS by-products (e.g., the space in landfills full of unrecycled products such as computer paper, ribbons, and printer cartridges). Then, too, libraries ought to consider their surplus supplies; don't dump it, donate it. Society is shifting from readily renewable cellulose products (i.e., paper) to sand and rust (i.e., computers) that may not be so easy to recover. Such products may be with us for a long time.

9.6
Conclusions

The most important single consequence of developing KBS for general reference work is the distinct possibility of improved access to information on the part of those whom the library serves. In the end, that is the *raison d'être* of our profession, and it is reason enough to work hard on developing intelligent question-answering systems, whether machine or human.

Endnotes

1. Based on responses by the eleven members of the 1991 Advanced Research Institute held at the University of Illinois Graduate School of Library and Information Science and sponsored by the Council on Library Resources.

2. The traditional response would be to use a set of test questions much like the Crowley–Childers studies have done with human reference service in the past.

3. See, for instance, Pamela McCorduck's *Machines Who Think: A Personal Inquiry into the History and Prospects of Artificial Intelligence* (San Francisco: W.H. Freeman and Company, 1979), 234f.

4. See Craig Brod, *Technostress: The Human Cost of the Computer Revolution* (Reading, MA: Addison-Wesley, 1989).

5. Edward Shils, *Tradition* (Chicago: University of Chicago Press, 1981).

6. Kaoru Ishikawa, *What is Total Quality Control? The Japanese Way*, trans. David J. Lu (Englewood Cliffs, NJ: Prentice-Hall, 1988).

7. "Workstations' Fast Growth," *Wall Street Journal*, March 1990, 1.

8. Bill McCrone on *NBC Today*, 11 December 1989.

9. "Sony's Federal Defense Contract is Good News for CD ROM," *InfoWorld*, 17 September 1990: 6.

10. Readers interested in pursuing neural nets might profitably consult the following works: D. Hebb, *Organization of Behavior* (New York: John Wiley and Sons, 1949); W. Ross Ashby, *Design for a Brain* (New York: John Wiley and Sons, 1952); F. Rosenblatt, "The Perceptron: A Probabilistic Model for Information Storage and Organization in the Brain," *Psychoanalytic Review* 65 (1958): 386–408; S. Grossberg, *Studies of Mind and Brain: Neural Principles of Learning, Perception, Development, Cognition, and Motor Control* (Amsterdam: Reidel Press, 1982); J.J. Hopfield and D.W. Tank, "Computing with Neural Circuits: A Model," *Science* 233 (1986): 625–633; R. Colin Johnson and Chappel Brown, *Cognizers: Neural Networks and Machines that Think* (New York: John Wiley and Sons, 1988); Tarun Khanna, *Foundation of Neural Networks* (Reading, MA: Addison-Wesley, 1990); and Robert Hecht-Nielsen, *Neuro-computing* (Reading, MA: Addison-Wesley, 1990). Microcomputer software, such as Brain-Maker and Neurosmarts for the PC and Mac environment, respectively, seem most promising. However, the major problem is developing an adequate training set of several thousand typical reference questions for the system to stabilize. I estimate a neural network approach to reference needs about 200,000 typical questions (10 questions/hour × 40 hours/week × 50 weeks/year × 10 years) to achieve real expertise.

11. An interesting counterexample is ELIZA, a natural language processing program, which many people endow with some humanlike qualities; see Joseph Weizenbaum, *Computer Power and Human Reason* (San Francisco: W.H. Freeman and Company, 1976).

12. One of the best studies of this topic is Eliot Freidson, *Professional Powers: A Study of the Institutionalization of Formal Knowledge* (Chicago: University of Chicago Press, 1986).

13. See Scott Beniger, *The Control Revolution: Technological and Economic Origins of the Information Society* (Cambridge, MA: Harvard University Press, 1986).

14. I am especially indebted to Bernd Frohmann, University of Toronto, for pointing out this specific scenario.

15. See, for example, Anand Swaminathan and Jacques Delacroix, "Differentiation within an Organizational Population: Additional Evidence from the Wine Industry," *Academy of Management Journal* 34 (September 1991): 679–692.

16. For more about how to overcome this limitation, see Donald A. Schön's *The Reflective Practitioner: How Professionals Think in Action* (New York: Basic Books, 1983).

17. Witness the large number of closures; see Marion Paris, "Perspectives on the Elimination of Graduate Programs in Library and Information Science: A Symposium," *Library Quarterly* 61 (July 1991): 259–292.

18. Anne Morris and Margaret O'Neill, "Information Professionals: Roles in the Design and Development of Expert Systems?" *Information Processing and Management* 24 (1988): 173–181.

Appendix A
Check List of Criteria for Selecting KBS Shells

    I. Cost
        A. Shell
        B. Training
        C. Run–time version
        D. Additional software
   II. Documentation
        A. Readability
        B. Skill level
        C. Index
        D. Real-world examples
        E. Cross-references
  III. Knowledge representation
        A. Rules
        B. Frames
            1. Examples
            2. Modularity
            3. Probabilistic knowledge
            4. Logic
  IV. Inference engine/methods of reasoning
        A. Backward-chaining
        B. Forward-chaining
        C. Induction
        D. Inheritance
   V. Developer interface
        A. Knowledge base creation
            1. Internal editor
            2. Extensibility
            3. Line entry
            4. Menu entry
            5. Graphics

      6. Compilability

      7. Help

  B. Knowledge base editing

      1. Full-screen editor

      2. Menu editor

      3. Syntax check

      4. Spell check

      5. Search utility

      6. Consistency check

      7. Global change facility

      8. Graphical representation of knowledge base

      9. Explanation facility (how, why)

      10. Apropos facility

      11. Saved cases

VI. End User interface creation

  A. Explanation facility

  B. Screen formatting utilities

  C. Graphics/animation facility

VII. Control

  A. Lockability

  B. Run-time version

  C. Access control/passwords

VIII. End user interface

  A. Response to system queries

      1. Natural language

      2. Fixed response

  B. Visual presentation

  C. Keyboard functions

  D. Multiple answers

  E. Uncertain answers

  F. Initial pruning/directed search

  G. Multiple conclusions

  H. Help

      1. How

      2. Why

      3. What If

  I. Fast/slow interaction

IX. Software

  A. Programming language

  B. Extensibility

  C. Links/hooks

  D. Embeddability

  E. Compilability

      F. Speed
      G. Run–time version
      H. Lockability
      I. Additional software needed
  X. Hardware
      A. Memory
      B. Host PC
      C. Additional hardware needed
          1. Color monitor
          2. Mouse
 XI. Training/company support
      A. Workshops
      B. Electronic mail
      C. Telephone hotline
      D. Consulting
      E. Documentation

Appendix B
A Guide to Expert System Development Tools

Songqiao Liu and Joo Yun Cho

There has been great interest in the use of expert systems shells to develop customized knowledge-based systems (KBS). These shells may be used for research, prototyping, or for developing end user applications. Despite this interest, there is a lack of objective information about commercial expert system shells. Aside from the occasional reviews that appear in AI and related journals and magazines, it is difficult to obtain a comprehensive overview and evaluation of the options available to the KBS developer. To this end, the criteria developed in Chapter 6 will be used to evaluate shells that are currently available.

The intent of this appendix is to aid the KBS developer who decides to use a semicustom approach in determining which shell might be appropriate for his particular situation. The shells selected have been identified mainly by reviewing magazines/journals, review articles, technical reports, and books on expert systems. The shells included here are those that are popular and often described in the literature. Emphasis has been placed on shells that actually have been used in developing operational or prototyping KBS, particularly for reference services. The scope of coverage is limited to shells for microcomputers. To help potential developers locate evaluation information on specific shells, citations to review articles, if any, have been included.

Except as otherwise noted, the information in this chapter is based on documentation provided by vendors, their replies to specific questions, their advertisements in AI journals/magazines, and review articles. As with any software acquisition, the prospective purchaser is well advised to verify that a given shell performs as claimed by actually testing it.

Moreover, since the world of computer software development is constantly changing, the developer should contact the vendor directly for the most recent information about specific shells, and check for the latest reviews and articles in journals and magazines. *AI Expert*'s "Expert System Resource Guide," which is published periodically, is an excellent source to consult for current company address and brief software information.

B.1
Alphabetical Listing of Expert System Shells

ACE
Knowledge Associates Ltd.
302 W. 259th Street, Riverdale, NY 10471
(212) 601-3393

Price $595.00
Hardware IBM PC or compatible; MS Windows 3.0 required.
Documentation Manual.
Knowledge representation Objects.
Inference engine Forward- and backward-chaining.
Developer interface Windows, graphics, pop-up menus; Dynamic Data Exchange; scripting language; context-sensitive help.
User interface Windows, graphics, menus; confidence factors.
Software Run-time system.
Training/Company Support Contact the company.

ARITY/EXPERT
DEVELOPMENT PACKAGE
Arity Corporation
Damonmill Square, Concord, MA 01742
(508) 371-1243/fax: (508) 371-1487

Price $295.00 for DOS; $495 for OS/2
Hardware IBM PC or compatible with 640 K memory.
Documentation User manual; online help.
Knowledge representation Rules; frames; fuzzy logic; hypertext.
Inference engine Backward-chaining.
Developer interface Built-in editor; windowed interpreter and debugger.
User interface Windows, graphics; confidence factors; explanation facility.
Software Written in Arity Prolog; complete links to external languages and databases; run-time system (no run-time fees).
Training/Company Support Contact the company.

AUTOINTELLIGENCE
IntelligenceWare, Inc.
5933 W. Century Blvd., Suite 900, Los Angeles, CA 90045
(310) 216-6177 or (800) 888-2996/fax: (310) 216-6177

Price $490.00
Hardware IBM PC or compatible with 640 K memory and a hard disk.
Documentation 200-page manual, and 40-page written tutorial plus interactive tutorial disk.
Knowledge representation Rules; interviews.
Inference engine Forward- and backward-chaining.
Developer interface Editing tool; automatic generation of a rule-based expert system based on examples and concepts.
User interface Menus, graphics; confidence factors; explanation facility.
Software Written in C; run-time system.
Training/Company Support Contact the company.

CLIPS
Patricia K. Mortenson, Marketing Coordinator
COSMIC, The University of Georgia
382 East Broad Street, Athens, GA 30602
(404) 542-3265

Price $250.00 (Program); $62.00 (Documentation)
Hardware IBM PC or compatible; Macintosh; VAX.
Documentation Extensive documentation.
Knowledge representation Rules.
Inference engine Forward-chaining.
Developer interface Integrated microEMACS editor; ability to generate C source code from a CLIPS rule base; utility program designed to facilitate the development and

maintenance of large rule bases; trace and debug facility.

User interface Windows, command line.

Software Written in C; can be embedded in other systems, such as a C or Ada program; run-time system.

Training/Company Support Free technical support.

Review Mettrey, William. "A comparative evaluation of expert system tools." *Computer* 24, no. 2 (Feb, 1991):19 (13 p).

Brooke, Thomas. "COSMIC CLIPS." *AI Expert* 3, no. 4 (April 1988): 71.

Golden, Jim. "CLIPS from Cosmic/NASA." *AI Today* (March/April 1988): 8.

CRYSTAL (DOS VERSION)
Intelligent Environments
2 Highwood Drive, Tewksbury, MA 01876
(508) 640-1090

Price $995.00

Hardware IBM PC or compatible.

Documentation Manual.

Knowledge representation Rules.

Inference engine Forward- and backward-chaining.

Developer interface Screen painter, rule editor, rule tracer/debugger; menus, graphics.

User interface Menus, forms, graphics; explanation facilities; certainty factors.

Software Written in C; interface with dBase and Lotus; run-time system.

Training/company support Telephone support and regular newsletter.

Review Humphry, Sara. "AI Tools for PCs Tackle App Development." *PC Week* 7, no. 8 (Feb 26, 1990): 86–88.

CxPERT 3.0
Software Plus, Ltd.
1315 Pleasant Meadow Road, Crofton, MD 21114
(301) 261-0264

Price $795.00

Hardware IBM PC or compatible.

Documentation 257 page manual, tutorial disk.

Knowledge representation Rules; frames; hypertext.

Inference engine Forward- and backward-chaining; inheritance.

Developer interface Open architecture that is 100% compatible with C; HyperWindows.

User Interface HyperWindows user interface; explanation and why facilities, online help; certainty factors.

Software Written in C; royalty-free run-time system.

Training/company support Free telephone technical support.

Review Nielsen, Paul. "Expert Systems Fortify Applications: Four Packages that Generate C Code Differ in Design, Ease of Use and Robustness." *PC Week* 8, no. 10 (March 11, 1991): 97–98.

Wilson, Lynwood H. "CxPERT." *AI Expert*, 2, no. 5 (May 1987).

ECLIPSE
The Haley Enterprise
413 Orchard Street, Sewickley, PA 15143
(412) 741-6420/(800) 233-2622/fax: (412) 741-6457

Price $499.00 (DOS Toolkit); $799.00 (386 DOS Toolkit); $999.00 (Windows Toolkit); $1499.00 (Windows NT, 386 Windows and OS/2 Toolkits)

Hardware IBM PC or compatible.

Documentation User manual with extensive source and examples. Online reference manual.

Knowledge representation Rules.

Inference engine Forward- and backward-chaining with automatic goal generator; Logical truth maintenance; data-driven pattern matching.

Developer interface Integrated EMCS editor; debugging utilities; Window 3.0 version adds a graphical development environment, and supports larger knowledge base using Windows's protected mode.

User interface Windows; explanation facility.

Software Call in from/out to C, Pascal, etc.; royalty-free run-time system.

Training/company support Custom consulting available.

Review Lane, Alex. "Ready? Rete! The Haley Enterprise's Eclipse Windows Toolkit." *AI Expert* 8, n10 (Oct, 1993):14–16.

ESIE
Edward A. Reasor, President
Lightware
P.O. Box 16858, Tampa, FL 33617
(813) 988-5033

Price $145.00
Hardware IBM PC or compatible.
Documentation 29-page user manual and 24-page tutor and 7-page novice guide on disk. Several sample KBS provided.
Knowledge representation Rules.
Inference engine Backward-chaining.
Developer interface Any flat-ASCII editor or word processor; trace and debugging utilities.
User interface Dependent on user: either Socratic interaction or menus.
Software Written in Pascal; Shareware, source code can be modified by the user for contribution of $145; run-time system.
Training/company support Technical support available.
Review Barr, Valerie. "Exploring expert systems." *Computer* 21, no. 11 (Nov, 1988): 68–73.

EXYS PROFESSIONAL 4.0
Nancy Clark, Marketing Director
EXSYS, Inc.
1720 Louisiana Blvd. NE, Suite 312, Albuquerque, NM 87110
(505) 256-8356 or (800) 676-8356/fax: (505) 256-8359 or (800) 256-8356

Price
  DOS:
    $995.00 (Development System), plus $1250.00 (Run-time license); $2100.00 (Development/Run-time Package); $3500.00 (Linkable Object Modules); $4750.00 (Linkable Package—includes Development/Run-time Package and Linkable Object Modules)
  Windows and Macintosh:
    $1495.00 (Development System), plus $1595.00 (Run-time license); $2900.00 (Development/Run-time Package); $5000.00 (Linkable Object Modules); $6500.00 (Linkable Package—includes Development/Run-time Package and Linkable Object Modules)

Hardware 386 or 486 PC running in enhanced mode with 3 MB hard disk, 2 MB RAM, and VGA monitor; Macintosh.
Documentation Manuals; videotape instruction; automated tutorials.
Knowledge representation Production rules; probabilistic knowledge
Inference engine Forward- and backward-chaining; frames; inheritance.
Developer interface Menu driven; algebraic expression; rule compiler and editor; online tutorial and help; screen design program; custom hyptertext files; automatic validation.
User interface Menu selection and fill-in-the-blank forms; UNDO command; report generator; confidence/certainty factors; hyptertext; online context sensitive-help and explanations.
Software Written in C programming language; interface with external database and spreadsheets programs; run-time system.
Training/company support Video tutorials; general or specialized training and customer support; maintenance contract.
Review Wendt, Larry. "We Had Joy, We Had Fun: EXSYS Professional." *AI Expert* 8, no. 10 (Oct, 1993): 17–19.
Siegel, Paul. "Exsys." *PC Tech Journal* 7, no. 1 (January 1989): 115–117.

1st-CLASS HT
1st-CLASS Expert Systems, Inc.
One Longfellow Center
526 Boston Post Road, Suite 150 East, Wayland, MA 01778
(508) 358-7722

Price $2495.00 (includes unlimited run-time license with no royalties)
Hardware IBM PC or compatible with 640K memory.
Knowledge representation Rules.
Inference engine Forward- and backward-chaining; 1st-CLASS plus induction.
Developer interface 1st-CLASS plus code generators; debug/trace capability; graphic capture and display; road map for easy chaining of knowledge bases; hypertext.
User interface Menus; graphics; hypertext.
Software Interfaces with dBase, Lotus-1-2-3, and other programs.

Training/company support Technical support available.

Review Dunkerley, Jim. "Software review: Programs in Motion's Fusion." *AI Week* 4, no. 12 (November 15, 1990): 5.

Pallatto, John. "1st-Class Eyes More Complex Expert Systems with Os/2 Tools." *PC Week* 6, n2 (Jan 15, 1990): 69–70.

Schmuller, J., et al. "E.S. Shells at Work—1st-CLASS." *PC AI.* 4, no. 5 (September/October 1990): 49.

Strickland, Dean. "1st-Class Expert System Development Software." *IEEE Expert* 4, no. 3 (Fall, 1989): 82.

Lane, A. "1st-CLASS Fusion." *PC AI* 3, no. 3 (May/June 1989): 10.

Ferranti, Marc. "1st-Class Brings Hypertext to Expert-System Structure." *PC Week* 6, no. 20 (May 22, 1989): 23–24.

Wright, Victor E. "Product watch: 1st-Class and 1st-Class Fusion." *PC Tech Journal* 7, no. 4 (April, 1989): 111–113.

FLEX
Clive Spenser, Marketing Director
LPA
Studio 4, RVPB Trinity Road, London, SW18 3SX, England
(441) 871-2016/fax: (441) 871-0449

Price

Windows 3.1 Series (Integrated Package, includes the relevant Prolog, flex and Prolog++ compilers): $2995.00 Developer Edition (includes a run-time generator for producing stand-alone applications); $1495.00 Programmer Edition (includes all the built-in primitives and environment).

DOS Series (Integrated Package): $3495.00 Developer Edition; $1745.00 Programmer Edition.

MacProlog Series (Integrated Package): $2995 Developer Edition; $1495.00 Programmer Edition.

Hardware IBM PC 386 or compatible with 640K memory; Windows 3.1; Macintosh.

Documentation Manual and user guide.

Knowledge representation Frames and slots; rules.

Inference engine Forward- and backward-chaining; multiple inheritance.

Developer interface Various editors; dialogues, forms, menus, windows; online help.

User interface Dialogues, forms, menus, windows; online help and explanations.

Software Prolog programming language; runtime system.

Training/Company Support Telephone and fax support.

Review Murphy, Thomas. "As you Know, I Love Prolog: LPA 386 Prolog." *AI Expert* (September 1993).

Kriwaczek, Frank. "Prolog Fights Back." *Expert Systems User* (May 1989).

Bartual, Richard. "LPA Prolog and Flex Expert." *Program Now* (February 1989): 43.

Rasmus, Daniel. "The Expert Is In." *MacUser* 5, no. 9 (Sept, 1989): 136–146.

GoldWorks III
Celia Wolf, President and CEO
Gold Hill, Inc.
26 Landsdowne Street, Cambridge, MA 02139
(617) 621-3300 or (800) 242-5477/fax: (617) 621-3300

Price $7900.00

Hardware IBM compatible 386 systems with 640K base memory and 8MB expanded memory; Windows 3.x or OS/2.

Documentation 12 manuals; video demonstration available.

Knowledge representation Frames; rules.

Inference engine Forward- and backward-chaining; multiple inheritance; object-oriented programming.

Developer interface Editor with multiple windows, multiple buffers, auto indentation, keyboard macros, and incremental search; debugging tools and graphics toolkit allows developers to build expressive dynamic graphics end user interfaces rapidly without much programming; tutorials and online help.

User interface Menus; explanation facility, and certainty factors.

Software Written in Lisp; interfaces with dBase, Lotus-1-2-3, and other programs; runtime system.

Training/company support Training and technical support.

Review Humphry, Sara. "AI Tools for PCs Tackle App Development." *PC Week* 7, no. 8 (Feb 26, 1990): 86–88.

Halstead, Rodd. "Develop Advanced Expert Systems." *Byte* 15, no. 1 (Jan, 1990): 219–222.

Tello, E. "GoldWorks II—Product Review." *PC AI* 3, no. 4 (July/August 1989): 55.

GURU 3.1
Denise Buhrmester, Marketing Coordinator
Micro Data Base Systems Inc.
Two Executive Drive, P.O. Box 6089, Lafayette, IN 47903-6089
(317) 463-2581 or (800) 445-mdbs/fax: (317) 448-6428

Price $7000.00 for DOS or OS/2 Development System (single user)
Hardware IBM PC, PS/2 or compatible with 640 K memory; 5MB hard disk. *Documentation* Reference manuals.
Knowledge representation Rules; metarules.
Inference engine Forward-, backward-, and mixed-mode chaining.
Developer interface Editing tools; debugging tools; databases, spreadsheets; menus, commands, natural language; user-defined input and output screen.
User interface Menus; commands; natural language; graphical representation; text processing; report generator; statistical analysis; explanation facility; certainty factors.
Software Written in KGL, a Fourth-Generation Programming Language; interfaces with dBase, Lotus-1-2-3, and KnowledgeMan; run-time system.
Training/company support Telephone support; training courses available.
Review Olympia, P. L. "Developing Smart EIS Applications." *DBMS* (July 1993): 81.
Taylor, Allen. "State-of-the-Art EIS Developer." *DBMS* (January 1992): 28.
Helliwell, John. "GURU: Brave New Expert System?" *PC Magazine,* May 27, 1991: 151–163.
Schmuller, J., et al. "E.S. Shells at Work—GURU." *PC AI* 5, no. 1 (January/February 1991): 40.

K-VISION
Richard L. Routh, President
Ginesys

1200 Woodruff Road, Suite C-9, Greenville, SC 29607-5731
(803) 288-8338/fax: (803) 458-9050

Price $49.95—$1495.00
Hardware IBM PC or compatible 386 system with 4MB RAM and VGA monitor.
Documentation User manual; reference manual; tutorial.
Knowledge representation Decision trees converted into rules; objects.
Inference engine Forward- and backward-chaining; multiple-level reasoning.
Developer interface Full editing capabilities, including sequence editor; natural language; math operators; automatic detection of incomplete knowledge.
User interfaces Graphic knowledge modeling; natural language; online help and instruction; user configurable interface; log recording and reporting; user entry protection.
Software Links to external data collection and other programs through the user's operating system.
Training/company support One-day and three-day training courses; 100 hours of consulting time included in price.

KAPPA-PC
IntelliCorp
1975 El Camino Real West, Mountain View, CA 94040-2216
(415) 965-5500

Price $3500.00 (Development Package); $450.00 (Run-Time Programs)
Hardware IBM PC or compatible with 640K memory and a hard disk; Windows required.
Documentation Two well-written and easy-to-use manuals.
Knowledge representation Objects, classes, subclasses, and instances; rules.
Inference engine Forward- and backward-chaining; object-oriented programming.
Developer interface Windowing environment; various structured editors for developers to edit, browse, and debug the knowledge base; help system, rule trace facility.
User interface Graphical and windowing user interface; explanation facility.
Software Written in C programming lan-

guage; interface with dBase, Lotus 1-2-3, and ASCII files, and external routines in C, Fortran, Pascal, and CAD packages; run-time programs can be embedded in other applications.

Training/company support Training and technical support available.

Review Heller, Martin. "Windows meets AI." *Byte* 16, no. 6 (June, 1991): 351–354.

Helton, Thomas. "Object-oriented expert-system tool: Kappa-PC 1.1." *AI Expert.* 6, no. 3 (March 1991): 65–67.

Faber, S., et al. "Kappa-PC - Vendor Forum." *PC AI.* 4, no. 6 (November/December 1990): 22.

Lydiard, T. J. "Kappa-PC." *IEEE Expert.* (October 1990): 71–77.

Humphry, Sara. "AI Tools for PCs Tackle App Development." *PC Week* 7, no. 8 (Feb 26, 1990): 86–88.

KDS 3.8
KDS Corp.
934 Hunter Road, Wilmette, IL 60091-1460
(708) 251-2621/fax: (708) 251-6489

Price $1,795.00

Hardware IBM PC, PS-2, or compatible with 640K memory and math coprocessor.

Documentation Printed manuals and sample disks.

Knowledge representation Rules; frames; facts; objects.

Inference engine Forward-, backward-, and mixed-chaining; blackboard.

Developer interface KDS applications can be developed using only plain English or other natural languages; built-in knowledge acquisition interface, editor, debugger, and automatic optimization options; graphics.

User interface Text; graphics; confidence factors; explanation facility.

Software Written in Assembler; interface with dBase, Lotus 1-2-3, and ASCII files; run-time system.

Training/company support Contact the company.

Review Rowe, Joyce M. "Basic Components of the Expert System." *Information Executive* 3, no. 3 (Summer, 1990): 55–58.

Brown, Lauren. "Training Gives Edge to Expert-System Developers." *PC Week* 5, no. 6 (Feb 9, 1988): 59.

KES 3.0
Software Architecture & Engineering, Inc.
1600 Wilson Blvd., Suite 500, Arlington, VA 22209-2403
(703) 527-4344

Price $4000.00

Hardware IBM PC or compatible with 640K memory.

Documentation Four professionally written and printed user manuals.

Knowledge representation Production rules; statistical pattern classification; descriptions.

Inference engine Backward- and forward-chaining; object-oriented data model; procedural control.

Developer interface Windowed interface; text editor; online help.

User interface Menus, graphics; run-time system; certainty factors; explanation, help, and why facilities.

Software Written in the C programming language; interface with external database and spreadsheets; can be embedded in the other software.

Training/company support Training and support available ($1200 is charged for the training).

Review Newquist, Harvey P. III. "C What Makes Software A&E run." *AI Expert* 6, no. 1 (January 1991): 67–68.

Schmuller, J., et al. "E.S. Shells at Work—KES." *PC AI* 4, no. 6 (November/December 1990): 38.

Newquist, Harvey P. III. "In Practice: No Summer Reruns, Continued." *AI Expert* 5, no. 10 (October 1990): 65–66.

KNOWLEDGEPRO GOLD
Knowledge Garden, Inc.
12-8 Technology Drive., Setauket, NY 11733
(516) 246-5400/fax: (516) 246-5452

Price $449.00

Hardware IBM PC or compatible with 640K memory.

Documentation Three-ring looseleaf manual with tabs to speed chapter selection and an extensive index.

Knowledge representation Topics, which are similar to frames or objects; hypertext.

Inference engine Backward-chaining; procedural control.

Developer interface Built-in editor, which uses standard Borland or Wordstar-like commands; Windows; menus; command.

User interface Menus; hypertext; command.

Software Written in Turbo Pascal; interface with external data and programs; run-time system.

Training/company support Telephone assistance; e-mail assistance on both BIX and CompuServe with good response.

Review Schmuller, J., et al. "E.S. Shells at Work—Knowledge Pro." *PC AI* 4, no. 1 (January/February 1990): 34.

Rasmus, D. "Knowledge Pro." *PC AI* 3, no. 5 (September/October 1989): 47.

Burg, J. "The Umbrella Insurance Analyzer." *PC AI* 2, no. 3 (September/October 1988): 12.

Shafer, D. "Ultimately Flexible Knowledge Representation Scheme." *PC AI* 2, no. 2 (July/August 1988): 37.

KNOWLEDGEPRO FOR WINDOWS (KPWIN)

Knowledge Garden, Inc.

12-8 Technology Drive., Setauket, NY 11733

(516) 246-5400/fax: (516) 246-5452

Price $549.00 for Windows; $1295.00 for Windows NT

Hardware IBM PC or compatible with 640K memory; hard disk drive; MS-DOS 3.1 or later; MicroSoft Windows 2.X or later.

Documentation A single, large manual that includes tutorial, reference, and appendix sections.

Knowledge representation Topics, which are similar to frames or objects; hypertext.

Inference engine Backward-chaining; multiple inheritance; object-oriented programming.

Developer interface Windowing interface; editor; debugger; Windows resource; font utilities; graphic interface tools; code is compatible with KnowledgePro (for DOS).

User interfaces Windows; graphics; hypertext.

Software Run-time system.

Training/company support Free telephone support.

Review Coleman, Tom. "A GUI Tool with Lots of Ideas." *PC User* 228 (9 February 1994): 68–69.

Shaw, Richard Hale. "KnowledgePro for Windows: Application Development Rooted in the Expert System Tradition." *PC magazine* (October 30, 1990): 46.

Shaw, Richard Hale. "KnowledgePro for Windows." *PC magazine* (January 15, 1991): 43.

Note Selected as "Best of 1990" by *PC Magazine* (January 15, 1991).

LEVEL5 OBJECT

Information Builders, Inc.

1250 Broadway, New York, N.Y. 10001

(212) 736-4433

Price $995.00 (Windows); $220.00 (Run-time system)

Hardware IBM PC or compatible with at least 640K memory; DOS 3.0 and Windows 3.x.

Documentation User manuals.

Knowledge representation Objects; rules; agendas; methods; demons; displays; hypertext.

Inference engine Backward-, forward-, and mixed-chaining; fuzzy reasoning; object oriented; customizable conflict resolution; point-to-point hypertext.

Developer interface Built-in editors; pull-down menu; knowledge tree; icon toolbox; debugging capabilities.

User interface Menus; windows; PF-key driven; confidence factors; explanation facility.

Software Written in C++; interface with dBase files; run-time system.

Training/company support Training and support.

Review McClanahan, David. "Level5 for Windows 2.5.2." *DBMS* 6, no. 2 (February 1993): 28–29.

O'Brien, Larry. "Level 5 Object for Windows." *Computer Language* 9, no. 9 (September 1992): 17–19.

Helton, Thomas. "Level5 Object: object oriented 5th-generation tool." *AI Expert.* 5, no. 11 (November 1990): 61–63.

LOGICTREE
CAM Software, Inc.
390 West 800 North, Suite 103, P.O. Box 276, Orem, UT 84059-0276
(801) 225-0080 or (800) 293-6777/fax: (801) 225-0286

Price $495.00; $50.00 (run time for single seat); $2000.00 (unlimited run time)
Hardware IBM PC or compatible with 640K memory and a hard disk drive.
Documentation Manual.
Knowledge representation Rules; Decision tree.
Inference engine Forward- and simulated backward-chaining.
Developer interface Graphical interface; multiple-path processing capabilities; user-defined report generation.
User interface Graphics; mouse support.
Training/company support Contact the company.
Review Keyes, Jessica. "Branching to the Right System: Decision-Tree Software." *AI Expert* 5, no. 2 (February 1990): 61.

MAHOGANY PROFESSIONAL
Emerald Intelligence
3915 AI Research Park Dr., Ann Arbor, MI 48108
(313) 663-8757/fax: (313) 663-5284

Price $495.00
Hardware IBM PC or compatible with 640K memory; Macintosh with 1MB memory.
Documentation Manual with a tutorial, and several small example systems.
Knowledge representation Objects; Rules.
Inference engine Backward-chaining, forward-chaining, and synergistic reasoning; multiple inheritance.
Developer interface Pull-down menus, forms; editing tool.
User interface Forms, windows; confidence factors; explanation facility.
Software Provide a set of hooks that allow users to link it to outside programs.
Training/company support BBS system and telephone support.

Review Caudill, Maureen. "Useful, Inexpensive, and Powerful Mahogany Professional." *AI Expert.* 5, no. 7 (July 1990): 61.
Shafer, D., et al. "Rules to Object: Mahogany." *PC AI.* 4, no. 1 (January/February 1990): 55.

NEXPERT OBJECT
Maureen Oliver, Direct Response Representative
Neuron Data
156 University Avenue, Palo Alto, CA 94301
(415) 321-4488

Price $5850.00 for DOS or Macintosh
Hardware IBM PC or compatible with 640K base memory and 8MB expanded memory; Macintosh.
Documentation User manuals.
Knowledge representation Objects; rules.
Inference engine Backward- and forward-chaining.
Developer interface Graphic interface; playback through a journaling feature; debugging tools; develop libraries; SQL queries; online help.
User interface Menus, graphics; explanation facilities.
Software Written in C Programming Language; interface with other programs and databases; can be embedded in other programs; run-time system.
Training/company support Training and technical support available.
Review Turner, Scott R. "Nexpert Object." *IEEE Expert* 6, no. 6 (Dec, 1991): 72–77.
Rasmus, Daniel. "The Expert Is In." *MacUser* v5, n9 (Sept, 1989):136 (11 pp).
Rasmus, D. "Nexpert Object—Part I." *PC AI* 3, no. 1 (January/February 1989): 49.
Rasmus, D. "Nexpert Object—Part II." *PC AI* 3, no. 2 (March/April 1989): 38.
Arcidiacono, Tom. "Expert System On-Call." *PC Tech Journal* 6, no. 11 (November 1988): 112–135.
Brown, Carol, and Sriram Subramanian. "Powerful, Visual Expert-System Shell." *IEEE Software* 5, no. 5 (September 1988): 98–100.

PC EXPERT PROFESSIONAL SOFT-
WARE ARTISTRY INC.
3500 Depauw Blvd., Suite 2021, Indianapo-
lis, IN 46268
(317) 876-3042/fax: (317) 876-3258

Price $500.00
Hardware IBM PC or compatible with 640K memory.
Documentation Printed manual.
Knowledge representation Rules.
Inference engine Backward-, forward-, and mixed-chaining.
Developer interface IDE (Integrated Development Environment) allows one to create, edit, run and debug expert systems from a single screen; knowledge base editor; pull-down menus, fill-in-the-blank screens, mouse support; tracing and debugging windows; online context-sensitive help.
User interface Menus, graphics, windows; confidence factors; explanation facilities.
Software Written in C Programming Language; interface with dBase and Lotus 1-2-3; run-time system.
Training/company support Technical support available.

REMIND
David Koenig
Cognitive Systems Inc.
880 Canal Street, Stamford, CT 06902
(203) 356-7756/fax: (203) 356-7760

Price $3000.00
Hardware IBM PC or compatible 386 system with DOS, Windows, or OS/2; Macintosh II; 4MB RAM and 4MB hard disk space; mouse required.
Documentation ReMind Developer's Manual; The Developer's Tutorial.
Knowledge representation Case representation.
Inference engine Induction; nearest neighbor matching; case-based reasoning.
Developer interface Data Import Tool; nine different editors; graphical interface; form editor and customized text editor; menus; online help.
User interface Graphical interface; menus; online help.
Software Written in C++.

Training/company support Available on request; three-day, hands-on comprehensive seminar available.

THE INTEGRATED REASONING
SHELL 1.3 (TIRS)
Igor Dayen
IBM Corp.
555 Bailey Ave., San Jose, CA 95030
(800) 426-7658 or (408) 463-4381

Price $8595.00 for Development/2 package; $859 for run time.
Hardware IBM PC or PS/2 running OS/2, with 5MB RAM and 6.5MB hard disk.
Documentation Extensive documentation available; online tutorial and help; sample applications.
Knowledge representation Rules; frames with inheritance; relations; parameters.
Inference engine Forward- and backward-chaining; pattern matching; opportunistic reasoning.
Developer interface Graphic interface; menu-driven installation; online help; source code template; trace and debugging facilities; national language support in Japanese and Korean.
User interface Graphic interface; Windows; online help; can use English, Japanese, or Korean.
Software Embeddable; can be called by any program.
Training/company support Contact the company.

TURBO SHELL 3
Eleanor Turino, Marketing Manager
Berkshire Software Company
44 Madison Street, Lynbrook, NY 11563
(516) 593-8019

Price $119.00
Hardware IBM PC and compatibles with a hard disk and minimum 384K of memory.
Documentation Manual and tutorial.
Knowledge representation Rules; frames.
Inference engine Fuzzy logic.
Developer interface Menu driven; editor; Knowledge Base Tree Generator.
User interface Menu driven; confidence factors; explanation facilities.

Software Written in Turbo Prolog; run-time system.

Training/company support Telephone support available.

VP-EXPERT

Paperback Software
2830 Ninth Street, Berkeley, CA 94710
(415) 644-2116

Price $249.00 plus $300 yearly licensing fee for an unlimited number of distribution copies.

Hardware IBM PC or compatible with 512K memory; CGA, EGA, or VGA is required to use graphics.

Documentation Manual.

Knowledge representation Rules, with added hypertext capability in the version 2.0.

Inference engine Forward- and backward-chaining.

Developer interface Built-in editor; inductive Front End, which can also create IF–THEN rules directly from examples in data files such as VP-Info, VP-Planner, 1-2-3, dBase, as well as examples in ASCII files; graphic primitives, which provides the ability to create custom graphics screen images; debugging tools; online help.

User interface Pull-down menus, windows, graphics; confidence factors; online explanation facilities such as How, Why, and What if.

Software Written in C programming language; interface with external database and spreadsheets programs. *Training/Company Support* Training and technical support.

Review Schmuller, J., et al. "E.S. Shells at Work—VP-Expert." *PC AI* 4, no. 3 (May/June 1990): 52.

Brody, Alan. "VP-Expert." *InfoWorld* 11, no. 25 (June 19, 1989): 74–75.

Angus, Jeff. "Expert Systems Take Off." *InfoWorld* 11, no. 17 (April 24, 1989): 41–44.

Shafer, D. "VP-Expert 2.0." *PC AI* 2, no. 3 (September/October 1988): 54–59.

Shaw, Richard H. "VP-Expert." *PC Magazine* 9 (16 January 1990): 43.

Aguiar, S. "Inside VP-Expert." *PC AI* 1, no. 2 (Summer 1987): 44.

XI PLUS 3.5

Inference Corporation
550 North Continental Blvd., El Segundo, CA 90245
(213) 322-5004

Price $995.00; $2495.00 for bundled package with all add-on modules.

Hardware IBM PC or compatible with 640K memory and a hard disk drive.

Documentation Manual and tutorial.

Knowledge representation Rules.

Inference engine Integrated forward- and backward-chaining with variables.

Developer interface Menu-based environment with color, windows, and online help; English-like syntax for defining rules; debug facilities.

User interface Menus, forms; Explanation facility.

Software Interface with dBase, Lotus, and other data files; run-time system.

Training/company support Telephone support available.

Review "XI Plus offers menu-driven development." *Software Magazine* 11, no. 5 (April, 1991): 122.

XSYS

Ray Weinstock, Senior Computer Scientist
California Intelligence
912 Powell Street, San Francisco, CA 94108
(415) 391-4846

Price $595.00

Hardware IBM PC or compatible.

Documentation Manual with examples; interactive tutorial.

Knowledge representation Rules (crisp and fuzzy); frames; tables.

Inference engine Forward- and backward-chaining.

Developer Interface Editing tools; trace and debug facilities; graphics.

User interface Menus, graphics.

Software Written in C; interface with dBase and Lotus; run-time system.

Training/company support Training and consulting service available.

B.2

Summary

The shells listed above represent a wide range in capabilities as well as in price. The developer must first evaluate his specific needs and the environment in which the KBS will operate and choose the shell that is best suited. A few of the shells deserve special mention and the reader's closer attention. These shells have not only received good reviews, but also have proven themselves by their longevity in the market. Moreover, they are widely used.

1st Class

1st Class has won rave reviews with its easy-to-understand spreadsheet-like format, sample knowledge bases, graphical decision trees, online help, and hypertext and hypergraphics. The National Agricultural Library developed AnswerMan, a KBS for ready-reference questions, using 1st Class in 1986. According to AICorp, 1st Class has become the preferred expert system tool for more than 8000 corporate, government, and academic users.

GoldWorks III

GoldWorks III has most of the advanced capabilities expected of a leading professional AI tool. The features of multiple inheritance, custom-designed user environments, goal-directed forward-chaining, bidirectional rules, object-oriented programming, and automatic dependency maintenance make it a serious candidate for many advanced KBS applications. However, its high price ($7900.00) may be out of many libraries' price range.

Kappa-PC

Kappa-PC is a powerful object-oriented programming tool with a well-integrated and easy-to-use development environment. It offers many significant facilities, including an object-oriented programming facility and active graphics. The lack of need for specific hardware, together with the system's range of facilities, suggest that it will become a main competitor in the KBS tool marketplace.

KnowledgePro for Windows (KPWin)

Selected as "Best of 1990" by *PC Magazine,* KPWin, at $695.00 to $1250.00, offers a robust development environment for both power users and developers. This is a package to which all libraries should pay special attention.

Level5 Object

Information Builders Inc. claims that ease of use and outstanding capabilities to quickly prototype and completely customize applications have made Level5 Object the most widely used expert system software in the world. In general, Level5 Object sets a high standard of robustness and user control. It is an outstanding tool that should lead to some truly interesting applications.

Nexpert Object

Nexpert Object is a powerful, comprehensive expert system shell. It offers a rich choice of knowledge representation, inference strategies, and integration into other programs, but it does require more than basic programming knowledge and is appropriate for more experienced KBS developers and users. For libraries with advanced equipment, generous budget (at least $6000.00 for the software), and plans to develop sophisticated KBS, Nexpert Object will be a good choice.

VP-Expert

Considering its power, ease of use, and price, VP-Expert is an extremely good tool. Paul Harmon (Editor, *Expert Systems Strategies*) says, "We recommend this tool with the greatest of confidence . . . the power is right, the ease of use is right, and the price is right."

Listed below are KBS shells that have in the past been popular choices for development but are either no longer available, or their availability is uncertain. Nevertheless, they are included in this separate list because some institutions may be owners of such software. Developers may want to use them to create their KBS.

ALEX (NO LONGER AVAILABLE)
Harris & Hall Associates
P.O. Box 1900, Port Angeles, WA 98362
(206) 457-4907

Price $675.00
Hardware IBM PC or compatible with 640 K
memory and a hard disk drive.
Documentation Xeroxed looseleaf manual.
Knowledge representation Rules; fuzzy logic.
Inference engine Forward- and backward-
chaining.
Developer interface Multiple windows, pop-up
menus; incremental compile, debugging
facilities; an expert system (Alex + +) written in Alex is provided to serve as a tutor;
source code included.
User interface Windows, graphics.
Software Written in Smalltalk; interface with
dBase and Lotus 1-2-3.
Training/company support Telephone support
available.

EASY EXPERT (AVAILABILITY UN-
CERTAIN)
Park Row Software
4640 Jewell St. Suite 232, San Diego, CA
92109
(619) 581-6778

Price $49.95
Hardware IBM PC or compatible.
Documentation User manual.
Knowledge representation Rules.
Inference engine ?
Developer interface Menu-driven editor; consis-
tency checker; online help.
User interface Menu driven; confidence factors.
Software Run-time system.
Training/company support Contact the com-
pany.

INSTANT-EXPERT(AVAILABILITYUN-
CERTAIN)
Lee Michaels, Director of Customer Relations
Human Intellect Systems
1670 S. Amphlett Blvd., Suite 326, San Ma-
teo, CA 94402
(415) 571-5939

Price $49.95
Hardware Macintosh; IBM PC or compatible.

Documentation User manual.
Knowledge representation Rules.
Inference engine Forward- and backward-
chaining.
Developer interface Creating rules using Windows, menus, and graphics; trace and debugging utilities; online help and explanations.
User interface Menus; Q&A; explanation facility; certainty factors.
Software Written in Modula-2; interfaces with
dBase, Lotus-1-2-3, and other programs;
run-time system.
Training/company support Training and technical support available.

INSTANT-EXPERT PLUS (AVAILABIL-
ITY UNCERTAIN)
Lee Michaels, Director of Customer Relations
Human Intellect Systems
1670 S. Amphlett Blvd., Suite 326, San Ma-
teo, CA 94402
(415) 571-5939

Price $498.00
Hardware Macintosh; IBM PC or compatible
with 640K memory.
Documentation User manual.
Knowledge representation Rules.
Inference engine Forward- and backward-
chaining; depth first search.
Developer interface Creating rules using Win-
dows, menus, and graphics; trace and de-
bugging utilities; online help and explana-
tions.
User interface Menus, windows, graphics;
Q&A; explanation facility, and certainty
factors.
Software Written in Modula-2; interfaces with
Graphic, Pict and Pict-2; run-time system.
Training/company support Training and techni-
cal support available.

INTELLIGENCE/COMPILER   (NO
LONGER AVAILABLE)
IntelligenceWare, Inc.
5933 W. Century Blvd., Suite 900, Los
Angeles, CA 90045
(310) 216-6177/fax: (310) 216-6177

Price $490.00

Hardware IBM PC or compatible with 640K memory and a hard disk drive.

Documentation 100-page manual, and 33-page written tutorial plus interactive tutorial disk.

Knowledge representation Rules; frames.

Inference engine Forward- and backward-chaining; inexact chaining.

Developer interface A compiler, editor, and knowledge manager.

User interface Menus, graphics; confidence factors; explanation facility.

Software Written in C; run-time system.

Training/company support Contact the company.

Review Mercadal, D. "Intelligence/Compiler." *PC AI.* 3, no. 3 (May/June 1989): 66.

LEVEL5 (NO LONGER AVAILABLE)
Information Builders, Inc.
1250 Broadway, New York, N.Y. 10001
(212)-736-4433

Hardware IBM PC or compatible with at least 512K memory; Macintosh.

Documentation User manuals.

Knowledge representation Production Rule Language (PRL) allows one to express knowledge using English syntax; mathematical capability and confidence weighing.

Inference engine Backward- and forward-chaining; goal outlining, and logical segmentation.

Developer interface Text Editor and Knowledge Base Compiler; debugging tools; reporting capability.

User interface Menus, windows, PF-key driven; confidence factors; explanation facility.

Software Written in Turbo Pascal; interface with ASCII files and dBase files; Can be embedded in a Focus application (Focus is a 4GL/DBMS, also developed by IBI); run-time system.

Training/company support Training and support available.

Review Barker, D. "Raising the IQ of dBase." *PC AI* 3, no. 1 (January/February 1989): 64.

Schmuller, J., et al. "E.S. Shells at Work - LEVEL5." *PC AI* 4, no. 2 (March/April 1990): 38.

PERSONAL CONSULTANT EASY (NO LONGER AVAILABLE)
Texas Instruments
(Austin, TX 78720-1088)
(800) 847-2787

Price $495.00; $3000.00 for site license

Hardware IBM PC or compatible.

Documentation Example-based tutorial-style manual.

Knowledge representation Rules; frames.

Inference engine Backward- and forward-chaining.

Developer interface Rule-entry language; integrated window-oriented editor; context-sensitive help; debugging tool.

User interface Menus, graphics; confidence factors, and explanation facilities.

Software Written in Scheme LISP; interface with dBase, Lotus, or external DOS files; run-time system.

Training/company support Technical support available.

Review Humphry, Sara. "AI Tools for PCs Tackle App Development." *PC Week* 7, no. 8 (Feb 26, 1990):86–88.

PERSONAL CONSULTANT PLUS (NO LONGER AVAILABLE)
Texas Instruments
(Austin, TX 78720-1088)
(800) 847-2787

Price $2950.00; $7500.00 for site license

Note Personal Consultant Plus is the larger, more powerful member of the Personal Consultant Series. Designed to take advantage of 286/386 DOS-based computers, it provides extended knowledge representation features, increased rule capacity, powerful access to external files, VGA graphics and mouse support, enhanced user manuals. It requires minimum 640K base memory. Please refer to Personal Consultant Easy for system features.

RULEMASTER 3 (AVAILABILITY UN-
CERTAIN)
Dr. Joe Stuart
Radian Corporation
8501 MoPac, P.O. Box 201088, Austin, TX
  78720-1088
(512) 454-4797

Price $595.00
Hardware IBM PC/XT/AT and compatibles.
Documentation Reference manuals and tutorial.
Knowledge representation Rules; examples.
Inference engine Backward- and forward-
  chaining.
Developer interface Induction File Editor; pull-
  down menus; automatic generation of rules
  from example sets; debugging tool.
User interface Pull-down menus, windows;
  confidence factors, and explanation facilities.
Software Written in C Programming Language; can integrate a database or spreadsheet into the knowledge base; run-time
  system.
Training/company support Technical support
  available.

SUPEREXPERT   2.2   (AVAILABILITY
UNCERTAIN)
Rod Campbell, Product Manager
SoftSync, Inc.
162 Madison Avenue, New York, NY 10010
(212) 685-2080

Price $199.95
Hardware IBM PC/XT/AT and compatibles;
  Macintosh.
Documentation Printed manual with tutorials
  and sample.
Knowledge representation Examples.
Inference engine Backward- and forward-
  chaining.
Developer interface Full text editor; spreadsheet
  interface; automatic generation of rules
  from example sets; debugging tool; tutori-
  als and sample applications included.
User interface Menus; confidence factors, and
  explanation facilities.
Software Written in Pascal, Forth; interface
  with any ASCII files; run-time system.
Training/company support Contact the
  company.
Review Keyes, Jessica. "Branching to the
  Right System: Decision-Tree Software."
  AI Expert 5.2 (February 1990): 61.

B.3
Useful Magazines and Journals to Consult

AI Expert, Miller Freeman Publications, 600 Harrison Street, San Francisco, CA 94107
The AI Magazine, American Association for Artificial Intelligence, 445 Burgess Drive, Menlo
  Park, CA 94025
Expert Systems: The International Journal of Knowledge Engineering, Learned Information Ltd.,
  Besselsleigh Road, Abingdon, Oxford, OX13 6LG, England
IEEE Expert, The IEEE Computer Society, 10062 Los Vaqueros Circle, P.O. Box 3014, Los
  Alamitos, CA 90720-1264
PC AI: Intelligent Solutions for Desktop Computers, Knowledge Technology, Inc., 3310 West
  Bell Rd., Suite 119, Phoenix, AZ 85023

Bibliography

All source material, primary as well as secondary, is cited in the endnotes following each chapter. This selective bibliography of the works that most influenced the author's thinking is divided into three sections: journal articles, books, and dissertations and theses.

Journal articles

Ackoff, Russell L. "The Art and Science of Mess Management." *Interfaces* 11 (February 1981): 20–26.

Berry, Dianne C. "The Problem of Implicit Knowledge." *Expert Systems* 4 (August 1987): 144–151.

Chi, Michelene T. H., P. J. Feltovich, and Robert Glaser. "Categorization and Representation of Physics Problems by Experts and Novices." *Cognitive Science* 5 (1981): 121–152.

Coats, Pamela K. "Why Expert Systems Fail." *Financial Management* 17 (November 1988): 77–86.

Crews, Kenneth D. "The Accuracy of Reference Service: Variables for Research and Implementation." *Library and Information Science Research* 10 (July–September 1988): 331–355.

Ericsson, K. Anders, and Herbert A. Simon. "Verbal Reports as Data." *Psychological Review* 87 (1980): 215–251.

Henderson, Deborah, Patricia Martin, Lauren Mayer, and Pamela Monaster. "Rules and Tools in Library School." *Journal of Library and Information Science* 29 (Winter 1989): 226–227.

Hilts, Philip J. "The Dean of Artificial Intelligence." *Psychology Today* (January 1983): 28–33.

Hutchins, Margaret. "The Artist-Teacher in the Field of Bibliography; An Application of Modern Educational Theories and Techniques to the Teaching of the First-Year Library School." *Library Quarterly* 7 (January 1937): 99–120.

Jahoda, Gerald, Judith Braunagel, and Herbert Nath. "The Reference Process: Modules for Instruction." *RQ* 17 (Fall 1977): 7–12.

Johnson, Paul E. "What Kind of Expert Should a System Be?" *The Journal of Medicine and Philosophy* 8 (1983): 77–97.

Johnston, Mark, and John Weckert. "Selection Advisor: An Expert System for Collection Development." *Information Technology and Libraries* 9 (1990): 219–225.

LeFrance, Marianne. "The Quality of Expertise: Implications for Expert–Novice Differences for Knowledge Acquisition." *SIGART Newsletter*, No. 108 (April 1989): 6–14.

Miller, G. A. "The Magical Number Seven Plus or Minus Two: Some Limits on Our Capacity to Process Information." *Psychological Review* 63 (1956): 81–97.

Mudge, Isadore G. "Instruction in Reference Work." *Library Journal* 27 (June 1902): 334–335.

Nisbett, Richard E., and Timothy D. Wilson. "Telling More Than We Know: Verbal Reports on Mental Processes." *Psychological Review* 84 (May 1977): 231–259.

Partridge, Derek. "The Scope and Limitations of First Generation Expert Systems." *Future Generations Computer Systems* 3 (1987): 1–10.

Perry, James W. "Defining the Query Spectrum: The Basis for Developing and Evaluating Information-Retrieval Methods." *IEEE Transactions on Engineering Writings and Speech* 6 (September 1963): 20–27.

Shneiderman, Ben. "Designing Menu Selection Systems." *Journal of the American Society for Information Science,* 37 (March 1986): 547–70.

Shneiderman, Ben. "We Can Design Better User Interfaces: A Review of Human–Computer Interaction Styles." *Ergonomics* 31 (May 1988): 699–710.

Simon, Herbert A. "How Big Is A Chunk?" *Science* 183 (1974): 482–488.

Steels, Luc. "Components of Expertise." *AI Magazine* 11 (Summer 1990): 28–49.

Steels, Luc. "The Deepening of Expert Systems." *AI Communications* 1 (August 1987): 10–16.

Taylor, Robert S. "The Process of Asking Questions." *American Documentation* 13 (October 1962): 391–396.

Taylor, Robert S. "Question-Negotiation and Information Seeking in Libraries." *College and Research Libraries* 29 (May 1968): 178–194.

Trotter, Robert J. "The Mystery of Mastery." *Psychology Today* (July 1986): 32–38.

Van Kaam, Adrian L. "Phenomenal Analysis: Exemplified by a Study of the Experience of 'Really Feeling Understood'." *Journal of Individual Psychology* 15 (1959): 66–72.

Winsor, Justin. "Reference Books in English." *American Library Journal* 1 (March 31, 1877): 247–249.

Books

Albury, Randall. "Commonsense Ideas of Objectivity and Their Social Significance." In *The Politics of Objectivity,* 5–17. Victoria, Australia: Deakin University Press, 1983.

Anderson, John R. *The Architecture of Thought.* Cambridge, MA: Harvard University Press, 1983.

Ayer, A.J. *The Problem of Knowledge.* London: Macmillan, 1956.

Beniger, Scott. *The Control Revolution: Technological and Economic Origins of the Information Society.* Cambridge, MA: Harvard University Press, 1986.

Boisot, Max. *Information and Organizations; The Manager as Anthropologist.* London: Fontana, 1987.

Brod, Craig. *Technostress: The Human Cost of the Computer Revolution.* Reading, MA: Addison-Wesley, 1989.

Brulé, James F., and Alexander Blount. *Knowledge Acquisition.* Artificial Intelligence Series. New York: McGraw-Hill, 1989.

Butler, Pierce. "Survey of the Reference Field." In *The Reference Function of the Library,* ed. Pierce Butler, 1–15. Chicago: University of Chicago Press, 1943.

DeMarco, Tom. *Structured Analysis and System Specifications.* Englewood Cliffs, NJ: Prentice-Hall, 1979.

Dreyfus, Hubert, and Stuart Dreyfus. *Mind Over Machine: The Power of Human Intuition and Expertise in the Era of the Computer.* New York: Free Press, 1986.

Ericsson, Karl A., and Herbert A. Simon. *Protocol Analysis: Verbal Reports as Data.* Cambridge, MA: MIT Press, 1984.

Feigenbaum, Edward. *Knowledge Engineering: The Applied Side of Artificial Intelligence.* Memo HPP-80-21. Palo Alto: Stanford University Artificial Intelligence Lab, 1980.

Feyerabend, Paul. *Against Method: Outline of an Anarchistic Theory of Knowledge,* rev. ed. New York: Verso Books, 1988.

Freidson, Eliot. *Professional Powers: A Study of the Institutionalization of Formal Knowledge.* Chicago: University of Chicago Press, 1986.

Galitz, Wilbert O. *Handbook of Screen Format Design,* 3d ed. Wellesley, MA: Q.E.D. Information Sciences, 1989.

Glaser, Robert, and Michelene T. H. Chi. "Overview." In *The Nature of Expertise,* ed. Michelene T. H. Chi, Robert Glaser, and M. J. Farr, xvii–xx. Hillsdale, NJ: Lawrence Erlbaum Associates, 1988.

Harrah, D. "Erotetic Logistics." In *The Logical Way of Doing Things,* ed. K. Lambert, 3–21. New Haven: Yale University Press, 1969.

Hayes-Roth, F., D. A. Waterman, and D. B. Lenat. *Building Expert Systems.* The Teknowledge Series in Knowledge Engineering. Reading, MA: Addison-Wesley, 1983.

Hekmatpour, Sharam, and Darrel Ince. *Software Prototyping, Formal Methods and VDM.* International Computer Science Series. Reading, MA: Addison-Wesley, 1988.

Herzberg, Frederick, Bernard Mausner, and Barbara B. Snyderman. *The Motivation to Work,* 2d ed. New York: John Wiley and Sons, 1959.

Hutchins, Margaret. *Introduction to Reference Work.* Chicago: American Library Association, 1944.

Ishikawa, Kaoru. *What is Total Quality Control? The Japanese Way.* Trans. David J. Lu. Englewood Cliffs, NJ: Prentice-Hall, 1988.

Janik, A. "Tacit Knowledge, Working Life, and Scientific Method." In *Knowledge, Skill and Artificial Intelligence,* 53–63. Berlin: Springer-Verlag, 1988.

Katz, J. J. "The Logic of Questions." In *Logic, Methodology and Philosophy of Science III,* ed. B. van Rootselar and J. G. Staal, 463–493. Amsterdam: North Holland, 1968.

Kelly, George A. *A Theory of Personality: The Psychology of Personal Constructs.* New York: W. W. Norton, 1963.

Kemp, D. Alasdair. *The Nature of Knowledge: An Introduction for Librarians.* London: Clive Bingley, 1976.

Kuhn, Thomas S. *The Structure of Scientific Revolutions.* Foundations of the Unity of Science, vol. II, No. 2. Chicago: University of Chicago Press, 1962.

Lakoff, George. *Fire, Women, and Dangerous Things; What Categories Reveal about the Mind.* Chicago: University of Chicago Press, 1987.

Lehnert, Wendy. "Problems in Question Answering." In *Cognitive Constraints on Communication,* ed. Lucia Vaina and Jaakko Hintikka, 137–159. Dordrecht: Reidel Publishing Co., 1984.

McClelland, David C. *Human Motivation.* Morristown, NJ: General Learning Press, 1973.

McCorduck, Pamela. *Machines Who Think: A Personal Inquiry into the History and Prospects of Artificial Intelligence.* San Francisco: W. H. Freeman and Company, 1979.

Norman, Donald A. *The Psychology of Everyday Things.* New York: Basic Books, 1988.

Parsaye, Kamran, and Mark Chignell. *Expert Systems for Experts.* New York: John Wiley & Sons, 1988.

Pekkanen, John. *The Best Doctors in the United States,* Rev. ed. New York: Seaview Press, 1981.

Polanyi, Michael. *Knowing and Being: Essays.* London: Routledge and Kegan Paul, 1969.

Polanyi, Michael. *The Tacit Dimension.* London: Routledge and Kegan Paul, 1967.

Popper, Karl. *The Logic of Scientific Discovery,* 3d rev. ed. London: Hutchinson, 1980.

Popper, Karl. "Learning Efficient Classfication Procedures," and Rosch, Eleanor. "Principles of Categorization." In *Cognition and Categorization,* ed. Eleanor Rosch and Barbara B. Lloyd, 27–48. Hillsdale, NJ: Lawrence Erlbaum Associates, 1978.

Schön, Donald A. *The Reflective Practitioner: How Professionals Think in Action.* New York: Basic Books, 1983.

Shils, Edward. *Tradition.* Chicago: The University of Chicago Press, 1981.

Shneiderman, Ben. *Designing the User Interface: Strategies for Effective Human–Computer Interaction.* Reading, MA: Addison-Wesley, 1987.

Shneiderman, Ben. *User-Friendly Computer Interfaces.* Carrolton, TX: Chantico Publishing, 1989.

Turing, Alan M. "On Computable Numbers, with an Application to the Entscheidungs-problem." *Proceedings of the London Mathematical Society* 42 (1937): 230–265; reprinted in Martin Davis, ed. *The Undecidable*. New York: Raven Press, 1965; reprinted in Darrel C. Ince, ed. *Mechanical Intelligence*. New York: North Holland, 1992.

Vavrek, Bernard F. "Communications and the Reference Interface." Ph.D. dissertation, University of Pittsburgh, 1971; reprint ed., *Communications and the Reference Interface*. Pittsburgh, PA: University of Pittsburgh, 1971.

Vroom, Victor H. *Leadership and Decision-Making*. Pittsburgh: University of Pittsburgh Press, 1973.

Waterman, Donald A. *A Guide to Expert Systems*. The Teknowledge Series in Knowledge Engineering. Reading, MA: Addison Wesley, 1986.

Weizenbaum, Joseph. *Computer Power and Human Reason*. San Francisco: W. H. Freeman and Company, 1976.

Wittgenstein, Ludwig. *Tractatus Logico-philosophicus*. London: Routledge and Kegan Paul, 1921.

Wrong, Dennis H. *Power; Its Forms, Bases, and Uses*. New York: Harper and Row, 1979.

Yourdon, Edward. *Modern Structured Analysis*. Yourdon Press Computing Series. Englewood Cliffs, NJ: Yourdon Press, 1989.

Zuboff, Shoshama. *In the Age of the Smart Machine: The Future of Work and Power*. New York: Basic Books, 1988.

Dissertations and Theses

Bush, N. W. "Investigation of the Relationship between Two Teaching Methods and Attitude Modification." Ph.D. dissertation, Florida State University, 1971.

Davis, Colin. "Attention, Memory, and Thought." TMs. An unpublished, September 1990, 12-page paper written in the School of Psychology, University of New South Wales, Australia.

Dube, Rajesh. "A State Transition Model for Rule Based Expert Systems." Ph.D. dissertation, Rutgers University, 1989.

Gardner, Karen. "Evaluation of Expert Systems: A Conceptual Framework for Evaluating Knowledge Representation Structure." Ph.D. dissertation, University of California, Berkeley, in progress.

Lippert, Renate C. "Refinement of Students' Knowledge While Developing Expert Systems." Ph.D. dissertation, University of Minnesota, 1988.

Moore, Maloy. "The Reference Interview: A Review." M.L.S. Specialization Paper, UCLA, November 1988.

Index

By Linda Webster, M.L.S., ASI member.

Entries include personal names; names of institutions, associations and companies; titles of works and computer programs; and subject concepts. Also included are concepts from the Appendices. Entries are arranged in letter-by-letter alphabetical order. Entries beginning with "Mc" are alphabetized as "Mc." Endnotes are designated by a lowercase "n" following the page reference.

Library and Information Science

(Continued from page ii)

About the Author

John V. Richardson Jr. grew up in Columbus, Ohio, the bibliographic center of the universe. Having minored in philosophy as an undergraduate, he studied propositional calculus as well as moral philosophy (i.e., choosing, deciding, and doing) with Earl Dennis and Andrew Oldenquist, respectively, and graduated from Ohio State University with a B.A. in Sociology in 1971. A student of Frances N. Cheney, he earned his M.L.S. from Vanderbilt University's Peabody College in 1972. Richardson then worked as a documents librarian and as a general reference librarian at the University of Kentucky. Wanting to know more about the intellectual foundations of his field, he undertook doctoral studies at Indiana University, earning his Ph.D. in 1978.

Involved with expert system tools and technology since 1986, Richardson now lives in Los Angeles and currently teaches general reference work, knowledge-based systems, and government information in the Graduate School of Education and Information Studies at the University of California at Los Angeles.